THE FLOOD YE.

THE FLOOD YEAR 1927

A Cultural History

Susan Scott Parrish

PRINCETON UNIVERSITY PRESS

Princeton and Oxford

Copyright © 2017 by Princeton University Press
Published by Princeton University Press, 41 William Street,
Princeton, New Jersey 08540
In the United Kingdom: Princeton University Press, 6 Oxford Street,
Woodstock, Oxfordshire OX20 1TW

press.princeton.edu

Jacket photograph: "Rolling Fork, Miss. 5-2-27," flood water covers streets and
railroad tracks, railroad cars sit on tracks. Rolling Fork, MS, 1927 Flood
Photograph Collection, courtesy of Mississippi Department of Archives
and History. Image of ripples courtesy of Shutterstock.

Owing to limitations of space, all acknowledgments for permission to reprint
previously published and unpublished material can be found on page 369, which is
an extension of this copyright page.

Library of Congress Cataloging-in-Publication Data

Names: Parrish, Susan Scott, author.
Title: The flood year 1927 : a cultural history / Susan Scott Parrish.
Description: Princeton : Princeton University Press, [2017] | Includes
bibliographical references and index.
Identifiers: LCCN 2016009841 | ISBN 9780691168838 (cloth)
Subjects: LCSH: Floods—Mississippi River Valley—History—20th century. |
Disaster relief—Mississippi River Valley—History—20th century. |
Mississippi River Valley—Social conditions—20th century. | Mississippi
River Valley—History—1865-
Classification: LCC F354 .P27 2017 | DDC 977/.043—dc23 LC record available at https://
lccn.loc.gov/2016009841

British Library Cataloging-in-Publication Data is available

This book has been composed in Minion Pro, Monotype Modern Std
and John Sans White Pro

Printed on acid-free paper. ∞

Printed in the United States of America

1 3 5 7 9 10 8 6 4 2

FOR BRUCE

Orestes: "Aye; the gods too, whom mortals deem so wise,
Are nothing clearer than some winged dream;
And all their ways, like man's ways, but a stream
Of turmoil. . . ."

Euripides, Iphigenia in Tauris, *1910*
verse translation by Gilbert Murray,
Oxford University Press

Performed by St. Margaret's School
at The Playhouse, Washington, D.C., May 28, 1927,
to raise money for Mississippi Flood victims

CONTENTS

ILLUSTRATIONS

THE FLOOD YEAR 1927

Introduction

One morning during the first week of May 1927, a publicist working for the American Red Cross boarded a small navy sea plane in Memphis and, as the sun rose, flew south along the Mississippi River to the city of Greenville. En route, from a vantage of three thousand feet, Taylor, the publicist, took in what he called "one of the most overwhelming tragedies nature has ever enacted."[1] Since August 1926, a strange coincidence of intense weather events passing over the center of the North American continent had filled the tributaries of the Mississippi to bursting. Flooding had occurred in the western and northern parts of the watershed in the fall, and by early winter people were experiencing high water in the eastern tributaries as well. In March, below the juncture of the Ohio and the Mississippi, as all the swollen tributaries emptied into the Lower Mississippi simultaneously, levees started to falter in Arkansas and the boot-heel section of Missouri. Easter weekend brought storms to the Delta region. Only days later, on April 21, came the largest crevasse of the flood—indeed the largest in the river's recorded history—in Mounds Landing, Mississippi. By this point, the *Chicago Daily Tribune* had called what was taking place in the alluvial basin south of Cairo the "most disastrous flood this country has ever had."[2] Memphis's paper the *Commercial Appeal* dubbed it the "greatest disaster that ever afflicted our country."[3] And a Louisiana newspaper, the *New Iberia Enterprise*, went as far as to say that this was "the greatest of all floods since the days of Noah."[4] Shortly after the April 21 break, "tragedy" began to turn into "scandal" as the nation's leading African American weekly, the *Chicago Defender*, started to publish dispatches about the "race hate" its reporters were witnessing in the Red Cross camps.[5] In Vicksburg on May 1, an evacuee was shot by a National Guardsman.[6] A story in which nature had been the protagonist, and the antagonist, was turning ineluctably into a story about humans.

Since the break at Mounds Landing, Taylor had been holed up in Red Cross relief headquarters in Memphis, doing his part in what he saw as a tremendous battle waged against a "conquering invader" along a thousand-mile line from Cairo to the Gulf of Mexico. Ensconced in his office, Taylor perceived the Red Cross's "huge relief machine function with a fascinating smoothness" as it rescued thousands from rooftops, trees, small bateaus, and disintegrating levees; as it delivered food with the same quick efficiency marshalled during wartime; and as it tackled the spread of disease through a massive public inoculation campaign. The template of the recent Great War in Europe, and in particular the nation's feat of large-scale organization in the midst of wartime emergency, is one that Taylor readily brings to bear on the current—but this time American—catastrophe. Situated at the nerve center of this prodigious relief machine, Taylor relished his agency's response as a remarkable modern mechanism in which sprawling and unpredictable circumstances could be connected and rationalized with the help of speedy communication and transportation technologies.[7]

But Taylor had yet to see the flood itself. That is what he intended to do on this early May morning. Flying south from Memphis, looking down from the sky, he began to notice little crowded islands of refugees, one full of animals "marooned and doomed" and surrounded by the carcasses of those that had already drowned. On a different island—likely a mound constructed for flood seasons by ancient inhabitants of the valley long before the arrival of Europeans—he made out human families but couldn't tell whether their arm gestures were signals of distress. All around these islands, he saw nothing but opaque brown water. The whole scene, it seems, was still a bit abstract.[8]

Soon enough, the pilot landed the plane in the water just off of Greenville's levee, a sliver of artificial land eight miles long with a crown only eight feet wide that had, in the past few days, become a precarious city of thirteen thousand.[9] Situated just thirty miles south of the Mounds Landing break, the levee was all that separated this population from the river on the one side and the new inland sea that covered much of the Yazoo-Mississippi Delta on the other. Greenville itself, as one journalist wrote, had been "turned into a swirling Venice."[10] Disembarking from the plane, Taylor was quickly surrounded by hundreds of people, most of whom were African American. Up until his landing, all of these evacuees had represented to Taylor nothing other than a series of logistics challenges—they had been abstract pieces in a "stupendous chess game." But he was about to be surprised. For it was not food, or medicine, or tents, or blankets that the people asked him for but rather information. The question on everyone's lips was: "Did you bring any newspapers?" As he remembered it, when he admitted that he "never thought about them wanting newspapers," everyone's "spirits fell."[11]

Once they had recovered from their disappointment, the crowd turned Taylor, this emissary from headquarters, into a vector of news, asking question upon question. In particular, the evacuees wanted to know "what was going on in the outside world—whether the levees farther south had broken, or whether any of the proposed trans-Atlantic flights had started."[12] Perhaps Taylor brought news that the water surging out of the Mississippi Delta at Vicksburg had caused large breaks on the Louisiana side of the river—that between this surge, and the water flowing over northern Louisiana from Arkansas, another inland sea was forming in the Sugar Bowl region of the Atchafalaya basin. Though Taylor could bring no information about transatlantic flights, it would be only a matter of days before news would, one way or another, reach this evacuated population that Charles Lindbergh had indeed made a successful solo flight to the other side of the Atlantic. While these men and women stood on the knife's edge of an epic modern miscalculation—one that Gifford Pinchot would, a month later, call "the most colossal blunder in civilized history"[13]—and while they wanted to understand better the geography and the human toll of the disaster, this marooned population wanted nonetheless to participate in the nation's, and the world's, virtual witnessing of a signal technological achievement. Taylor had seen this crowd as a mass of bodies and bodily needs. He had not imagined them as consumers of globally significant information or as part of a contemporary public. Less still did he imagine this crowd—and crowds like them throughout the Delta—as poised to *produce and disseminate* meaning out of their experience. But that was exactly what happened in the days, months, and years to come.

If Lindbergh's solo flight, mediated at a distance for a global audience, was one scenario of the modern, this haphazardly amassed population at a Red Cross camp was another. When we think about early twentieth-century catastrophes, we typically consider World War I, the financial collapse of 1929 along with the Great Depression, and the rise of fascism and genocide in Europe and the Near East. These have represented, and continue in our historical memory to represent, key problems of the modern age: mechanized combat and slaughter, unrestrained speculative capitalism, totalitarian governments, and the unstoppable global extension of crises. My conviction is that we are now prepared to see in this 1927 environmental disaster another signal, and abiding, problem of modern life. *The Flood Year 1927* brings eco-catastrophe into our discussions of modernity, its experiences, and its cultures. Rather than a blow-by-blow narrative of the event itself—a typical feature of disaster historiography—my book explores how this disaster took on form and meaning as it was nationally and internationally represented across multiple media platforms, both while the flood moved inexorably southward and, subsequently, over the next two decades. I begin by looking at the social and environmental causes of the disaster, and by briefly describing the sociological certitudes of the 1920s into which it broke. I then investigate how this disaster went public, and made publics, as it was mediated through newspapers, radio, blues songs, and theater benefits. Finally, I look at how the flood comprises an important—but until now underappreciated—chapter in the history of literary modernism.

My immediate goal is for readers to understand what a major cultural phenomenon this was. Historians have so far uncovered the details of what happened, especially out of sight in the upper echelons of local and federal government, to cause the flood to unfold the way it did.[14] Less work has been done, though, to explain how what was arguably the most publicly consuming environmental catastrophe of the twentieth century in the United States assumed public meaning. Disasters, as Kenneth Hewitt argues, tend in technocratic societies to be viewed as "unplanned holes" within essentially stable human-environmental relations when, in reality, they are crises brought on by and within everyday practices.[15] They show not what is abnormal or accidental but rather what has *become* the norm coming invariably undone. Disasters, therefore, show us the unsustainable in the everyday and test whether cultural reserves exist for people to confront the breaches in—and thus redesign—these diurnal structures. The nation's multifarious responses to the flood, therefore, indicate much about the United States in 1927 and, in particular, how unresolved the interregional and interracial crises leading up to the Civil War still were.

Many other events around this time bring these lingering crises to light: the Scopes Trial of 1925, for example, and the numerous urban race riots of 1919. What the flood uniquely allows us to see is how the "Nature" that stamped with inevitability definitions of races and regions, modernity and tradition—the "Nature" that grounded dominant U.S. social geography—was revealing itself to be a human invention with deep design flaws. Because the Mississippi watershed is a continental land feature funneling matter, and material practices, of the North, West, and East into the Gulf South, its hydro-geography turned the river's Delta into a place that made national (and global) environmental regimes visible. That the river's—or the levee system's—engineering had been federally designed, moreover, made it politically effluent in yet another way. The Mississippi River has long been a "naturalcultural contact zone," to use a phrase from Donna Haraway.[16] But in 1927, as this techno-organic hybrid catastrophically faltered, each term within that "zone" and the history of their contact seemed to demand a new and openly contested scrutiny. The river was a noisy medium, but everyone heard its blasts and murmurings differently.

My other goal, then, is to use this very concrete case study to encourage readers to meditate on a more elusive, abstract, but increasingly important issue, namely: *how do disasters become meaningful?* How do—and how should—humans communicate with themselves about politically charged eco-catastrophes? What are the stages through which mass-mediated societies encounter disaster? Do certain media entail better, or more productive, or more democratic epistemologies of crisis? What can we learn from 1927 about how to make transformative expression, and knowledge, out of disaster today and in the future? This flood was the first to occur in a "mediascape"[17] enough like our own to make it a critical place to look to understand, and to consider modifying, our own contemporary modes of disaster communication and consumption. Moreover, the shape this disaster took—with extreme weather events, high waters, a faultily designed infrastructure, and poor, racially marked evacuees struggling in a southern resource frontier—increasingly characterizes the Global South in a present and future era of global climate change.

I started working on this project in the fall after the New Orleans levee disaster of 2005. Since that event, and the Indian Ocean tsunami of 2004, global attention has been drawn to a series of other environmental catastrophes: the Haiti earthquake of 2010, the BP oil spill of that same year, the 2011 Fukushima Daiichi nuclear disaster occurring in the wake of an earthquake and tsunami, and Superstorm Sandy of 2012. The Flood of 1927 likewise occurred within a stretch of years characterized by the deadliest spate of disasters in U.S. history to date, one that comprised 938 events, lasting from 1881 to 1928, years roughly coeval with the Second Industrial Revolution. Lowell Juilliard Carr, the sociologist studying the social consequences of catastrophe who produced this figure in 1932, was struck by their frequency in the United States, "where nature is supposed to be most completely subdued." Such figures were enough, he surmised, to make us think twice about our "so-called conquest of nature."[18]

Though these disaster-intensive periods—in the early twentieth century and early twenty-first century—are associated with different immediate causes, they can both be placed along a continuum within the new planetary epoch that scientists have recently dubbed "the Anthropocene," a term meant to indicate the scope, intensity, and irreversibility of human alteration of planetary life begun around 1800 with intensive agriculture and deforestation, pollution, the combustion of fossil fuels, and other modern practices.[19] This term indicates that we have started to conceptualize the human, the human's relationship to nature, and the human's relationship to historical periods anew. We may have thought that with the intensive reengineering of natural processes begun in the early modern period, humanity had graduated into eras marked solely by anthropocentric political, intellectual, technological, or economic change—the Age of Empire, the Age of Reason, the Industrial Age—but we find that these human "Ages" have actually produced a reimmersion in an environmental conception of selfhood, of limitations, and of ineluctable entanglement. We never transcended biological processes, never became more modern than they are.[20] Form is something that biology makes in, out of, and with us.

In the early modern period, Europeans stood knocking on the door of nature's "inner chambers" (to quote Francis Bacon), believing nature to be a fairly fixed and ultimately knowable thing.[21] An entire Euro-Western epistemology was built around the belief that human alteration of natural environments improved and reclaimed nature to its destined purpose. Science seemed to abet humanity's material life, to quell humanity's ancient susceptibility to accident. And upon material liberation rested the Enlightenment's claim for science's role as political liberator.[22] In this way, a belief in a limit-imposing natural order was replaced by a trust in human design.[23] Now, in the twenty-first century, we stand surrounded by a "second nature,"[24] a dynamic creature partly of our making whose behavior is no more predictable for that. Ulrich Beck has described this shift—from Enlightenment's faith in our human ability to reengineer nature to make life more secure to a more recent sense that modernization has made us all *less* secure—as a transition from a "science society" to a "Risk Society," a shift he associates with the first use of nuclear weapons in 1945. Risks after this year no longer "accumulated . . . at the bottom" but became so generally sensed that a revolution in thinking about scientifically produced danger occurred. The sciences then entered "the reflexive phase" as their "*claim to enlightenment was demystified.*"[25] The Great Mississippi Flood allows us to see that almost two decades before 1945, science was being publicly associated with a "colossal blunder," and "risk" was already making its appearance as the new norm in some intellectual circles. It also shows us that in this new order, the consequences of risk would continue—against Beck's theorization—to be unequally distributed.[26] Moreover, those at "the bottom" in the rural South had never felt themselves to be living in a "science society" and thus perceived technological failure in the Great Flood differently. Given such modern conditions, in which "the human" has achieved a new mixture of intense agency (engraving its practices on the biosphere with geological force and duration) and intense vulnerability (as we find our everyday consciousnesses, knowledge-making processes, and political structures now outmoded in this crunch time of potential irreversibility) without the intellectual traditions to understand what this uneven agency means,[27] it seems appropriate to place this 1927 event within a new kind of timeline, or narrative, of human/natural history representing the emergence of the Anthropocene. The contours of the 1927 disaster—its racial and regional manifestations, its political and media handling, its repercussions to human conceptions of self—show us what life within the Anthropocene has become. We see in the 1920s an early arrival of a "Risk Society," but different from the one Beck described.

Within such a narrative, some things that once looked peripheral now seem central. Some people who once seemed lost to history now seem to be key participants in it. Inhabitants of the Delta in 1927—white planters but even more so poor whites and African Americans—were imagined by the rest of the country to be historically retrograde, caught in "Lost Cause" nostalgia, outmoded Christian fundamentalism, or feudal social and labor relations. The Harlem Renaissance spokesman Alain Locke, for example, described the northward migration of southern blacks to be not only a geographical move "from countryside to city" but also a temporal move forward "from Medieval America to modern."[28] Northern pundit H. L. Mencken imagined all southerners to represent "a hostile tribe on our borders,"[29] as if they were a throwback to the barbarian hordes. Sociologist Georg Simmel was one among many who characterized the small-town and rural inhabitant as "emotional," as "rooted in the unconscious levels of the mind [which] develop most readily in the steady equilibrium of unbroken customs"; he contrasted this figure with the "metropolitan type" whose "intensification of consciousness" is brought on by "the profound disruption with which the fluctuations and discontinuities of the external milieu threaten" him.[30] And recall Taylor's surprise that the crowd on the levee wanted newspapers, let alone news about cutting-edge aviation.

To combat such views typical of metropolitan commentators, historians of the Western Hemisphere plantation zone (stretching from Maryland to the northern part of South America) have built an argument since the 1940s that the plantation was one of the first modern places on earth. Sugar colonies housed one of the first forms of factory production; migrant and multicultural populations from around the Atlantic world produced together, and against each other, creole cultures alongside a new construct of race, and race-based slavery; landscapes were quickly obliterated to produce monoculture crops for a world market, bringing on both environmental turmoil and a dawning ecological awareness;[31] and financial speculation attached to commodified labor and plants produced the profits that would launch industrialism.[32] In other words, modernity is marked not only by industrialization, urbanization, mass consumerism, and mass mediation in nineteenth-century North Atlantic centers but also by the production of cash crops for a world market in which poor, racially marked laborers are rendered vulnerable by their being caught in a degraded environment that their labor has helped to alter, a phenomenon begun in the plantation zone in the sixteenth and seventeenth centuries.[33] Modernity not only is a threshold entered through technological and political progress but also consists of new experiences of dislocation, reification, vulnerability, and creolization within a "second nature."[34]

In 1927, the almost exclusively African American population that Taylor encountered was not only holding out on a man-made levee. As the source of cotton labor, they had been prevented, by the planter interest, from evacuating onto an empty rescue barge and were later, by the National Guard, kept from flight and forced to work in what the Red Cross called a "concentration camp."[35] The term "concentration camp" had first come into use in the suppression of colonial insurrections some thirty years earlier in Cuba and South Africa.[36] Its most horrific application, of course, would begin in Nazi Germany six years after the flood, in 1933. Giorgio Agamben has controversially described the concentration camp as "the hidden paradigm of the political space of modernity" because it combines the state's inherent totalitarian potential with its ostensible role in regulating the health and security of its population.[37] And yet, as a consideration of these 1927 Delta concentration camps indicates, there is a distinct history to the American, as opposed to the European, version of biological management. Michel Foucault has argued that governments from the late eighteenth century forward began to assume a "biopolitical" function, addressing subjects at a mass scale and attempting to "control the random element in biological processes"—birth and mortality rates, contagion, environmental instability—by maintaining an "overall equilibrium" through "complex systems of coordination." And yet this new regulatory function of government continued to coexist with an older, disciplinary "right of the sword." The Nazi death camps used old sovereign power perversely to kill citizens under the logic of maintaining social welfare; Nazi "biopower" distorted the Darwinian theory of evolution to imagine that the "death of the bad race . . . is something that will make life in general healthier."[38]

A different biopolitical history pertained in the American plantation zone. There, governmental control over "the random element in biological processes" did not "become racist" in the twentieth century. Rather, plantation powers had invented race in the late seventeenth and eighteenth centuries to make a buffer zone between itself and this biological uncertainty.[39] Bodies marked as "black" and physical labor became fused categories, while "whiteness" established distance from a host of biological perils through this labor tool. Whites protected themselves, their property, and the category of whiteness itself by positioning black bodies to absorb various manifestations of biological chance: pest infestations, unpredictable weather, infertile soil, tropical earthquakes, fluctuating crop yields, contagious disease, unexpected fires in sugar manufacture, and risky oceanic transit. Within European biopolitics, governments used probabilistic reasoning to mitigate biological and other forms of chance for an *entire* population; plantation powers, by contrast, designed one part of the population to protect the other.[40] Agricultural laborers always, to a certain extent, perform this buffering function for landholders, but in the American plantation zone, where for centuries the laborer's body and bodily reproduction were owned, and where that body's "nature" was concocted by its owner, people of African descent came to assume an unusually absolute function of being that nature which protected another class of people from nature's unpredictability.[41]

In the 1927 Delta concentration camps, then, neither southern planters nor cooperating institutions like the National Guard and the Red Cross could have imagined that white health could be achieved through the total "death of the bad race." Though scores of individual black people were, in the decades leading up to 1927, ritualistically killed on the pretext of keeping black and white lineage apart, the planter interest was keenly aware that the region's economic health utterly depended upon the continuing life and proximity of black labor. The Red Cross concentration camps were—to modify Agamben's phrase—a political space of rural plantation modernity. And as blacks went from being inoculated in camps to reinforcing levees, their role as a living buffer zone between whites and nature's dangerous vagaries was made literally manifest.

What I plan to make clear in this book is that for African American rural laborers, existing in this strange zone—having had their own "second nature" defined by others while being forced into an intimacy with an unpredictable plantation nature mostly of their own physical creation—also allowed these laborers to know their environment with great empirical acumen. This deep experiential knowledge, however, made as it was in a Jim Crow society, did not earn the status of rationality. Rural, southern rural, and especially black southern rural people were understood by metropolitan commentators to be fossilized and curious specimens of a pre-Enlightenment epistemology when in fact plantation laborers had a long history of seeing modernity's limitations, costs, and dangers. Though we have recognized the metropolitan artists and pundits in the North Atlantic who communicated the disintegration—during and between the world wars—of Enlightenment-seeded modern projects (like democratic rationality, or the European imperial order), we have little understood how this rural, southern, American crisis of 1927 produced a separate but equally significant response to modernity's troubles.[42]

Paul Gilroy, extending the work of the Caribbeanist scholars mentioned earlier, made the case some twenty years ago in his book *The Black Atlantic* for reenvisioning modernity as not an exclusively European product. He urged that scholars assume the "transnational and intercultural perspective," represented by a broader Atlantic geography, to grasp how modernity emerged in an "intimate association" with slavery, colonialism, and scientific racism.[43] Jace Weaver has recently mapped out the existence of a corresponding "Red Atlantic" by tracing the importance of indigenous Americans to the growth of the trade, technology, and political modeling that helped create the modern West.[44] Despite the critical importance of this recovery of an intercultural Atlantic history, we still need to focus more attention on the particular insights that non-Europeans contributed on the subject of the drastic environmental changes that occurred in the Atlantic world alongside colonialism and the establishment of plantations.[45] Environmental justice scholarship, the New Orleans levee disaster, and the increasingly visible overlay of global climate change hotspots with old maps of extractive empire put scholars in a position today to hear in the archives of Atlantic history the green inflection in which the "dissident assessment" of modernity has taken place.[46] We can hear in the archives not only a political critique of the failures of the Enlightenment project of universal liberation but also an environmental critique of the Enlightenment project of reducing Nature to an instrument of human profit. If the ship was the key "chronotope" of Gilroy's study, the *raft*—understood as a catchall for any makeshift floating device, like a downed airplane, coffin, piece of roof, or stolen rowboat—is the chronotope of this one.[47] While the ship represented for Gilroy the purposive circuits of an exploitative but materially and culturally burgeoning modernity, the raft, which reappears again and again in the 1927 flood archives, indicates to me how underresourced and colonized people around the globe have been the first to need to improvise structures for survival in the wake of material depletion.

One reason I raise this issue of a multicentered and eco-literate modernity is to establish at the outset that the flood zone in the Lower Mississippi Valley was by no means a disconnected, peculiar, remote hinterland, as words like "bottomlands," "Deep South," and "Medieval" suggest and as the customary location of this material in the disciplinary subfield of "Southern Studies" might indicate.[48] Global trade connections between the Delta and the "cottonopolis" of Manchester, England—including the fact that the largest cotton plantation in the world was located in the Delta and owned by a Manchester company[49]—

meant that the *Manchester Guardian* followed the flood more carefully than many a U.S. paper.[50] New Orleans was a major shipping and banking center, a strategic nexus in a worldwide circuit of goods and capital. Herbert Hoover, the commerce secretary put in charge of rescue and relief efforts by President Calvin Coolidge, transposed to the Delta his experience managing the health of a mass population of Europeans during and after wartime. Many reporters sent to cover the flood brought with them their memory of the battlefields of Europe. Southern Vaudevillians most important to disaster fund-raising—like Will Rogers—had spent their careers in international entertainment circuits. The authors who thought most deeply and critically about this flood, William Faulkner and Richard Wright, engaged with the aesthetics of European leftist artists and intellectuals to draw out the resonances between convulsions overseas and convulsions at home. Thus, in terms both material and cultural, the Delta flood zone was fully enmeshed in a contemporaneous global skein.

Taylor, the publicist, described the flood as a "tragedy" that "nature had enacted." In fact, the unpredictable, and temporarily destructive, features natural to any river had been severely exacerbated by industrial-scale alterations of the watershed taking place since the nineteenth century. As I explain in chapter 1, deforestation, wetlands drainage, and monoculture farming seriously reduced the storage capacity of the watershed's soil. Added to this intense environmental alteration, designers of the flood protection system elected *not* to mimic an alluvial basin's own mechanisms for slowing water's movement and for holding and dispersing water in times of overflow. They decided instead to straighten and impound the river within a towering levee system. In the decades before the flood, then, Euro- and African Americans had gradually transformed a natural disturbance-maintained regime, characterized by periodic overflows, into a massive hydraulic mechanism—what one Mississippi journalist called a "trough aqeduct [*sic*]" rolling like "an elevated railroad" high above the land— that, when breached, could cause catastrophic damage.[51] Because modern engineering, agriculture, and silviculture all coalesced in their misapprehension of the complex behavior of the watershed, this catastrophe was significant as a very public science experiment, and a highly leveraged resource extraction enterprise, gone wrong. To put it in the terms of the "biopolitical" discussed a moment ago, the U.S. government, combined with timber and agricultural interests, had sought to "control the random element in biological processes" by turning the river into a rationalized drainage pipe but, in so doing, managed to turn the river into an even more unpredictable cataract.[52]

The mediation producing this flood for the public was distinctly new. Unlike the deadlier U.S. floods in Johnstown, Pennsylvania (1889), Galveston, Texas

(1900), and the Lake Okeechobee area of Florida (1928), which all occurred in a matter of hours, this flood moved so slowly and lasted so long—Faulkner would call it "the flood year 1927"[53]—that national audiences could be pulled in, through newly established media circuits, to the events as they occurred. Indeed, real-time, virtual disaster consumption began with this flood. Moreover, because no Federal Emergency Management Association (FEMA) yet existed, and because Congress refused to convene to appropriate emergency funds, all money for relief efforts had to be raised from that virtual national audience. Indeed, the word "audience" fails to capture the ways in which citizens from Los Angeles to New York City participated in the prolonged event, for the public linked together by the catastrophe mattered to—and actually altered—its unfolding.

The speed with which the media could shape public perception of what was occurring in the Delta was a product of some quite recent innovations in communication and transport technologies. Taylor, for example, described the various technologies put into use on April 25 to connect the chaotic stretches of the Lower Mississippi: "Telephones frantically ringing; a wireless sputtering incessantly . . . ; aviators rushing in to report new levee breaks; . . . Leased wires to Vicksburg, Natchez, Baton Rouge, New Orleans, Alexandria . . . bringing in every minute of the day and night news of overwhelming disasters."[54] While wired telegraphy was some ninety years old, the other means of communication were phenomena of only the preceding decades. Radio had gone national only weeks before, thanks to Hoover. All of this information pulsing through his office, Taylor suggests, was answered with commensurate dispatches of relief, making the headquarters "busy, throbbing, humming, [and] noisy."[55] Combined with these technologies, other media such as newsprint, musical recordings, and film were charged into service to, as the Red Cross's director of public information put it, "mobilize the resources of the entire nation in behalf of [this] disaster-stricken population."[56] Indeed, as I discuss in chapter 4, this "super-flood"[57] was so protracted and media technologies so swift that Bessie Smith's "Back-Water Blues"—the song that became *the* ballad of the flood—was inspired by personal experience, written, sung, and etched onto a wax disc, then advertised in white and black newspapers in both the North and South, purchased, and set on Victrolas *two and three months later* by listeners in the Delta, just as the flood crest was ponderously working its way down the Lower Mississippi.

This new combination of swift mediation and protracted calamity allows us to witness an early version of what Rob Nixon recently termed "slow violence." By this phrase, he characterizes environmentally linked distress that occurs "gradually and out of sight, a violence of delayed destruction that is dispersed across time and space," and, as such, "is typically not viewed as violence at all."[58] Taking the phenomena of the toxic drift and the biomagnification of DDT, warned about in 1962 by Rachel Carson, as an origin point of this late modern environmental reality, Nixon distinguishes it from the fast and sublime spectacles that contemporary media traffic in.[59]

Between these two models, the 1927 flood offers a hybrid case. Though media producers—from journalists to carnival exhibition designers—tried to quickly package this flood as the dazzling spectacle that, for example, the Galveston deluge seemed to have been, it was too slow to satisfy consumers who had been thrilled by scenes of swift destruction since the beginning of the century. Though the flood's pace was narratively advantageous at first—allowing the public to feel the suspense of an unfolding event—it wasn't long before this protracted cyclicality became a communications problem. Along the Mississippi, levees broke, and broke, and kept breaking. Flooded acres and numbers of evacuees were counted and, the following week, counted again. After about two months, media pundits started to complain about the "iteration of the same sequence"[60] and invoked Aristotle's rule of dramatic unities to pronounce this disaster aesthetically unsatisfying. It was just too sprawling and repetitive. Moreover, much early hype about the flood uncoupled it from human causation. Also like the contemporary instances of slow violence that Nixon describes, this earlier flood occurred in a "resource-rich, regulation-poor, war-fractured societ[y]." It, too, induced the widespread problem of "displacement without moving."[61] And it, too, raises the critical question of how those afflicted by, or close to, the submerged and drawn-out violence of the Delta experience were able to make matters visible to a distant—and increasingly disaffected and attention-sapped—audience.

Though many journalists, like Taylor, represented the flood as a deliberate natural onslaught, and though many ministers attributed the flood to God's anger, the Flood of 1927 was noteworthy in that it eventually was hailed as a humanly caused calamity. Unlike the Johnstown and Okeechobee floods, both also man-made disasters, in which the powerful industrialists involved in the first case and the Florida boosters in the second sought to avoid publicity, in 1927 southerners with access to the national media determined to bring attention to the flood—and to its human causes. White southerners saw it as a fully political event and made that point heard. Just two years after the Scopes "Monkey" Trial, when the categories "southern," "fundamentalism," and "anti-science" were fused together in the national mind—when outsiders believed that for every southerner, "The earth is God's stage," as Wilbur J. Cash would quip[62]—it was primarily southern editorials that deciphered and declared the human role in the flood. In particular, pundits argued, the federal government had failed miserably in its management of a watershed covering two-thirds of the nation, and it was the South that, yet again, suffered.

Moreover, because the course of the flood moved from north to south, retracing the 1863 river-borne assault on the Confederate strongholds of Mississippi and Louisiana, this flood had the peculiar power to make sixty-four-year-old history feel unfinished—to make it feel even biologically reenacted. Many in the white Delta looked at the water destroying their crops, scattering "their" labor, drowning their animals, and sinking them into greater debt, and saw it as Yankee water. Southerners in states farther away from the river had sympathy for such a position.

Advocates for southern black farm laborers likewise found old politics written all over the flood. As conditions in the evacuee camps spelled for their black populations both forced labor and violently guarded movement, it seemed to many that slavery had returned to Dixie and that northern institutions were abetting its reestablishment. W.E.B. Du Bois, for example, in an editorial he wrote for the NAACP's *Crisis* magazine, would place a caption that read "The Slave Ship, 1927" beneath a photograph of a rescue barge moving down the Mississippi. A *Pittsburgh Courier* editorial declared: "Despite the Civil War and the 13th, 14th and 15th Amendments, the cotton barons it seems are determined to hold their black slaves in bondage."[63] Ida B. Wells, Walter White, William Pickens, Jesse O. Thomas, and others made similar public analyses. The white South convinced many beyond their borders to take up their view, while the black press faced a harder time reaching across the color line to make their case more broadly.

White Americans in the North and West were also quick to summon memories of the Civil War as a way to involve themselves in the South's current battle. Imaginatively reenacting the 1860s conflict allowed them not only to revisit a victory but also to rewrite the terms of that victory. Instead of the destroyers of a plantation splendor they themselves had come to romanticize and feel nostalgia for, whites in the North and West of the country cast themselves, in the words of the *New York Times*, as "an army of rescuers."[64] The northern invader was, in Herbert Hoover's nationwide radio address, reenvisioned as a "water enemy" attacking "the people of our south," against which "the engineers" and "strong and experienced men from every important center" were "directing" a "great battle."[65] Administering to their needy white brethren would help heal old wounds and return accord to the national house. White southerners found such noblesse oblige and such belated engineering and professional acumen from the North—including the role-playing it involved—to be dim-witted and aggravating. In a surprising inversion of the cultural geography, the white South was using science to demand increased federal involvement in Dixie while the North and West dwelled in their own chivalric reverie.[66] Though the death toll from the flood was more limited than that of other twentieth-century environmental disasters, it was the way that this flood—for northern, southern, white, and black publics—uncannily rematerialized the defining American nightmares of slavery and civil war that made it so culturally engulfing.

This disaster produced a complex configuration of overlapping and contending reading and listening publics who made meaning out of the event in a variety of ways (the subject of chapters 2 and 3). Added to this virtual print and auditory realm, thousands of people, inside and outside the South, gathered in live rituals of gift-giving. "Monster Benefits" were staged in Hollywood, Atlanta, Chicago, Boston, New York, and New Orleans. People put on circuses in Indiana, amateur theatricals in D.C., an opera concert aboard a transatlantic ocean liner, and boxing benefits in Rhode Island. Of all, the most typical, and successful, type of benefit performance was delivered in the Vaudeville variety mode. Without knowing that this was Vaudeville's dying gasp, performers—from blues singers to comedians to escape artists—offered venues in which spectators around the nation could and did think about the South, about race in America, about media consumption, and about the environmental politics of the flood.

Many of these Vaudeville fund-raiser acts appearing outside the South centered on a predictable minstrel invocation of a lovable, pitiable, and risible Dixie. To the contrary, as I explain in chapter 5, Vaudevillians who found themselves caught within the flood zone practiced a meaningful and participatory "environmental theatre" for the surrounding communities.[67] Up north, the Vaudevillians who hailed from the South but had traveled the national and international circuits of the live entertainment industry brought to their benefit acts the kind of experience that afforded them a distinct acumen. The "Cowboy humorist" and fancy roper Will Rogers, son of a man who was both a Confederate soldier and a Cherokee leader in Oklahoma Territory, raised more money for flood victims than any other individual. Through his daily newspaper columns and his gala appearances in New Orleans and New York City, he mustered a national response that was critical and sentimental at the same time. Rogers managed simultaneously to cajole, accuse, and amuse his audiences as he encouraged them to feel the obligations of citizenship. The black comedians Aubrey Lyles and Flournoy Miller, raised in Tennessee just miles east of the flood zone, and crossover artists to white Broadway, were headliners in a

"Monster Vaudeville Benefit" at the Lafayette in Harlem, a theater that drew in both black and white audiences. Conveying their humor through something they called a "syncopated argument," Miller and Lyles used a series of off-tempo swerves in logic, and the exaggerated ridiculing of ignorance, to trigger realizations in their audience about the hazards of black life in the United States. As audience members "got" their wit, they got to thinking, and relished the whole process enough to want more.

Contrary to the assumption that the most productive public encounter a society can have about its crises occurs through print media that encourage rational debate, I argue in chapter 5 that the history of performances surrounding the 1927 disaster suggests otherwise. The disembodied realm of the newspaper coupled with a disinterested form of reporting, in particular, have been understood to engage a reading public in a deliberative process that allows hidden truths to emerge. In such arguments, from Walter Lippmann to Jürgen Habermas, "entertainment" in general, and theater in particular, are believed to foster a passive and escapist stupor in a merely pleasure-seeking audience. The field of performance studies has, for the last few decades, been answering this antitheatrical prejudice on the part of theorists of the democratic public sphere by arguing for the many ways in which embodied performances make possible profound kinds of cultural reckonings and cognitive transformations. Historians of disaster have made the link between disaster and theater: they point out that these destabilizing events turn the societies in which they occur into a kind of enormous theater to stage "expiation" and thus "ward off danger and reestablish normality." Print journalism, radio, and live performance were in 1927 *all* part of those ritual efforts to place blame and give gifts; rationality or irrationality was not particular to any one medium. And if disasters "lay bare the longue durée as a society mobilizes its deepest cultural reserves in response to a crisis in its habitual forms of real and symbolic exchange,"[68] then my study of how publics and individuals made meaning out of the Mississippi Flood of 1927 will help assess how the nation's "deepest cultural reserves" reckoned with what was problematic in its "habitual forms" of economic, intellectual, and social life. I also contend that this crisis not only helped artists tap into existing "reserves" but even forced them to devise new questions, new thoughts, and new aesthetic strategies.

To put it another way: the Flood of 1927 had the ability to call into question key intellectual paradigms then in ascendance. There were widespread, cross-disciplinary scholarly and intellectual investments in the concept of *equilibrium* in this period. Derived from a conservative, nineteenth-century interpretation of Darwinian evolution, natural scientists developed a model that accounted for biological changes over time by theorizing that such change was purposive and stabilizing. Nature complicated itself as it progressed, and this process actually created a more concordant, subtly interdependent, and stable world. Practitioners in the social sciences took up this concept of Nature's "patient self-rectification"[69] as a model for how human societies evolve and function. Thus sociologists who studied disaster in this period contended that such events worked like a therapeutic reset button, making social organisms more balanced and integrated. As it became increasingly clear during the spring of 1927 that two major American systems were designed for dangerous results, and kept producing calamity after calamity, whether in recurrent Mississippi floods or flares of Jim Crow violence, direct witnesses and distant commentators who followed the disaster closely articulated a vision of reality—an ontology—based upon chance, and a risk-based maneuvering within such chance, rather than upon equilibrium. They saw that in the plantation zone it was the laboring bodies of poor whites, and still more so poor blacks, that, as it were, absorbed risk itself. Their stories, acts, and songs asked the world to notice this sleight of hand too.

In the dozen years following the Mississippi flood, in the early but enduring work of Faulkner and Wright, these authors visited and revisited this flood and created out of it fictional worlds run on catastrophic coincidence, mad gaps in empirical processes, tricky currents skewing spatial and mental orientation, and new risk-centered forms of perception. This model of a more unpredictable, chance-driven, even chaotic world would not catch on in the field of ecology until the 1970s. Ahead of the shift in scientific paradigm, both Wright and Faulkner (as I argue in chapters 6 and 7) articulated this model as they braided together rural and small-town Mississippi experience, blues expression, the national mediation of the flood during 1927, and their contact with contemporary transatlantic intellectual, literary, and visual enterprises. While European literary modernism, Dada, Surrealism, and other avant-garde movements made their audiences think about war, industrialization, consumerism, and the rise of fascism, environmental catastrophe was not yet a major European cultural concern. Wright and Faulkner, by contrast, lived in a nation where "nature [wa]s supposed to be most completely subdued" but was in fact showing tumultuous signs of distress; they lived in "Nature's Nation" where risks had accumulated, geographically and socially, at the bottom.[70] Thus they brought to an evolving global Modernism a rural and cosmopolitan meditation on a new kind of catastrophic environmental consciousness.

Moving through various media—weather, river, radio, newspaper, live comedy act, recorded song, poem, novella, novel—this book does not stress a distinction between Nature's event and humanity's culture, or between a human subject and his or her environs. Philosophically, I agree with John Dewey in his assertion that "environment is not something around and about human activities in an external sense; it is their *medium* or *milieu*."[71] Conversely, the environment, or an evolving biology, takes us as its medium as well. There is no position outside the circuit. I therefore describe a decades-long "material-discursive" event in which "material phenomena" and "discursive practices" snag and crisscross and knot.[72] When a levee broke in 1927, for example, it was simultaneously a biological phenomenon involving water and earth *and* a human expression involving technological design (the levee structure), environmental design (the transformation of the watershed), social design (the composition of laborers on the levee), and rhetorical design (the explanation and dissemination of the event). The various media mentioned earlier are not lined up like objects in space moving increasingly and distortingly away from some original truth of *what Nature did*. Rather, all these media, and the humans participating in them, converse with and affect and create each other.

As is clear in chapter 1, the work of trying to arrive at a baseline story of factual history relies itself on collaging letters, reports, newspaper accounts, committee investigations, and so on. In traditional historiography, the more "private" those media—a letter, for example, from one Red Cross official to another—the more revealing it is taken to be, thus establishing another dichotomy between *what actually happened* and *the public representation*, which is understood to be at a distortive remove from truth. Behind-the-scenes transactions of those in power *are* critical to understand. But we should not presume that such sequestered political power controls the sustained and broader cultural power of meaning-making. What this book offers, then, is not the "true history" of an event but rather—using the method that modernists employed to capture the simultaneity of variant truths across a social field—an arrayed account in which I investigate how groups, working across multiple media and genres, and often in conflict with each other, made the flood significant.[73]

In contending that a major catastrophe offers us an exceptionally good opportunity to analyze social and cultural patterns of the Western world in 1927, I am not that unlike the sociologists in the 1920s and 1930s who performed case studies of disasters to understand how social organisms work.[74] Their premise, however, was that organisms are inherently self-stabilizing and that a disaster jolts that process into action by getting problems quickly out in the open to be solved. The social model I have derived from the archives of this flood is different: the flood did not galvanize into existence a newer, better balance (between humans and nature, black and white, North and South, wealthy and poor), even if it did cause the federal government to rejigger the levee system. Instead, it suggested that nature's unpredictability could not be engineered into placidity. It suggested that catastrophe was the abiding, everyday reality of Jim Crow. It suggested that the gap between "problem-solvers and problem-laymen,"[75] between system designers operating at a distance from the consequences of their decisions and those who had a more direct and immersive experience of those consequences, had grown too vast. And it suggested that a paradigm shift was occurring, such that visions of equilibrium needed to make way for perceptions of, and strategies for negotiating, a world of unpredictable change. In the new Risk Society hailed by Beck, the sciences no longer monopolize rationality but instead make way for the claims of amateurs who can circulate these claims in a "*science, media and information* society."[76] When amateurs looked at this flood, they saw broken systems; when most technocrats and engineers did, they saw clues for tweaking the existing machinery.

The "problem-solver" par excellence of the 1927 flood, Herbert Hoover, was, as he admitted, "too busy really to see this flood at close range," engaged as he was with building up the "great relief machine." He regretted, for example, that a white composer "didn't write a plaintive dirge which the negro refugees might sing in the camps," calling it a "great oversight."[77] He somehow missed the fact that such an influential song *had* been written, and sung into history, by Bessie Smith and that dozens more had appeared during the spring months. If he neither saw nor heard nor read the other "problem-laymen" and laywomen of the flood—Will Rogers, Miller and Lyles, Richard Wright, and William Faulkner, along with numerous other Vaudevillians, singers, and journalists—we, at least, can encounter them now. And we can examine how they drew various publics into the orbits of their thinking. I wager they have something to teach us still.

ONE

Modern Overflow

In a May 1, 1927, feature story in the *New York Times* Sunday magazine, re-porter Herschel Brickell announced, "Once more war is on between the mighty old dragon that is the Mississippi River and his ancient enemy, man." Brickell continued: the dragon is "something sentient," "something of unmeasurable power and unfathomable ingenuity," and, in his current battle, full of "rage and viciousness."[1] Illustrating the story was a contemporary photograph of the river in flood, shot near Memphis, Tennessee, but also, just below it, a reprint of an 1868 Currier & Ives lithograph called "High Water in the Mississippi," to which had been added the phrase "In Days Gone By" (Fig. 1.1). Through the curtain-like trees, the 1927 viewer—perhaps a Manhattanite drinking her Sunday morning coffee?—peeped at a gallant steamboat, a columned Great House, and a close-up scene of free Negro folk caught in a picturesque predicament of floating roofs and tugging mules—she saw, even as she looked at an image of catastrophe, a tableau bedecked in plantation nostalgia. To think of the South from the distance of Manhattan was somehow to think *back*—back to 1868, back further to a storied battle on the river in 1863, or maybe all the way back, to an "ancient" time when chivalrous men tilted at dragons.[2] It was hard for northerners to imagine the South as modern, and harder still for northerners to see the flood as an industrial disaster partly of their own making.

Economic and social commentator Stuart Chase was one of those northern-ers who did look critically at the flood as a sign of systemic trouble. In a 1936 book titled *Rich Land, Poor Land*, Chase contemplated not only the 1927 flood but also the still unfolding Dust Bowl, averring that his was a time of environ-mental "boomerangs." Trained as an accountant, he imagined American nature as a long-accruing depository that European settlers, equipped with a fallacious sense of resource "infinity," had quickly emptied out. While Europe was shaped "at a snail's pace over centuries," North America, beyond the Appalachians, "was settled with railroads and steam, at a gallop, over decades." At the end of

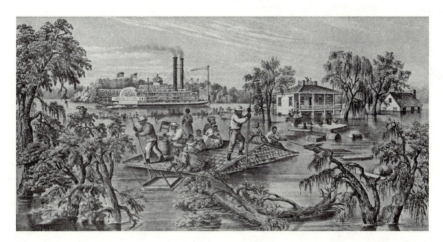

1.1. Frances F. Palmer, "High Water in the Mississippi," lithograph, published 1868 by Currier & Ives, reprinted in black and white in Herschel Brickell, "Again the Old Dragon Mississippi Fumes," *New York Times*, May 1, 1927, SM9.

those decades of industrial development, he wrote, "The boomerangs are now returning thick and fast."[3] As Brickell's dragon attests, the river in 1927 might have seemed a conscious, vengeful, primordial agent bursting its chains. It was easier to think that the only thing humanity had done to the river was try to restrain it and that the river was still its ancient, fighting self. Chase, however, perceived correctly that a river is not a willful agent but rather one neutral part of various natural and humanly altered cycles, systems, and histories. To understand 1927 in the Delta, then, we have to understand that industrial "gallop" which occurred throughout the Mississippi watershed after the Civil War.

Though developers throughout the entire watershed, as well as federal engineers and distant investors, were all implicated in the volume of water descending upon the Delta, it was there, especially in Arkansas, Mississippi, and Louisiana, where the shape of the disaster would take on the contours of the regional social order. According to contemporary scholars of disaster, these events exhibit the "*characteristic* rather than accidental features of the places and societies where they occur"; risks and consequences hence flow from ordinary—rather than *extra*ordinary—life.[4] Focusing on the flood as a social rather than environmental crisis, the secretary of the Chicago branch of the Red Cross, Maurice Reddy, wrote confidentially in a letter to headquarters that summer: "Of course, I think we have to realize that conditions in the South have been bad for several years and that the flood may have been 'the straw which broke the camel's back.'"[5] Looking at the flood zone from Chicago, Reddy imagined a strained social system that had been pushed into collapse by an external event. Commentators more aware of the ways in which the Delta—its Jim Crow structure, its forms of indebtedness, and its distribution of wealth and property— was perpetually at risk of sliding into violence and de facto enslavement did not perceive the flood to be the final breaking of a functional system afflicted by recent decline. Instead, the flood forced out in the open—for those willing to look—the chronic and longstanding social and economic precariousness of the Delta. The flood made visible the combination of history and natural history that had produced it.[6]

Boomerang

A map of the Mississippi watershed looks like an asymmetrical, intricately branched, giant crown of a tree improbably poised on the shortest of trunks (Fig. 1.2). The river's drainage area covers about 40 percent of the United States, drawing from thirty-one states between the Rocky and the Allegheny mountains and from two Canadian provinces.[7] Its tremendous reach makes it not only a regional but a fully continental land feature. The Missouri and the Ohio rivers make up its major northern tributaries, while below the junction at Cairo, Illinois, where the river levels out and slows, it is primarily the St. Francis, Arkansas, Red, and Yazoo rivers that contribute to its volume. Between Cairo and the Gulf, the lower river does not actually resemble the "trunk" the map suggests. In fact, there is nothing solid or stable about it. The floodplain, from Illinois south, is naturally a dynamic environment, comprising what ecologists call a "disturbance regime," meaning that the periodic occurrence of floods—the "disturbance"—created and maintained an environment that depended on these floods' sedimentary and fluid deposits.[8] The environment of this Delta region, therefore, is not exactly a "terra firma," the National Geographic Society was wont to explain in 1927, but instead "a quaking morass of jelly-like silt through which the river meets the sea."[9] The rich alluvial soils and swamps of the river's bottomlands were brought into being over thousands of years by sediment-bearing water moving southward in continually shifting channels and meander patterns and by the river's aperiodic flooding beyond these mobile banks. A rich "heterogeneity" of vegetation and habitats was a healthy feature of these bottomlands, produced as the curvilinear river kept shifting its earthen signature.[10]

The river itself, even when not in flood, is complex and unpredictable. The Mississippi has multiple velocities at its different levels, multiple, independent

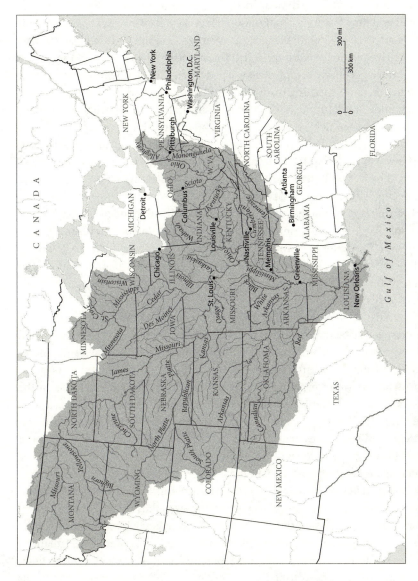

1.2. The Mississippi watershed. © Princeton University Press.

currents moving in different directions, and multiple depths within a single stretch. Consequently, violent undertows and giant whirlpools form. The river carries a tremendous sediment load that, in turn, redirects where the river moves and how fast it moves. Friction affecting velocities can arise from multiple sources: the wind, the banks, the riverbed, and the motion of sediment.[11] As one river engineer put it in 1851: "The surface of the river is not therefore a plane, but a peculiarly complicated warped surface."[12] Another observer of river turbulence, and its issuing from a host of competing and unpredictable influences, understood turbulence as "akin to a clockmaker's shop with a huge number of clocks each ticking at a different, irrational rhythm."[13]

As the river bends, it continually deposits soils on the inside of curves and cuts away at outer banks. Eventually, as this process makes the curves more acute, the river will often cut through bends, redirecting its own course and producing leftover ox-bow lakes and swamps. These resulting slackwater areas, full of ridges and sloughs, made up of former stream beds or scoured out in time of flood, acted to contain or drain water in time of succeeding floods; moreover, the dense hardwood forests they supported could take in and dissipate some of a flood's force. As historian John M. Barry explains, "Without levees, even a great flood . . . meant only a gradual and gentle rising and spreading of water."[14]

The Mississippi watershed, even in what we can ascertain of its natural, unmodernized state, then, is full of unpredictability. Delta scion Will Percy called the river "the shifting unappeasable god of the country."[15] Complex and unforeseeable weather patterns across the continent contribute to its uneven flow; storms in the western plains or in the Alleghenies affect water levels in the Lower Valley; the river is perpetually reshaping the land, which, in turn, shapes the river; in all, it is—or was—a regime maintained by its chance-dependent patterns of disturbances. In the course of the nineteenth century, though, major shifts in land use and the built environment designed to make the lands of the watershed more profitable, and, in theory more predictable, nevertheless made the Lower Valley more potentially dangerous to humans. Industrial deforestation, the mowing under of prairie grasslands, wetlands drainage, commercial monoculture, population settlement near the river, and a levees-only engineering policy conspired to produce this profitable but highly precarious situation.

Forests absorb water. To be more precise, "the litter on the forest floor, grasses, herbs, shrubs, rotting logs, twigs, leaves, flowers, even rocks and pebbles, all [retard] the runoff of the rains and snows." After 1800, that "slowly building humus" of the forests that covered the middle of the continent began to disappear.[16] The lumber industry, moving westward from the denuded hills

1.3. A lumber raft, Duluth, Minnesota, 1903–4. Postcard. Detroit Publishing Company. Miriam and Ira D. Wallach Division, New York Public Library, New York. New York Public Library/Art Resource, NY.

and mountains of New England, first concentrated on the forests of New York and Pennsylvania. As early as 1805, lumbermen began to cut down the white pine stands of this region, moving them to market along the Allegheny and Ohio rivers to the Mississippi. These tributary streams seemed "almost covered for miles with floating rafts" of logs during springtime high water. This extraction reached its peak in the 1830s and came to a close around 1870, having exhausted the area's pineries. Lumbering by midcentury had begun to move to the upper Midwest.[17]

From the Black, Wisconsin, and Chippewa River regions of Wisconsin, felled pine trees traveled to the Mississippi.[18] By 1850, lumbering had become the main industry in Minnesota, especially in the St. Croix pineries between the Mississippi River and Canada. Lumber drawn from the upper Midwest would be the dominant source for the nation's wood-dependent growth until 1890 (Fig. 1.3). St. Louis was the central trading port for Upper Valley timber heading to the developing, and tree-poor, prairie communities farther west.[19] As these lumbering activities moved from one stand of first-growth pines to another, selective tree-cutting turned into the swifter but improvident practice of clear-cutting as lumbermen developed increasingly industrial techniques of extraction, milling, and transportation.[20] These water routes by which the timber was moved reveal the resulting geography of watershed vulnerability. In other words, the rain- and snowfall previously stored by the forest soils would, once those forests were gone, move swiftly along the same tributary river routes to the Mississippi that the felled trees had traveled.[21] As logs had moved, so too would high water.

The industrial logging of the Mississippi's southern watershed commenced in earnest in the 1880s. Historical geographer Michael Williams explains that "the acceleration in commercial lumbering came with the sudden and massive transfer of capital, technology, and know-how from the North." Southern governments failed to check absentee extraction and exportation of their major resources, allowing a situation to develop of "semicolonial dependency" on northern financiers.[22] Investigating southern timber resources for a federal census of 1880, Dr. Charles Mohr presciently reported that in the Mississippi bottomland, "The cutting of these cypress forests is not wisely regulated under the ownership of the state. . . . [which] sells for 50 cents what on its face is worth to the purchaser hundreds of dollars, and which, when deprived of its value and rendered forever worthless, will be turned back to the state again." A local agent in Mississippi as early as 1884 sounded this warning note: "English and Northern capitalists are fast purchasing our magnificent pine forests. The avarice of capitalists and the great number of saw-mill men, if not in some way checked, will ere long destroy the grand pine forests of this section." By 1900, the South had eclipsed all other regions in lumber production, comprising 32 percent of the national total.[23] Highly efficient machines, like the steam skidder, could pull six hundred trees out of the forest in eight hours. This machine worked, as one observer noted in the early 1920s, like "an octopus of steel with several grappling arms running out 300 or more feet"; the "octopus[es]" dragged massive trees through the woods, "lay[ing] low everything in their way." What remained of the forest, the observer bleakly summarized, was "like the shell torn area of France."[24]

The Delta bottomlands of southeastern Missouri, eastern Arkansas, northwestern Mississippi, and northeastern Louisiana, which at first seemed too impenetrable for cultivation, came to attract outside capital investment in the later nineteenth century. Not only were lumbermen interested in the bottomland forests, but investors were now poised to "reclaim" the rich alluvial soil for cotton.[25] Along with deforestation, they needed to drain the wetlands and then protect the exposed soil from the very flooding that had constituted and nourished it. Allegiances of outside investors, big southern planters, and economically depressed but resource-rich postbellum southern states came together to accomplish these ends.

By the 1920s, much of this clear-cut land throughout the watershed lay waste. Colossal fires began to appear across the country on cutover territory, but most such fires were in the South.[26] Where trees were clear-cut in the southern watershed of the Mississippi, forests ceased to function as impediments to flooding. As Thomas D. Clark has pointed out, the mid-1920s represented "a major crossroads": "Never in the whole scope of southern history had such a large proportion of the land been caught in so harsh a crisis."[27]

In the plains region, through which the western tributaries run before joining the Mississippi, the transformation of the prairie grasslands into industrial-age wheat and corn belts likewise dramatically decreased the storage capacity of western watershed soils. The roots of the grasses, especially the six-feet-deep roots of the tall grasses, produced a mat to hold water (and humus) in. Beginning with large-scale cattle ranching in the 1860s, which depleted much of the grass, the prairie was then developed into small-scale farms beginning in the 1880s. Early twentieth-century mechanization and intense demand for wheat beginning during World War I accelerated a transformation toward large-scale, industrial farms. In the second half of the 1920s, wheat production increased 300 percent.[28] As Stuart Chase summarized this situation in 1936, considering that year's Mississippi Flood, the Dust Bowl, and the Flood of 1927: "The natural grass cover has been torn to ribbons by steel plows and the hooves of cattle and sheep. The skin of America has been laid open. Streams . . . heavy with silt, run wild in flood to the sea."[29]

Alongside industrial deforestation, removal of grasslands, and the spread of monoculture,[30] drainage of natural water reservoirs occurred in the watershed in this same period. On small farms in the Midwest in the early nineteenth century, drainage of wetlands was piecemeal and slow, often carried out by hand. With the introduction of steam dredges in the 1870s and 1880s, the draining of wetlands steadily accelerated. Moreover, this technology was expensive enough that it helped push out the small farmer, make way for industrial-scale agriculture, and usher in tenancy. Between 1880 and 1920, an "active propaganda" for capital-leveraged agricultural drainage was waged in midwestern newspapers and farming journals; the vision it promoted was that of "malarial wetlands" being miraculously transformed into America's "most bountiful cornfields." By the time of the flood, "all but a few, very small patches of wet prairie lay within the boundaries of organized drainage enterprises."[31]

As the natural means of water storage throughout the Mississippi's extended river system was being depleted by the loss of roots and reservoirs, engineers set out to manage the increased threat of severe flooding. Despite a series of sophisticated studies done in the nineteenth century to ascertain the surest methods for flood management—methods that often involved mimicking the river's natural migratory behavior that created zones for excess water storage—

1.4. "Mississippi River Improvement, 1890." National Archives 77-A-9–21. Courtesy of Office of History, HQ, U.S. Army Corps of Engineers.

the Army Corps of Engineers ultimately forsook the best wisdom produced in those studies. They rejected the building of reservoirs, outlets, and cutoffs that would have dissipated the main channel's force, indeed going so far as to close natural outlets, and relied instead on an unfounded assumption that a levees-only solution would increase the speed of the river and make it function, as one engineer said in 1912, like a "giant hydraulic dredge," scouring out and deepening the river's channel and thus "carry[ing] floods to the sea, where we want them to go, without damage to us."[32] Instead, silt deposited on the bed of the river merely raised the level of the water, requiring the levees to be built even higher. And, as the main channel grew in height, it would send its waters *backward* up the Mississippi's tributaries during flood, extending the horizon of damage.[33] In trying to lessen the risk to property inherent in a floodplain, this "levees only" policy paradoxically turned natural disturbance into potential catastrophe. For, as environmental historians note, the "more engineering that is done to control a river's path, the greater are the floods when they burst the barriers"[34] (Fig. 1.4).

Labor and Race

Developers of the ovoid bottomland to the east of the Mississippi that comprises the Yazoo-Mississippi Delta drew in a majority African American labor population to effect this environmental transformation. During the early postbellum stages of this process, frontier conditions, combined with Reconstruction politics, meant that African Americans could leverage their much-needed labor to achieve material and social advances. The 1880s, however, represented a negative turning point as planters consolidated and entrenched their power. As James C. Cobb summarizes: "An ambitious and grasping planter-business-professional elite" created at the end of the nineteenth century "an ironic combination of economic modernization and racial resubjugation." Planters maintained the upper hand in a number of ways. While in other parts of Mississippi between 1900 and 1925 roughly 20 percent of blacks owned their own farms, in the Delta that percentage declined from 7.3 to 2.9 in that same twenty-five-year period.[35] By the end of the 1920s, the great majority of farms in the Yazoo Delta—95 percent, in fact—were worked by tenants who did not own the land.[36] Sharecropping was the arrangement of choice for the planter because, unlike a pure wage-labor situation, it kept laborers on the planter's land throughout the crop cycle; it made the laborer share in—and to some extent absorb—the risk of lower agricultural yields; it allowed the planter, who typically forbade his tenant from selling his cotton elsewhere, to set the price of the tenant's crop; it allowed unscrupulous planters to fix the ledger books that a poorly educated tenantry could neither read nor tabulate differently; and, as it mired the tenant in year-to-year debt, it kept that cropper legally bound to stay put, amounting to a situation of debt peonage.[37] For these reasons, the sharecropping, or crop-lien, arrangement behooved the planter still more than paying workers on a wage basis or renting out his land for cash. The planter oligarchy buttressed their interests politically by supporting African American disfranchisement and by allowing a climate of racial violence to develop such that a lynching occurred every 5.5 months in the Mississippi Delta.[38] Though hierarchy did not break down into a simple white over black caste distinction in this period[39]—the notable presence of ethnic minorities in the merchant class and the existence of professional-class blacks and working-class whites all complicate such a binary—the majority of black farm laborers who had migrated to the Delta with the hope of sharing in the cotton boom found themselves crushed under the heels of poverty, debt, planter manipulation, a largely race-based political exclusion, and "an atmosphere of violent impermanence."[40]

In the parts of the Delta region across the river, from the boot heel of Missouri to the Tensas basin of Louisiana, the New South Cotton Kingdom followed a slightly different pattern. These counties also saw in-migrations of laborers, often from the less fertile hill country, seeking economic opportunity. The Louisiana bottomlands were less cleared and drained than other parts of the Delta, and hence less populated; areas that were planted to cotton there were worked by majority-black laborers. In Arkansas and Missouri, by contrast, the Delta counties were majority white, and there was slightly more widespread landownership on the part of farmers. However, 88 percent of cotton land in Louisiana, 83 percent in Arkansas, and 80 percent in Missouri were worked by tenants, making the great majority of black and white rural agricultural laborers in other parts of the Delta susceptible to a similar cyclical indebtedness felt in Mississippi.[41] Though in the 1880s and 1890s in Arkansas there was room for assertiveness on the part of laborers who had made allegiances across racial barriers, even if "vulnerable to violence and repression," in the 1920s, as cotton prices declined, that maneuvering room was all but lost.[42] In the 1920s, cotton production in other parts of the world—Egypt, India, Brazil, Iran, China, and the Sudan—was cheaper, putting added economic pressure on the U.S. South.[43] Planters tried to compensate for this downturn in profits by having their tenants plant more and more cotton for smaller and smaller returns. Indeed, by the time of the Flood of 1927, planters were especially reluctant to lose hold of their indebted sharecroppers to outmigration and were particularly anxious about their own indebtedness.[44]

In Louisiana, on land bordering the Mississippi and the Atchafalaya rivers, sugar was the staple crop. In the postbellum period, most farm labor was performed by African American wage workers. Because of the possibility of labor stoppage at harvest time, there was sporadic successful labor agitation until the 1887 Thibodeaux massacre, a violent response by local white militia and planters to a 10,000-person strike during the November harvest, in which somewhere between eight and fifty strikers were shot and killed. This event marked a turn toward white willingness to enact violent repression of laborers' collective action and to enforce an attitude of future black labor "humility."[45] Suffrage, though frequently and violently contested, remained a narrow means by which African Americans in sugar country could still exert influence.[46] In terms of the sugar culture, overreliance on the D-74 varietal of cane, which had begun in the 1890s, caused a plummeting of crop yields (from 324,000 tons to 47,000) when disease struck the varietal between 1921 and 1926, making planter debt, in the years leading up to the flood, unusually burdensome.[47]

The particular history of labor in the Delta cotton and sugar regions that were inundated by the Flood of 1927 are part of a larger and longer history of race relations in the Deep South following Reconstruction. After African Americans lost the federal armed protection of their civil rights, they continued by and large during much of the 1880s to be able to hold on to a modicum of political agency as they were courted by both patrician whites in the Conservative camp and working-class Populists. Georgia-born Populist congressman and leader Tom Watson made a strategic cross-racial appeal typical of this moment when he said, trying to recruit Negro voters to the movement and convince laboring whites of their common cause: "You are made to hate each other because upon that hatred is rested the keystone of the arch of financial despotism which enslaves you both." Watson spoke of the "accident of color" and the movement's determination to "wipe out the color line."[48] Between 1889 and 1915, however, racial "Radicalism" overwhelmed the working-class alliances of Populism as well as Conservative paternalism.[49] Economic recession in the late 1880s turned into depression; this, combined with a fear of a new generation of young black men born and raised outside of the "civilizing" effects of slavery, worked to produce among a majority of whites a sweeping fear of black retrogression, ready to leap out in lurid acts of violent and sexual criminality. Ensuing—though not total—black disfranchisement and Jim Crow segregation statutes were symptoms of a white determination to cordon off political agency and to draw a public color line, upheld by *Plessy v. Ferguson* in 1896. This geographic separation in turn worsened white paranoia and removed political motivation on the part of whites to find common cause with voting blacks. Watson, the former Populist, became a bigoted demagogue, fomenting views against blacks, Catholics, and Jews. Patriarchal rule, white male sexual hypocrisy, and a tradition of extralegal rites of "honor" also played a part in the complex.[50] Responding to the bestial vision of black people that whites had created, mob lynching—ritualized communal acts that included among the perpetrators women, children, and the professional classes—rose to its height in 1892 with 156 black victims in one year.[51] Race riots in Wilmington (1898), New Orleans (1900), and Atlanta (1906) partook of this trend toward violent mob enforcement of white domination. As the nation at large pursued its own imperial control of nonwhites in the Caribbean and the Philippines, and as it forgot the more radical promises of the Civil War, white citizens throughout the United States forged a racial solidarity across sectional lines along with a resubjugation of those whom the Civil War had ostensibly freed.[52] African Americans responded by either a drawing inward or a movement outward: establishing all-black towns and communities, building up civic organizations (churches, benevolence societies and lodges, schools, Republican groups, and newspapers), or joining African colonization societies (especially popular in Mississippi and Arkansas).[53]

Historian Joel Williamson has argued that an abrupt end of Radicalism occurred around 1915. African Americans migrated north in increasing numbers for the industrial jobs produced by World War I while occurrences of lynching dramatically declined. "The Negro," he argues, "practically disappeared as anything more than a cipher in southern white calculations"; if he appeared at all, it was not as a "black beast" or as a progressive Booker T. Washington figure but rather as a child or "neo-Sambo." Though whites would commit what in their minds was "the violence necessary to keep blacks in place" on the lowest rung of the social and economic ladder, this violence was now more pragmatic than obsessive. Aside from these incidents, whites assumed a Conservative, inattentively paternalist posture. According to Williamson, what interested southern whites more was not the terrorization of the black mass but the romantic cohesiveness of the white mass, the achievement of a cross-class white confederation, and the obscuring of historical relations between white and black peoples and cultures.[54] This post-1915 ideological mood among southern whites will help us understand, when in the next chapters we look at the media responses to the flood, why the white southern press represented the flood as an attack on a romanticized white community and made tactical use of black "Sambo" figures as comedic relief from this white drama.[55] Though Williamson's account reckons with a general shift in white thinking, it does not fully account for the ongoing *experience* of the majority of African Americans in the Deep South in the 1920s.

Walter White, a light-skinned man of partly African descent who was a member of the NAACP leadership, writing his study of lynching in 1927–28, presented the southern situation of the 1920s in more urgent terms. An average of 38 lynchings a year in the 1920s and periodic race riots were, he argued, cause for public concern and reaction. In particular, White had reported on the 1919 riot in the Delta town of Elaine, Arkansas, in which a peaceful gathering of black sharecroppers, members of the Progressive Farmers and Household Union of America, seeking fair payment from landlords for their cotton crops, turned into a violent clash. Within a day, some one thousand white males from nearby counties and across the river in Tennessee and Mississippi responded to the call for armed support. Soon thereafter, the Arkansas governor arrived with 583 soldiers, including World War I veterans. While five whites died, somewhere between 20 and 856 black men were killed. Black survivors were prosecuted in unjust trials until they were finally released in 1925.[56] In *Rope and Faggot*, White describes the present time of the late 1920s as one of continuing crisis—for the black citizenry of the South, for the white mind and soul, for southern white female advancement, and for the southern justice system. But for White it was also *potentially* a time of progress in race relations, due to liberal scholars at southern universities, liberal elements of the southern press, white southern women denouncing "chivalry" in their names, public shaming by northern pundits, agitation from northern organizations like his own NAACP, and the pressure of black outmigration.[57] The crisis still very much existed, White thought, but its increasing public exposure and analysis opened the way for change.

If to Walter White national attention on the South in the 1920s augured potential improvements, white southerners had extraordinarily mixed feelings about once again being the "problem" region the rest of the nation needed to solve. This sense of the South-as-problem dated back to the antebellum period, but, as historian Natalie Ring explains, it was especially as the United States was drawing other tropical, staple-producing regions into its imperial periphery at the turn of the century that it turned its reformist eye southward, *within* the nation, whence the region became a "colossal laboratory for social change"—for modernization, "readjustment," and "uplift." An internal, New South creed of "industrial progress, racial harmony, and sectional reunion" developed in tandem with these external reforms as southerners courted capital from northern and European investors.[58] By the 1920s, though, the awkward symbiosis of external and internal reform carried on since the 1890s became more polarized. In the words of Fred Hobson, the 1920s were the "most crucial decade" within the South since the 1870s because southerners were feeling especially assailed by the rest of the nation for committing "crimes against progress"; the South had come to be ridiculed as "a region of belts—the Bible Belt, Hookworm Belt, Malaria Belt, Chastity Belt."[59] As University of North Carolina sociologist Howard Odum put it at the time, "propaganda" on the South in these years was "one of the chief indoor sports of unstable folk in other climes."[60] According to George Tindall, a "neo-abolitionist image of the benighted South" emerged in the 1920s, producing in southerners a "defensive temper" throughout the decade.[61] The years surrounding World War I had ushered in immense changes—with black outmigration and armed military service, women's suffrage and the rise of the New Woman, and an apparent end to Victorian values in Jazz Age culture—that brought out more conservative, even reactionary, elements in the South. The Scopes Trial of 1925, in particular, seemed to pit a backward, fundamentalist Dixie against an aggressively iconoclastic and secular North. While some southern liberals and academics—especially Odum and his students—stepped up the process of internal scrutiny, in general, the tenuous discourse of collaborative, interregional white reform familiar in the Progressive Era had become seriously strained.

In the years immediately preceding the Flood of 1927, then, a kind of acute precariousness characterized the Delta region. The previous forty years had seen drastic environmental transformation, turning a swampy, forested lowland into leveed and drained New South cotton and sugar kingdoms. The Delta—constituted and sustained by river flow and overflow—was ostensibly reclaimed by its developers from aperiodic disturbance only to be made vulnerable to a higher order of catastrophic danger. Even before the super-flood of 1927, flooding had been a factor: annual spring sandbagging and levee reinforcement, punctuated every few years by serious overflow, meant that Delta life was, despite the levees, patterned by an unpredictable crisis cyclicality. The price of cotton, while high in the years between 1900 and 1920, fell throughout the 1920s, miring planters—and still more, their legally undefended tenants—in overproduction and debt. Rather than overproduction, diseased Louisiana sugar suffered from severe underproduction in the years leading up to 1927, causing planters their own economic setback. In cotton country, possibilities for working-class farm ownership, and even cash-based renting, declined. As one labor historian has put it, the failure of labor reforms, put off in the more prosperous first two decades of the century, became "all too apparent during the 1920s."[62] While the widespread white obsession with black "retrogression" during the Radicalism of 1889–1915 had somewhat exhausted itself, the violent intimidation of black men and women had not ended. African American farm laborers knew that if they organized to ameliorate their working conditions, they still risked the kind of violent white mob backlash and legal injustice apparent in Elaine in 1919. Black outmigration had become a viable escape valve, yet, as African Americans peopled labor centers in the North, it became clear, in the outbreak of race riots around the country in 1919 (in Omaha, Washington, D.C., and Chicago), that these problems were national in scope. Finally, while some white southerners continued to draw up plans for a viable role the South could play within an American modernity, others, feeling assaulted by outside cultural forces and economic colonialism, retrenched.

High Water Everywhere

From the late summer of 1926 through the winter of 1927, an unusual amount of rain and snow fell on the center of the continent, filling and then overflowing tributary rivers and filling the Mississippi itself to capacity. As early as September and October 1926, flooding occurred throughout the plains and Upper Valley states, in Nebraska, South Dakota, Kansas, Oklahoma, Iowa, Illinois, and Indiana.[63] In December, heavy snowfall in Montana and South Dakota shifted southeast, producing floods. In March 1927, more blizzards traversed eastward from the Rockies to Virginia and tornadoes formed in the Lower Valley. Levees began to slough into the Mississippi and serious flooding occurred in southern backwaters when tributaries that could no longer empty into the Mississippi began to flow in reverse. Black plantation laborers—and, eventually, any able-bodied black male within sight—amounting to thirty thousand persons were directed, often brutally, to reinforce the levees. Convicts from Parchman Prison in the Yazoo Delta added to the labor force. Guards patrolled levees to ward off saboteurs from opposite banks. Already, even before any major crevasses took place in the Lower Valley, there were thirty-five thousand flood refugees.[64]

Soon enough, in mid-April, water began to undermine levees. Just south of Cairo in the Delta region of Missouri, two crevasses occurred near New Madrid (see Fig. 1.5). In Arkansas, over five million acres flooded, largely because the Arkansas River was pushed backward by the Mississippi, producing overflow almost as far inland as Little Rock. Levee breaks also occurred throughout the St. Francis River basin,[65] along the Arkansas bank of the Mississippi, and on the White River. The overflow in the southern part of the state then spilled south over Louisiana. On the eastern banks just south of Memphis, six days after the "Good Friday Storm" of April 15, water forced a gap three-quarters of a mile wide in the levee at Mounds Landing, inundating the entire lower Yazoo-Mississippi Delta for what would become months. Unofficial reports estimated that between one hundred and several hundred African Americans working on the levees were drowned that April 21. As the towering barrage of water 100 feet high—"approach[ing] Niagara Falls in its volume"—began to flatten out across the Delta, the chief engineer of the Mississippi Levee Board in Greenville warned: "Wall of water going south is very dangerous and unless people move to levees quickly, they will be drowned." This was, according to Barry, the "greatest single crevasse ever to occur anywhere on the Mississippi River."[66]

The water that moved impassively overland through the Delta would ultimately return to the Mississippi, downriver, at the outlet of the Yazoo River at Vicksburg, and would proceed to exert its force along the west bank of the river in Louisiana. Here was, according to a *National Geographic* reporter, a "foul and swirling sea, bearing on its yellow tide the offal, animals, trees, and trash, the fences, bridges, houses, barns, and chicken coops scoured down by 54 flooded tributaries."[67] The powerful of New Orleans, then a major banking center, home of the second largest port in the nation, and the wealthiest city in the South,

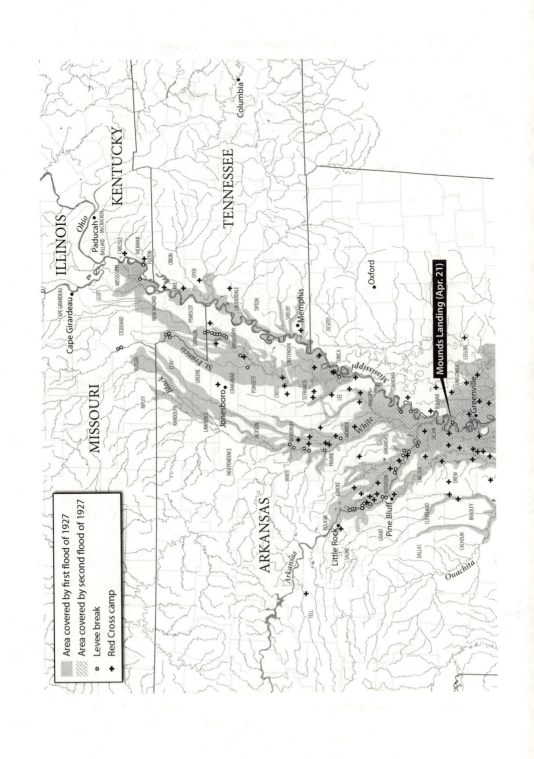

Area covered by first flood of 1927
Area covered by second flood of 1927
○ Levee break
✛ Red Cross camp

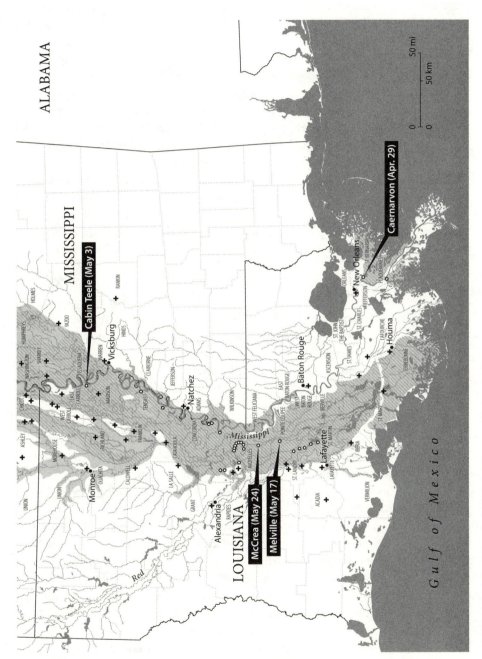

1.5. The Mississippi Flood of 1927. © Princeton University Press.

devised a plan—ultimately sanctioned by the federal government—to protect the city from the flood heading its way. On April 29, thirteen miles below New Orleans, they dynamited the levee at Caernarvon in order to flood the relatively less populated Acadian region of St. Bernard and Plaquemines parishes and to protect the crescent city. If authorities had waited just days more, they would have realized that there had been no need to create another refugee population: overwhelmed by the water pouring out of the Delta at Vicksburg, a chain of levees in Louisiana had begun to break, flooding the Sugar Bowl just west of the Mississippi in the Atchafalaya basin and taking pressure off the main river. Breaks at Cabin Teele (May 3), Bayou des Glaises (May 12), Melville (May 17), and McCrea (May 24) created a second inland sea to match the first that already covered the eastern part of the Delta. The four major basins that make up the Delta—St. Francis, Yazoo, Tensas, and Atchafalaya—were all underwater. Though by the end of May the major crest of the flood had passed, the whole region, with its levees unrepaired, was re-flooded by the typically higher waters of June.[68]

In anticipation of these breaks, Louisiana towns mobilized. As Tallulah, Louisiana, journalist Helen Murphy, living in the path of the Cabin Teele break, put it, in a line resonant with the drama of Calvary: "Everywhere people were working, nailing, hammering, lifting, struggling." Typical of the best scenarios of flood preparation throughout the region, Murphy's prosperous white neighbors—"hourly dreading, hourly expecting an overflow"—got themselves, their goods, and their cattle to higher ground. Murphy herself moved to the upper floor of her house, putting goods on scaffolds, turning a bathroom into a makeshift kitchen, and cajoling her cats and chickens to come aloft into her and her husband's "modified Noah's Ark." The typical "household machinery" broke down as her two female servants, "black Martha and yellow Mary," "defected" for the "somnolent idleness" of "gov'ment rations." Soon after the crevasse, Murphy recalled: "I looked north, and far over the fields a glistening sheet was unrolling steadily and the dull roar of rushing water broke on my ears." Not long after, the water was "rushing through the ditches, filling the low places till by night our streets were long mirrors, reflecting eerie shadows." And then came the loud chorus of frogs, emitting "every gradation of sound." With allusions to biblical plagues, scourges, and crucifixions, and her use of terms like "sacrificing," it is no surprise that Murphy imagines the nearby "tall smokestacks of the oil mill pointed heavenward like grim accusing fingers."[69] "Why hast thou forsaken us?" seemed to be the implicit question.[70] This was a question, moreover, that recapitulated southerners' postbellum Lost Cause query: why had God let us lose the war?[71]

According to Murphy, hundreds of thousands of others, situated lower down and marooned by high water, took to anything remotely solid left in sight: trees, rooftops, ancient Indian mounds, railway boxcars, cotton gin lofts, and fragile levees. In Tallulah, "Mexican Joe" had disappeared after his "little shack, down by the woods, [wa]s submerged up to the comb." Closer to Cabin Teele, "several hundred Negroes and a few white people, with their accompanying train" of domesticated animals, placed their belongings around them on a levee; "they have been through deadly peril ... [and] gazed on sickening sights."[72] Near Pine Bluff, Arkansas, aviators reported seeing "about fifty Negroes ... marooned on a drainage ditch levee"; they watched as the levee started "crumbling on both ends" and listened to "the distress cries."[73]

Boats, railroads, and planes were all put into service as guardsmen and lay folk attempted to rescue people from these precarious sites. *Times-Picayune* reporter Lyle Saxon noted on May 17 a steamboat, towing barges alongside, "like a huge floating island filled with as miserable a freight as any ship has borne": a mostly black, rural population, who carried their worldly wealth in the form of "a mixed cargo of mules, horses, cows, and calves. . . . The[se] gore each other and low incessantly."[74] As the *Times-Picayune* narrated on May 18: Acadians, deliberately flooded by New Orleans, as they waited for rescue barges, looked at ancestral homes inundated to the rooftop, old bayous washed out by the water; "in French they shout or sob: 'My home, my corn, my pigs, cows, my blessed church—gone—gone.'"[75]

Small towns, levees, and barges were turned into places with the crowding, urgency, noise, minute-by-minute suspense, and contingent meeting patterns typically reserved for large cities and industrial centers. Such was the aural environment in Tallulah, with "the roar of the motor boats, the click of the oars, the drone of airplanes"; "locomotives shrieking and shunting, cars chugging back and forth, ... and an incessant whirring of saws and battering of hammers! A magnificent symphony of distress and unrest" after which the remembered soundscape of Manhattan, "the rumble of the subway, the roar of the L, ... were not so bad after all."[76] One African American farmer interviewed in Pine Bluff, Arkansas, stated that, at the Red Cross camp, "I never seen so many folks in mah life."[77] Mississippi journalist Harris Dickson declared: "A concentration camp may be even more punctual than New York City at producing its sporadic crowd."[78] Not only the amassing of strangers but also the unfamiliar technologies present in these facilities increased the evacuees' sense of disorientation.[79] Hundreds of thousands of people were marshaled into rows of crowded tents, public health regimens, timed meals, and labor details, and all were made to be the auditors of loudspeaker announcements, radio broadcasts,

1.6. Red Cross Camp at Vicksburg, Mississippi, May 3, 1927. Courtesy of the Archives and Records Services Division, Mississippi Department of Archives and History.

educational outreach, and hygiene campaigns (Fig. 1.6). This massing of evacuees represented striking forms of modern state-managed crowd behavior.

To confront this humanly engineered super-flood, it was incumbent on the Red Cross to piece together what the *New York Times* called, with no irony, "reconstruction machinery."[80] While President Coolidge never visited the flood districts and resisted the urging that he convene a special session of Congress to deal with the emergency, he did appoint Herbert Hoover, his secretary of commerce, to orchestrate all disaster mitigation, relief, and recovery efforts and put him in charge of the Red Cross to do so. An engineer by training, who had managed food distribution in war-torn Belgium a decade earlier and then a postwar relief program across Europe, Hoover had a mind well suited to coordinate what *National Geographic Magazine* would call a "big intelligence machine."[81] Indeed, the *Survey Graphic* assessed that Hoover had "the best organizing brain in the country."[82] *World's Work* called him "that master-organizer."[83] Hoover was the paradigmatic technocrat of the era, someone who put faith in the power of well-designed systems and organizations to solve any and all problems.[84] Issuing out of what he called "central control," Hoover put faith, as he said in one of his two nationwide radio broadcasts, in "the command of modern engineering knowledge" and "all our modern equipment . . . to do something we never before attempted in the history of floods."[85]

Aside from this touted structural control of water, Hoover's system involved the deployment of reconnaissance and rescue teams; the establishment of 149 Red Cross concentration camps run for 325,554 people living on-site and an almost equal number being provided for outside the camps; the deployment of the National Guard and the Coast Guard and the creation of separate state flood relief commissions, each with its own "flood czar"; the movement of supplies from across the country for immediate shelter, sustenance, and medical care and then for rebuilding and planting in the Lower Valley; the transmission of communiqués over local airwaves and wireless sets with urgent information; and public relations and fund-raising campaigns broadcast across the national radio system, which Hoover had helped establish and, just that winter, link. Though the federal government would appropriate $300 million in its 1928 flood control legislation and ultimately spend much more than that in ensuing years,[86] it was, in 1927, the Red Cross, relying on this elaborate communication network and the mobilization of its dispersed committees, that needed to raise private funds from around the nation to finance this "huge relief machine." In the words of a Red Cross writer: "Like a stupendous chess game, the enemy had to be check-mated at all times from two points," namely from the point of both recent and oncoming devastation. A relief system was thus designed to outmaneuver an invading "enemy," an enemy that was in fact really the serially occurring dereliction of humanly designed systems.[87]

In total, during this months-long flood in the Lower Valley, water covered 27,000 square miles, land in seven states where about a million people lived (almost 1 percent of the nation's population); thirteen major crevasses occurred; roughly 637,000 people became homeless, approximately 555,000 of whom were people of color; somewhere between 250 and about 1,000 people died; and 50 percent of all animals in the flooded areas drowned. And financially, direct property losses totaled $250–500 million, while indirect losses brought that figure up to $1 billion.[88]

Though the whole region was devastated, lower-income black women, men, and children experienced—among human groups—the most direct physical consequences of the ambient danger: the wider geography of distress collected especially in their bodies. As a journalist at the *Chicago Defender* put it: because of Jim Crow, "our people are double sufferers."[89] African American farm laborers had less secure dwellings and less opportunity for evacuation. In fact, they were typically barred from flight by planters concerned not to lose their labor. It was African American men—made to "delve in the muck and the danger"[90]— who did the lion's share of the physical work of flood prevention and cleanup, often at gunpoint. Louis Davis's experience was typical: a young African American man visiting Monroe, Louisiana, during high water, Davis was arrested as a vagrant, forced to work for three days on the levee, and kept in jail by night. His nephew recalled, "After they turned him loose, he came home and just sat down and boo-hooed like a baby. Those people had caught him down there and worked the devil out of him."[91] Others wrote by letter to Ida B. Wells, the anti-lynching crusader, journalist, and Mississippi native then living in Chicago, that blacks without the protection of powerful whites "were being treated like dogs" or, as another said, taken "for everything but human beings."[92]

Mindful that the NAACP's Walter White—who had interrupted work on *Rope and Faggot* to investigate flood conditions in Mississippi—was about to make public his findings, Hoover suggested to the then head of the Tuskegee Institute, Robert Russa Moton, that he appoint a Colored Advisory Commission to investigate conditions in the Red Cross camps.[93] Moton chose leading, mostly southern, black citizens of a conservative bent, among whom was Claude Barnett, founder of the Associated Negro Press, from Chicago and Jesse O. Thomas, field secretary of the National Urban League, from Atlanta. Working in small groups, these sixteen men and women fanned out to camps across the Lower Valley. Other investigators besides White and the members of the commission included an unnamed white woman working for the NAACP's *Crisis* and J. Winston Harrington reporting for the *Chicago Defender*. Neither Wells nor W.E.B. Du Bois toured the flood zone, but both, as I explain in chapter 3, used the print medium to draw national attention to the treatment of African Americans in the refugee camps.

The most basic fact that became clear, over the course of the dealings between a white, mainly northern, Red Cross leadership and a black, mostly southern, Colored Advisory Commission, was that each group defined "relief" quite differently. The goal of the Red Cross, according to Robert E. Bondy, the executive in charge of Memphis Headquarters, was to bring any inhabitant of the flood zone back to a position "as near like the position he occupied before the disaster as is nearly possible."[94] Hoover concurred with this conservative policy when he said: "To go beyond what we are doing in our present reconstruction plans would mean that we were trying to take over the whole problem of the Delta."[95] As Moton wrote in a letter to Hoover, the commission, by contrast, saw the flood as providing the chance to rectify "an unsound and in many instances an unfair economic situation." Moton expressed, strategically, the commission's hope that "in the measures undertaken for reconstruction," a new plan will be devised to "liberate both the white planter and his Negro tenant" from the cropping system that exposes them both to "the hazards of an unstable economic condition."[96] For the Red Cross, then, *restoration* of the pre-flood status quo was the goal; for the commission, *liberation* from just such an "unsound," "unfair," and "unstable" economic order was necessary.[97] For Hoover, a grand designer of efficient modern systems, the idea of the property redistribution and the credit system overhaul necessary to put the region on sounder economic and social footing did have appeal. He intimated as much when interviewed by a southern journalist from the *Atlanta Constitution* in July.[98] And he dangled the promise of just such a radical redesign of the Delta in front of Moton to keep him from releasing the commission's full report.[99] Yet as relief efforts were receiving typically glowing coverage in the mainstream white press, Hoover was becoming presidential timber. Ultimately, the political strategist in Hoover, a Republican who could not risk alienating the vote of the white Democratic South, won out over the disinterested system designer.[100] Indeed, if Hoover's "reconstruction machinery" had used the disaster to engineer increased opportunities and protections for African Americans, it would have smacked to southern whites of postbellum Reconstruction; and property redistribution would have aligned Hoover with the most "radical of the radical Republicans" of the 1860s.[101] In such a political climate, neither property redistribution nor credit reform occurred.

The Red Cross, true to its stated goal of restoration, effectively instituted and upheld Jim Crow practices within the camps. Certain camps appeared more functional than others: Natchez, Mississippi; Marianna, Arkansas; and Lafayette, Louisiana, received praise. They were clean, well-managed, and comfortable, offering opportunities for recreation and education and allowing African American social service workers to act as advisors; in this last was "not only sincere sympathy born of kinship to the refugees, but quick comprehension of the methods to be used."[102] It seemed that even the most responsive white administrators in these functional camps, however, needed to be forced to look critically at an everyday racial hierarchy they had come to see as natural—exemplified, for instance, in black nurses receiving lower wages than white.[103] More frequently reported, however, were situations of a more dramatic racial imbalance.

Claude Barnett and Jesse O. Thomas arrived at the Sicily Island Camp, in the cotton section of northern Louisiana, unexpectedly. They were traveling nearby, and though the Red Cross indicated that the camp was closed down (marking it as "no camp" on the itinerary), the two men decided to see for themselves. "We learned from informants that in the camps which had been notified of our coming, everything was in readiness for our reception." If Sicily Island was still in operation, the hope was, "we would get a chance to see and hear things which we probably would not have . . . [were] we piloted by an official." Getting to the camp, their train had been "six hours going eleven miles" in darkness, with the water "up to the lowest steps of the car." They continued: "The Jim Crow coach [was] half occupied by whites, and the remainder packed with negroes some sitting three in a seat . . . the noise of the water boiling over the track terrifying one woman until she screamed and put down the window to shut out the sound, with the people refusing to sing because of what seemed to be a sullen resentment of their treatment."[104]

It turned out there were in fact still 3,000 refugees at Sicily Island, 90 percent of whom were African American. The chairman of the Sicily Relief Committee had gone to the Black River on a fishing trip; the two local Red Cross officials in charge of the camp were absent. One "Meadows," the white man in charge of the commissary, "confronted us with laughter and said insinuatingly, 'You boys don't need anything here, not with all those clothes you have got on.'" Presented with their credentials, Meadows "flew into a rage. 'What in the hell do you think of this?', he shouted to the loungers in the office. . . . 'Isn't this the damdest thing you ever saw? What G—D—S—of a B— do you suppose signed this letter?', he demanded." Barnett and Thomas were then directed to a Lieutenant Clark, who was apparently hiding in a car "watching our approach and in which he started away as soon as we made for him." After finally encountering him and being told they might look around, they were directed to one "Deacon," a black man who turned out also to be absent. "We were glad to have this opportunity of interviewing the refugees without direction or supervision. There had been all along the suspicion in our minds that the refugees to whom we had talked had at other times expressed the opinions which they thought our guides wanted them to express rather than what they really felt."[105]

What they observed or heard was the following: all the work of the camp was performed by blacks; better-quality food was reserved for whites; donated clothing was "secretly" made available for white women to "pick over the choicest articles," who took "the most of them"; while all whites had sleeping cots, blacks had either to supply their own mattresses or sleep on the ground; and the toilets were in "obnoxious condition." Though some had had rations cut off while their land was still flooded, "the chief difficulty at this camp was the sodden apathy and lack of sympathy of those in charge."[106] Barnett and Thomas's at times satirical exposé depicts a vacuum of white leadership; white outrage at well-to-do urban blacks assuming a position of potential critical authority; separate and unequal accommodations; an unfair distribution of labor and relief supplies; and Red Cross collusion in returning workers to land prematurely so as to be ready for plantation labor.

At other camps, still more serious Jim Crow abuses occurred. Black refugees were often required to gain a white co-signature in order to receive rations or be granted freedom of movement.[107] In certain cases, landlords charged their tenants for Red Cross supplies or applied the apparent cost of these supplies against old tenant debts.[108] The Red Cross agreed to bar from its camps labor agents who might recruit blacks away to new places of employment.[109] Frequently noted was the menacing presence of armed National Guardsmen, a presence sometimes read as excessive intervention even by local white planters.[110] At camp Crowley in Louisiana, the report stated that National Guardsmen apparently had been "too free with a few of the colored girls. . . . . [though] it was impossible to sift these rumors to the bottom"; word of an "attempted assault upon colored women" by the Guardsmen emerged likewise out of Vicksburg.[111] Black men were forcibly conscripted into labor, which, during the flood, had prevented their safe and deliberate evacuation from the levees.[112] A public notice issued by William Alexander Percy, scion of the influential Delta planter family, who was in charge of the Greenville levee, stated: "All Negroes . . . outside of the levee camp who are able to work should work. If work is offered them and they refuse to work they should be arrested as vagrants."[113] Ida B. Wells, relying on letters and visits from refugees, averred in July 1927 that the Red Cross was "encouraging and condoning a system of discrimination, of peonage, and of robbery of funds."[114] Walter White, having toured the Mississippi camps, judged, in an article in the liberal white weekly *The Nation*, that "Those in immediate charge of flood relief, whether wittingly or not, are . . . permitting the relief organizations to be used by plantation-owners further to enslave or at least to perpetuate peonage conditions."[115] Apparently to avoid just such conditions, some three thousand refugees escaped out of the Vicksburg camps by night.[116]

The commission report called attention to northern white women administrators who were particularly discriminatory in their behavior. Of a social worker from New York, Cordelia Townsend, in charge of Red Cross activities in Melville, a letter to Moton from commission investigators stated: "We do not believe that there can be found anywhere in the flood area a situation where the attitude toward colored people is more brutal." The report detailed how "hundreds of houses for whites have been rebuilt" while only seven houses of African Americans had been repaired; consequently, African Americans slept in flood-damaged shacks with "scarcely sufficient clothes to hide their nakedness."[117] Townsend was subsequently dismissed because of the revelations.[118] The camp at Pine Bluff, Arkansas, was likewise headed by a white woman from New York City, Catherine B. Monroe. Monroe left the distribution of Red Cross supplies "entirely in the hands of the farm owners," who proceeded to charge their laborers for these free supplies. The report continued: "A typical statement made by Miss Monroe was that the 'darkies' in that County preferred that white people would serve them in preference to 'niggers', and this policy was being religiously followed by her."[119] Such instances of northern white discrimination, the authors underlined, did not "indicate that it is a safe plan so far as colored people are concerned to have the affairs in the hands of local whites."[120] Instead, the report repeatedly urged the need for the establishment of trained African American personnel to assess and oversee distribution of food, clothing, farm supplies, and public health and home economics information. The report detailed the successes achieved through such black communal self-direction: "Conditions were best in those camps where the officials in charge had invited the assistance and cooperation of leaders among the local colored people."[121]

Acts of racial violence were committed throughout the flood zone. In New Orleans, J. W. Mershon, an African American insurance agent, was shot to death by whites after he demurred doing levee labor so that he could fulfill his duty to clients.[122] In the Vicksburg Camp on May 1, African American Marshall Dunbar was shot in the stomach and arm by a private in the National Guard, apparently defending himself from Dunbar's attack with a tent pin.[123] African American brothers Jim and Mark Fox, accused of having slain a sawmill superintendent, were lynched and burned in Mississippi.[124] Also in Mississippi, African American Dan Anderson was lynched. The *Chicago Defender* attributed the act to white "wrath . . . aroused over the recent flood."[125] Later that summer, a resolution was signed by leading white female citizens of the state, declaring: "As southern women we hold that no circumstances can ever justify mob action and that in no instance is it an exhibition of chivalric consideration for the honor of womanhood."[126] In Little Rock, Arkansas, in early May, a black man named Carter was the victim of mob violence; his mutilated body was dragged through the black section of town and there set on fire. Whites used the furniture of neighborhood homes to feed the flames; only the arrival of the National Guard broke up the rioting.[127] The local Associated Negro Press correspondent Theodore Holmes was run out of town by whites.[128] Rail ticket sales in Little Rock soared to $2,000 the next day as African Americans began an exodus out of the region. That same day, in a front-page editorial, the *Arkansas Gazette* denounced the mob action.[129]

Walter White opined that these events were both "the inevitable products of a gigantic catastrophe" and a "part of the normal picture of the industrial and race situation in certain parts of the South."[130] This yoking together of the catastrophic and the normal in this characterization implies that, in White's mind, behavioral extremes characteristic of emergency situations were not unfamiliar in the rural Deep South but had become normalized, and ritualized, into everyday practice.[131] Normal life hewed to catastrophic patterns. Visible "blackness" meant you were more likely to be living or working in a precarious part of the landscape; it marked men out for forced labor under gunpoint, marked women out for the threat of sexual assault by National Guardsmen, and marked both out for containment in concentration camps.

On June 2 through 4 in Chicago, several thousand people—statesmen, planners, and reporters—gathered for the Chicago Flood-Control Conference. The mayor of Chicago, William Hale ("Big Bill") Thompson, along with St. Louis mayor Victor Miller and New Orleans mayor Arthur O'Keefe, had devised the meeting "to arouse sentiment for Federal action," to tackle, in a nationally concerted manner, the problems of flood control. Thousands of delegates were called from "virtually every city in the Mississippi Valley," representing what O'Keefe called its "best interests and influences."[132] In November, Chicago's mayor led a group of 2,000 to the nation's capital in ten special railway cars, accompanied by "an accordion player, a banjo player and eight singing policemen," to spur action on flood control legislation.[133] Months later, on May 15, 1928, Coolidge signed a bill into law that appropriated $300 million for a restructuring of the levee system and that did not require cost sharing by the Mississippi Valley states.[134] The levees-only policy had proven a failure, so the new design would mimic, and accommodate, a flooding river's tendency to seek outlets during its run to the sea as this design created reservoirs and emergency outlets along the river from Missouri south.[135] This bill represented a new consensus that the river was a federal responsibility.[136]

By July 1927, though floodwaters had receded, the region had hardly recovered. As a British reporter from the *Manchester Guardian* put it: "The fertile fields of early spring are now great desolate wastes of mud, in which appear windowless, doorless houses, many of which have been moved from their foundations and partially or completely overturned. Much good land has been covered with barren sand . . . [and] in the drier regions, whipped by the wind into great fantastic dunes. Here and there, half-submerged in the slime and mud, are the decaying bodies of farm animals, poisoning the air with their stench." Refugees returning home to this scene of mud and sand, destruction and putrefaction, must, he concluded, "begin again like pioneers in the wilderness."[137] He might have added, though, that a "wilderness" has tremendous stored biotic energy off of which pioneers thrive. And though the alluvial silt—this apparently accursed "slime and mud"—would perform its function of replenishment within the river's disturbance regime, the Delta bottomlands typified a second nature in distress much more than a primordial wilderness. Carcasses of farm buildings and animals revealed "domestication" itself to involve not a pacifying of natural processes so much as a catastrophic intensification of them. Even as late as March 1928, a full year and a half after the heavy precipitation over the plains states had produced the water that would later flood the Delta, some seventy-one thousand flood victims in Mississippi were still receiving food from the Red Cross. Planting food crops had not been viable in 1927, and credit had yet to be advanced by planters and bankers in 1928 against the following fall harvest.[138]

Writing in the *National Geographic Magazine*, Frederick Simpich called the 1927 flood a "major geographic phenomenon of our time." Simpich also took the long view, however, and noted that "since time began," hydrology "has warped the fate of men and nations."[139] Indeed, the distribution of water across the earth by geological and climatic conditions has influenced, throughout history, where humans have sought to dwell, plant, and trade. The human attempt to safeguard that human culture which river conditions had made possible long involved the engineering—adulteration or improvement, depending on one's vantage—of those rivers. As old as riverine culture, though, was river disaster, for disturbance regimes *will be* disturbance regimes. If river overflow is a hydrological fact preceding human history, anthropogenic floods represent a historic occurrence of ancient pedigree. To put it differently, modernity does not mark a phase in which disasters stopped being natural and started being cultural. At the end of the first century BCE, for example, the poet Horace had described the Tiber River's "batter[ing] the royal monument and the Temple of Vesta" in Rome, a consequence of mountain deforestation and pastoral development. Disasters were understood to be cultural even then.[140]

If levee-bursting overflows are ancient, the Flood of 1927 was modern because global industrialism intensified the scale of this older pattern: the clearcutting of the forests of a massive, continental-scale watershed with steampowered equipment in mere decades; industrial-scale wheat, corn, and cotton monocultures; a one-thousand-mile levee system built four stories high; and, possibly, industrially produced climate change that contributed to the initiating and extreme weather events. All these factors made water in both the atmosphere (rain, snow), the lithosphere (on and under the ground), and the hydrosphere (in the rivers) behave with what seemed an unnatural intensity. The 1927 flood could also be called modern because of the particular social and cultural conditions at play in the event. Telephones, the wireless, and the radio, combined with aerial surveillance, made communication about the flood across vast distances almost instantaneous. Because catastrophes are mediated events, acquiring their identity and their scale through communication, these technologies speedily *produced* the geographic extent of the disaster.[141] The international credit system, along with speculative and consumer markets, meant that inundated cotton and sugar fields in the Delta affected, for example, Wall Street, mills in Manchester, England, and competing tropical producers of these staples the world over. Nationhood was the distinctly modern political geography in which the flood occurred, for the catastrophe occurred very much as a national drama—a drama in which the U.S. citizenry publicly wondered about what obligations national union entailed. Moreover, this flood was modern because it involved a belief in race-based personhood. Injustice, violence, and poverty are age-old, but aligning hierarchical castes and a spatial zoning of these castes with a "science" of racial classification was a product of the Atlantic world from the seventeenth century onward.[142] Race was, in short, like the D-74 cane cultivar or the radio broadcast system, a modern product.

Finally, the Flood of 1927 was modern because of the particular moment in intellectual history into which it broke. In the decades leading up to the flood, Nature was meant to be on a purposeful journey toward equilibrium. That is to say, the majority of natural scientists working in Darwin's wake chose not to follow up on Darwin's observations about random chance in evolution and instead emphasized processes of gradual stabilization.[143] Englishman Herbert Spencer, a Victorian of towering influence who wrote across the fields of biology, philosophy, sociology, and psychology, proposed that, at all scales of life, organisms were evolving toward greater differentiation and complexity, all the while producing an ever more concordant network: "universally a patient self-rectification," as he described it.[144] Along with this vision of organismic and cosmic self-perfection developed a parallel faith that humans, through technological development, were gaining a progressively better control over their social and natural worlds. As editors of the journal *World's Work* wrote in their inaugural 1900 issue, theirs was a time of "the perfection of method and of mechanism" that will "spread well-being among the masses." They embraced "the newly organized world" and saw the United States as its center. In the nation's imperial "extension of democracy and the rise of science," the journal urged, one sees "a new adjustment of man to man and of man to the universe."[145] University of Chicago sociologist Thorstein Veblen attributed this dominant scientific belief in processes of perfecting change to the modern "technological processes" of the Machine Age.[146] Indeed, ecologists tried to incorporate the human adoption of technology into its view of gradual self-stabilization: using mathematical models indicating precise equilibria, they conceived of nature as a manageable mechanical system.[147] As one early systems-theorist put it in the 1920s: "Man and machines today together form one working unit, one industrial system."[148]

The spate of environmental disasters occurring between 1880 and the mid-1920s did not, strangely enough, disturb this model of gradual stabilization and increasing human control. Sociologists who studied major disasters argued that it was inherent in the social body to produce a more cohesive form of organization after it had been disorganized by severe crisis. Samuel Prince, for example, basing his thesis on the case study of the 1917 Halifax explosion, held that "fluidity is not the usual state of society"; rather, it is induced by catastrophe, during which "life becomes like molten metal. It enters a state of flux from which it must reset upon a principle." The fluidity brought on by crisis allows a social organism to quickly re-form and perfect itself.[149] The young sociologist, it seemed, would prescribe catastrophe for all social bodies as a galvanic episode. Other sociologists agreed that with disaster comes a "realignment of social forces which will make for a better organized community working more effectively toward the solution of its various problems."[150] In these examples of sociological responses to disaster, the evident backfiring of technological control, of industrial materials, and of human communication and judgment, all with catastrophic consequences, did not induce skepticism in the progressive equilibrium model of modernity. Rather, by focusing on processes of reorganization after disorganization, these investigators paradoxically used massive human error to reinforce a vision of social balance.

James C. Scott describes this combination of trust in scientific progress, an ordering of human society as if reducible to natural laws, and a mastery of nature as a "high-modernist ideology," reaching its apogee, specifically in the United States, as "designers of the new order" mobilized for involvement in World War I.[151] Such American technocratic managerialism was typified in the figure of engineer, geologist, and system-designer Herbert Hoover. Hoover represented par excellence that early twentieth-century trust that technological, scientific, social, and natural progress could all reinforce each other in their path toward equilibrium.

What did the appearance of chance in the 1927 flood do to this model of purposive change and of organismic harmony? Tied as the event was to complex and aperiodic weather patterns; to an unpredictable and altered rhythm of melt and flow from multiple segments of a watershed; to the river's own "peculiarly complicated warped surface"[152] and chaotic turbulence; to unpredictable collapses of earthen defenses; and to the exigencies of human response—given all of this, how did defenders of the social and natural science model of equilibrium respond? What did the spectacular collapse of engineering systems, in this case dealing with a continental land feature, *do* to the period's intellectual investment in purposive systems that blended human and technological energy? Would observers around the nation react by seeing the collapse of physical and social protections as a call to create stronger systems? Or would such collapse produce a profound skepticism about human knowledge, about human control over the natural world, and about humanly invented social arrangements? How did people make intellectual meaning out of the flood: was it part of a bigger game plan or just a chance occurrence? If it showed nature's own gamble at work, did that allow humanity a part in the universe's operations?

This sketch of the dominant trend in the natural and social sciences in the years leading up to the flood will allow us, in the chapters ahead, to place certain responses to the flood within their historical moment; it will allow us to recognize certain responses as historically situated. It will also allow us to see how the magnitude of the flood had the capacity to call some of these dominant intellectual certitudes into question. We will soon see that, for certain observers, the Flood of 1927 brought into being an entirely different vision of the world than the one I have just described.

DISASTER'S PUBLIC

The 1927 flood was a public occurrence in two senses. First, it unfolded as a series of public events, affecting the population of seven states, a population often pressured into collective spaces like levees, barges, and concentration camps. Second, this disaster, like all modern disasters, created another public much larger than the contiguous one comprised in the disaster zone: those who read newspapers and magazines, listened to radio and records, watched movie reels, and attended Vaudeville benefits. As all of these forms of mediation occurred in the Delta, too—refugees received messages broadcast over loudspeakers, scanned news copy for information about other parts of the flooded territory, listened to recorded sermons and blues songs, and attended local benefit performances—the first, physically affected public was also drawn into that larger, virtual public.

While chapter 1 offered a history of that group of people directly and materially affected by the flood, the next four chapters analyze how the media variously called into connection the broader public, or publics, of the flood. Because of changes in media technology leading up to 1927—like the interconnection of a nationwide radio circuit just as floodwaters were gathering in the tributaries—the difference between reality and representation was increasingly hard to locate, thus lending to media events their own convincing substance.[1]

Rather than examining representations (cartoons, editorials, radio addresses) in isolation, my goal is to understand how these representations delivered meaning, or provided opportunities for those it reached to make meaning.[2] I am interested in the wider national, and indeed international, disaster public in part because its donations—in the absence of FEMA—actually fueled relief and recovery efforts, making the people who comprised this public not only passive spectators but effective agents. More than that, this public is important because it was the vector through which social, scientific, and environmental "data"—strewn upon events—traveled and took on meaning, credibility, and longevity. Because the flood evinced such profound troubles in social and technological systems, troubles that are still with us today, it seems quite relevant to ask: how did occurrences become "news," narratives, collective understandings, images, and facts? And what can we learn from the mediation of the 1927 flood to help us see how a complex public might communicate with itself about its catastrophes?

The first point to note is that the "Great Flood" was produced and disseminated within a media climate that was the product of the Great War. Media theorists in the postwar years, and still today, associate World War I and its machine-age propaganda with a crisis in the belief that democracy rests upon, and is secured by, a rational, well-informed public. While a nation's decision to enter a war is overtly controversial and thus understandably raises questions about public persuasion, a nation's response to an internal and apparently natural disaster seems, at first glance, uncontroversial. There should be no debate about giving gifts of aid. Such gifts define at the most basic level what shared citizenship within a nation requires. Thus all communication surrounding the generation of that aid can appear to be absent of propagandistic elements; it can seem a neutral lubricant of decent citizenship. The fact that governmental and media messaging about the flood, even in its early phases, was anything but neutral helps us understand how disasters within nations can be manifestations of chronic but unacknowledged civil wars. Disaster propaganda aims to manage this reality.

The 1920s skepticism about war propaganda is thus remarkably applicable to the journalistic archive of the 1927 flood. It helps us understand how Hoover, the Red Cross, and its "relief machine" manufactured popular investment in the idea of disaster response as a national battle against an invading enemy. Though a world war, far away from U.S. soil, and an apparent "act of nature" occurring in the heart of the American continent might appear to be wholly dissimilar events, the flood was in fact imagined by most publicists as a blameless war but experienced by residents of the Delta as a fully politicized form of aggression. While the nation-binding propaganda surrounding American involvement in World War I was revived in 1927 to muster the nation together as an "army of rescuers," memories of an older conflict—the U.S. Civil War—were also close at hand. For those outside the South, this new rescue narrative helped to reposition the 1860s conflict; for whites in the South, the War of Northern Aggression seemed a fitting lens through which to understand their renewed physical experience of disaster; and for African Americans, the flood made evident the unfulfilled promises of the Union victory.

What I intend to reveal in this part of the book is that 1920s theories of propaganda, and of propaganda's necessarily passive audiences, could not account for the complex and contested ways in which this event went public. Because the evidence for assessing events in 1927 was much closer at hand than it had been in the overseas war and was immediately available to laypeople caught up in disaster, this event spawned a different American public reckoning than had World War I. The categories "expert" and "layperson" were jostled so much as to actually reverse roles. As I will soon show, one finds all over the print journalistic archive of 1927, especially arising from southern white, northern black, and environmentalist editorials that relied on victim testimonials and other empirical data, critical dissection of the dominant flood narrative in which Nature was the aggressor and the white North was the rescuer. Moreover, 1920s media theorists who decried the sacrifice of public rationality on the altar of degraded *entertainment* failed to understand that Vaudeville comedy and blues concerts actually could generate and popularize skeptical counternarratives.[3]

Today we still harken back to the 1920s debate between journalist and political advisor Walter Lippmann and philosopher John Dewey—whose touchstone was the war—as the paradigmatic discussion about the fallibility of communication and hence of judgment within modern publics. Much that Lippmann warned about, in terms of state-managed information in a time of war, continues to be relevant today. By presenting an alternative case in the chapters to come, one that derives not from distant war but from near eco-catastrophe, I find that Walter Lippmann's thesis only goes so far and that John Dewey better points the way to understanding how communities *can* make provocative meaning as they become part of disaster publics. Given events of the early twenty-first century, we are now primed to see that how we communicate about environmental disaster is as important as how we communicate about war.

Supporters of the war at its beginning embraced a positive definition of propaganda to describe what their own nation was engaged in. Indeed, H. G. Wells went as far as to contend in 1914 that "the ultimate purpose of this war is propaganda, the destruction of certain beliefs and the creation of others."[4] Each nation sought to propagate its sacred idea of civilization over and against its opponent's practice of barbarism and to defend its method of information dissemination over against the enemy's production of lies.[5] As Mark Crispin Miller has trenchantly said, propagandizing the war "was an extraordinary state accomplishment: mass enthusiasm at the prospect of a global brawl that otherwise would mystify those very masses, and that shattered most of those who actually took part in it."[6]

During the war, wary or dissenting commentators came to criticize information protocols they saw to be distortive occurring both within other nations and within their own. In the United States, the prowar effort involved not only censorship but also the creation of a vast multimedia publicity campaign. A week after declaring war in the spring of 1917, President Woodrow Wilson established the Committee on Public Information (CPI) and put Colorado newsman George Creel in charge; also on the committee were the secretaries of navy, state, and war.[7] As Creel himself explained in 1920, the CPI was "a vast enterprise in salesmanship" that aimed—with the use of oral suasion, a daily newspaper, motion pictures, stereopticon slides, posters, and Wilson's instantly telegraphed speeches—to convince countries abroad of the idealism of America's motives and to "weld the people of the United States into one white-hot mass instinct with fraternity, devotion, courage, and deathless determination."[8] Because of false or exaggerated war dispatches produced by the CPI, the *New York Times* began to call it "the Committee on Public Misinformation," and some used the word "creeling" to indicate fact-bending distortion.[9] In Berlin, Paris, Zurich, and New York City, antiwar activists associated with Dada expressed their dissent specifically as subversions of media representations or as "media pranks": along with performances, Dadaists invented techniques of photomontage, in which they cut apart published photographs and then recombined the parts to produce shocking indexes of bodily disintegration and trauma.[10] The effect of their art was to challenge technology's claims on reality and "outrage the public."[11]

In the wake of war, its mass casualties and disfigurations, its controversial peace treaty, and its patent nonfulfillment of the ideals for which it was fought, media critics came to possess what Brett Gary has described as a "new consciousness about the relationship between modern communications technologies and public manipulation."[12] There descended a mood of "chastened democratic faith" on the part of liberal intellectuals[13] even while the professional fields associated with the newly discovered powers of machine-age propaganda flourished.[14] The year 1928, for example, saw the publication of both *Falsehood in War-Time: Propaganda Lies of the First World War* written by British MP Arthur Ponsonby and the book *Propaganda* written by Edward Bernays, the American founder of public relations, in which he embraced the conclusion that managerial elites needed to "organiz[e]" the "chaos" of the world for bewildered masses.[15] In 1927, the year of the flood, Harold D. Laswell, the University of Chicago political scientist and communications theorist, wrote *Propaganda Technique in the World War*. Laswell called propaganda "one of the most powerful instrumentalities in the modern world." He pointed out that though print had supplanted archaic ritual as a means of "weld[ing] thousands and even millions of human beings into one amalgamated mass of hate and will and hope," and though its content appealed to the masses' belief in their own popular sovereignty and individual reason, propaganda nonetheless used disguised forms of "pseudo-rational appeal." In the modern world, he summarized, "more can be won by illusion than by coercion." What was more, the sheer quantity of mechanically reproduced and disseminated representations of events in general was beginning to make actual life seem less real than mediatized images of that life. With the arrival of sound film in 1927 came what Guy Debord has called "the society of the spectacle."[16]

The most influential debate about public communication to emerge in the postwar decade was that conducted by Lippmann and Dewey. Just as for Las-

well and Bernays, at stake was the critical issue of how public knowledge functioned—or whether it could function at all—within a mass-mediated democracy. Lippmann, journalist, founding editor of the *New Republic*, and a war-time
advisor to Woodrow Wilson who was deeply disillusioned by the process that
produced the Treaty of Versailles, wrote *Public Opinion* (1922) and *The Phantom Public* (1925) in order to address the problem of "how to make the invisible
world visible to the citizens of a modern state."[17] Columbia University philosopher, educational innovator, and reform activist John Dewey wrote a book-
length treatise in response, which he revised during the flood, called *The Public
and Its Problems* (1927).[18] For Lippmann, to put it simply, "news" and "truth"
were not one and the same. Truth consists of "circumstances in all their sprawling complexity." Lippmann elaborated that these "circumstances" are "unseen"
and full of "disharmonies," operating according to "innumerable systems of
evolution, variously affecting each other, some linked, some in collision, but
each in some fundamental aspect moving at its own pace and on its own terms."
These extremely complex patterns of "truth" never "spontaneously take a shape
in which they can be known." Occasionally, though, some "aspect" of this complexity will "[obtrude] itself," in an act or signal event. This obtrusion is the stuff
of news, but much happens to it as it makes its way to public reception. Private
interest attempts to shape it. Members of the press, susceptible to their own
"subjective lenses" and to an abstracting perceptual inclination Lippmann
dubbed "stereotyping," further alter this obtruded aspect. And finally, there was
the problematic public. To Lippmann, democracy rested on a dangerous illusion that there existed a unitary public that could operate like a single executive
mind, "sovereign and omnicompetent," and that could consult its "conscience"
or its will in order to act well. What existed instead were "lay publics" or "random publics."[19]

Though Lippmann's experiences with failed diplomacy and misleading propaganda during the war should have, it seems, directed his ire mostly at heads
of state and the diplomatic corps, he directs his cynicism instead at these "lay
publics." He expresses his disdain especially by imagining these publics as kinds
of theater audiences. In one version of this characterization, the public is "a deaf
spectator in the back row, who ought to keep his mind on the mystery off there,
but cannot quite manage to keep awake"; in another instance, Lippmann la-
ments that the public will "arrive in the middle of the third act and will leave
before the last curtain, having stayed just long enough perhaps to decide who is
the hero and who the villain of the piece."[20] Such a feckless audience responds
primarily to its desires and emotions, and takes away only what its own experience allows identification with. In *Public Opinion*, Lippmann's only way out of

this mess is provided through his concept of "intelligence work," in which the "experts" of the media must strictly separate themselves from "those who make the decisions." The journalist "is there to represent the unseen"; if he can do that, "he confronts the people who exercise material force with a new environment." How this representation happens, especially when the unseen can never be appreciated whole or directly because it is an unevenly evolving strand-set rather than a unitary thing, is left unclear. By the time Lippmann wrote *The Phantom Public*, three years later, hope for the disinterested expert's "intelligence work" was replaced by a grim admission that the most these random publics can do is give their fragile attention once a "crisis has become obvious." The publics cannot be the judge of this crisis. All they can do is "[cancel] lawless power" as they "take account of a protest made on behalf of a relatively large number of persons" by looking to see if that protest's "spokesman is authorized" by being unopposed. Finally, in *American Inquisitors* (1928), he lambastes the press for relinquishing a belief that "any public event really matters very much" as they give in to the public's desire for "entertainment." Agreeing that pundit H. L. Mencken has sized up this cynicism better than any, he summarizes: "the booboisie and the civilized minority are at one in their conviction that the whole world is a vaudeville stage."[21]

While Lippmann satirizes much of what was newly worrisome in the 1920s about mass media democracies, it was John Dewey who continued to imagine ways in which social communications could remain meaningful. In so doing, he offers us an especially helpful set of ideas for getting at the complexity of the nation's flood uptake and talk. Dewey agreed with much of Lippmann's analysis of modern life. He sensed that the public was "scattered, mobile and manifold" and worried that the Machine Age had produced "physical tools of incalculable power" whose "instrumentality becomes a master and works fatally as if possessed of a will of its own." Unlike Lippmann, though, Dewey saw the crux of the problem with the twentieth-century public to consist of modernity's assault on the integrity of local communities. World War I, in particular, beset previously stable communities with "forces so vast, so remote in initiation, so far-reaching in scope and so complexly indirect in operation" that these forces could not be "referred to their origins" and hence "regulate[d]." These forces were "felt" and "suffered" but not "known." Diagnosing the origin of crises in a world connected via "vast, innumerable and intricate currents of trans-local associations"—associations that only become felt during crisis—presented the major problem for modern social awareness. This was a particular conundrum for Dewey because, contrary to a Lockean model in which solitary acts of sense perception slowly accrue inside the individual as a storehouse of knowledge, Dewey believed that it was only though "association and communication" that knowledge could be produced. If knowledge is social but modern society attenuates social "ties" beyond apprehension, what could be done? "Poetry, the drama, the novel" provided one way out for Dewey's "random public." These forms interrupted "routine consciousness" and taught "the highest and most difficult kind of inquiry and a subtle, delicate, vivid and responsive art of communication." The other method by which an "inchoate" public could become "articulate" was through a reinvestment in embodied local publics, who, via face-to-face discussions, digest news into "meanings" as that news "pass[es] from mouth to mouth." Though both Lippmann and Dewey help us understand the challenge of seeing "the unseen" and referring "forces" "to their origins," in an era of complex global interconnectivity, what I find especially valuable is Dewey's contention—one he shared with various Modernist artists—that, in such a world, art can still disturb routinized thought and invite difficult inquiry.[22]

In another major work of interwar media criticism that held out the possibility of the public's activation—rather than stultification—by contemporary media, "The Work of Art in the Age of Mechanical Reproduction" (1936), Walter Benjamin applauded the ways that new technologies invited their users to feel a greater stake in, and control over, how the content was produced and took on meaning. Not only because of Benjamin's continuing influence on so much work in cultural history and media studies today but also because he delivered a Berlin radio address on the 1927 Mississippi flood (coverage I will later discuss), it is crucial to engage with his media theory. Benjamin, in the words of one scholar, "aligned mass production with an idea of the democratic multiple."[23] He associated premodern live rituals, consecrated by the aura of a singular object, with forms of cultic or autocratic subjection. By contrast, new media—photography and film—allowed their processes of making, or montage, to be detected by viewers, who then position themselves with some cognitive discernment vis-à-vis the work of art or information. The visual technology itself—by its powers of arresting or slowing motion, isolating and magnifying details—"introduces us to unconscious optics as does psychoanalysis to unconscious impulses." Because of the forensic powers of the camera, these new media "[permit] the audience to take the position of a critic" or "expert" who conducts a kind of "testing." Benjamin found unconvincing "the same ancient lament that the masses seek distraction whereas art demands concentration" for he contended that this critical attitude happened *during* distraction, as one "noticed the object in incidental fashion." In the print sphere, he likewise saw a transformation occurring—for example, in published "letters to the editor"— such that "at any moment the reader is ready to turn into a writer."[24]

Though such was the potential of the new mass media to Benjamin, the film industry, with its "illusion-promoting spectacles," and fascism, with its "*Fuhrer* cult," each in its own way tried to tamp down this new form of mass critical reception. Benjamin's final, and most radical, assertion was that if the new democratic media were appropriated by autocratic power, and by a power that refused to consider a "change [in] property relations," it could only result in war: "Only war makes it possible to mobilize all of today's technical resources while maintaining the property system."[25] My contention, in the chapters to come, is that it is not only war but also large-scale environmental disaster—the closest thing to peacetime war imaginable—that is likewise the result of a fundamental crisis in public communication and a crisis in economic relations. And the same way a country's initial response to war mobilizes everything to disguise these causal factors, the initial media push surrounding a national-scale disaster is likewise full of "illusion-promoting spectacles" and the cultic lionization of supreme problem solvers.

Since the 1960s, theorists of the mediated public sphere have turned their attention to industrial and environmental disaster. Though this criticism attends to an era of media technologies—mass television consumption and the Internet—that postdate 1927, they nevertheless offer theses about disaster communication that are useful for our own inquiry. Many take the growing affinity of mass media for disaster as a sure symptom that news has turned into mere spectacle. Jürgen Habermas argued that with twentieth-century forms of mass mediation came a paradoxical "refeudalization" as "critical publicity [wa]s supplanted by manipulative publicity," by news as a "staged display" that invited identification rather than deliberation. Disasters, in particular, had become more prominent, constituting "immediate reward news" that was "dressed up" as entertainment.[26] Daniel Bell in the mid-1970s echoed Habermas's concern about the new dependence on both narrative visualization and calamity: "The visual media impose their pace on the viewer and . . . invite not conceptualization but dramatization." Especially with the media's over-attention to "disasters and human tragedies, it invites not purgation or understanding but sentimentality and pity, emotions that are quickly exhausted, and a pseudo-ritual of pseudo-participation in the events."[27]

A number of other scholars have lately turned to disaster mediation to query whether such mediation tends to work like a summoning of loyalty or an opening up of problems to view. There is a general recognition that because large-scale disasters can destabilize vast "imagined communities,"[28] the media coverage typically functions like a ritual intended to cohere a public potentially divided by the political inequities implicit in the disaster. The controversy surrounds whether such rituals reinforce, and even exacerbate, an untenable status quo by their staging techniques, by their "meaning monopoly" that forestalls critical thought, *or* whether these mediated rituals of recovery can bring out in the open new kinds of witnesses, new knowledge, new alliances, and possibilities for new meanings. A number of scholars point to the kind of "charitainment" that kicks in immediately following a disaster. In this recent scholarship, the 2010 Haitian earthquake and the 2005 New Orleans levee disaster are the dominant objects of analysis, making social inequalities involving race, class, and imperial history especially relevant. Such scholars argue that "these Hollywood-style spectacles depoliticize philanthropy by suggesting that philanthropy is about cyclic acts of consumption . . . and leisure"; the spectacles involve emotion-producing visuals as opposed to argumentative reasoning; such events "separate social problems from their spatial dimension and structural causes"; and they "reframe[e] compassion as a competitive game of giving" and as a project of "self-construction."[29] In making the benevolence of the giver and the dependence of the receiver hypervisible, the mediation of charity makes the giver's complicity in the problem, in the disaster, invisible.[30] In general, the Euro-western "media's desire to cultivate Others [has] helped to frame a racialized discourse of pity" that emphasizes the "helplessness" of people of color.[31]

Other scholars have asserted that disasters actually bring out the power of the ordinary citizen to produce transformative knowledge and ritual meaning. Simon Cottle reasons that though disaster mediation typically includes "'scale and body counts', 'tragedy and trauma', 'heroism' and 'miraculous escapes' and 'elites on parade,'" it also has the potential to "open up possibilities for social reflexivity, political critique and censure."[32] Pantti and Wahl-Jorgensen, in a survey of the British coverage of man-made disasters in the second half of the twentieth century, found that while most of the time "ordinary people . . . tend to be represented as apolitical and passive spectators to a political drama over which they do not have any influence," disasters can by contrast allow nonelites to act as the "'primary definers' of the story of blame and accountability" as they "direct criticism at power holders in society," forming a "disaster citizenship" in which there is a "democratized systemic critique of complex social processes."[33] And Coonfield and Huxford likewise hold that the meaning of a mediated disaster is not determined by its source but occurs in the ways various communities ritually take up the news and perform what it means as part of their everyday worlds.[34] These locally devised rituals transform trauma into communal affirmation and, in the words of anthropologist Victor Turner, perform the modes of interaction that must pertain "if there is to be any kind of coherent social life."[35]

The consensus in these studies of large-scale disaster mediation after World War II is that the upheaval these events inflict seems to demand a ritualistic reintegration of populations into coherent meaningful publics. The shallowest form of ritual, the "pseudo-ritual," is the top-down glitzy parade that props back up the hierarchical status quo and opens up no space for genuine investigations. Another problematic ritual form involves the anxious, hasty hunt for the "culprit."[36] The more socially healthful form of ritual is the kind that allows for the population to scrutinize itself, make new kinds of witnesses audible, and, in Cottle's words, think "subjunctive[ly]" about what "should or ought to be."[37] In order to be genuinely affirming, then, these rituals must take the man-made disaster as an index of internal societal malaise, as an occasion to listen for alternative sources of knowledge, and as a prompt for transformation.

Part of what has made such new theses about disaster publics possible is that they call upon work done after Habermas on what mass publics are and how they work. Scholars across the humanities like Rita Felski, Nancy Fraser, Michael Warner, Todd Gitlin, Gerard Hauser, and Catherine Squires have offered various nuanced models for thinking about what Hauser calls the "complex multilogue of disparate voices indigenous to complex and pluralistic societies."[38] In this work, the public sphere is a contentious network comprised by a dominant public and multiple "subaltern counterpublics"[39] that interact with—and at times overlap—each other. These counterpublics change over time, moving from protective group formation—or "enclaving" activities—using "hidden communication"[40] strategies to more open engagements with other publics and means of communicating. The boundaries between publics can be more or less permeable, and this, too, can change over time. Any given individual may move among multiple publics and modes of discourse. Rather than blood kinship or spatial immediacy, what connects publics is a "normative stranger-sociability" that can be paradoxically "intimate."[41] Publics can be deliberative, oppositional, and critical, but they can also be drawn together by recreation, pleasure, and camaraderie. Moreover, these "civic public spheres" can themselves turn into "new political publics."[42] Opposition can hone rational-critical speech but also call to consciousness articulations of a "poetic-expressive character."[43]

These recent insights into the complex operations of publics, and disaster publics especially, within societies that are simultaneously pluralistic and hierarchical provide ways of understanding how the Flood of 1927 *did* seem to configure, all at once, as if at the flip of an all-powerful speaker switch, a complex but coherent "public," but proved incapable of maintaining this charged network for very long. Environmental disasters, especially before they are revealed to be man-made, do the work of *naturalizing* publics. Strangers are presented as kin, their place as if it were your own. As these more organic communal affiliations circulate, however—as the public feels itself to be natural after all—nature itself finds itself in crisis. Or, to put it differently, as publics are made to feel primordially bonded in their ancient fight against Nature's forces, questions arise about how natural this "Nature" is and thus how cohering a war against it can be.

TWO

A Northern Army of Relief

On May 14, 1927, *Billboard* magazine ran an advertisement on behalf of the Ohio-based Charles T. Buell & Company for what they called a "marvelous attraction." The company had assembled a "Walk-Thru Exhibition" for carnivals, storerooms, and parks of "America's Greatest Calamity." They promised that their exhibit would be the "Greatest Money Getter of the Season. The Raging Waters; Flooded Districts; Dynamiting Levees; Refugees; Flood Babies; Whole Towns Submerged; Rescue Work of the Red Cross, etc." What the kit included for $125 were "twenty-four viewing boxes with views. . . . wonderful enlargements for flash . . . a Striking 6x10-ft. canvas banner, in bright colors; lecture, etc." The sales pitch was capped off with this question and answer: "Remember the Johnstown Flood? Well, this is bigger yet. Good anywhere in America. Will pay for itself over Decoration Day and give you a big profit, too."[1] This advertisement shows the potential within catastrophe for "marvelous attraction." Because the carnival exhibition used visual reproductions of eye-enveloping scenes—Dynamiting Levees! Raging Waters!—it tapped into its viewers' attraction to the sublime experience, transporting them into the presence of calamity even as they felt their own physical safety. As much as the modern American public identified itself with systems that seemed to control the world for human progress, certain mediators of this flood—like Buell & Company—bet that the public would find the massive failure of such modern systems deeply attractive as well. A super-flood seemed to be a kind of self-generated spectacle such that one needed only place a "viewing box" of one kind or another around the event to produce a thrill-craving audience.

The Red Cross wanted the flood to be a great "Money Getter" too. In fact, to prevent the flood from causing greater devastation of life, it needed national, and international, publics to become riveted to the event. As I mentioned earlier, Congress refused to appropriate any special funds for rescue and relief efforts.[2] President Coolidge, however, put his secretary of commerce, Herbert

Hoover, and under him, the secretaries of war and treasury, in charge of Red Cross relief efforts and mustered the National Guard to carry out its directives. The Red Cross, commanded by the executive branch and aided by the military, then enjoined privately owned media channels—newspapers, magazines, radio broadcasting companies, moving picture theaters—not only to disseminate the messages crafted by its Public Information bureau but also to be official channels for collecting donations from the public. The federal government was constructing a "great relief machine" that required the media to operate; the media, in the words of the director of public information, Douglas Griesemer, needed "to mobilize the resources of the entire nation in behalf of a disaster-stricken population."[3] But how could publicists narrate the flooded Delta into life? They had to do more than simply sell a spectacle; instead, they had to convince donors that they were invested in the outcome of the unfolding event. Our immediate question here, then, is this: confronted with the flood, with its complex and indirect set of causes and its sprawling ramifications, its potential erasure of the individual, of human-ness, its self-evident indictment of American technology and science, and its potentially unlovable southern protagonists, how did the media and entertainment industries produce public engagement out of these events?

In 1917, Woodrow Wilson became the chief propagandist for U.S. involvement in the eastern hemisphere war. Lippmann wrote enthusiastically that only Wilson "could have lifted the inevitable horror of war into a deed so full of meaning."[4] American participation would assure that the conflict did not terminate as an imperial or vindictive territorial grab but would establish a lasting peace. Creel and his Committee of Public Information disseminated this narrative, even skewing facts to do so, by every available technological means. The 1927 flood likewise needed to become "full of meaning." It required another "vast enterprise in salesmanship" that could "weld the people of the United States into one white-hot mass instinct with fraternity."[5] This relief machine did not need to sell a vision for a geopolitical world order. Instead, the Red Cross's News Service, with the help of the commercial media, needed to craft a vision—or, to quote Laswell and Benjamin, an "illusion"—of national solidarity and a related illusion about the volitional drive of nature. In the words of Edward Bernays, the "chaos" inherent in the event needed to be "organiz[ed]" into narrative form for the masses.

James Fieser, the acting chairman of the Red Cross, sent a wire in late April to his staff: "Essential push all publicity angles next week or ten days for sake of financial drive."[6] The drive would last much longer than seven or ten days. In some ways, the protracted nature of the calamity worked in favor of its publicists. People far away from the Delta were not simply being asked to send money to help clean up debris after the fact; rather, they could be pulled into the suspense of an unfolding saga. And with the almost instantaneous technology of wireless and radio, audiences could feel virtually present in the drama. If the campaign worked and the right affective levers were pressed, donations commensurate with the disaster would flow in, and material support could then flow out to the necessary Lower Valley sites. Herbert Hoover, in order to make appeals for citizens' dollars, "borrowed" the entire nationwide radio circuit twice—a circuit he himself had recently established—to transport his voice into millions of homes. He had his staff carefully track press coverage and report on it to him frequently.[7] Newspapers in every city of the country opened up column and photo space for the flood and became official reverse conduits for the public's donations of funds. On their pages were banner headlines; maps that tracked the southward-moving progress of the flood crest; photographs of refugees; cartoons; feature stories; editorials; and frequent lists of donors. Urgings like this one from the *Los Angeles Times* issued forth: "let it not be said that she [Los Angeles] ignored the call of agonized victims in the worst catastrophe that ever befell any section of the United States."[8] Cities, working through their leading dailies, competed to be the first to meet relief quotas set by the Red Cross.

As the publicity push was carried out over the ensuing weeks, then, which angles would work best to draw in the public? First of all, publicists skirted the issue of the flood as evidence of a federal engineering blunder by representing relief efforts as a massive and flawless technocratic mechanism assembled by the country's best experts. While the experts planned and organized the relief, that relief was imagined to be delivered by a familial figure: "Uncle" Sam or a Great Mother. The government exercised its "biopower"—its control over masses of bodies—in the camps as a protective parent. At the broadest level, military scenes dominated the narrative. The flood was imagined as a fight between modern organization and primordial forces, as a battle between modern and ancient. High water was an "invading enemy" attacking the whole nation. Because the enemy was not human, it would be a war without blame but one that could "weld" the masses nonetheless. The recent experiences of world war were summoned forth here: not only in the fact that the same governmental structure of publicity was set in motion once more—as well as the key American figure of war-time relief, Herbert Hoover—but also because this battle, in America and for Americans, appeared to be genuinely humanitarian in ways that the Great War had ultimately failed to be. More potently still, this war offered the chance for American donors—all imagined as "the North"—to rewrite the terms of a still older victory as they became an "Army of rescuers" saving the Southland.

Mediascape

This was an era, as media historians have put it, of "proliferating, ubiquitous, nearly inescapable print."[9] There were 2,200 dailies in the United States in the late 1920s.[10] The Associated Press served 1,200 of them, controlling roughly 58,000 miles of leased wires across the newly expanded imperial nation, from, as it boasted, "the Philippines to Porto Rico."[11] By 1926, the AP was gathering not just news copy but photographs, feature stories, cartoons, and comics into its clearinghouse. The organization prided itself that "only minutes now separate readers from the most distant point in the world."[12] The Associated Negro Press, eight years old by 1927, with eighty charter members, was inaugurated and run by Chicagoan Claude Barnett (who served on Hoover's Colored Advisory Commission).[13] Among urban dailies, the *Chicago Daily Tribune* disseminated its news to more than 700,000 readers on weekdays and to more than a million on Sundays. The *New York Times* reached upwards of 300,000 readers during weekdays and more than 600,000 on Sundays. About 135,000 people opened the *Los Angeles Times* every morning, with numbers likewise increasing on Sundays.[14] The *Chicago Defender* reached more than 200,000 readers weekly, while *The Crisis* went out to 100,000 monthly.[15] By 1920, the literacy rate among African Americans was at 77 percent; communal oral reading raised the reach of the dailies and weeklies farther still.[16] Readership varied across class lines: newspapers were the most popular form of reading matter among blue-collar workers and workers without a college education, who tended to spend about an hour a day reading them. Though college-educated readers likewise purchased the daily news in large numbers, they tended to spend less time with their papers on a daily basis.[17] Of the print magazine, the *World's Work* editor Walter Hines Page wrote that it "is the best instrument that has yet been invented or developed or discovered for affecting public opinion in our democracy. It gives the only way in which serious men can continuously reach the whole reading public."[18] Analyzing magazines more recently, Richard Ohmann argues that magazines "helped ease the passage into industrial society for working people of moderate means" while "they helped capitalists make that society a less menacing environment for their project of development."[19]

Lines of communication crossed regional, class, and racial boundaries. The "Negro press" did not, for instance, make up the entire media landscape for

African American readers. In the South, white-owned dailies carried substantial news related to the African American community, typically sectioned off with headings like "Negro News Events" or "Colored Notes."[20] African American readers outside of the South read the white-owned papers as often—if not more often—than they did black-run papers like the *Chicago Defender*, *The Crisis*, the *Baltimore Afro-American*, the *New York Amsterdam News*, or the *Pittsburgh Courier.*[21] An African American writer such as Walter White wrote his account of flood conditions in the leftist periodical *The Nation.* The main exposé of the Red Cross and the National Guard that was published in the NAACP's *Crisis* was investigated by a white female reporter. Moreover, a significant technique of reportage in the press agitating for racial reform was to quote and reprint pieces, across the political spectrum, from white-owned papers and white-authored bureaucratic documents.

Newspapers and their readerships also crossed regional boundaries. Southerners accessed reporting from around the country and the world via wire services and the Associated Press; they also read pieces reprinted from northern publications. For example, *Chicago Daily News* reporter Craig Dale wrote a series of articles critical of white southern moral hygiene in the refugee camps that caused "a rumpus in the South";[22] it could cause a "rumpus" because newspaper reading was cross-regional. Mississippi journalist Harris Dickson's feature stories on the flood ran in the *Los Angeles Times*, the *New York World*, the *Atlanta Constitution*, and elsewhere. The *Chicago Defender* used a network of railroad porters to deliver local papers from around the country to its Chicago headquarters and then widely distribute the *Defender* outside the midwestern capital; in fact only one-third of its distribution was inside Chicago.[23] During the flood, for instance, copies of the *Defender* were bought up and burned by whites in Little Rock, Arkansas.[24] Thus publications crossed both racial and regional boundaries, making for a messy skein of lines connecting news producers and news consumers. Often in the mainstream northern and coastal white-owned press there was an obliviousness of its actual multiracial and multiregional readership.

Print media in 1927 were replete with imagery—photographs especially but also maps and cartoons. Lest we associate newspapers and magazines of the 1920s exclusively with verbal print, and thus with "disembodied self-abstraction,"[25] which was an aspiration of journalism's origins during the Enlightenment, it is important to note how full of visual information and commentary newspapers and magazines were then. Maps and photographs appear to truthfully represent—or transport—the real. Yet of course photographs and maps frame truth, make choices about inclusions, exclusions, angles, and so on.

Editorial cartoons announced their perspective more forcefully and could wear either their satire or their sentiment outwardly.

Radio was a newly nationalized and regulated medium in 1927. In February of that year, a Radio Act was signed into law that gave the new Federal Radio Commission the power to divide the country into zones, assign frequencies, and control licensing. A year earlier, the National Broadcasting Company was created as a commercial enterprise. The radio medium, operating exclusively through sound and the ear rather than on visual material and the eye, did not present human subjects as embodied in ways similar to photography, film, and the stage. Though race, gender, and class identities can be carried, or simulated, in the voice, the body on the radio was trickier to access and seemed to authenticate socially produced assumptions less automatically. An audience member might let certain voices into his or her consciousness in a way that he or she may not if that voice were attached to stigmatized bodies. Moreover, before the era of broadcast television, radio was the only medium that could be experienced at the same time by a mass of people; in 1927, therefore, it was uniquely positioned, in the words of radio historian Michele Hilmes, to "assert actively the unifying power of simultaneous experience [and] to communicate meanings about the nature of that unifying experience."[26] It was not a fully disembodied medium, however, for it connected distant voices and ears into a kind of present exchange. Because the recorded speech could sound like a physically present voice, appeals made in this way had the particular power to seem direct and immediate. The executive branch, having decided not to finance relief operations, needed to commandeer the communications infrastructure of the nation to involve the public in the work and the cost of relief. The state needed to use commercially owned networks to mediate between a "disaster-stricken population" and the rest of the nation. Newspaper and radio outlets made themselves available to do this work of mediation, and simultaneously noted and promoted their function as the vital pathways in a top-down, diffusive program of national coherence.

The New Reconstruction Machine

In the model of society outlined in the few years preceding 1927 by sociologists who studied disaster, these disasters function positively to "make for a better organized community" and to turn the community into "a family on a larger scale, [so that] the interests of each member are interwoven with those of all."[27] To these theorists, disasters had an evolutionary function, making the social organism more balanced and integrated. Disasters on a cross-regional scale, like the 1927 flood, should hypothetically turn the nation, in fact, from a political invention, an imagined community, into a large-scale organism. The public, though actually a population of strangers, could, because of disaster, feel tied together like kin. Moreover, as one territory in the country drew everyone's attention no matter their geographic distance, the public could feel as if it were all in the same place at the same time. In addition, phrases like "relief machine" and "intelligence machine" reflected a sense that a crisis could also make a society function like a good modern machine: complex, internally coordinated, and predictable. A word, and indeed a concept, that seemed to fuse the realms of mechanization and organism—and to capture the positive dynamism of each—was "organization." What the visionaries of the Flood of 1927 imagined was that humanly designed organizations would not merely relieve the immediate distresses of the human and built environments but would bring about a better "realignment of [the] social forces" of the nation, would galvanize the nation into equilibrium.[28]

Hoover first addressed the entire nation about the flood via radio from Memphis on April 30, 1927. The *New York Times* noted how the aural medium "brought the appeal intimately to the people."[29] He summoned listeners to participate in a "national fight against the most dangerous flood our country has ever known in its history." Though skirmishes were lost where breaks had already occurred, the battle was very much ongoing, and engineers were in its charge. Hoover located exactly where the crest—or the front line of "the water enemy"—was at the very moment of his speech; it just happened to be at Vicksburg, the site of a great former battle which once tore the nation apart. Today, though, listeners could become part of a "great national organization" that would bring not devastation, but "reconstructions," for, as he said, "a catastrophe has come to the people of our south."[30] (Hoover would soon tell a luncheon audience in New Orleans that he used the term "reconstruction" "advisedly" because he believed "we may give it a new significance in the relation of north and south.")[31] Leading the organization were experts, "strong and experienced men from every center." The Red Cross is "your organization," he summarized; "it is your hand carrying out the will of your great heart." A generous American will, directed by modern, urban technocrats, could be soldered together into an organization—or a kind of intelligent organism—as it countered "the invasion" of the water enemy. The very phenomenon of the engineer's voice on the radio network offered a model for that quasi-human, quasi-infrastructural intelligent national organism at work. This voice summoned a "heart" to compel a "hand" to save part of its body, its "south."[32]

Hoover strove to make the flood that galvanic event of the sociologists' model: the crisis that reintegrates. In the weeks that followed, this message was taken up and extended by the commercial news media. This transmittal of the news, it should be noted, is not utterly neutral; it is not just about conveying information. When a large territory is completely destabilized by catastrophe, journalism achieves a kind of ritual function as it finds itself called to transform a biological occurrence into a cultural occasion to reaffirm the bonds and the values of the suffering community.[33]

Just as Hoover represented the "water enemy" as a nonpolitical threat to the entire nation, so too did journalists. Though comparisons were made to the recent European antagonists of the world war, more constant was a representation of the river as a primordial and evil animal bent on human destruction. The *Wall Street Journal* pictured the Mississippi as a "squirming, twisting snake."[34] For the *Atlanta Constitution*, the river was "a giant, bloated snake, ugly and menacing."[35] *New York Times* reporter Herschel Brickell—as I mentioned at the start of chapter 1—declared that "Once more war is on between the mighty old dragon that is the Mississippi River and his ancient enemy, man." Brickell concluded: "It is proper to speak of this struggle of man to save his life and his possessions from the dragon as war."[36] Louisiana writer Helen Murphy, writing in the *Atlantic Monthly*, called the Mississippi a "ruthless river," an "old enemy."[37] Will Irwin of the *World's Work* described the river's movement as a "long siege."[38] Frederick Simpich, surveying the flood in a forty-six-page article for the *National Geographic Magazine*, described the "yellow, sewerlike waters," "the evil, yellow sea," as "diabolically deliberate." Simpich reasoned that if it weren't for the warning system enabled by "modern invention, more lives must have been lost in this flood than America gave to the battlefields of Europe." He judged that "fiercer . . . by far than any war ever waged against a hostile kingdom" was the fight the nation mounted against the Mississippi.[39] And as an editorial in the *Washington Post* put it: "It is essentially a question of national defense against the savage power of nature."[40] To avoid directing blame inwardly—something that might quash the communal spirit of relief—blame is directed at an external, nonhuman agent. These writers, even as they drew from mythologies that used to coalesce ancient peoples, position the 1927 event as a war of the modern versus the ancient, "modern invention" versus that "old enemy," that "twisting snake." This war *for* modernity thereby showed the moderns to be as irrational, as enthralled as old Adam.

To repulse this external siege, the rest of the country outside the "stricken" zone[41]—understood as "the North"—would put together what relief organizers and journalists, following Hoover, called "reconstruction machinery." Recall that though suffering was worst in the states of Arkansas, Louisiana, and Mississippi, storm and flood damage had occurred in the plains states as well as throughout the Mississippi and Ohio valleys, including in Ohio, Illinois, Iowa, and the former border state of Missouri. This hydrogeological unit of the Mississippi watershed was forgotten in order to envision *this* war (between the river and southern people, defended by a northern army) as an event to remedy the older war fought between North and South. The *New York Times* reported in June that Hoover would "see that the reconstruction machinery is well oiled and running in perfect harmony there" to aid people whom Hoover pictured as "this great army of unfortunate people."[42] Northern commentators seemed to want to replace memories of the fraught, and ultimately unsustained, process of postbellum Reconstruction with a more politically neutral but somehow more substantial form of material reconstruction and modernization. An AP dispatch out of New Orleans in May explained that the "greatest machine . . . in the nation's history was [being] organized in the southland."[43] Framing national relief, relief that was also issuing from southern donors in great quantity, as an avant-garde northern machine on southern soil reinforced old dichotomies: northern invention, modernity, and solution as set against southern nature, dependency, and backwardness. Apparently word of the New South had failed to reach the rest of the nation. Terms like "organization," "harmony," and "machine" bespoke a Spencerian model of a forward-moving equilibrium northerners could galvanize.

The dominant way in which the public was imagined to be sharing a household with distant misery was by revisiting, and setting right, the older saga of the "house divided." The chairman of the Los Angeles Red Cross, as he urged the citizenry "to give and give and give," reminded them exactly where the "torrential flood" was occurring: "in virtually all of the old Confederate States."[44] This statement was, needless to say, a mischaracterization but one that got a great deal of traction. Hoover put it still more plainly when he said that giving aid "should be the task of a generous north to a resolute and courageous south . . . and we of the north have the right and duty to bind their wounds."[45] This phrase—"bind their wounds"—would have been familiar to many. It recalled the closing words of Abraham Lincoln's 1865 "Second Inaugural Address," in which he exhorted his listeners that "with charity for all . . . let us strive on to finish the work we are in; to bind up the nation's wounds . . . to do all which may achieve and cherish a just, and a lasting peace, among ourselves, and with all nations."[46] If Lincoln hoped, in March 1865, that soon the task would be national self-healing from the ravages of intestine war, Hoover, some sixty years later, harkened back to this vision of sectional reunion brought about through the work of relief but this time explicitly cast "the north" as the healers and "the south" as the wounded. Reunion would occur through northern ministry and southern suffering. Hoover positioned all donors—whether they lived in Vermont or Southern California or Virginia or Georgia—as a northern army of relief.

Giving as Taking: Southern Revival as Northern Absorption

Hollywood did not miss a chance to turn the flood into symbolic spectacle. A spread in the *Los Angeles Times* from May 11 advertising a "Monster Flood Benefit" run by Will Hays, the chief publicist of Hollywood's morally reformed image, is a case in point (Fig. 2.1). On the top half of the page (not shown) are shots of screen stars, establishing the tutelary deities of the event. The photographs of the flood zone, placed just below in the page layout, draw the disaster close in space: the viewer sees white families, and especially mothers and "tiny tots," being cared for by the Red Cross. Both the reason for and the yield from the donors' money is in evidence through a kind of scenic intercutting. More interesting still, though, is the comic strip placed just below, called "Our History in Pictures." It depicts scenes from the Civil War leading up to Lee's surrender at Appomattox Court House. Moving back and forth in point of view as the strip has its viewer experience the conflict through both Confederate and Union proxies, it positions the war as "our history." It also has its viewers retrace especially those scenes leading up inevitably to reconciliation. This plot—of southern defeat followed by national reunion—is played out again in the flood photos. Only this time, the "defeat" has no human antagonist and no victors. "Union" forces are recast as an army of relief workers saving the refugees whom Hoover called "this great army of unfortunate people." If this layout draws the (defeated) South and (a luminous) Hollywood close in space, it also draws a neutralized spring of 1865 into the present scene. The old contest is restaged as a new, sublimated contest of philanthropy. America's aristocracy has moved from the plantation not only to Wall Street but also to Hollywood, and the all-white South is recast as an object of paternalism.

Another example of this visual rhetoric of reunion—of a renewed intimacy between the white South and the rest of the country discovered in the catastrophe—appeared a couple of weeks later in the *Los Angeles Times*, placed next to an Associated Press story out of New Orleans (Fig. 2.2). Because this graphic

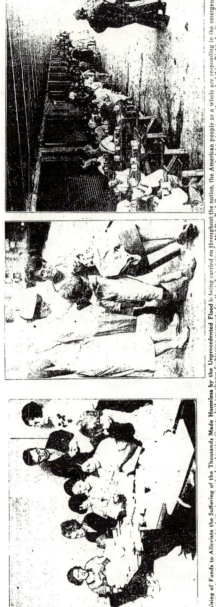

2.1. "Hollywood Bowl, Scene of Monster Flood Benefit Saturday Night," *Los Angeles Times*, May 11, 1927, 12. © 1927 *Los Angeles Times*. Reprinted with permission.

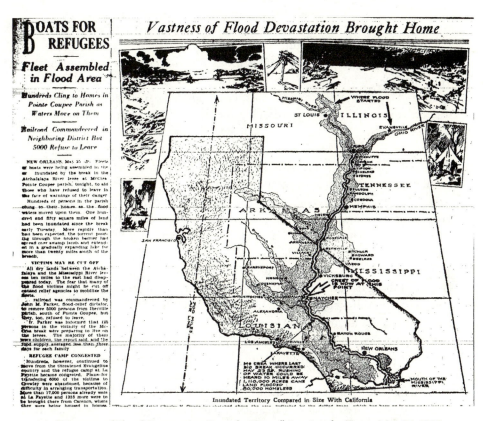

2.2. "Vastness of Flood Devastation Brought Home," *Los Angeles Times*, May 26, 1927, 2. © 1927 *Los Angeles Times*. Reprinted with permission.

representation, like that of the "Monster Benefit," participates in eliciting donations, it functions as part of the gift culture produced by the flood. First of all, it eschews the difficult historical and environmental investigation of "Where [the] Flood Started" (a phrase visible on the upper right-hand corner) to place its origin points in the river itself. The crest, described as "now at this point" (in Natchez), identifies the drama as in medias res. This "superimposition" of a map of California over the Lower Mississippi Valley is intended to give "a clearer idea as to [the] tremendous nature of the devastation" by bringing it "Home"; it is tacitly meant to be an education in spatial scale. To this end, the caption verbally asks its readers to imagine "the whole of Southern California below the Tehachapi" underwater.[47] Visually, it places "Los Angeles" in the state of Louisiana, just northwest of "Lafayette" and within miles from the most recent levee break. What is also curious is the arrowed line running from north to south on the left side of the map, for while it mimics the lines indicating state boundaries, it actually functions as the deceptively slender indication of a vast and hidden fold. A seven-hundred-mile territory of plains and mountains—the great upthrust of the Continental Divide—disappears in this new graphic seam. This superimposition offers the illusion that California is *in* the Mississippi drainage basin and that the great majority of California falls within the former Confederate states. Or, to flip it around, viewers see the former Confederacy absorbed into the far West. This map is designed to produce Californians' sympathy for residents of the Lower Mississippi; to eradicate physical space and thereby eradicate affective distance; and to instill a geographic and hence (vicarious) personal identification. What begins as a neutral question of scale is taken over by a suggestion of affective relocation. It also imagines the South to have been symbolically absorbed into a greater Hollywood.

Associated Press copy partly surrounding the map spoke of disappearing land, a "shifting inland sea," and a "broken barrier," all suggestions that things once geographically separate could become newly close. The *Los Angeles Times*, akin to passing a hat after a performance, finished its reporting by an appeal: "Los Angeles needed approximately $30,000 . . . to subscribe fully its $350,000 voluntary goal for the relief of the flood-stricken Mississippi River Valley."[48] Reports of various efforts "to swell the Mississippi Flood Fund" followed: children's neighborhood plays, women's bridge tournaments, air carnivals, and rummage sales. These details particularized a public brought into visibility, and hence being, through its will to alleviate southern suffering.

A feature of drawing distant sections of the nation closer in affective geographic cohesion entailed severing a global conception of citizenship. One of the most avid northern proponents of flood relief was the Republican mayor of Chicago, "Big Bill" Thompson. As noted, he had led a tour of the Mississippi Valley during the lesser flood of 1922; he called together a "flood summit" in June 1927 in Chicago to hash out flood prevention policy; and he led a kind of jamboree down to D.C. to lobby for flood prevention spending. Whether the motive behind his passion for the Lower Valley had to do with southern Illinois's own inundation early on in the super-flood, or his state's standing to gain from watershed management appropriations, or trying to turn himself into presidential timber is unclear. Before the flood, "Big Bill" had made a name for himself as a proponent of the "America First" campaign, which seemed primarily aimed at expurgating all mention of Great Britain from U.S. history textbooks.[49] In the spring of 1927, he pressed for a new north-to-south reconnec-

We went cuckoo over the Armenians, Russians and Poles.

2.3. Nate Collier, "We Went Cuckoo over the Armenians, Russians and Poles," *Washington Post*, May 8, 1927, 8. Illustration for Will Rogers's article "Dimes for Flood Victims."

tion that was meant to trump lesser transnational obligations. Such public support of aid between the states to promote national integrity was echoed in many other sources. As a *New York Times* letter to the editor asked on May 12: "Is this domestic danger, which is of much greater magnitude than that existing in Nicaragua and China, less deserving and are the lives and property any less sacred and valuable?"[50] A cartoon from the May 8 issue of the *Washington Post* posed a similar question: should we be fleeced of our garments for nations in Eurasia and have nothing left to donate when our own people on the Mississippi are crying out in need (Fig. 2.3)?

The federal "relief machine" was humanized in visual print culture around the country as the Red Cross, Uncle Sam, and the South were embodied in familial and religious dramas of reunion and salvation. In Foucauldian terms, the "biopower" of the state wore the costume of white consanguinity and Christian spirituality. In a *Columbus Dispatch* image from May 5, "The Distressed Southland" was embodied as a white refugee family, cowering without any paternal protection (Fig. 2.4). A Christic source of illumination appears across the water as "Columbus" discovers a land made primitive in its emergency. What is promised is that the nation as Anglo-Saxon Christian family will be united and redeemed again. An April 25 lithograph from the *Denver Post* shows patriarchal but spry Uncle Sam trudging into darksome waters to save his fair southern child. Finally, on May 10 the *St. Louis Daily Globe Democrat* pictured "the Greatest Mother in the World," a monumental but ministering Red Cross, giving forth loaves to all her tiny southern children (Fig. 2.5). All of these representations strive to make the sociologist Prince's prediction come to pass: namely, that out of "a state of flux" induced by disaster, the

2.4. "Columbus Understands an Appeal Like This," *Columbus Dispatch*, May 5, 1927. Reprinted with permission.

"community" will become again "just a family on a larger scale." Because of the geographic scope of the flood, that "community" assumed national, continental proportions. In the case of the 1927 disaster, the southern part of the national family was envisioned as feminine, white, and dependent, in need of protection from a federal father, mother, or brother. The national white press— as it energized the public "Relief Machine"—imagined the nation reintegrating white brethren in Dixie.

2.5. Jay N. "Ding" Darling, "Next to Your Own the Greatest Mother in the World," *St. Louis Daily Globe Democrat*, May 10, 1927. Courtesy of the Jay N. "Ding" Darling Wildlife Society.

The Bossman of the Flood

In this scenario, Hoover was the likeliest flesh-and-blood candidate to play the national patriarch. But Hoover was not an easy man to humanize as the hero of reunion. He seemed more than anything else to be a walking brain, the neural center of a "big intelligence machine." The most thorough attempt to give humanity to the "master organizer" persona during the flood was, perhaps surprisingly, created by a southern author, Truman Hudson Alexander, the managing editor of the *Nashville Tennessean*, who had reported on the Scopes Trial two years before while simultaneously acting as an attaché to the then governor of Tennessee. Promoters of the New South saw the Scopes case as a bungled publicity stunt by local Tennesseans, one that had intensified the North's sense of the South as a place of backward fundamentalists.[51] Alexander had come to understand the importance of the South's promoting its own modernity, its own part in the modern nation. In his article "Herbert Hoover Wins Hearts of Folks in Flood District," the first of a series on "builders of the modern south," published not only in southern papers but also in the *New York Times*, Alexander fashions Hoover into a new kind of amalgam of Big Planter and Federal Boss. The scene opens at Pine Bluff, Arkansas. (Recall that the Red Cross camp at Pine Bluff was called out by the Colored Advisory Commission for leaving distribution of rehabilitation supplies "entirely in the hands of the farm owners," who at times charged for these supplies, and that the racist New Yorker in charge of the camp repulsed the involvement of black social workers.) A "crowd of negroes" has assembled to give Hoover, whom Alexander styles "the boss of the Mississippi flood," a "loving cup." "In token of appreciation and gratitude for his wonderful work and sympathy during FLOOD OF 1927 By the Colored People of Arkansas," says the inscription. Out of the assemblage of African Americans in which, in fact, the leading professional class were very much present,[52] Alexander selects for an interview one "Uncle Eph," "wiping his shining ebony countenance with a bandanna handkerchief," for whom mention of his crop was a natural trigger of talk. What Uncle Eph reveals to—or, better put, performs for—Alexander is a serf-like reverence for the paternal protection of the bossman of the flood: " 'Sho' would have had a hard time didn't Mr. Hoover come to fetch us de high ground,' said Uncle Eph now that he sensed the white gem'man wished to talk to him." Not only did Hoover bring the high ground to the folk, but it was "Mr. Hoover feeding us." In fact, Eph summarizes, "Mr. Hoover sho' thought about ever'thing."[53]

The scene then switches to Hoover's private railroad car, equipped with radio, telephone, typewriters, and staffers, speeding to New Orleans. As Hoover sits in conversation, his "glance strayed at intervals to the huge loving cup which had been bought with grimy nickels and dimes and 'four bit' pieces of the negroes of Arkansas. His face . . . bore an air of eternal youth such as America had seen upon the face of Lindbergh and the other great adventurers of our time." Though "his mind clicks like a machine [and] [h]is forehead is that of a great engineer and builder," his eyes are "the eyes of Joseph, the dreamer of dreams." Hoover "surveyed the cup with eyes kindling with sentiment" and said, "almost apologetically, 'One must have some household gods.' " He then judged that "It was a great oversight that some white composer . . . didn't write a plaintive dirge which the negro refugees might sing in the camps. . . . It would have become the great epic of the floods." Hoover went on to speak positively about the South's "economic renaissance," underway these last twenty-five years. He attributed it mostly to external capital—from the Northeast, and from Great Britain—but averred that local leaders were needed who better knew how to direct that capital: "before the Civil War the South had leadership in plenty but in the long poverty afterward it had little opportunity to develop leaders." Along with the cultivation of white southern strongmen, the "vocational education" of the "colored people" needed to occur, and "large blocks" of land needed to be "broken up and colonized by small owners." The river "can and will be controlled" with "the boldest engineering plan ever attempted." Later on in the journey, at dinner, the topic fleetingly arose, without altering the collective mood, of "a lynching some miles from this place." Indeed, as Hoover admitted: "I have been too busy really to see this flood at close range."

Hoover and Alexander together are using this opportunity to publicize a vision of southern modernity—or, one could say, a southernized version of American modernity—in which a regional leadership would emerge who could deftly direct external capital to create economic growth and to ameliorate the lives of the black underclass via small property ownership and vocational education. The big southern planter is not necessarily a part of this picture, nor is the existing southern black elite. What might pass notice, though, is that the Hoover of Alexander's making has come to occupy the role of the planter as the plantation is made national and symbolic in scope. Alexander called forth "Uncle Eph" to declare it. In return, blacks get to play the lowercase "gods" who will help transform the nation into a "household." If only a white artist could come up with lyrics for them, these minor gods—something like a play's chorus—could fill the house with song.[54] Hoover is a new kind of modern avatar, moving over the face of the waters in a railroad car equipped with the technology to activate a nationwide communications and relief infrastructure. "The negro" keeps him human by keeping alive the sentimental patriarch within. The Delta's large plantations need to be broken up, but the nation can become a new kind of plantation household: modern, capitalist, efficient, and with African Americans sufficiently educated to play their vocational part.[55]

Comic Relief

Alexander was not the only journalist to produce scenes of black dependence on white rescue. Such vignettes were typically intended to play as comic minstrel interludes within the larger saga of national reunion. These skits would

NEGRO NOAH GETS WET FEET

*Ark Built in Preparation for Mississippi Flood Fails to Float
So Parson and His Flock Land on Railroad
Embankment Instead of Ararat*

MEMPHIS, May 12. (*P*)—Exhorted by their parson, a community of negroes in the lowlands near Parkin, Ark., emulated the example of Noah when they heard the flood was approaching and hastily built an "ark." Into the crude vessel, they crowded themselves and all their worldly belongings, including chickens, dogs, cats and mules. While they waited for the flood, they prayed and rejoiced.

The flood came, but the ark refused to float. Water poured in from a hundred leaks in the uncaulked hull and with the flood a foot and a half deep on the floor of the flat-bottomed craft, its occupants fled to a railway embankment.

News of the "ark" was received at Red Cross headquarters from relief workers.

MURDERER KILLS SELF

CLEVELAND (N. D.) May 13. (*P*)—Sayles Hastings, 50-year-old farmer who shot his neighbor, W. F. Flint, to death yesterday and seriously wounded the latter's 16-year-old son, committed suicide in his granary today as a posse advanced on his farm home.

2.6. "Negro Noah Gets Wet Feet,"
Los Angeles Times, May 14, 1927.

amuse and satisfy white readers into opening their purses. The Red Cross publicist mentioned at the start of the book, Mr. Taylor, disseminated the story, gathered from relief workers, of a group of African Americans in Parkin, Arkansas, a town on the St. Francis, who had built a raft only to discover that it was not river-worthy. As the Associated Press told it on May 12, this group had been "exhorted by their parson . . . [to emulate] the example of Noah . . . and hastily built an 'ark.'" They put all their "worldly belongings" on board, where they "prayed and rejoiced." Alas, as the waters came, the "ark refused to float. Water poured in from a hundred leaks in the uncaulked hull," and the group "fled to a railway embankment."[56] While Red Cross publicists were every day attempting to communicate the efficacy, and the salvific quality, of their own "relief machine," they framed this vernacular form of self-help as a Noachic travesty. Professionals at the Red Cross have built a "humming" machine whereas credulous black folk are neither modern builders nor God's chosen ones. Editors at the *Los Angeles Times* saw in this story the opportunity for blackface lampoon (Fig. 2.6). The derision here leaves little need for analysis, but one may note that the cartoonist has captured this minstrelized routine in a moment when the actors' physical and linguistic acts are at their most futile.

The most scandalous type of black figure to show up in the white press was the minstrel type for whom the flood was actually a vacation. The "disaster" was

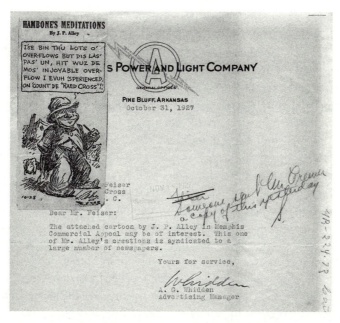

2.7. J[ames] P[inckney] Alley, "Hambone's Meditations," *Commercial Appeal*, enclosure within letter from A. G. Whidden to James L. Fieser, American Red Cross vice chairman, October 31, 1927. U.S. National Archives & Records Administration, Red Cross Papers, DR-224/72 Mississippi River Valley Flood 3/30/27 Newspapers, Clippings, Etc., Central File, 1917–1934, box 742, Collection ANRC.

a godsend, freeing him from work and allowing him to bask in the federal munificence. It was all a sweet reminder of plantation days when white folks took good care of him and he could be his natural, happy-go-lucky self. This cartoon by J. P. Alley appeared in Memphis's *Commercial Appeal* in late October as part of a widely syndicated series (Fig. 2.7); interestingly, Alley was part of the editorial team that had won a Pulitzer Prize in 1923 for opposing the Ku Klux Klan.[57] "Hambone" tells his audience that this "wuz de mos' injoyable over-flow I evuh 'sperienced, on 'count de 'Raed Cross'!!" The series suggests that for Delta blacks, Red Cross concentration camps were an unbeatable tent show, one that didn't even charge admission. This image reached Red Cross headquarters in Washington, D.C., folded in a letter from an advertising manager named A. G. Whidden at the Arkansas Power and Light Company in Pine Bluff. Whidden, a professional promoter, addressed the letter to James Feiser, the Red Cross acting chairman, as an image that "may be of interest."[58] The suggestion seems to be that "Hambone" might be working as a positive mascot for the organization.

In both this cartoon and that of the Noachic travesty, white-produced flood minstrelsy is received and disseminated by national papers. Picturing black incompetence and dependence serves, by contrast, to publicize white technological mastery and paternalistic munificence.

Delta author Harris Dickson wrote a syndicated series of twelve articles depicting the flood zone, a series the *Los Angeles Times* promoted as "The drama of the great flood . . . set forth comprehensively for the first time . . . by Harris Dickson, famous southern writer."[59] By 1927, Dickson had made a name for himself not only as war reporter for *Collier's* but also as the creator, for the *Saturday Evening Post*, of an African American ne'er-do-well character facetiously named "Old Reliable."[60] Of Dickson's Delta expertise, the *New York Times'* Herschel Brickell wrote that he "knows more about the valley floods than most engineers."[61] A key objective of the series was to reveal, as Dickson put it, "all of these motley people, farmers, volunteers, Red Cross workers, everybody that is jumbled together in this chaos," as "just common human folk" with whom readers could sympathize and laugh, for indeed, "a saving grace of humor shines cheerily through it all." His articles were intended to pluck *characters* out of this distant mass event and set them in relief. Because a "mass loses individuality," and "magnitude . . . dull[s] . . . sympathy," he needed, as he put it, to find an "individual" caught up in "an instance."[62] There *are* moments of pathos and grace in his vignettes: in one tableau, an African American couple throws overboard from a rescue boat a new sewing machine and a phonograph to make room for other refugees;[63] in another moment, Dickson appreciates the "gallant blacks" who operated skiffs in "treacherous currents."[64] More typically, though, Dickson turned the Red Cross camps into virtual Vaudeville stages. Readers paid their entrance fee by purchasing the daily paper and their exit fee by donating to the Red Cross via that same paper. Typical of Vaudeville's multiethnic rotations of acts in which Americans encountered lampoons, in swift rotation, of "the Irishman," "the Jew," "the Dutchman," and "the Negro," Dickson likewise staged a "motley" assemblage of amusing characters (Acadians, dialect-speaking Anglo American farmers, memories of long-departed Spaniards and Pirates). Dickson was trying to make the South charming and intriguing in order to enjoin Americans to aid in relief of the water's conquest. His most reliable means, though, of drawing the nation close was to stage black "folk" as the comic relief of relief operations. If this was a gamboling plea for help, they also unburdened Dickson of the uncomfortable task of directly begging for assistance. He could make his plea vicariously through his black-faced surrogates.

In the Mississippi backwaters, he figuratively makes an impromptu stage platform out of an "almost totally submerged" cabin: "There's the phonograph playing merrily. Jazz tunes. On a scaffolding built up into the roof a dozen men and women sit around it. Very black people with very white teeth. And happy. Having a good time, eating out of pans and listening to Broadway. / 'no, suh, boss, thankee, suh,' one of the black men called down. 'Us don't want to go no place, but I'd be powerful glad to git some rations.'" Dickson concludes: "Seven feet more of water drove them all to Vicksburg."[65] So Dickson follows, where he finds at the Red Cross camp a kind of costuming department: the "naked are clad [here], frequently producing most humorous effects." "Into the clothing room comes a white man, much sunburned, wearing shirt and breeches." The "farmer grinned: 'I'm wearing' a fat lady's undershirt, and can't wriggle no kind o' way to make it fit. Them little straps keep a slippin' off my shoulders.'" Along with this scene of accidental drag (that makes lightly risible the issue of disaster-induced southern emasculation), we are presented with "a coal black person, promenading in pride, barefooted, and sporting a full evening suit," a figure reminiscent of the black urban dandy of minstrel tradition known as "Zip Coon."[66] The preposterousness of black folk dressing *up* in rank is again displayed when a sedan-full of "donated, cast-off hats" produces "mobbing" and "turmoil": "A mass of negro women buzz around it—heads, bobbing heads. . . . [I]t appears that the sedan itself is also packed with heads, as if a miscellaneous petting party were jumbled together on the back seat."[67] More physical comedy occurs as black refugees slip in and out of openings in the mess tent, trying to affect a literal run-around of the rations system. Finally, Dickson describes the scene on a large rescue barge as an "incongruous farce!" One colored person comes aboard, having saved "only his gilded birdcage. Empty, no canary." Then a "dignified black preacher is boosted aboard the barge, wearing a longtail coat with a flirtatious and undulating swing, and white tie. Square-rimmed spectacles and a dilapidated silk hat." Once a revival gets going on board, the crowd emits a "groan, a weird uncanny jungle chanting. . . . Hundreds join in, swelling barbaric rhythm."[68] As Dickson winds down his appeal to readers, he envisions Delta history as the story of "a redeemed wilderness"; "Instead of a barbaric jungle, civilization flourished." What is called for now, after the flood's erasure of that work, is a "reconquest of a jungle."[69] In the list of donors printed in the *Los Angeles Times* next to the twelfth and final installment, the very final donor mentioned in the tally is a "Civil War Nurse," giving $1.[70]

As we shall later see, other writers and performers would respond to the disorienting "mass" "chaos" of this event by trying to get inside the mind of individuals caught up in the emergency. Rather than a first-person subjective narrative in which reader and character are conjoined, Dickson opts to create the spectatorial situation of a small Vaudeville theater or minstrel show, in which comedic troupes briefly appear, produce a laugh, and then exit. Averring that whites are "unable to trace [blacks'] mental processes," Dickson doesn't try to get inside any black minds but tries to create comedy out of the way he imagines "a negro comes in contact with trouble," namely unwillingly and physically, "because he gets bumped into [it as] a rear-end collision."[71] He has African American "actors" put on the Jim Crow costume of the threadbare but high-stepping gentleman, a man made comical through planter aspiration. For the most part, Dickson construes black participation in the consumer market, in organized religion, in refinement, and in cosmopolitan culture as various forms of "farce." Thus readers are meant to understand, along with the "reconquest" of that physical "jungle" brought back by the flood, Deltans like Dickson have before them the abiding "white folks' business" of thinking on behalf of blacks and getting them out of trouble. The list of donors shown next to Dickson's twelfth installment works visually as a kind of print-generated applause for a final curtain. And the "Civil War Nurse"—of indeterminate allegiance—is called forth to cheer on the process of disaster-brokered national reconciliation.

As mentioned earlier, recent theorists of disaster mediation have argued that news stories and images can work to provide templates that the public can take up and act out in their daily life within local communities.[72] Though Dewey and recent theorists of disaster mediation have hoped that discussions and rites in these face-to-face communities might represent an opportunity for sorting through and giving meaning to widespread, mystifying events—a chance to transform trauma into communal affirmation—it can also happen (as the following examples illustrate) that local rites will affirm the identity and values of the local community while failing to understand the trauma of distant sufferers. Beyond the journalistic dissemination of Hoover's message about the flood as a unifying struggle, white publics outside the disaster zone began to act out this drama of southern reincorporation. If the Red Cross's publicity machine wanted the lay public to bring the flood "home," some private fund-raisers nevertheless chose to bring a different kind of Dixie home—a Dixie untroubled by disaster. In *this* version, the South had yet to lose the war; life on the plantation was a pastoral, premodern idyll; and white paternalism and black dependence were in perfect, tuneful harmony. On June 27, the *New York Times* announced that "To Aid Flood Sufferers," a benefit "Dance on Wednesday Night Will Revive Memories of Old South."[73] The morning after, the paper reported that "many New Yorkers returned from their country homes in Westchester, Long Island and New Jersey to attend the dance last night at the home of Mme. B. de Petschenko" at 31 Riverside Drive (on the corner of 75th Street). The hostess, a

Russian émigrée who was later deported for embezzling proceeds from a differ-ent philanthropy,[74] prepared "an entertainment program and supper menu in the southern fashion" aided by a committee, many of whose members "were former residents of the south. Southern music was provided for dancing"[75] and many appeared in "old-time Southern costumes."[76] The music was played by a quartet known as "Deacon Johnson's cheerful entertainers." Typically known as "The Deacon," the African American band leader, mandolin player, and second tenor hailed from Pine Bluff, Arkansas, a town that was underwater at the time he appeared at Mme. Petschenko's apartment. He had migrated north in the 1890s, attended McGill University, and, once in Manhattan, worked his way up from playing the rathskellers to being a major booker of "Race" talent.[77] Ac-cording to the *Chicago Defender*, Deacon Johnson "is better known in the high-est financial and social circles of New York City's great white plutocracy than almost any other Race man" for he "is to them a gilt-edged security for the finest in private entertainment." His motto was: "So cheerful, tuneful, sweet and harmonious."[78] Apart from his musicianship, it seems that "the Deacon's" suc-cess—much like the character in Faulkner's *The Sound and the Fury* with the same name—derived from his ability to embody and to stage "Memories of the Old South" that quieted its associations with racial and sectional conflict and amplified its associations with tunefulness and harmony. Perhaps "Wall Street" craved to see its own "plutocracy"—set in an urban, modern, multiethnic me-tropolis—as moving with such apparent grace; perhaps "Wall Street" needed the likes of Deacon for it symbolically to assume the role of the nation's undis-puted aristocracy. In describing the exclusive evening, the *New York Times* helped publicize how the event paid homage to—but also tried to absorb—antebellum southern prestige.

Iphigenia in D.C.

The most profound example of a northern amateur rite that tried to give mean-ing to the distant catastrophe was the mounting of Euripides' *Iphigenia in Tauris* (ca. 414 BCE) by a Protestant all-girls school called St. Margaret's in Washing-ton, D.C., on May 28. All manner of citizen-initiated events and neighborhood fund-raisers were carried out across the country in the "performative spaces . . . of everyday life"[79] in the spring of 1927, but none captures with more eloquence the broader white northern attitude about the flood as a propitious occasion for a rite of national reconciliation. In fact, it was on the day that the play was staged that Secretary Hoover broadcast an appeal from New Orleans to "every state in [the] union" about the "north com[ing] to the aid of the south." *Iphige-nia*, as its English translator—Oxford classicist Gilbert Murray—remarked in 1910, "is a romantic play, beginning in a tragic atmosphere and moving through perils and escapes to a happy end," a play whose lyrics are full of "the clash of waters."[80] In chapter 5 I address in greater depth how theatrical professionals, especially those with knowledge of the flood zone, produced rituals of reckoning during the flood; I place my discussion of *Iphigenia* here because it exemplifies so well Hoover's disseminated message of postwar reunion.

Euripides' tragedy was staged with an all-female cast at a private venue across from the British embassy on N Street called The Playhouse where, eighteen months before, Langston Hughes had given a pre-publication reading of his poetry collection *The Weary Blues*, introduced by Alain Locke.[81] The Playhouse was also frequently the venue for a kind of avant-garde psychophysical healing culture; in the 1920s, lectures were given titled, for example, "Vitalic Culture," "The New Psychology," and "the Tarot," advertised in the religious section of the paper under the nondenominational heading of "New Thought."[82] The notice about *Iphigenia* in the *Washington Post* indicated that there would be "rhythmic dancing" by a "chorus of maidens." Proceeds would go to "increase the contribution already made for the Mississippi flood sufferers."[83] The director of the play was the school's principal and owner, Mrs. Frank Gallup, a graduate of Vassar College who, having won "the classical fellowship for graduate work," traveled through Greece, Turkey, Sicily, and Italy "under the leadership of archaeologists."[84] The choreographer of the rhythmic dancing was Mary Newell Schultz, who performed ballet and "Oriental dance in recitals all over the world in the late 1920s,"[85] and the music was composed by the principal's daughter, Ruth Gallup, who had studies at the Paris Conservatory of Music. Staged and performed by a female cultural elite, this was not a popular entertainment of democratic self-fashioning as were the variety shows of Vaudeville, yet the play represents how a group of white female intellectuals and artists living in the nation's capital envisioned the catastrophe and its epic prehistory. The tragedy allowed this Washington group to put national history into archaically profound aesthetic form while it sidestepped questions of blame.[86] I imagine Mrs. Gallup, in particular, mentally thumbing through the classical canon of tragic plays she knew until she found in the story of Agamemnon's household, riven by internal conflict and geographic separation, but restored to union by a younger generation, the fitting plot of the American flood's own nation-binding destiny. The resonances, indeed, are almost uncanny. As we shall see in chapter 6, William Faulkner, in *As I Lay Dying* (1930), would call upon the same tragic Athenian family to envision the flood's social environment, albeit with a less cheerful prognosis.

Iphigenia is based on an ancient Attic ritual of a near sacrifice at the altar of Artemis, in which a victim is touched on the throat with a sword but ultimately spared. The play thus fittingly takes as its subject two near sacrifices, that of Iphigenia and Orestes, sister and brother, the first of whom is nearly murdered by her father to help Greeks prosper in the Trojan War and the second almost done in by his sister, whose role in Tauris is to prepare strangers for death. Actual killing has occurred, too: the mother avenged her daughter by killing the father, and the son avenged the father by killing his mother. This younger generation still seems to live within the bitterness of the household curse.

Not only did the theme of the "house divided" make it an apt play in 1927, but also its emphasis on water as a medium of destruction. In the opening scene, Iphigenia relates a dream she had of "my father's house" in which "the level earth was swept / With quaking like the Sea"; she "saw the cornice overhead / Reel, and the beams and mighty door-trees down / In blocks of ruin round me overthrown." Agamemnon's original sacrifice of his daughter was undertaken to calm the "warring water," and Iphigenia's washing of strangers in water was a prelude to their sacrifice. Finally, water is linked to exile, for Iphigenia is "Far in the Friendless Waters."[87]

In their mutual condition of exile, familial disintegration, and near-death, and their mutual involvement in blood sacrifices, both sister and brother judge the world to be ruled by an inscrutable divinity. The 1927 flood, as I will later detail, raised the specter of a cosmos ruled by purposeless chance. In her first speech to the still unrecognized Orestes, Iphigenia wonders: "Who knows when heaven / May send that fortune [death]? For to none is given / To know the coming nor the end of woe; / So dark is God, and to great darkness go / His paths, by blind chance mazed from our ken." Orestes pushes this bleak ontology one step further: "Aye; the Gods too, whom mortals deem so wise, / Are nothing clearer than some winged dream; / And all their ways, like man's ways, but a stream / Of turmoil." It is not just that divine intent seems, because of the faulty medium of our knowledge, to be conditioned by chance. Like mortals, the gods' decrees and actions are merely part of a contingent and turbulent flow.[88]

The dramatic catastrophe—or turnabout—of this play lies not in the household's internecine violence but in the scene of recognition through which further familial slaughter is avoided. Indeed, much as the 1927 flood was imagined, the scene pulls off a salvational reversal: Iphigenia changes from her brother's sacrificer to her brother's savior; and Orestes, bearing knowledge of kin and the means for homeward travel, rescues Iphigenia from exile and oblivion. It is a recognition that returns the dead to life. Orestes rejoices: "Back from the dead this day! / Yet through the joy tears, tears and sorrow loud / And o'er mine eyes and thine eyes, like a cloud." It is a recognition that affirms consanguinity as Orestes announces: "One blood we are; so much is well." Orestes remarks that, in their own avoidance of further intrafamilial bloodshed, "things fell / Right by so frail a chance." Perhaps it is a sign that "Chance [shall] yet comfort me, / Finding a way for thee / Back from the Friendless Strand, / Back from the place of death—." For her part, Iphigenia determines "To ease thy pain, / To lift our father's house to peace again, and hate no more my murderers—aye, 'tis good. / Perchance to clean this hand that sought thy blood, / And save my people." Once the two are yoked again in their shared knowledge and history—of one blood and one mind—they plot to outwit a now mutual foe and to bring the icon of divinity back to their restored household. As they gain their pelagic liberation, the medium of water changes from that which is associated with death and exile to that which allows reunion and absolution. To Iphigenia, water "beareth ease / Flowing through Earth's deep breast . . . / By these shall the dead have rest." If water initiated the curse, it now makes possible its expiation.[89]

Iphigenia in Tauris is a play in which the dramatic reversal—the catastrophe—becomes the means by which the larger, historical catastrophe hanging over the Greek *oikos* can be reversed. A house in ruins is set aright. Water moves from being an agent of death and separation to a source of reunion. And blood, too—at first turned against itself, finally becomes "one." Chance, though it starts out "blind," swerves in the nick of time to ally itself with "peace." Human knowledge, at first "mazed," eventually partakes in an open-handed divine will. For the audience of the play in May 1927, the drama might very well have suggested that a nation still shadowed by memories of internecine conflict and geographic alienation, whose sections had but an imperfect knowledge of each other, could, by their response to the current disaster, turn warring water into the waters of peace. The bitter reading of this flood was that both humanity and divinity were perpetually—and fundamentally—adrift on a "stream of turmoil." Turbulence was the signal constant of the cosmos. Knowledge and peace in such a world was impossible. And yet, fortuitously, in this tangle of failed cognition and imperfect anticipation, brought on by the cosmos's own unpredictability, a recognition could occur. An old shared history could be spoken of and revived. This environmental catastrophe could affect a dramatic catastrophe of happy historical reversal. In short, Mrs. Gallup staged this flood as a postbellum restoration plot.

* * *

Just a few years before the Mississippi flood, French social theorist Marcel Mauss wrote his *Essai sur le Don* (*The Gift*), in which he proposed that societies establish solidarity and hierarchy through the exchange of gifts. Mauss focused on "archaic" societies but believed that the social patterns he found in such cultures "are constantly turning up under new guises," even after the invention of capital, individualism, and mechanization. What is noteworthy about the gift is that it is not a one-way payment but rather the opening salvo of a two-way obligation, thus involving both parties in a dramatic contest of prestige. How a people acquits itself in this contest determines whether that bond is one of equals or one of masters and subordinates. Also important about the gift is that it "retains a magical and religious hold over the recipient. The thing given is not inert. It is alive and often personified, and strives to bring to its original clan and homeland some equivalent to take its place."[90] Mauss's theory helps bring out the sublimated power struggle present even in apparently humanitarian acts of giving. Rituals of gift exchange perform a kind of hidden battle: they determine power relations without bloodshed, but they exist as political negotiations between potential adversaries nonetheless. As northern-born political executives like Coolidge and Hoover encouraged, through media channels, the nation to imagine itself as an "army of relief," guided by technocratic urban experts, coming to the rescue of an "army of unfortunate people," it restaged the ideal, Wilsonian version of World War I. It sidestepped the question of federal technological failure by touting humanitarianism itself as a "humming machine." Still more emphatically, it restaged the Civil War as a peacetime humanitarian conquest. While President Coolidge pronounced that "the North and South have been brought closer together in the bonds of sympathy and understanding. The heart of an entire nation has been quickened,"[91] he failed to acknowledge this northern penchant for reenactment. The flood seemed to wash the North clean of the old, guilty blood of victory while it replayed that victory all over again. Such a conquest, under the guise of healing the previous war, actually reenacted its outcome of victory and defeat. As "the North" gave aid, it took "the South" inside itself. Having since the 1880s entertained itself with a Dixieland fantasy as a favorite tonic for northern urbanism, industrialism, multiethnic strife, and general historical flux, this fantasy was easy to summon in response to the flood. Costumes and stage sets were ready. Acts were already formed. These acts just received a special spotlight, attended to as if they were in some way real, in the months of April and May and June 1927. In such incantations of the South, the white citizenry represented the lost but now retrieved members of a national family, while its black citizenry appeared as the jesters who entertained at this rite of white reunion. The war behind these gifts was thus less quiet than it might typically be in Mauss's model. The theater of gift-giving enacted, for people in New York, or Los Angeles, or Chicago, a symbolic repatriation of the South into the nation. As "the North" gave, it took pleasure in its chance to *play southern* and to absorb old southern forms of prestige. Such was the particular invitation to "solidarity" these gifts performed.

In the influential model of Jürgen Habermas, print journalism is the medium that enabled, during the Enlightenment, the formation of a deliberative and rational bourgeois public sphere. To the contrary, the visual and dramatic media engender in their audiences forms of cognitive passivity as they draw beholders into a spectacle. What this archive shows is how much print journalism could shape what both Laswell and Benjamin would call an "illusion." It wasn't only that visual material—cartoons, maps, illustrations, and photographs—was an inseparable part of a print consumer's experience of the flood, or that the dramatic rites the public staged to enact itself as an "army of relief" were pictured, narrated, and promoted in the print medium, or that the "results" of these rites were visualized and tallied in lists of donors. The papers were the institutional channel through which the work of ritual passed; the donations were materialized in ink as a virtual rite of prestige. Even within the lengthy verbal forms of the newspaper—in Alexander's and Dickson's narrative portraits of the flood zone, or journalists' descriptions of the Mississippi River—these representations did not rhetorically invite deliberation. Instead, newspapers and magazines produced their own myths, sentimental stagings, and minstrel romps. As I will show in the next chapter, print journalism, as it turned the flood from natural disaster to scandal, *became* a medium that conveyed investigation, analysis, and dispute. But it was not inherently or exclusively rational or disputatious. As did all the media in the first weeks of the disaster, print gave itself over to the rites of reunion.

THREE

Cross Talk in the Press

On May 20, Secretary Hoover ordered the evacuation of some 35,000 people from McCrea, Louisiana.[1] While this mass of people began their flight away from the fragile levee standing between them and the swollen Atchafalaya River, another flight, also historic but much more favorably symbolic, was underway. Early that morning, a young airmail pilot, Charles Lindbergh, took off from Roosevelt Field on Long Island and flew his single-seat, single-engine *Spirit of St. Louis* in a nonstop arc from New York to Paris. Upon his landing, the world went completely giddy.[2] When the young hero made his triumphal return to the U.S. capital, broadcasters had to perch at the top of the Washington Monument just to get high enough to take in the scope of the gathering crowds. People clustered around radios and loudspeakers to take in the media event that their own attention helped to make.[3] As a cartoon from the June 1 issue of *The Nation* conveys, the intrepid Nordic spirit that harnessed wind and water on its westward discovery almost a thousand years before was alive and well (Fig. 3.1). Nordic America had at last produced a commensurate gesture, even perhaps a superior gesture, so elegant, individual, and apparently free of elemental reliance. Lindbergh's flight made all of America feel that, with the right mixture of daring, divine ordination, and technological ingenuity, this human animal could become angel.

After Lindbergh's flight, the mainstream white public outside the flood zone began to express dissatisfaction at the particular forms of representation that modern mass catastrophe seemed to produce. On May 29, in the same breath in which the *New York Times* applauded "LINDBERGH's flight, the suspense of it, the daring of it, the triumph and glory of it—these are of the stuff that makes immortal news," the paper complained of the flood that "the very sweep of such a tragedy makes it hard to grasp it in its full significance. We read day after day of new breaks in the levees, of more acres flooded, of so many thousand new refugees. Our senses become dulled by iteration of the same sequence of detail,

3.1. Hendrik van Loon, "The Return Visit," *The Nation*, June 1, 1927. © 1927 The Nation Company, LLC. All rights reserved. Used by permission and protected by the Copyright Laws of the United States. The printing, copying, redistribution, or retransmission of this Content without express written permission is prohibited.

and it is difficult for those of us who have never been in a flood to get the real picture of it. The very numbers involved blur the image."[4] A June 15 editorial in *The Nation* agreed: "people can stand only so much calamity. After a while it begins to pall and finally it has no meaning whatever." And what's more, "we have had spectacular flights to think about."[5] L. C. Speers of the *New York Times* reported on the "desolation, absolute and complete" he found in Melville, Louisiana: "It's water, slime, sand, mosquitoes and sand flies for all four points of the compass."[6]

And even Harris Dickson had to admit, as he opened his own series of articles, that "10,000 mangled bodies, grotesquely strewn along a battlefield, may leave the beholder quite unmoved. By their very numbers those ghastly things have ceased to appear human, no longer to be regarded as flesh and blood." In short, "Individual peril makes its vivid impression," but it is harder to respond to "a mud-bespattered mass of human beings, six times the population of Albany, N.Y."[7] And modern disaster, like modern warfare, was a mass event that produced spatial disorientation rather than human-based identification: "Landmarks have shifted. . . . A store has disappeared by which I might have located a certain cross-road. . . . The lake looks like a field. The field is indistinguishable from a lake." If the scene smears cognition, it is also true that "the solitude above which we soar appalls imagination. A water-conquered country, a dead, dumb, silent country, far lonelier than the hell-swept fields of France."[8] He implies that the current liquid obliteration of life in the Lower Mississippi is uniquely total.

The flood had become unsatisfying news because of both its scale and its duration. The individual humans involved were difficult to decipher amid the "very numbers," within the "sweep," and underneath the "pall" of mud. There was no "real picture," crisp "image," or "distinguishable" scene. And, after the crevasses had passed, there was not even any sound, only "dumb, silent" inundation. Moreover, these disorienting dispatches repeated themselves on what seemed like an unchanging loop. Perhaps the American public had become accustomed to these types of dispatches during the Great War; "natural" disasters, however, were supposed to obey the rules of classical tragedy. But here were—to use Rob Nixon's phrase about eco-catastrophes marked by slow violence—"formidable representational obstacles."[9]

What was also unsatisfying was the messy cadaverous muck of human failure. Modernity appeared to perfect advantage in Lindbergh's man-machine "romance."[10] By contrast, modernity appeared to epic *dis*advantage in this catastrophe. All was declension here, not ascent. Man was returned to the mud from whence he came. The waters did not drown away evil. One could say that "meaning" was not really absent from the disastrous events. The meaning—or meanings—were just unwelcome. Mid-June, the time of *The Nation* editorial, marks the end of the civic rites of gift-giving that had begun on April 24 with the first nationwide radio appeal. The last big benefit was Will Rogers's in New Orleans on June 1. And Harris Dickson's final installment, his last-ditch effort paper Vaudeville benefit, appeared across the nation's papers on June 19.

It was not only Lindbergh's flight that made the flood seem like less of a "marvelous attraction" and more like a testament to human error. In the midst of the "frolics" and "Monster Benefits," news began to emerge from the Delta about the abiding and at times violent "enforcement" of the color line. In addition, northern whites began to represent southern whites not so much as long-lost kin but rather as a sociological project, or worse, as an encroaching antagonist. White pundits throughout the Mississippi Valley, who from the flood's beginning saw the disaster as a product of federal neglect and scientific hubris rather than of natural cyclicality, gradually gained the nation's ear. Environmental writers across the country began to agree that this flood was a man-made debacle. The "Great Relief machine" cohered within itself a national, and international, civic public for about seven weeks. And then it broke asunder. This is not to say all concern for and awareness of the flood disappeared in individual minds. But that formation of individuals into a ritualized, gift-offering mass came apart.

Meanwhile, as the social issues and human practices that had turned cyclical overflow into disaster in the first place began to manifest themselves still more visibly in the disaster's developments, a print practice of exposure and blame emerged. Here, reformative action was the goal. Exposure happened in part through special witnesses: in the environmental and sociological realm, these were professional experts; in the racial realm, lay experts spoke the hidden truth. Equally, exposure occurred by using the written or print record of adversaries as the most damning form of incrimination. In the early stages of the disaster, the Red Cross's publicity "machine" worked via cycles of disaster messaging output and monetary input: publicists of the flood transmitted stories to papers around the country, which in turn became conduits for relief donations. Ideally, as Taylor put it, this publicity machine would "function with a fascinating smoothness."[11] As the Red Cross and Hoover lost control of the messaging, a new configuration of public discourse came into being. As sectional conflict brewed, white southerners started to publicly react to northern coverage; as racial conflict intensified, black papers in the North began to quote and critique white southern coverage; and as evidence of land management and engineering blunders accumulated, environmental pundits across the nation took those making watershed policy to task. As such, a cross-regional pattern of print consumption and barbed quotation transpired. This second phase of disaster publicity worked as a multidirectional, lateral, and contentious network. Strangers had been pulled together in the first weeks of the flood within tableaus of rescue and reunion; in these later weeks and months, strangers who perceived themselves to be part of translocal "communities of danger"[12] found commonality. As anthropologist Mary Douglas has observed, "blaming behavior is geared into the making of community consensus."[13]

Blaming, moreover, was a completely necessary part of bringing into public discussion the social, technological, and environmental problems that had caused such a calamity. It was an important social tool, and also a forensic one. Americans—experts and pundits from across the country and southern lay folk—asked not only "what caused the flood?" but "who?" Part of the analytical work these groups did was to claim that the flood was not a "natural" disaster—that such calamity was not random, and needn't be so cyclically repeated. To these groups, then, it was crucial that cultural response involved not only gift-giving but also an attribution of blame so as to avoid repetitions. Catastrophic Mississippi flooding occurred every decade or so. If no public blaming took place, how could matters change? Given that all large-scale disasters that strike human communities are, to a certain extent, man-made—humans decide to build cities on fault lines and in hurricane zones—blaming is a necessary part of modifying those decisions. Because blaming can be based on partial and socially inflected information channels, and because it can be targeted at customary or vulnerable scapegoats, it needs to be exchanged, refuted, and tested. Moreover, if gifts can come without understanding, without engendering reflection about how the givers may have had a hand in the calamity, then the gift adds the proverbial insult to the injury.

Yankee Water

When Will Rogers told northern readers, "The cry of the people down there is, 'We don't want relief and charity; we want protection,'"[14] he was expressing the indignation southerners felt at much of the rhetoric of the relief machine. Southerners, though they at times allowed themselves to participate in the staging of a lovable Dixie, in general resented the federal government's and the North's unwillingness to see themselves as the conjoined source of the disaster. Earlier than anyone else, southerners read this flood not as divine or natural but as definitively anthropogenic. Americans outside the flood zone were not just obliged to be charitable out of their noblesse oblige; they needed to understand that a watershed drawing from two-thirds of the country entailed responsibility outside the Lower Valley. To southerners, patronage from the North felt harmful both because it seemed oblivious to the facts of watershed hydrogeography and because it smacked of old northern victory.[15] Those attentive to watershed mismanagement, and to the entire valley's falling victim to bad environmental and engineering policies, saw the flood as a second attack from the North, this time by way of a liquid proxy. Repatriation to this group meant federal assumption of the burden of the near-continental Mississippi system.

Though this southern position would grow increasingly insistent as policy meetings were convened in June and in the late fall, southern pundits were poised, even in the flood's early days, to make this point. On Easter Sunday, April 17, four days before the Mounds Landing crevasse, an editorial in the Memphis *Commercial Appeal* opined: "Control of the flood waters of the central area of the United States—from the Rockies to the Alleghenies—is the government's problem."[16] The Memphis paper reiterated this point again and again through the spring as the flood moved down toward the Gulf. On April 24, an editorial declared:

> It seems obvious that neither the head of the nation nor any one of his responsible advisors realize either the nature or the immensity of the problem that faces the nation. For it is a national problem. . . . [This is no] unprecedented visitation of nature's wrath. It is a continually recurring disaster whose recurrence points an accusing finger at the whole nation.
>
> . . . the states of the Lower Mississippi Valley are bearing today, as they have borne in many other years, the burden of a great part of the nation. These states are suffering death and destruction so that all of the other states from the Rocky to the Alleghany [sic] mountains may be relieved of a large part of the same catastrophic evils. . . . For the Mississippi river is the drainage system of almost the whole of the country.[17]

A month later, the *Appeal* argued: "It is not the first time the south has suffered and been penalized for no offence it committed and because of no fault of its own. . . . This flood has brought damage that cannot be repaired. It has brought sorrow that cannot be assuaged. There is loss that cannot be restored. But it will not have been in vain if it has served to catch and hold the attention of the nation by reason of its vastness."[18] The phrase "will not have been in vain" echoed Lincoln's language in the Gettysburg Address as he outlined his vision of a war made meaningful by the conservation of a nation. Likewise, the sacrifices of this flood could be made meaningful if the nation came to understand that the watershed linked north and south. As editors of the *Appeal* signified upon Lincoln's address, they were making the subtle case that if the nation could fight a war about the maintenance of a political construct (nationhood), here in 1927 was an instance in which hydrogeography actually made a natural case for union, and for mutual obligation. A week later, the *Appeal* printed Hoover's comment, made in public in New Orleans, that the reconstruction "should be the task of a generous north to a resolute and courageous south . . . and we of the north have the right and duty to bind their wounds,"[19] also, as I mentioned earlier, an allusion to Lincoln. Finally, in mid-June, *Appeal* editors reasoned: "It would be unreasonable for the government to say to a destitute soldier who lost both legs in war that the government would pay for one leg if he would pay for the other."[20] The logic here is: if the nation owes its recent war veterans an honorable protection for representing it in conflict, doesn't the nation owe the Lower Valley protection against its assault by the entire valley's waters? Suggestive, too, is the idea of the lower South as a disfigured victim of an old war whose consequences are still felt. The similarity of the southward-moving flood to the movement of the northern forces in the 1860s made many white southerners feel that disasters are just another name for political warfare.

Editors of the *Atlanta Constitution* echoed the Memphis paper on May 15: "The unvarnished truth is the great disaster in its entirety is directly chargeable to congressional neglect."[21] And a month later: "The river belongs to the whole nation. . . . As a potential and capricious enemy of the lives and property of millions of our citizens it must be combated and checked and conquered by the national power and resources as surely as those agencies would be employed against a hostile army, navy and air fleet."[22] An op-ed piece written by a Protestant clergyman in the *Constitution* expressed feeling for "the inhabitants of this beloved valley, which, in years gone by, have been trampled by war, poisoned by pestilence, and submerged by floods." The river's challenges constitute "a dare to the united human sympathy of America to forget sectional interests . . . and bring the united thought and power of a nation to meet this supreme task." The flood is "a dare to the very genius of our nation—a perplexing problem to be solved." Soon, "assembled spiritual forces [will be] triumphing over the temporary physical catastrophe."[23] "United human sympathy," "united thought," "the very genius of our nation," and "assembled spiritual forces": here a southerner characterizes the various states in their physical geography as an immaterial, transcendent unity. In so doing, he uncannily, or cannily, plays back northern antebellum rhetoric that had sought to make the Union indivisible. Did you really mean it when you said it, this Atlanta minister implicitly asks? This, too, is how a house undivided stands.

Mississippian Harris Dickson, at the end of his twelve-part series on the flood zone, declared: "Americans do not relish working to build up a home, then having some tyrannical power snatch it away." He continued: "Glance at a map of Father's vast watershed. Note that our lands lie in the mouth of an enormous funnel. Then remember that every creek and gutter from Western Pennsylvania to Wyoming empties its water into the top of that funnel. We get the drainage from thirty-two States." In conclusion: "two-thirds of this Union combines its flood to drown us. So we do earnestly insist that those who dump water into the funnel should help to minimize its disastrous results."[24] After the many installments in which he deliberately costumed and staged southerners in a kind of paper minstrel show, Dickson must have felt that he had called forth a sufficient reserve of love for his region to be able to make demands upon that love.

Southern observers sought to make the point again and again that this was not the first time the Mississippi had acted as a baleful conduit of northern aggression. Louisiana journalist Hodding Carter wrote, in his history of the Mississippi, that "northern leaders," during the Civil War, "had vision enough to make the conquest of the Mississippi their most persistent offensive objective." Doing so in 1863, the North had reopened cotton traffic to New England mills, separated the Southeast from the Confederate Southwest, and given northerners access to the Gulf and to formerly enslaved people. "In that shameful decade of Reconstruction," Carter elaborated, "the river was peculiarly suited to the corrupt purposes of the carpetbagger and scalawag, and the radical intent of their vengeful masters in Washington; and their talons clung longer to plunder and political control here than elsewhere in the South." Northerners vengefully plundered the Lower Valley because its planters especially represented "the hated southern slave-owning aristocracy which must be ground in its own pride."[25] Carter wrote this characterization in 1942, but he is giving voice to longstanding southern attitudes that were felt equally at the time of the 1927 flood.

Indeed, few observers failed to notice that the Red Cross refugee camps at Vicksburg, Mississippi, were pitched on the site of the Confederate Cemetery where more than 18,000 war dead were buried (see Fig. 1.6). Here, with some 77,000 men in total, Grant had defeated Pemberton in the weeks-long siege of Vicksburg that ended in Confederate surrender on July 4, 1863. During the largely waterborne siege, Mississippians faced assaults from the river, as well as food shortages and public health issues in an enclosed encampment (Fig. 3.2). After the fall of Port Hudson, Louisiana, a few days later, Union forces gained full control of the river. To this news, Lincoln had responded: "The Father of Waters again goes unvexed to the sea."[26] These Union victories along the Mississippi, combined with the defeat of Lee's troops at Gettysburg in that same week, represented to many the turning point in the Civil War. In September 1927, a *National Geographic* reporter noted: "At Vicksburg the refugee camp is pitched high on green hills where long ago Grant fought Pemberton. Here, after threescore years, again long rows of tents are set up, the bugle calls, and armed sentries voice their challenge."[27] Maria Mattingly Maloney, a Mississippi-born author who was then working for the *New York Herald Tribune*, wrote in her travelogue of the disaster zone, "Orphans of the Mississippi," that "this is the greatest tragedy that has come to America since the World War. It is the greatest tragedy on American soil since the Civil War." She continued: "I went out to [Vicksburg]. . . . Five thousand white people were camped on the bluff above the river at the point where Gen. Grant overcame the Confederate forces, in what is referred to in this part of the country as 'the war.'"[28]

A rumored break in the levee at Milliken's Bend, Louisiana, prompted another southern, female journalist who had lived many years in New York City, Helen Murphy, to think of "the skirmish between Grant's forces and Confeder-

3.2. "Grant's Transports Running the Batteries." Image from Alfred H. Guernsey, *Harper's Pictorial History of the Civil War*, William L. Clements Library, University of Michigan.

ate guerrillas" at precisely this spot and of the "ashes of carnage" that resulted. Studying the recurrent devastation of the overflow, Murphy wondered, "rebelliously, if we must always be a poor, shabby, struggling people, battling against a force too great for us." At sunrise, she mistakes one of her neighbors atop his garage for a praying "muezzin" and, in another moment, imagines that the "saffron colored winding sheet" wrapped about the town will, soon enough, "unroll." The curse of water, patterned on the historical curse of northern aggression, keeps her people down; they are a shabby caste, perpetual but ineffectual rebels. Imagined as pious internal exotics, Muslims or Hindus or ancient Israelites, they are made holy by their "great trial" and await "deliver[ance]."[29] Editors of *The Gulf Coast Guide* likewise showed the painfulness of being imagined as somehow *outside of* the nation's geography of obligations: when *Barron's* magazine sarcastically insisted that southern flood states repay relief funds with the same austerity as did European "dilapidated allies" after World War I, the *Guide* quipped that "we then wonder just whose water this is that comes pouring down upon us from the sheds of thirty states."[30]

Papers from around the country and the world espoused the southerners' assertion that the Mississippi River watershed was a continental feature requiring a coherent national strategy and that it was the human mismanagement of this watershed that caused the 1927 catastrophe. These commentators saw the flood as not merely the result of an engineering mistake but as the product of decades of environmental practices in the upper part of the watershed. On April 18, an editorial of the *Chicago Daily Tribune* called "The Lesson of the Mississippi Flood" put it simply: "The damage is felt downstream, but the responsibility is upstream." He added: "The Mississippi valley is a geographic unity, but politically it is too often divided." The editor urged the construction of reservoirs that could also produce hydroelectric power.[31] Writing in *The Nation* on May 11, engineer Walter Parker argued that the levees-only policy had "gone bankrupt." He reviewed that, in the late nineteenth century, "the forests were being cut from the watershed, . . . low places were being drained, marshes and lakes destroyed, sewerage systems installed, [and] drainage run-off hastened in every way." Parker described how reservoirs and outlets had been gradually sealed off and, with each new flood, the levees built higher; "Thus the process which enriched the Northern landowner has resulted in the destruction of many valuable Southern plantations."[32] He urged "source-stream control" and southern spillways.[33] The *National Geographic* quoted a Louisiana planter as saying: "Up North of us . . . they build levees that turn lots of marshes into farms; but, when high water comes, this system often turns a lot of our farms into marshes."[34]

On May 14, Great Britain's *Manchester Guardian* explained of the Mississippi's more than four-thousand-mile drainage basin that "the forests in the upper reaches had been largely destroyed," increasing water runoff and loss of soils (amounting to "118,000,000 tons of silt a year"), which literally and figuratively "degraded" the continent.[35] Two days later, the *Los Angeles Times* described "an intricate network of bayous which, prior to their inclosure by levees, served as spillways for escaping surplus[es]," until levees had blocked such helpful discharge, trying to hold within its masonry a river that now coursed high and perilous *above* the land.[36] In early June, at the Flood Control Congress in Chicago, Gifford Pinchot, the first chief of the U.S. Forest Service, called the levees-only policy then in place on the Mississippi the "most colossal blunder in civilized history." At the same conference, Minneapolis writer T. G. Winter commented, in reference to deforestation, wetlands drainage, and river containment throughout the valley: "The great floods now ravaging the Mississippi Valley are considered by many to be an 'act of God.' They are, on the contrary, most distinctly the work of man." Lyle Saxon, *New Orleans Times-Picayune* reporter, quoted both of these sources as authorities in his book-length account of the flood, *Father Mississippi: The Story of the Great Flood of 1927*, completed in the summer of 1927.[37] In December, the *Washington Post* quoted this statement from the *Forestry News Digest*: "Every forest fire in the Mississippi basin tends, sooner or later, to augment flood conditions. Every abandoned or ne-

3.3. J. P. Alley, "Poor Business," *Commercial Appeal*, June 10, 1927. Commercial Appeal/Landov.

glected piece of poor hillside farm land has the same tendency. Destructive lumbering and overgrazing which leave naked soil behind them, are sure to contribute . . . to some flood crest." The *Post* article quoted W. B. Greeley, the chief of the U.S. Forest Service, urging: "We must not fail to restore . . . the natural storage."[38] Transferring the job of storage from healthy forests and marshes throughout the watershed to man-made levees in its lower reaches had been a colossal failure. If southerners saw it with their own eyes, environmental critics throughout the nation could agree.

Through visual culture, southern papers satirized the federal government by lampooning Washington's status as a locus of expertise. A cartoon in the Memphis *Commercial Appeal* of June 10 showed Calvin Coolidge making a "sounding," not of the river's depth but rather of political "sentiment" (Fig. 3.3). He is labeled as an "engineering politician," a phrase that transforms the disinterest that ought to pertain to the science of engineering into the self-interestedness of politics. In a May 29 cartoon, the Memphis paper questions the northern epistemological map of the country in which the North is a place of reason and the South of backward fundamentalism and anti-education (Fig. 3.4). It labels the overflowing water as "The Floods of Rationalism," implicitly asking: are these the brilliant results that a rationalist mind-set achieves? The *New Orleans*

WATERS THAT WILL PASS AWAY.

3.4. J. P. Alley, "Waters That Will Pass Away," *Commercial Appeal*, May 29, 1927. Commercial Appeal/Landov.

Times-Picayune, on May 31, reprinted a cartoon from the *Chattanooga Times*, a paper that had been at the epicenter of the Scopes Trial coverage (Fig. 3.5). Uncle Sam seats his backside on top of a partially submerged house and assumes the position of Auguste Rodin's sculpture, colloquially called *The Thinker*, which had made its first American appearance during the 1904 St. Louis World's Fair. Uncle Sam ponders "The Problem," indifferently holding, or letting go, various proposals for flood management: "Stronger Levees," "Impound the Water for Power Utilization," and "Reservoirs." His thinking seems ridiculously abstracted from the materiality and the urgency of the problem, and the scale of The Thinker's body allows him to be impervious to vernacular experience. Again, the federal "center of calculation" is woefully impotent.

Northern papers printed similar satirical and critical cartoons. The *New York Tribune* ran a cartoon on April 27 that exemplified its verbal editorial opinion: "Relieve the Flood Sufferers, But the Cure Lies at the Other End" (Fig. 3.6). Two fiendish Goliaths, "Blind Deforestation" and "Drainage of Lakes and Marshes," pour torrents of water into the valley, submerging houses and creating droves of refugees; all Uncle Sam bothers to do is throw handfuls of coins

3.5. Morris, "The Thinker and the Problem," *New Orleans Times-Picayune*, May 31, 1927. Reprinted from the *Chattanooga Times*. Courtesy of the *Chattanooga Times Free Press*.

3.6. Jay N. "Ding" Darling, "Relieve the Flood Sufferers, But the Cure Lies at the Other End," *New York Tribune*, April 27, 1927. Courtesy of the Jay N. "Ding" Darling Wildlife Society.

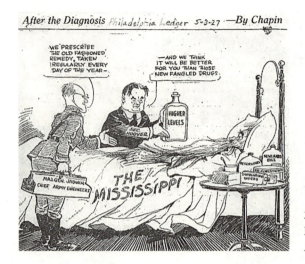

3.7. Chapin, "After the Diagnosis," *Philadelphia Ledger*, May 3, 1927.

and paper money at the roofs, a gesture that mimics rather than remedies the giants' own assault. This image, moreover, reveals the strained logic behind all the cartoons that showed deluges of coins to promote public giving. On May 3, "After the Diagnosis" appeared in the *Philadelphia Ledger* (Fig. 3.7). It showed an ancient and ailing Father Mississippi ministered to by two engineers: Herbert Hoover and Major General Jadwin, the chief of the Army Corps of Engineers. Rejecting "those new fangled" remedies—reforestation, reservoirs, and so forth—they smugly offer "the old fashioned remedy," namely, higher and higher levees. A cartoon that the *New Orleans Times-Picayune* reprinted on May 22 from the *New York Herald Tribune* shows "Cal," or President Coolidge, looking to hire an "expert" to help him with flood relief (Fig. 3.8). Before him stands a pathetic candidate for the position: a personified "Extra Session of Congress," who is "expensive but noisy," "addicted to politics and filibustering," and so on. Needless to say, he is not the man for the job.

What arose out of this recognition of the valley's "geographic unity" was a sense of its potential political solidarity. L. R. Martin, from Natchez, Mississippi, wrote in an op-ed piece in the *Chicago Daily Tribune* on April 23: "The people in this section appreciate in the highest degree your editorial on 'The Lesson of the Mississippi Flood.' At last a bright light appears to be dawning on our present dark horizon and that is the close linking of our interests in the valley with those of the great city of Chicago."[39] If the southern section had been drawn together by plantation agriculture and, to its mind, a necessary dependence on an enslaved labor force, here was a new kind of bio-linkage, not born out of climate and growing seasons but out of the watershed as ecosystem. As

3.8. Jay N. "Ding" Darling, "Nothing Just Now, Thank You!" *New Orleans Times-Picayune*, May 22, 1927, reprinted from *New York Herald Tribune*. Courtesy of the Jay N. "Ding" Darling Wildlife Society.

southerners invoked, again and again, the fact that the Mississippi drained off the waters of thirty-two states, an area stretching from Montana to Pennsylvania, they became the ones to invoke the bio-linkage of a watershed that crossed the Mason-Dixon Line. They urged here a hydrological configuration of space and, along with it, social debt, communal responsibility, and dispersed costs, rather than a state- or section-driven concept of linkage. The Mississippi Valley linked New Orleans with Chicago, Memphis with rural Minnesota, and Greenville with the mountains of Pennsylvania.

Southern pundits who appeared in print in 1927 were not turning their back on science to embrace a fundamentalist reading of the floods. This ran counter to the picture that emerged from the Scopes Trial, thanks especially to H. L. Mencken's charged coverage.[40] While there were those in southern pulpits who didn't miss the opportunity to declare in their Sunday sermon that "God sent the flood" because He saw "the inroads of free love," "the petting parties," and "the dress of some of our women,"[41] the dominant southern print diagnosis of the flood's origin, in both word and image, was secular and based on the environmental fact that a watershed is a connected system. What southerners did fail to discuss was how they had allowed their own part of the watershed to be degraded as they colluded with northern and British financiers in turning the

Lower Valley into a quasi-colonial resource frontier. Moreover, as all of the interested parties in the valley joined forces to demand action from Washington, there was little talk of drawing from the fortunes some had made in logging and large-scale monoculture farming, which had caused the extreme troubles with water storage. Even as wetlands drainage, deforestation, and agriculture were abstractly cited as the cause of the catastrophe, the personified source of blame was Uncle Sam. If these actions were "what" caused the problem, he was the "who" responsible for fixing it.

The Color Line

For the powerful white interests in the Delta, this flood was about property and crop values. It was not a physical crisis of life and limb. For poor whites, including Acadians, and poor blacks who represented the overwhelming majority of sufferers, the flood represented direct threats to their bodily integrity and to their personal freedom. What made refugee status and the emergency environment especially acute for African Americans was their place on the wrong side of the color line. On April 19, editors of the Memphis *Commercial Appeal* opined that "when some great crisis looms and threatens the people of an entire community or section, men forget to hate each other . . . and [instead] join forces. . . . The spirit of the brotherhood of man wells strong within and their better selves come to the surface."[42] Directing this point, Representative William Nelson, a Democrat from Missouri, professed on April 28 that "in the saving of human life, in great humanitarian undertakings, we know no color line."[43] What all the "Race" men and women, and their supporters, who looked into the social conditions in the flood zone agreed upon was that such statements were patently false.

An editorial in the *Chicago Defender* stated: "Now while the whole Southland is under the greatest devastating flood in its history, the color line is given its most rigid enforcement" (see Fig. 3.9).[44] An editorial in the *Pittsburgh Courier* urged: "In times of stress, people reveal their souls. . . . the flood has brought home to Negroes the fact that the white South is still adamant in its attitude toward the Negro. This spirit withstands floods, fires and hurricanes. Physically it may be a New South, socially and psychologically it is the same old South."[45]

If "the War" was on the minds of southern whites, and the "Old South" was playing well at benefits outside the South, papers concerned with racial discrimination also invoked—albeit in a wholly critical manner—scenes of antebellum days. Those attentive to black suffering in the floods strove to demonstrate that a kind of neo-slavery was alive and well, long after 1863: the Civil

3.9. Rogers, "Will There Be Discrimination in the Mississippi Flood?" *Chicago Defender*, June 4, 1927, 1.

War was not far away; it was not even won. Genuine patriation of African Americans had to entail the right of free movement and the right to control their own labor. The exposé that ensued, of life on the levees and in the "concentration camps," was not isolated to black authorship in a black press with exclusively black readers. White authors who wrote for the black press and black authors who wrote for white-owned papers on the left were part of this public. Moreover, one of the signature rhetorical moves to bring to light Jim Crow conditions was to quote from, and signify upon, white sources.[46] Just as the southern white planter interest created a "public" for itself in the press, but also realized its place in a broader valley-long public, and indeed a national public advocating for federal accountability of the river, African American flood sufferers in the Delta became comprised in larger groupings via publication. These national groupings, moreover, extended beyond a strictly black membership. In this way, a contiguous "community of danger" built virtual allies. This public talked beyond its borders, and it also disputed issues within its bounds. In short, there was no consistent, harmonious, racially homogenous, and separate, black vox populi.

A number of investigators, both black and white, were sent to look into conditions for black refugees: along with Hoover's Colored Advisory Commission, J. Winston Harrington reported from the flood zone for the *Chicago Defender*;

Walter White, one of the leaders of the NAACP, toured the flooded areas, and wrote up his findings in *The Nation*; Theodore Holmes reported for the Associated Negro Press; Jesse O. Thomas for *Opportunity*; and finally, an undisclosed white woman made an investigation of the Mississippi and Arkansas camps for *The Crisis*. Ida B. Wells, W.E.B. Du Bois, and William Pickens all wrote about the flood but were not eyewitnesses to events. Across all of the public coverage in black-run presses was the argument that a reenslavement of southern blacks had occurred and that the federal government, in the form of the Red Cross and the National Guard, was abetting its reappearance.

Walter White, writing for *The Nation*, opens his article with a rhetorical softball, announcing that the Negro was having "an essentially fair deal" in terms of relief supplies and medical attention. The phrase "fair deal" advertised White's "reasonableness," creating a parlay with his predominantly white readers. White continued: "It is in the handling of this problem of labor that legitimate ground for complaint is to be found"; using impersonal and passive constructions, White gingerly legitimates his own circumscribed "complaint." Soon enough, though, White gets to his main allegations: "Conscripted Negro labor did practically all of the hard and dangerous work in fighting the flood." Despite this, "Those in immediate charge of flood relief, whether wittingly or not, are . . . permitting the relief organizations to be used by plantation-owners further to enslave or at least to perpetuate peonage conditions." White quotes at length from the Jackson, Mississippi, *Daily News* (April 30) and the *Vicksburg Evening Post* (May 5) to show how white southern papers worked to reassure planters that the large Red Cross–run camps were protecting their labor from labor agents and abetting planters in returning labor from whence it came. These circumstances, White summarized, are both "the inevitable products of a gigantic catastrophe" and a "part of the normal picture of the industrial and race situation in certain parts of the South." Such a situation threatens to "crystallize a new slavery almost as miserable as the old."[47] White strategically paces his revelation, easing his readers in with a characterization of the situation's fairness; offering specific evidence; quoting white southern papers to show how openly the restriction of Negro movement was avowed. He can then end with a characterization of the South as a place of normalized catastrophe and of a "new slavery." White's article was reprinted in the *Chicago Defender* (July 2) and the *Baltimore Afro-American* (May 28). And some of White's remarks, delivered at a press conference on May 27, were printed in the *New York Times* and the *New York Herald Tribune*.[48]

Disagreement within this counterpublic arose over what had caused the flood. A Chicago preacher in early May professed that "God has poured His irresistible waters over the fields of the South to punish the white people for their mistreatment of the Negro."[49] William Pickens fired back with a damning rebuttal in the May 18 edition of the *New York Amsterdam News*. On May 4, the same paper had printed a letter Pickens had sent to President Coolidge suggesting that because it was a disaster in which "the Negro masses are so dearly concerned," and because "color" still divided the South, that a "Negro officer" be appointed as a "right hand help" to whoever was put in charge of relief operations. "It would prevent a great deal of suffering and avoid much American scandal," he added.[50] Pickens wanted his letter to the president printed in order both to increase public pressure for the involvement of leaders of the black community and to flag for his African American readers the Jim Crow scenarios that threatened to transpire.

Pickens knew the South well; he had been raised in a working-class family in South Carolina and Arkansas, had managed to work his way toward a bachelor's degree from Yale University, and had then served as a college professor and administrator at southern universities and become a prominent member of the NAACP. Two weeks later, in what could be considered the most succinct and comprehensive characterization of Jim Crow conditions in the flood, he accurately predicted what would ensue:

> The fatal flood has swept away for [blacks] everything but left the white man's land. The biggest loser is the Negro. Not only the flood, but the Red Cross and the martial law will be his enemies, and "forced labor" will mean black labor. Blacks will be put to work helping to clear the white man's property without wages or reward.
>
> Being poor and homeless, they will be yoked with new debts in order to get a start. Except for the few who will be able to escape through the trap doors of "martial law," they will all find themselves more completely enslaved than before the flood. "Relief" will be given to them niggardly and last after all the whites have been taken care of. . . .
>
> How in the name of God can a Negro preacher ascribe this horror to God and expect anybody to love God for it? It looks rather as if the devil took charge of this river and this whole business.
>
> Besides, it is a drawback to a people to be taught that some special providence is fighting their battles against their oppressors. That is a bad doctrine. People must feel the need of fighting their own battles. God is not "on the Negro's side." He thinks just as well, to say the least, of white people.

Furthermore, it is just as degrading a superstition to think that nature's perils are caused by somebody's sins as to think that storms and crop failures were caused by witches. Certainly if God meant to hit white people of the South by this flood, He made a wide miss on one of His biggest throws.[51]

Pickens's argument is hung around secular self-reliance, the empirical evidence of history and science, and a repudiation of the notion of a special relationship between God and the Negro. He quotes the black providentialist interpretation and shows how that undermines black agency and how wrongheaded is its logic given that black suffering will greatly predominate over white.[52]

Another disagreement carried out across the black counterpublic was that between the *Chicago Defender* and *The Crisis*, which both advocated a defiant exposé of white abuse, and leaders of the Colored Advisory Commission, who favored using the quiet threat of publication to procure Hoover's aid. Ida B. Wells, the Mississippi-born antilynching crusader, wrote a series of articles for the *Defender*. She had received advance copies of the commission's report from Claude Barnett, which she found inadequate in a number of ways that she spelled out for *Defender* readers. She begins by noting that the "bad conditions" found by the commission are "touched upon very lightly." The report's judgment that "local committees [of the Red Cross] frequently have misinterpreted their [the national body's] policies" lets the Red Cross's leadership off the hook too easily; by upholding local practices, the Red Cross is "encouraging and condoning a system of discrimination, of peonage, and of robbery of funds." In an interesting moment of gender shaming, she writes that it is up to "black men to report these conditions" or else the public will be "hoodwinked." She compares their praise of the Red Cross to a doctor "admiring that part of the body that needs no attention" while ignoring the "infected wound." She doubts "that a 'Colored committee' could afford to tell the truth and still live down there."[53] She holds to account other newspapers for not making "any protest" and assuring Hoover "that everything is all right." She wonders why prominent blacks in Pine Bluff are giving Hoover a loving cup "while their own people are being treated like slaves."[54]

To get at that "truth" that is too toxic for the black men of the commission to tell, Wells positions herself as a go-between to a purer source of truth. She encloses a private letter from a flood sufferer in "hiding" in Greenville, who asks that his letter be printed anonymously in the next issue of the *Defender*. He says, of the commission: "Had I had a chance to get to see one of them, he would have had something to tell, if he would have told it." He describes how

Greenville whites use prosperous blacks, who are coping during the flood, as "catspaws" to attest to an overall climate of racial fairness. Local black ministers publicly praise the Percys and urge blacks not to leave Greenville. "We who are under the lash know better." The writer tells of having hid lest he be "made to work like a dog under a gun and club and tagged like a bale of cotton." "Not one Mexican, Italian, Greek or any other race but the Colored Race" was forced to work for food. "My people . . . are treated worse than convicts" in this place that is the "gridiron of hell." The only way to say it is that "our people are in slavery." He intimates that "I am afraid for what I have written," so he attaches his name on a slip of paper, asking that Wells "tear my name off" before passing the letter on for publication. Wells frames his letter by asking that readers contribute to this man and his family's "escape."[55]

In an article two weeks later, she described a refugee who arrived on her doorstep in Springfield, Illinois, having been shot in the leg for threatening to flee a camp in Louisiana. He did get out, and made his way by foot, truck, and car to Wells's door.[56] Though this is a different man, his own motion completes the saga of liberation begun by the first captive. Wells moves from the discrediting of tepid reports to revelations of the real "truth." She authenticates her sources by visualizing the drama of their fugitive plight and by mentioning the written hand of the one and the wounded leg of the other. If the commission's deference to a patronage network of whites dilutes their words, Wells promises direct, bodily proximity to the truth—the truth that slavery was in force again in the South. Both the figure of the testifier, hidden on the wrong side of the Mason-Dixon Line, and that of the escaped fugitive are, in fact, tropes of the slave narrative genre. She does not just convey facts; rather, she tells the story of these two Delta men *as* slave narratives in order to convince her readers that slavery is back.

After the journalist fulfills her duty to transmit the truth of direct experience, this information must turn into public "questions," "demands," "cries," and "action." She writes that "all the Defender and I can do is to tell the Race about these conditions. It is up to you who have the power of organizations to keep on with . . . demands." She proposes a series of questions "every one of the 12,000,000 people of our Race in this country should be asking themselves and using their brains to find answers for. Then, after they get the answers they should get busy in an effort to have the whole country know the facts and use their power to have these conditions changed. Nobody else is going to do anything about it if we don't." She avers that "the only way to bring public opinion to action is for those whose race is suffering to cry aloud, and keep on crying aloud until something is done." Finally, Wells makes the critical point about how gift-giving publics need to understand their political potential: "The South needs, and is asking help in this, her time of trouble. It is the psychological moment for us to demand that the South do justice to our people before she receives help from the nation."[57] She contends, like Mauss, that the gift creates a two-way obligation. Gifts cannot "irrigate [the] social system"[58] if the system is too faulty. But they *can* work as a lever for reform. What "the Race" should see is that "the victim" receiving the most beneficial aid was the planter. The planter, well connected in Washington, made use of the powers of the state to rehabilitate but also to confine his labor force so that it could be delivered right back to his hold. The nation's giving, by both blacks and whites, protected not the laborer as much as the planter's labor system. Thus, if the planter needs the nation's help, *that* is the moment to negotiate with him for reform.[59]

Along with direct quotation, many journalists and pundits in the black counterpublic made use of white quotation. William Pickens, in a June 22 *Amsterdam News* article, quoted Mississippi governor Dennis Murphree's telegram in which he objected to having a single black physician on the Flood Rehabilitation Committee. Pickens remarks that this brief telegram "exposes the South's unfitness to be 'let alone' in its dealing with the Negro better than any Northern or Negro 'radical' could ever have exposed it." He summarized: "The best meanings of a foolish man's words are not drawn from their syntactical construction, but from their other implications."[60] It is not so much how folly sounds but, more deeply, how it works. J. Winston Harrington, a reporter for the *Chicago Defender* stationed in Greenville, Mississippi, exposed the Jim Crow situation in part by reprinting unjust white decrees. For example, he cites the "Labor Notice" decreed by William A. Percy (mentioned in chapter 1), which stated: "All Negroes in Greenville outside of the levee camp who are able to work should work. If work is offered them and they refuse to work they should be arrested as vagrants."[61] This was not the standard for white men in Greenville.

The Crisis thoroughly involved itself in white mediation to draw out its facts. As the official publication of the NAACP,[62] *The Crisis* bore the strong impress of its editor from 1910 to 1934, W.E.B. Du Bois, but was also connected to an organization Du Bois cofounded with a cadre of wealthy liberal whites, among whom were Mary White Ovington, William English Walling (who devised the magazine's name), and Oswald Garrison Villard. Du Bois wrote editorials about the flood in the summer and fall of 1927 but did not travel to the flood zone himself. No doubt he read the reporting in rival black news outlets, probably met with Walter White, who had toured the flooded states in late spring, and probably talked with Claude Barnett. Most important, Du Bois sent down a white female investigator who made two trips to the refugee camps in Mississippi and Arkansas in May and October 1927.[63]

In Du Bois's editorials, he argued that "slavery still exists in the Mississippi Valley."[64] "We hope," he asserted, "that every Negro that can escape from the slave camps guarded by the National Guard and the National Red Cross for the benefit of the big planters of Mississippi and Louisiana and the lynchers of Arkansas will leave this land of deviltry at the first opportunity. Let them ride, run, and crawl out of this hell."[65] He voiced his "grave suspicions" that the Colored Advisory Commission "will be sorely tempted to whitewash the whole situation" and will make "no real effort to investigate the desperate and evil conditions."[66] For proof, he quoted white-owned southern papers, which were trying to get planters, still keeping their tenants in unofficial camps and inundated plantations, to bring their tenants to the more centralized official Red Cross camps. These papers assured the planters that the camps would *not* allow their Negro croppers to be seduced away by roving labor agents.[67] Listening in on the white Delta public conversation, and reprinting it—effectively transporting what was transparent and open to one regional public and republishing it elsewhere—allowed Du Bois to expose truth by simply shifting the geography of print. He used print networks—rather than Wells's epistolary and face-to-face linkages—to move Jim Crow facts from their parochial sheltering.

Having charged the Colored Advisory Commission with offering less revelatory information than even white-owned southern papers, and with failing to be truly investigative, *The Crisis* followed up by publishing its own three-part series, "The Flood, the Red Cross and the National Guard," based on "an Investigation Made by the N.A.A.C.P." The white female investigator understood that she would have a distinct advantage over African American observers when it came to peering into white behavior and psychology. This investigator opens the first installment by establishing the scene in "the lovely hills" of Vicksburg "where once the Confederate and Union armies were camped," and hence establishes herself as a kind of northern spy bundled across southern lines, moving about in disguise amid the tent camps of her, and her readers', old enemy. Above the Red Cross Headquarters, "a spreading magnolia tree opened its waxy blossoms." The apparent picturesqueness of the scene will likewise be "opened" up by her pressure. She wanders amid the tents of the white Camp Hayes, filled mostly with sharecroppers and tenant farmers as indebted to the planter as were black rural laborers. She listened to one revivalist state, "I love this place . . . it's just like camp meeting," and to others who felt comfortable enough in her presence to give voice to their "race hatred." Though these tents may seem to some to be places of spiritual revival or material relief, the author's invocation of the old scene of enemy encampments conveys her suggestion that the social battles fought in that conflict have still to be won.

When in Louisiana, she assumed the alias of a Red Cross worker from the

Vicksburg camp. As she spoke to a white man in Melville, she "applied the stimulus, 'of course you Southerners understand Negroes as we Northerners can't', and he responded immediately. It seemed that that was only too true but that unfortunately most Northerners did not realize it. Their Red Cross workers in fact had come in and attempted to carry out a most outrageous plan by which white and colored cases were to be treated alike. The Committee, of which he was a member, had had considerable difficulty in educating them but had at last succeeded and anticipated no trouble in that line. No plan involving equality between white and colored would be tolerated in that town for a minute."[68] Feigning deference to white southern racial understanding, she played the part of a northern sympathizer and plied a "true confession" out of her interlocutor, a confession she rendered in free indirect discourse. He told her how local Red Cross committees were able to bring national officials around to their method of conduct. Most interesting, the last line of this short scene ("No plan . . .") manages to simultaneously voice the Louisiana man vehemently insisting on the preservation of a just inequality *and* the *Crisis* investigator, in a wholly different tone, summarizing a condition of injustice. She counted on her readers being able to hear her tone pushing from behind, and distending, his utterance.

The *Crisis* author continued her rhetorical strategy of revelation by the critical quotation of white thinking as she began to excerpt National Guard documents on the subject of camp discipline. One black refugee, Dunbar, was shot in the stomach and arm on May 1. Documents attested that a "Private Moore was forced to shoot Dunbar to save his own life," for Dunbar had attacked him with "a tent pin." The author also included testimony surrounding the case of Matilda Heslip, an African American woman who, in trying to fulfill the labor order of one Guardsman, ran afoul of others when she got in the way of kitchen operations, "raising a disturbance." Because of her obstinacy and "impudent" language, "force," in the form of blows to her arm and head, was needed to keep "discipline, . . . so necessary to the successful handling of these camps." The *Crisis* author, in juxtaposing these two cases, avers: "It is doubtful whether a self-defense plea would have served in the case of Matilda Heslip . . . had she shot the soldier who struck her with a stick the exact size of the one with which Dunbar struck the guardsman."[69] By placing two events, structurally similar but racially reversed, next to each other, the author can offer and underline textual proof of double standards that resulted in Guardsmen violence against black refugees. Though the *Crisis* investigator would outline where conditions were just—in particular where African American medical workers were allowed some control of relief efforts—her main critique centered upon what she took to be the Red Cross's cowardly defense

3.10. "The Slave Ship, 1927," *The Crisis*, February 1928. The author wishes to thank the Crisis Publishing Co., Inc., the publisher of the magazine of the National Association for the Advancement of Colored People, for the use of this image first published in the February 1928 issue of *Crisis Magazine*.

of their participation in abetting peonage, namely "that they did not create the social conditions in the South and it is not their function to reform them." The Red Cross claims that it can only "relieve temporary suffering." The author calls this out as an illusion, for the organization will invariably "strengthen or weaken . . . existing social institutions."[70] Like Wells, this writer sees the relief provider, the gift-giver, as having her or his hand on a key political lever. This white *Crisis* writer devised a disguise of the northern sympathizer in order to catch what she saw as the essence of southern white thinking—"race hatred" or race prejudice—in its unadulterated form. In so doing, she hoped to shame national organizations that were practicing a form of southern ideological sympathy she found intolerable. The War was definitely not over; what was worse, key national institutions were now pitching themselves on the side of infamy, and abetting bondage. The photograph, and the editorial caption, used to illustrate the second installment of the exposé series makes this point unmistakable (Fig. 3.10).

Nordic Tribalism

The influential and irascible pundit H. L. Mencken suggested in a May 23 Baltimore *Evening Sun* editorial that the reason he believed the South was not a very sympathetic victim was because of everything the region had done in recent years to alienate itself from the nation's modern mentality. As we shall see in chapter 7, it was the paper war this editorial triggered—when the Memphis *Commercial Appeal* fired back with "Another Mencken Absurdity"—that awakened the broader consciousness of Memphis resident Richard Wright in May 1927. Mencken's editorial appeared two years after his reporting on the Scopes Trial in Tennessee, in which the most salient "descent" for Mencken was that of southern intelligence, and ten years after he threw down his first gauntlet at the South in his 1917 essay "The Sahara of the Bozart." In his article on the flood, Mencken set out to analyze why, as he saw it, "the flooding of the Ku Kluxers has . . . brought forth no deluge of gold from the North." First of all, he averred, Deltans' suffering was their own fault. Because they were warned, "most of the dead committed suicide." More generally, the South is the "habitat of the least advanced white people now living in the United States." All southerners want to do is "annoy and prosecute everyone else. They have been hot for Prohibition, they have marched with the Klan, and, by means of anti-evolution laws, tin-pot revivals and other such barbarous devices, they have tried to outlaw every variety of common sense. In the whole region, so far as the record shows, not a single intelligent human being is to be found." Given that, "is it any wonder that the New Yorkers refrain from sobbing now?" Southerners will not "get" that their unlovability is their own fault; instead, they will "blame the Beer Trust, the evolutionists, or the Pope." It is the South's fault that we are "a country that has lost solidarity, and no longer houses a happy family." These twentieth-century religious feuds "are fully as bitter as those which culminated in the Civil War, and it is perfectly possible that they may have the same issue." The Mississippi "yokel" is not a bad fellow, but he has "been played on for years by the worst scoundrels . . . now at large in the United States" and "made to see red" when he contemplates "his betters" in the "big cities." Indeed, Mencken concluded, these backward whites "now seem, not like our own people, but like a hostile tribe on our borders." An inhabitant of the formerly slave-owning border state of Maryland, Mencken removes all traces of "the South" from his own state and redefines that cast-off South as a premodern "tribe," full of rogues and dupes. He sees the victims as "fools," whites who should have known better.[71] If the disaster did not turn the nation into a family, it's because the South has been waging a fundamentalist war on culture, sense, urbanism, and modernity.

Though Mencken was uniquely, even gleefully, barbed, he was not alone among the northern intelligentsia in his sense of a developmental gap between north and south. As spring turned into summer, and as unfolding flood turned into sodden aftermath, the sociologically inclined elements of the northern media looked southward to the Delta as if they were looking at the very "bottom" of the national hierarchy, anticipating how professional expertise could be diffused from modern centers to ameliorate the folkways, and cure the social diseases, of those bottomlands. The earlier rhetoric of "relief" for "suffering" hardened into a narrative of sociological cleanup. Nor was the narrative informed by Ida B. Wells's enterprise of social justice, of advocating from within a group *for* a group. Here, it was not so much immediate relief being summoned from a lay public as it was a renewed, long-term attentiveness on the part of the North to the South's problems, laid bare by the flood. The breaks in the levees became gaps in the solid wall that had, until the spring, hidden the Delta from outside view. These investigative journalists articulated a vision of northern paternalism and a diffusionist program of modernization and amelioration. Its logic intensified, and professionalized, the popular response to the flood as evinced in April and May.[72]

Arthur Kellogg, the managing editor of *Survey Graphic*, wrote two accounts of the flood zone in the July 1927 issue of the magazine. *Survey Graphic* was a companion publication to *The Survey*, a journal of the social work profession. In "Behind the Levees," Kellogg called attention to the camp at Vicksburg as a site for a "new meeting of North and South" and added that unlike the old meeting there in which General Grant starved the entrenched Confederate population into submission, "northern money today plays a big part in feeding the southern refugees."[73] In his second article, "Up from the Bottomlands," which is more a study of abiding Delta social and economic issues, he introduces this region as being not just geographically south but also "at the bottom of the United States." Here, he says, the people are "sick," not occasionally like the rest of the country but instead perpetually "plagued with diseases." To cure the problem, Kellogg envisions more "extension work" in the Delta run by the Agriculture Department involving the dissemination of "expert advice" moving outward and downward from a centrally controlled site of knowledge (along the lines of the Smith-Lever Act of 1914 inspired by Seaman A. Knapp). The main subject population of his vision of improvement is African American farmers. He calls one farmer "a dumb fellow" and speaks of the signal "imitativeness of the Negro . . . making him an easier pupil to deal with than the white farmer." He avers that these black farmers should not be left alone to "compete in the world's market against migrant Mexicans in Texas and Oklahoma,

Indians in Brazil and Peru, fellaheen in Egypt and the untouchables of India."[74] In this article, Kellogg was essentially shaming American readers into supporting a top-down, city-to-country, north-to-south, professional-to-folk, diffusionist project of educational uplift of the Delta Negro, understood as inferior but imitative, to make sure that the man on the "bottom" rung of America stayed above the peasantry of other imperial powers.

A series of six articles printed in the *Chicago Daily News* in August extended this picture of a "sick" South. Basing his facts on a document written by a member of a "hygiene society" to the Red Cross medical supervisor in Memphis, reporter Craig Dale outlined the "almost unprintable" "aftermath of the flood."[75] Not only did "the landscape [resemble] the aftermath of war," but there was "a quite evident cracking and crumbling of the whole economic and sociological structure of the stricken south."[76] He quotes military and health officers in Louisiana as stating that towns were "becoming rotten with prostitution," "disease," "vice," and "[p]romiscuity." Indeed, "the black cloud of crime [is] hovering and widening over all."[77] "If we can get these people to clean up physically and socially," one official averred, "we can save them."[78] In his depiction of African American farmers, Dale creates the following primitive tableau: "Swaying and singing in a sort of aboriginal rhythm . . . they indent the soft and muggy black bottom gumbo with their equally black heels." "And as he steps, he sings . . . 'Nobody knows the trouble I see.'"[79] Dale describes an African American woman afflicted with pellagra as a "walking mummy," who "greedily . . . suck[ed]" a side of raw bacon with "toothless gums."[80] What all of this alarming data seemed to call for was a sociological crusade to rescue a South stricken not only by the recent flood but by a chronic moral and physical hygiene problem.[81]

* * *

Investigative journalism did the important work, in many of the examples I have just given, of getting empirical data into print. Yet, as this last dispatch from Craig Dale shows, the perception and transmission of "facts" are not necessarily neutral. The southern attribution of all floodwater as northern was scientifically incorrect and allowed southerners to ignore their own participation in watershed endangerment. In another example, when northerners read southern poverty as a "hygiene" problem rather than the mark of southern states having become a vulnerable resource frontier in the postbellum period, or of race-based property distribution inequality, they were "moraliz[ing] danger" rather than historicizing it. One function of cross-regional journalistic distribution and reception was that it pushed any single accusation or "fact" into a realm of testing, and potential rebuttal. It could also strengthen distant geographical alliances: making the national black "community of danger" internally aware and responsive, or the watershed states' linkage as a vulnerable region apparent. And yet there were limits to how the movement of news across space translated into its movement across the color line: only Walter White's article in the left-leaning *Nation* exemplified such a crossing. Though there were some white readers of the black press, one does not find the narratives and critiques produced in black papers influencing how the mainstream white press represented the flood. One important mark of this situation is that while southerners and environmentalists could band together and get Congress to pursue a new flood prevention method in 1928 despite Hoover's own continued belief in a levees-only strategy,[82] African American investigative journalism—while it did cause Hoover to remove the most egregious Red Cross volunteers from their posts[83]—could not bring about the more crucial long-term legislative changes necessary to prevent peonage or lynching.

In January 1928, an editor of the *Baltimore Afro-American* wrote a piece in which he contended: "The United States is run by propaganda."[84] As I argued earlier, this had become a refrain of the post–World War I period, but this writer was referring to the flood, not the war. In particular, he found an example of his statement in the congressional debate then taking place over the flood prevention bill. He predicted that Congress would forget arguments about why states bordering on the Mississippi River should bear some of the financial burden for infrastructure improvement. All Congress would remember, as they prepared to make their decision, was that the cowboy humorist Will Rogers came before the Reid subcommittee and described "the Mississippi valley dwellers as 'half drowned.'" Rogers had told the committee, moreover, that "the people" "all over the country" felt the same way as he did.[85] The *Afro-American* editor then came to this conclusion: "Congress has dallied with the antilynching bill for three or four years. If those to be benefitted especially by this legislation could employ Mr. Will Rogers to perform before Congress in joint session and Mr. Al Jolson to sing a 'mammy song' in the congressional cloak room before the bill is brought out for a vote, there is a chance of making headway. Of course the flood relief bill has not passed yet, and may not pass. The antis may bring forth Fred and Dorothy Stone to entertain congress while Paul Whiteman and his band jazz 'It ain't Gonna Rain no More.'"[86]

"Making headway," he argues, does not happen because of facts and disinterested deliberation. Instead, legislation gets passed because an entertainer summons forth "those to be benefitted" in the most winning performance. If this author is to be believed, politics is a contest of fantasies. The editorialist is being largely satirical here, but he brings up a crucial point about change within mass-mediated democracies. Public perceptions and attitudes, which directly and indirectly, quickly and slowly, affect legislation and policy, are shaped by entertainment. Theorists of the public sphere in the tradition of Lippmann have viewed entertainment as anathema to the rational critical debate they argue is necessary for a well-functioning democracy. This author seems to agree, as he categorizes the presence of comedians and musicians in the halls of public opinion as a form of "propaganda." But what if the performer were not Al Jolson, appearing in burnt cork and purveying plantation nostalgia? What if the entertainer were "Blues Empress" Bessie Smith, singing of her own flood experience? And what if the suasion took place in a venue that seemed more fitting for "the people" to arrive at their feelings? What if popular entertainment, which arguably had even more power to cross over the fault lines of a pluralistic democracy than did the still stubbornly enclaved spaces of investigative journalism in 1927, could "make headway" with mass perception?

FOUR

Bessie's Eclogue

One day in the second week of February 1927, Bessie Smith walked into the kitchen of her Philadelphia row house with a pencil and paper in her hand. Her sister-in-law Maud Smith was there, at 1926 Christian Street, and likely her brother Clarence, who was the manager of her touring show, *The Harlem Frolics*, and also the straight man in one of the show's comedy routines. All of them, along with twelve chorus girls, a seven-piece band, the comedy duo of Tolliver and Harris, and Eggie Pitts and his Dancing Sheiks had been on the road together since before Thanksgiving.[1] They had been traveling the Midwest and South in their specially built railway car, seventy-eight feet long and painted a bright yellow with the star's name emblazoned in green on the side.[2] Smith was in her heyday that winter, drawing crowds of more than fifteen hundred into the company's capacious tent, filling theaters in the bigger cities, as she played both for "whites-only" and for majority black audiences (see Fig. 4.1). Her shows were broadcast on the radio in the bigger southern cities like Atlanta and Memphis.[3] And her records were intensely popular on both sides of the color line in the South, generating advance excitement for the *Frolics*.[4] As the *Pittsburgh Courier* stated: "Miss Smith is a great favorite in Atlanta. Few white homes here are without her records."[5] Now, the second week into February and back in Philadelphia, after months on the move, Smith could rest. Her next engagement, a show called "Bessie Smith and Her Yellow Girl Revue" at the Lincoln Theater in Manhattan, wasn't until March 2.[6]

But she didn't rest. As Maud Smith remembers it, "Bessie came in the kitchen one day, and she had a pencil and paper, and she started singing and writing." As she sang and wrote, wrote and sang, she figured out the words she wanted, which vowels to vault into and which to compress, which words to give the uneasy flats and which the temporary resolutions. She made syntax stretch and shrink to fit a four-bar phrase, and figured out which lines needed repeating. She chose the character she would become in the song, as well as

4.1. Michael Ochs, "Bessie Smith." Michael Ochs Archives/Getty Images.

the narrator. All that attention mattered, for what Bessie Smith was writing, as she walked around her row house in Philadelphia, was soon to become *the* anthem of the Great Mississippi Flood. In fact, according to music historian David Evans, "Back-Water Blues" ultimately "took on a life of its own, becoming *the* flood blues, an all-purpose generic blues on the flood theme." Covered by multiple artists throughout the 1930s, 1940s, and after, it became over time "one of the best known of all blues songs."[7] Given its release early on in the 1927 super-flood cycle and its nationwide distribution while the disaster was still unfolding, this song was a key vehicle for communicating ideas and attitudes about the flood *while it was occurring* to a large multiracial, multiregional public.[8] As it invited identification with a female refugee (a "poor old girl"), offered a neutral natural history of disaster, and brought an aural rendition of the extreme weather to far-off listeners' ears, it invited a complex vicarious experience of the event. It connected the low-down feeling and worried mind so typical of the blues to the geographic experience of being in the troubled lowland space of a flood, thus connecting pervasive blues tropes to environmental experience. It positioned a particular blues way of knowing nature as an unwanted, dystopic calling and let listeners in on how it would feel to be so called. Moreover, it did so without identifying a source of human antagonism or oppression and without conspicuously racializing the disaster. As we shall see in later chapters, Smith's song not only influenced the spate of flood songs produced in the months and years that followed but also shaped a

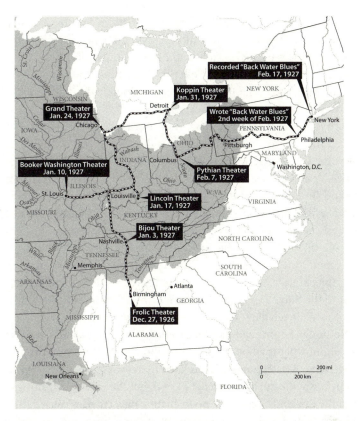

4.2. Bessie Smith's 1926–27 concert tour and recording itinerary. © Princeton University Press.

form of knowing and saying that made its way into the flood fiction of William Faulkner and Richard Wright.

* * *

What was remarkable about the tour Smith and her company had just taken through the southern and midwestern states was not so much Smith's marital quarrels with her husband, Jack Gee, or the diva's apparent "hedonistic spree" in Cincinnati[9] but the fact that her private Pullman car traversed, again and again, virtually all of the swollen eastern tributaries of the Mississippi River (see Fig. 4.2). As her sister-in-law remembered it, the company had its closest brush with calamity when it "came to this little town, which was flooded, so everybody had to step off the train into little rowboats that took us to where we were staying. It was an undertaker parlor next door to the theater, and we were supposed to stay in some rooms they had upstairs there. So after we had put our bags down, Bessie looked around and said, 'No, no, I can't stay *here* tonight.'" The undertaker's was packed with her admirers, though, and "they were trying to get her to stay, so they started hollerin', 'Miss Bessie, please sing the Back Water Blues, please sing the Back Water Blues.' Well," admitted Maud, "Bessie didn't know anything about any 'Back Water Blues.'"[10]

Through a careful reconstruction of her touring schedule, David Evans has determined that the town Maud Smith was describing was Nashville, Tennessee, where the Cumberland River overflowed on Christmas Day 1926 and kept rising until New Year's Day, displacing ten thousand mostly African American persons and inundating two hundred city blocks. Smith arrived by rail from Birmingham, Alabama, sometime between December 28 and 30 but needed to be rowed ashore because the Nashville station was underwater. She performed twice on the thirtieth at the Bijou Theater, the first time for a black audience and the second time for a white one. The undertaker's parlor where the troupe, and many black Nashvilleans, had to take refuge was, as Maud remembered, next door to the Bijou on Fourth Avenue North. Bessie Smith and her company stayed in Nashville ten days, witnessing the high water and the rescue and relief efforts. No doubt Smith read papers, listened to the radio, and heard personal accounts about what the flooding had done to people's lives and property. Unlike in the Delta disaster zone months later, there was good interracial communication in Nashville during the relief period, but the race-based siting of black houses in the lowlands, and their poor quality, nevertheless caused disproportionate black suffering.[11] Smith had grown up in a low-lying section of West Chattanooga, a section of the city called Blue Goose Hollow, between the Tennessee River and the city's railroad tracks, so she understood from childhood experience how Jim Crow urban planning invariably left African Americans more exposed not only to industrial waste and insect-borne diseases but also to periodic inundation.[12]

It was not just Nashville, and distant memories of Chattanooga, that Smith was writing about, however.[13] The entire length of the Ohio River, actually a more voluminous tributary to the Mississippi at Cairo than the main branch of the river, was pulsing with floods from late December through much of the winter. Pittsburgh, where the Allegheny and Monongahela meet to form the Ohio, was inundated on January 23. Five days later, the overflow reached downtown Cincinnati.[14] Earlier in the month, the flooding Cumberland and Tennessee rivers had sent their high waters into the Ohio downstream of Cincinnati. Thus, crest upon crest moved down the Ohio for weeks. The Illinois River, which also feeds the Mississippi from the east, had reached flood stage in the early fall and remained there for 273 days.[15]

Bessie Smith's *Harlem Frolics* tour traveled from Birmingham, Alabama, to Nashville in late December; from there it went northwest to St. Louis, then to Louisville, arriving in Chicago on January 24. From there, the show moved to Detroit, on to Columbus, Ohio, with perhaps a detour in Cincinnati, and then home to Philadelphia. As their car coupled and uncoupled itself from various trains, this troupe of singers, dancers, and comedians crossed the Tennessee, the Cumberland, the Ohio, and the Mississippi rivers; they crossed again the Mississippi and the Ohio, and then the Wabash and the Illinois, and once again the Ohio and finally the Monongahela before they exited the Mississippi's extensive eastern watershed on their way home to Philadelphia.

By the time she was back at 1926 Christian Street in the second week of February, Smith had accumulated quite a lot of flood knowledge. Not only was she raised in an inundation-prone lowlands, but in this winter of 1927 she had lived among evacuees for ten days in Nashville and then went on to traverse, over about five weeks, the extent of a riverine system pulsing with overflows. While living at the undertaker's, as Maud explained, Smith "got the title [for "Back-Water Blues"] from those people down South."[16] One assumes, though— if a crowd was requesting a specific song of that title from her—that she got more than just a title from her audience. This is not to suggest that she purloined a fully formed country blues song of that name and called it her own but that the crowd at the undertaker's shared something musical and, you could say, something empirical with her that night: phrases, catches, anecdotes, and ways of making meaning out of displacement. They multiplied her direct experience.

These were the lyrics Smith put down on paper during the second week of February:

When it rains five days, and the skies turn dark as night
When it rains five days, and the skies turn dark as night
Then trouble's takin' place in the lowlands at night

I woke up this morning can't even get out of my do'
I woke up this morning can't even get out of my do'
That's enough trouble to make a poor girl wonder where she want to go

Then they rowed a little boat about five mile cross the pond
Then they rowed a little boat about five mile cross the pond
I packed all my clothes throwed them in and they rowed me along

When it thunders and lightnin and the wind begins to blow
When it thunders and lightnin and the wind begins to blow
There's thousands of people ain't got no place to go

Then I went and stood upon some high old lonesome hill
Then I went and stood upon some high old lonesome hill
Then looked down on the house where I used to live

Back water blues done called me to pack my things and go
Back water blues done calls me to pack my things and go
Cause my house fell down and I can't live there no mo'

Mmmmmm I can't move no mo'
Mmmmmm I can't move no mo'
There ain't no place for a poor old girl to go

On February 17, Smith recorded this song for Columbia Records in New York City. Her accompanist on piano was a remarkable innovator and talent, James P. Johnson. This was their first collaboration. "Back-Water Blues" was released by Columbia on March 20, with a song called "Preachin' the Blues" on its flip side (Columbia 14195-D). Levee breaks were just beginning to occur along the Mississippi below Cairo (at Laconia, Arkansas, on March 29 and at Dorena and New Madrid, Missouri, two weeks later). On April 2 an advertisement, with its image of a kerchiefed and countrified Bessie Smith crammed in a rowboat with her few salvaged worldly possessions, appeared in the *Baltimore Afro-American* (Fig. 4.3). Addressing a black readership, the copy confided that though the winter's high waters in the Mississippi's tributaries might be getting familiar, "folks, you don't know how mean and moanin' it really can be 'till you let your ears drink in 'Back-Water Blues' as Bessie Smith mixes the notes." It emphasized: "*People, here is the record you want.*" In mid-May, once it became clear that the 1927 flood was an unprecedented disaster, advertisers started to use the flood more explicitly to sell this song. An advertisement in the *Pittsburgh Courier* by a major race records distributor touted that "'BACK WATER BLUES' brings to your mind the heart-rending scene of thousands of people made homeless by the mighty flood."[17] As of mid-June, the *Baltimore Afro-American* noted that Bessie Smith's "Back-Water Blues" and her cover of "Muddy Water (a Mississippi Moan)" were "in the score of best sellers of the past week . . . owners of the record shops attribute the present popularity of these records to the publicity given to the Mississippi river floods which are laying waste to many former haunts of record buyers."[18] Orders for "Back-Water Blues" were close to twenty thousand. It was soon covered by Lonnie Johnson, Viola McCoy, and Kitty Waters.[19] Smith led her *Harlem Frolics of 1927* tour back to the South in May and June, moving all over North Carolina, from Asheville east, and into Virginia. "Back-Water Blues" was enjoying "phenomenal sales,"

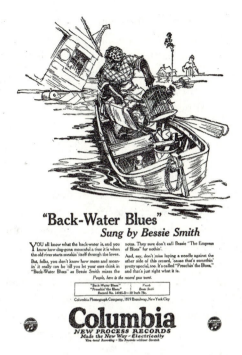

"Back-Water Blues"
Sung by Bessie Smith

YOU all know what the back-water is, and you know how dog-gone mournful a time it is when the old river starts sneakin' itself through the levee.

But, folks, you don't know how mean and mean-in' it really can be 'till you let your ears drink in "Back-Water Blues" as Bessie Smith mixes the notes. They sure don't call Bessie "The Empress of Blues" for nothin'.

And, say, don't miss laying a needle against the other side of this record, 'cause that's somethin' pretty special, too. It's called "Preachin' the Blues," and that's just right what it is.

People, here is the record you want.

"Back-Water Blues"	Front
"Preachin' the Blues"	*Bessie Smith*
Record No. 14195-D—10 Inch 75c.	

Columbia Phonograph Company, 1819 Broadway, New York City

Columbia
NEW PROCESS RECORDS
Made the New Way - Electrically
Viva-tonal Recording - The Records without Scratch

4.3. Advertisement, "Back-Water Blues," *Afro-American*, April 2, 1927, 7. Courtesy of the Afro American Newspaper Archives and Research Center.

which likely boosted attendance at her tent shows. No doubt audiences wanted her to sing the song wherever she toured. Throughout August and September, she moved south and west, touring in Georgia, Alabama, and Texas. It was her "most successful" tent show tour ever.[20]

The phenomenon of "Back-Water Blues" becoming *the* anthem of the 1927 flood is noteworthy for several reasons. It brings the modernity of this flood into focus. The fact that the flood's most popular song could be inspired, composed, recorded, released, disseminated, and consumed across the nation all within the duration of this super-flood shows both the massively systemic nature of the watershed distress and the speed and reach of media and transportation technology in 1927. Those African Americans whom Harris Dickson described listening to "Broadway" on their phonograph while the flood rose all around them in the backwaters of the Mississippi Delta likely also had a copy of Bessie Smith's flood hit.[21] She sang to them about how leaving their house would feel before they had even felt it. Those sharecroppers were experiencing the flood both as a material occurrence—something that soon caused their evacuation to Vicksburg—and simultaneously as a mediated event. As the physical event issued out of tributaries in the North, so too was Smith's part in the media mega-event "produced" up north, in Philadelphia and New York City. The local and directly experiential was part of a much broader, and circulatory, cultural system. Advertisers promised that if the public listened to Smith's song, they would "know how mean and moanin' [a flood] really can be"; they would "know" how this flood felt and hence, to a certain extent, what it meant. Smith's knowledge, derived from personal and direct experience, and influenced by other southern black witnesses, provided a kind of access—emotional and cognitive—to real experience; her art turned it into vicarious experience and potential meaning.

Smith's audience was made up not only of southern flood refugees but also of African Americans born in the South who had migrated northward to such cities as Chicago, Baltimore, and Pittsburgh. It was made up of southern blacks outside the flood zone and northern blacks who had never been south. Whites across the nation were part of her audience, but especially southern whites, both people in the Delta disaster zone and outside of it. As these different listeners, and at times live audience members, heard Bessie Smith sing "Back-Water Blues" in the spring of 1927, they formed a particular kind of cross-racial, blues-mediated flood public. Along with newspapers, radio, and flood benefits, the blues circuit—both live and virtual—connected listeners into a complex and heterogeneous assemblage.[22] In the South, white and black consumers of this music would not have, in the main, listened to Smith's live singing together. And Columbia 14195-D would have spun on Victrolas in houses ritualistically mapped out by race. Imagine, for instance, the record playing in the parlor of an insurance agent and his wife in a white section of Atlanta; the African American woman cleaning up from their dinner in the nearby kitchen could also hear Bessie Smith's voice. All are, more or less, part of the same aural environment, but each has his or her own way of identifying with the protagonist of the song. The woman at the sink may have heard "Back-Water Blues" as *her* song because its lead "character" was created and performed by an African American woman, describing a fragile lowlands situation particular to the black community. The couple in the parlor may have heard it as *their* song because Smith was a southerner bemoaning a tragedy that regional papers had spilled ink to establish as yet another case of southern suffering at federal hands. Because Smith's voice, emitting from the Victrola or the radio, was bodiless, and yet intimately present and suggestively meant *for* each listener, typical lines of racial identification were scrambled.

Elsewhere, beyond this one conjectural listening tableau, what kind of understandings of the flood experience did such a blues public have? What kind of understanding did this particular song suggest? Before we address what this song might have *done* culturally, we must think through how and why Bessie Smith wrote it, and sang it, the way she did. We must think through, too, the aesthetic choices that James P. Johnson made as he accompanied Smith's voice on piano.

Of Smith's singing, one of her biographers has said that "no one had a voice as powerful and compelling as Bessie's."[23] Gunther Schuller, a composer, horn player, and conductor, remarks on the "the tragic, weighted quality" of her voice and hears in Smith's singing the "finely controlled microtonal nuances of the blues notes." Moreover, Smith possessed "an extreme sensitivity to word meaning and the sensory, almost physical, feeling of a word." Still more remarkable was her pitch control as she moved in and out of vowels: "the way she could move into the center of a pitch with a short, beautifully executed scoop or 'fall' out of it with a little moaning slide."[24] Of the narrative element in her songs,[25] Albertson argues that "no other singer of her day could tell a story as convincingly" such that the narratives within them "became shared personal experiences."[26] Schuller concurs that Smith excelled in "complete compositional forms and narrative continuity." Moreover, "like a great actress, she created the illusion of total improvisation"; in other words, she made listeners feel that she was telling her own story spontaneously, "even though every move may have been in some manner prepared and studied."[27] Of her singing, white writer and Harlem habitué Carl Van Vechten remembered in 1947, with significantly less insight into performance modes than Schuller, that "this was no actress, no imitator of a woman's woes; there was no pretense. It was the real thing—a woman cutting her heart open with a knife until it was exposed for us all to see, so that we suffered as she suffered, exposed with a rhythmic ferocity, indeed, which could hardly be borne."[28]

Bessie Smith remembered the time she sang for a gathering at Van Vechten's apartment in 1928 somewhat differently. According to her niece, she commented in the week following the event: "Sheeeeiiiit, you should have seen them ofays lookin' at me like I was some kind of singin' monkey!"[29] From the perspective of Manhattan sophisticates, Smith provided a kind of anthropological encounter with a ferocious, and sacrificial, "real thing"; no wonder she felt like that audience had fantasized her into a jungle primeval.

New Orleans jazz guitarist Danny Barker heard in Smith's singing not the tearing away of culture but rather the reservoir of a deep cultural tradition of southern Christian liturgical performance. He observed, "If you had any church background, like people who came from the South, as I did . . . you would recognize a similarity between what she was doing and what those preachers and evangelists from there did, and how they moved people. . . . Bessie did the same thing on stage . . . she could bring about mass hypnotism."[30] Ralph Ellison corroborated this impression when he recounted, "Within the tighter Negro community where the blues were a part of a total way of life . . . she was a priestess, a celebrant who affirmed the values of the group and man's ability to deal with chaos."[31] Smith's father was, in fact, a Baptist clergyman (and an iron foundry laborer) before his untimely death, and the family seems to have attended church until their mother's passing a few years later. Their daughter Bessie would have thus been exposed as a child to hymns, spirituals, and shouts, and she would have seen firsthand the power a sacred music soloist could exert on the emotions and the spiritual regeneration of a congregation.[32] It was this sacred performance tradition that Smith combined with listening to the work songs of washerwomen (her mother's job) and factory laborers, popular rent party tunes, and minstrel show and Vaudeville numbers she learned in Chattanooga and touring with Ma Rainey as a teenager to create her own, very deliberate, secular-sacred performance techniques.[33]

We do not know if Smith or Columbia Records requested James P. Johnson as her accompanist for "Back-Water Blues." Johnson had grown up in New Jersey and moved as a young teenager into New York City, where he began playing at Barron Wilkin's Cabaret in Harlem. Though he was not a southerner, he would make a career of fusing southern themes with cutting-edge "modernistic"—to borrow another of his titles—musical composition. Johnson had composed the "Charleston" for the 1923 Broadway hit *Runnin' Wild*, the music for *Plantation Days*, and other southern-themed songs such as "Carolina Shout" (1921); he would soon create a long choral work inspired by coastal Georgia called "Yamacraw—a Negro Rhapsody," which was made into a movie short starring Bessie Smith,[34] and collaborate on a one-act opera with Langston Hughes called *De Organizer* about the unionization of southern sharecroppers. Because African American experience in general, but especially in the South, was already an abiding subject for Johnson, one presumes he took up the opportunity to accompany Bessie Smith singing about the flood in Nashville with imaginative energy. Johnson was one of the foremost practitioners of the Harlem "stride" style of piano. As music journalist Nick Morrison explains, stride pianists "took the basic left-hand 'oompah' rhythm of ragtime, but played it with more swing and complexity." The left hand responded to the melodic improvisations on the right hand in a contrapuntal fashion, requiring a "broader use of the bottom end of the piano"[35] and making that hand seem to "stride" to cover distances on the keyboard at great speed. Johnson's virtuosity, in particular, derived from his ability to imagine and to execute the superimposition of multiple rhythms.[36] Bessie's biographer calls Johnson's playing "complicated, highly rhythmic," and "richly embroidered."[37]

One of the most striking features of this song is the way the interplay between voice and instrument renders the human relationship to a troubled environment. As with the typical 12-bar blues following an AAB stanza pattern, each line begins with vocal measures and transitions into an instrumental response or commentary; the second line echoes the first but has a slightly lower and more level pitch. The practice of repeating the first line loosely derives, it is thought, from traditions like call and response and hymn lining out in the African American church.[38] Smith performs, with her voice and her choice of words, the part of both refugee and third-person narrator.[39] Johnson, meanwhile, responds in two ways. Whenever Smith sings of rain, thunder, skies, or wind, he turns the piano into a weather machine. For rain, his fingers are lightly and quickly percussive, moving around the higher notes and trilling as if he's striking patches of sky into pattering sound. For thunder, he moves to the lower notes and produces between his hands a reverberative transfer that mimics a deep echo. In both instances, Johnson makes the keys sound out a wide and layered aural map of the sky's drama—of elemental behavior. In other lines, as Smith sings of her, or her protagonist's, ensuing predicament, of trouble or confusion, Johnson has the instrument provide an aural register of the subject's interior—her mental, emotional, and psychological atmosphere. As Johnson's piano playing moves back and forth from, as it were, outer to inner weather, he connects them sonically.[40] Indeed, as the piece progresses, the sonic signature of the two kinds of weather gradually becomes indistinguishable. "The human" imagined in this song is by no means an autonomous agent, what we might in a philosophical tradition identify as a pristine delimited Cartesian *cogito*. Rather, the "I" has a permeable skin, and thus both an exterior and an interior susceptible to environmental events.

Before this moment of atmospheric permeation, Smith tells, through her word choice and through the pattern of emphasis she creates with her voice, a story about the territorial consequences of weather. The first five stanzas have a "when . . . then" structure, in which the various "thens" signify the necessary and incontrovertible outcome of the "when" (as in a law of logic, mathematics, or nature). This pattern is established in the first stanza. The best way to understand this is to listen to the recording, but I have also tried to show, through a typographic equivalent, each word Smith emphasizes by increasing her volume, by sustaining the note, or by drawing the vowel out over a run of varying notes (a vocal technique called melisma) or through oscillation (vibrato); if there is extensive melisma or vibrato, I indicate it with a ~.

> When it **rains five** days and the **skies** turn **dark** as night
> When it **rains five** days and the **skies** turn **dark** as night
> Then troubles takin' **pla~ce** in the lowlands at night

By invoking the logical structure of causation (when x, then y), Smith introduces her narrator as a person whose knowledge is based on deep experience, someone who is a vernacular expert. The narrator makes a scientific and social observation: when there is this much rain moving from the atmosphere to the earth's surface, rivers will overflow their banks, and the lowest-lying terrain will be the first inundated. Figural "night" will materialize on earth (so "as" turns to "at"). While the narrator reports the intense rain, she is reinforced by Johnson's aural demonstration of the extreme weather. In the final line of the stanza, the phrase "takin' place" has an interesting double meaning. It works as a temporal phrase, indicating that an event will occur, but it also works as a spatial marker, showing that "trouble" literally will take the place where the lowlands used to be. Place is a location, but it is also an outcome of natural and human history.

After the narrator has made these expert observations, she recedes, and the first person emerges.

> I woke **up** this mornin', can't **e**ven get out of **my** do'
> I woke **up** this mornin', can't **e**ven get out of **my** do'
> There's en**ough** trouble to make a poor girl wonder where she want to go

The "I" is a "poor girl" who lives in the lowlands. Night has given way to morning, and, just as the narrator predicted, "trouble" is at the girl's door while vexation is in her mind. Specifically, she "wonder[s]," not about why or when but about "where," where she can situate herself. She feels the spatial foundation of self, its "where," to be disappearing.

In the next stanza, which begins with "then," she describes more spatial consequences of the precipitating environmental event. The "five" days of rain have turned into "five miles" of groundwater.[41] "They," the rowers, are neither antagonists nor saviors; they merely transport her vaguely "along," detaching her from a located self.

> Then they **rowed** a little boat about **five** miles **cross** the pond
> Then they **rowed** a little boat about **five** miles **cross** the pond
> I packed **all** my clothes, throwed them in and they **ro~wed** me along

Then the fourth stanza, like the first, provides a natural and social history lesson. As with the first, the piano accompaniment offers the atmospheric—you could say, empirical—simulation for the listener.

> When it **thun**ders and lightnin' and the **wind** begins to blow
> When it thunders and lightnin' and the **wind** begins to blow
> There's th**ou**sands of people ain't go~t no **place** to go

By shifting back into the third-person expert narrator, Smith can, by zooming out from the "poor girl" to encompass "thousands of people," extend the force of her observations. It is not just one unmoored "I" we have to worry about; in fact, "there's thousands" like her. As her voice sustains the word "place," she reminds her listener of her earlier use of it in stanza one ("troubles takin' place") and of its abiding importance to this song.

In the fifth stanza, we return to the girl's voice, as she takes us through her removal to higher ground. She uses the "thens" not exactly in the mode of causative logic of the third-person narrator but rather to indicate a series of movements.

> Then I **went** and stood upon some **high** old loneso~me hill (heeill)
> Then **I**~ went and stood upon some **high** old loneso~me hill (heeill)
> Then looked down on the **hou~se** where I **u**sed to live (leeive)

Though it is a "high" "hill," it is also "old" and "lonesome"—not really a refuge, or a realm of spiritual transcendence, as much as it is a site of isolation and exile. Indeed, when she pronounces the word "hill" ("heeill"), she does it—ironically—with a descending fall-off to her voice. When, in the repeat line, she shifts her emphasis from the word "went" to the word "I," she seems to do it not out of defiance or assertion as much as to make clear her aloneness. From this abject place, she "looked down" and, in a sense, looked *back* in time, as she looks at her unsalvageable past. In this line, "down" and "house" rhyme internally, and the way Smith employs melisma while singing "hou-ouse," she gives the painful "ou" sound another, descending, echo. Looking back with longing, she does, like a latter-day Lot's Wife, seem at this point to disintegrate.

In the first line of every stanza up to this point, her voice has jumped up dramatically in pitch, volume, and duration on the third word: "rained," "up," and so on. Her voice vaults into this word each time and then makes a gradual, uneven descent until its fall-off in the last syllable of every line, a rising and sinking that may also be Smith's vocal approximation of a body riding a series of waves. The distance her voice travels, from high to low, is always exactly one octave down in the root chord. Thus each of the five stanzas begins with an upthrust followed by a sinking. The sixth stanza breaks this pattern, and the specific word that breaks the pattern is "blues." Smith goes down into the word and sustains, or warbles on, the long "u" sound.

> Backwater blue~s done called me to pack my things and go
> Backwater blues done calls me to pack my things a~nd go
> Cause my **house** fell down and I **ca~n't** live there no mo

"Back-Water blues" is a personified force, exerting a "call" upon the speaker not toward missionary purpose but rather toward a kind of knowing dislocation. "Blues" or "the blues" are often personified in blues lyrics to signify, in Adam Gussow's words, "willful violators of every single psychic boundary the isolate black subject seeks to erect." In another of Smith's songs, "In the House Blues," Smith sings, "Catch 'em, don't let them blues in here / They shakes me in my bed, can't set down in my chair."[42] In numerous blues lyrics, that violator is implicitly a kind of white violence or oppression.[43] "Back-Water" is another kind of "in the house" blues, a willful violator of domestic and bodily safety; though Smith does not explicitly link "Back-Water" with white aggression, she may be making use of what would have been an association for her more initiated listeners to subtly racialize and hence politicize the floodwater. Finally, in line three, the first-person speaker, using the word "cause," has at last adopted the causative logic of the third-person narrator. Through her direct experience of this flood, and now standing off at the distance of ratiocination on that "old lonesome hill," she has turned into the vernacular expert, into someone who understands environmental cause and social effect. Her former, wondering, surging naïve self is gone.

In the final stanza, as with the sixth, there is no upthrust toward the beginning of its first line. In fact, there aren't even any words, just a prolonged, rising then dipping moan. The "mmmmm" sound slides into and becomes the "I," making it the ending sound, or the open-mouth exit, of the moan instead of a distinct pronoun. Then the "m" in "move" and "mo" serve to reverberate the moan across the line.

> m**mmm**mi can't move no mo'
> m**mmm**mi can't move no mo'
> There **ain't** no place for a **poor** old girl to go

As the girl, who has absorbed the narrator's wisdom, and hence her function, issues forth this melismatic "m**mmm**m" sound, she breaks down another expressive barrier, that between the human and the elemental. "Mmmm" could be animal, human, or outer atmosphere. Here, it is an extrusion of pain that sounds like an intrusion of the elements. Though the "old girl" may be stripping herself of human culture as she loses language in her moaning, she is—for listeners who know the traditions—also invoking a key sonic element of the blues and, before that, of nineteenth-century field hollers. Johnson, moreover, responds in kind on the piano keys to her moan.[44] In the first and fourth stanzas, Johnson mimicked the environmental sounds of rain and thunder. In the other intervening stanzas, he comments upon the unfolding drama with playing that conveys suspense, tension, and at times a kind of martial insistence. In this final stanza, responding to her first line, he returns to the up-and-down cascading on the lower keys he had used earlier to imitate thunder, but for the first time it also sounds just like her voice, something made easier by the fact that she has temporarily lost that distinct human capacity for speech, for arbitrary signification. In these bars, piano, voice, and atmosphere are all one. To put it another way, Johnson uses his piano accompaniment to show how the elements have penetrated this "I," how this "I" has become elemental.

Finally, the endings of these last three lines recapitulate those of the sixth stanza, but they also indicate an inversion. If, in the sixth stanza, the speaker couldn't stay anymore, now she can't move anymore. If she was in the midst of going before, now she sees that there's "no place" to go. Over the course of the song, the "old girl" has ascended to the high hill to see and comprehend but figuratively descended to the "no place" where this kind of blues knowledge is.[45] She has lost her "hou-ouse," the solid word rippled into lament. The matrix of her former self has collapsed. She has been called to, or inducted into, a blues way of knowing. There may be insight there, but it is no place for living.[46] This ending without resolution, in a moving/stuck, high/low quandary draws, too, from the blues form, which is characterized, in the words of Abbé Niles, by the "rather bizarre and contrasting effects of internal finality and final incompleteness."[47] The ending also reflects the blues' characteristic "stubborn refusal to go beyond the existential problem and substitute otherworldly answers."[48]

This final condition of the female protagonist—elementally fused, self-dissipated, and deeply knowing—would be, in the hands of a Romantic or Transcendentalist writer, an ecstatic achievement. Think, for instance, of that canonical passage in Ralph Waldo Emerson's "Nature" (1836):

> In the woods, we return to reason and faith. There I feel that nothing can
> befall me in life,—no disgrace, no calamity, (leaving me my eyes,) which
> nature cannot repair. Standing on the bare ground,—my head bathed by

the blithe air, and uplifted into infinite space,—all mean egotism vanishes. I become a transparent eye-ball; I am nothing; I see all; the currents of the Universal Being circulate through me; I am part or particle of God. The name of the nearest friend sounds then foreign and accidental: to be brothers, to be acquaintances,—master or servant, is then a trifle and a disturbance.[49]

For Emerson, being "nothing" and seeing "all" happens as a consequence of divine and natural incorporation. Those "currents of the Universal Being," that self-reparative "nature," that "God," elevate him upward and "bathe" him. Here is an elemental baptism that makes worldly issues—class, kinship, friendship—all "accidental" in comparison. By contrast, Smith's speaker, experiencing American nature almost a hundred years later and from a lower echelon on the socioeconomic and racial hierarchy, is more engulfed than uplifted. Smith writes of a single human's immersion in a highly disturbed nature—a nature after industrialization, after decades of deforestation in the Northeast, upper Midwest, and South, after wetlands drainage and after the baleful impounding of the Mississippi River. This nature cannot repair itself after such intense anthropogenic interference. Moreover, those who profited from the disturbances are not in harm's way when the "calamity" occurs. It is at that point at which whether one is "master or servant" *matters* because it will determine your geographic location, the strength of your house, and your possibilities for recovery. This is all to say that a twentieth-century blues kind of environmental subjectivity and epistemology is markedly different from a nineteenth-century Transcendentalist one: it is about the sinking feeling of losing a "where" to be one's self rather than the transportive feeling of finding yourself where God is.[50]

The tradition of nature writing, and specifically of environmental lyrical verse, that Smith's song actually belongs to is that of the classical eclogue or pastoral.[51] The ancient pastoral poem is about a community living on the margins that knows, as Raymond Williams has put it, "winter and barrenness and accident," that is, "the real social conditions of country life."[52] Pastoral verse is derived from Mediterranean peasant traditions of competitive singing and, more specifically, from the Hellenistic Greek poet Theocritus; it came to be characterized by singer-herdsmen in dialogue, meditating on the demolitions of love, the fickle nature of patrons, and the insecurity of land tenure. There is much in common, in particular, between the world of the sharecropper in the twentieth-century South and that of Virgil's first-century BCE Roman Republic, and between Smith's blues and the ancient poet's *Eclogues*. Neither describes a milieu of rustic simplicity and idyllic innocence; rather, both rural environ-

ments are "permeated through and through with . . . human infelicity, catastrophic loss, and emotional turbulence." Virgil's *Eclogues*, in particular, were
written around 37 BCE amid the "violent disintegration of the political fabric"
occasioned by the republic's civil war.[53] One of the consequences of that war for
the rural tenantry—both small farmers and herdsmen—was the threat of land
confiscation and redistribution to returning soldiers. Eclogues I and IX address
the trauma of territorial displacement that we see in Smith's own song. In the
first Eclogue, one of the shepherds, Meliboeus, has just been exiled from "the
realm I called my own" and from "My poor man's roof" (9, ll. 68–69). For this
displaced singer, "The land / Is crying havoc, and I'm sick at heart" (4, ll. 11–
12). The protagonist of the ninth Eclogue, Moeris, likewise experiences a forced
removal from the small farm and from the local spirits who altogether make
him who he is. This Eclogue in particular explores "the mitigating role of poetry
in the face of catastrophic loss."[54] Moeris's interlocutor expresses the wish that
his friend's land will be preserved—not materially but in and as a song. The
dispossessed farmer responds: "In Mars's weaponed world, our songs prevail
the way / Chaonian doves do with the eagle in a fray" (9, ll. 11–15). Despite
Moeris's dim view about the power of verse, Virgil himself seems to offer these
scenes, in which a pastoral poetry of loss is socially performed and passed
along, as a kind of portable vestige of the land, or at least of the singer's former
condition of territorially derived happiness. Williams makes the point that ide-
alizations of rural life do exist in the classical genre of pastoral, but they do so
as a wishful antidote to loss. These small moments of compensatory dreaming,
however, mistakenly "[become] the 'source' of a thousand pretty exercises on an
untroubled rural delight."[55] In the early modern period in England, for instance,
this lobotomized version of pastoral could depict the countryside as a restorative, apolitical retreat from the city even as enclosure laws were dispossessing
a vulnerable rural tenantry.

One could say that the relation of a complex ancient pastoral and its sham
derivatives has much in common with the relationship between the southern
blues traditions and the much more idealizing tunes about Dixie moonlight
and magnolias.[56] The former express how "The land / Is crying havoc, and [the
singer's] sick at heart," while the latter do not. Both Virgil's *Eclogues* and Smith's
"Back-Water Blues" lay out the paradox of knowing land loss—of having
knowledge and song but "no place . . . to go." Ralph Ellison observed that "the
blues is an impulse to keep the painful details and episodes of a brutal experience alive in one's aching consciousness, to finger its jagged grain, and to
transcend it, not by the consolation of philosophy, but by squeezing from it a
near-tragic, near-comic lyricism. As a form, the blues is an autobiographical

chronicle of personal catastrophe expressed lyrically"; in as much as this "brutal experience" or "catastrophe" is connected to land use, this description likewise holds for the pastoral eclogue.[57]

Throughout the spring and summer of 1927, Bessie Smith's song played on phonographs in the South, the Midwest, and the North, in the flood zone, and outside of it. Her song made a wide flood public, both embodied and virtual. Given that the early, noncritical coverage of the flood in the white northern presses tended to imagine the typical victim as a white woman, or a white family, awaiting reincorporation into the national fold, Smith's refugee persona must have troubled, or somewhat corrected, such a distortion. And as Harris Dickson's decidedly minstrel-show rendition of the black refugee population had been syndicated to papers around the country, its staging likewise would have come in for adjustment as listeners in Los Angeles or New York City heard Smith's (and Johnson's) plaintive, authoritative, and virtuosic presentation of displacement. Moreover, her song—and the blues tradition more broadly—offered a first-person lyric invitation to identify with the speaker; the song invites the "you" listening to become the "I" singing, and many listeners probably literalized this prompt by opening their mouths and singing along. Finally, as I suggested earlier, Smith doesn't call out any egregious behavior here: "thousands of people" are homeless, but this situation seems—at least given the syntax—a logical result ("when" . . . "then") of five days of rain than of human malice or neglect, or structural socioeconomic inequity, or the geography of Jim Crow. The third-person narrator's account is a truncated natural history of rain's behavior in a floodplain, not a searching exploration of decades-long anthropogenic degradation of the environment. White presence, if there is any, appears in the form of a vague "they" who pick her up and row her "along" to higher ground.

The popular blues genre allows Smith to tell a story about the black experience of lowland flooding to a more cross-racial and capacious audience than any journalistic medium could or did—than either white newspapers were willing to or black papers could reach. And this genre demanded a sonic intimacy with black pain. But it could do so precisely because it put no white character in its story who was explicitly responsible for that pain. As such, in Smith's song, the flood is less humanly caused, and less an occasion for overt political blaming, than it appears in the white southern editorials that began issuing from presses in late April. While not invoking a rhetoric of blame, blues singing nevertheless exerted cultural and social pressure. In 1964, Ellison would remark that in the blues we see "politically weak men successfully imposing their values upon a powerful society through song."[58] In this case, Smith was a woman from a politically restricted caste who did not so much "impose" as share the broader American "value" of territorial security, of sovereignty within one's house; she used song to include African Americans within that "value." As Angela Davis has said of the blues genre, "'Protest,' when expressed through aesthetic forms, is rarely a direct call to action." And yet "critical aesthetic representation of a social problem must be understood as constituting powerful social and political acts." Of the 1927 flood in particular, Davis argues, occurrences that might have remained "merely private misfortunes" became, through the medium of blues songs, "social, collective adversities" and hence "catalytic events."[59] Adjusting this formulation slightly, I would point out that because this flood created mass populations of displaced persons forced together into what were more populous spaces than many evacuees were accustomed to, "misfortune" was rarely "private"—it was already "social [and] collective." Come May in the Delta, through word of mouth in the "concentration camps," group reading, and transmission of the *Defender*, as well as sacred music shared within and outside the churches, evacuees communicated to themselves about the meaning of this flood. Because Smith's "Back-Water Blues" was released so early in the super-flood cycle, she helped establish, from her December experience in Nashville, the broader event as collective—rather than private—even before massive displacement occurred in the Delta: before, that is, miles of tents were pitched and patrolled by armed guards in places like Greenville and Sicily Island. Within the lyrics of her song, by oscillating between the first-person lyric mode and the reportorial mode (which told of "thousands of people") she could take a mass event and make it matter to individual listeners who together made up a national public. Though African American southerners, including those who had migrated north like Ida B. Wells and William Pickens, knew how quickly a private event (like the accusation of sexual assault) could ramify outward to afflict the entire community, and also knew who suffered most when high water came anywhere in the South, it seems right to suggest that Bessie Smith's song primed a multiregional and multiracial public to appreciate the magnitude and the sorrow of the 1926–27 catastrophe.

As Smith took her song on the road in that late spring and summer of 1927, as she traveled from North Carolina and Virginia to Georgia, Alabama, and Texas, the force of embodiment—both in terms of Jim Crow and patriarchal hierarchies—impinged on her tent shows in a way that it did not with the virtual dissemination of her music. On the other hand, her live presence as the climatic, much-anticipated act of an hours-long show, and her magnetic power, added a ritualistic quality to the event that could not be communicated through a waxen 78 rpm disc. Recall Barker's comment that Bessie Smith, like the great

Baptist clergymen of the South, "could bring about mass hypnotism" and Ellison's observation that "she was a priestess, a celebrant who affirmed the values of the group and man's ability to deal with chaos." Daphne Duval Harrison has added that for Smith, and other blues queens of the 1920s, live public singing in front of a black audience worked to "exorcise the blues feelings in a communal ritual with other black folk."[60] It seems likely, then, that as Smith performed in front of large crowds of African Americans, her carefully crafted flood blues—which sonically performed what it meant to let a disturbed environment permeate your "place" and your consciousness—both "called" catastrophe into the tent and also temporarily "exorcised" its community-destroying power.

It was not only the black southern community that needed affirmation of its group's value and integrity or an exorcism of its woes. Southernness in general seemed under assault from aquatic and federal forces, and from misplaced northern "sympathy." As separate audiences of blacks and whites filled *The Harlem Frolics* tent, and the more plush playhouses, they saw before them a virtuosic southerner whom the country had embraced as an "Empress"; they saw someone more wealthy, cosmopolitan, and talented than themselves, so that for either audience to experience Smith as one of their own—as in some sense representing them—was indeed an expanding, affirming celebration and one assurance that the South had a vital place in modernity. She made southern suffering seem momentous to both races. And yet, outside the tent, or off the stage, Smith was still a black woman in a patriarchal Jim Crow world. Her personal bravery and toughness, and her fame, could often obviate this hierarchy, but not always.

One night in July, as Bessie Smith was performing for a majority black audience in Concord, North Carolina, one of her musicians detected six Klansmen trying to untie the tent from its stakes. Consequences would have been very serious if fifteen hundred people were trapped under a fallen canopy. Apparently Smith, once warned of the intrusion, shouted at the hooded men, "What the fuck you think *you're* doin'? I'll get the whole damn tent out here if I have to. You just pick up them sheets and run!" After they'd retreated, she summed up with "I ain't never *heard* of such shit." Her niece remembers that Smith scolded her prop boys with these words: "You ain't nothin' but a bunch of sissies." Maud, her sister-in-law, recalled that Bessie "confronted the Klan with her hand on her hip . . . and shook her fist at them!"[61] On another occasion in Texas, her temerity and anger did not this time frighten away but actually provoked her antagonists. While performing at a theater in Dallas in September, Smith had a verbal outburst with a white stage manager. Because the curtain wasn't lowered at the right time, the carefully orchestrated moves of her twelve chorus girls were muddled, making the show look so foolish that the audience started to laugh. Furious, Smith apparently rushed over to the stage manager, who was talking to his wife, and yelled: "Are you drunk, you was late getting that curtain down, standing here talking to that white bitch." He reared back to hit Smith, but she knocked him over first. Hearing of this, a number of white men ambushed her after the show, took her to a nearby empty lot, and attacked her with a whip. It was only a police car, with company members trailing behind it in another vehicle, that interrupted the attack. Smith refused ever to appear in Texas again and canceled the rest of the tour.[62]

While Bessie Smith was traveling through the South in May and June 1927, and the catastrophic Delta flooding was in every newspaper around the country, record companies like Victor, Okeh, Paramount, and her own label, Columbia, rushed to record more flood songs and to promote previously recorded spiritual material.[63] Just after the first major crevasse above Greenville, Okeh blues artist Lonnie Johnson recorded in St. Louis "South Bound Water" and covered Bessie Smith's song on the B side (Okeh 8466). Country music singer Vernon Dalhart recorded "The Mississippi Flood" on April 27, and other country singers, also from outside the Delta, weighed in with "The Story of the Mighty Mississippi" and "The Terrible Mississippi Flood." In Chicago during May, the Texas country blues singer Blind Lemon Jefferson recorded "Rising High Water Blues" (Paramount 12487). Also in May, Blue Belle's "High Water Blues" (Okeh 8483) and Sippie Wallace's "The Flood Blues" (Okeh 8470) were set into wax, as was Laura Smith's "Lonesome Refugee" and "The Mississippi Blues" (Victor 20775) and Barbecue Bob's "Mississippi Heavy Water Blues" (Columbia 14222-D) in June. And blueswoman Alice Pearson, who appears to have had direct contact with the flood, either in Greenville or Memphis, recorded "Greenville Levee Blues" (Paramount 12547) and "Water Bound Blues" (Paramount 12507) in Chicago in July.[64] The baritone Paul Robeson recorded a version of the Negro spiritual "Deep River" on May 10 (Victor 20793). Also very popular in May and June was more religiously oriented material that happened to be recorded in February: Rev. J. M. Gates's sermon "Noah and the Flood" (Okeh 8458) and the Norfolk Jubilee Quartette's "The Old Account Was Settled Long Ago" taken from the black hymnal Gospel Pearls (Paramount 12499).

Either because all but one of these artists had no direct experience of the catastrophe or because of the rush to record something topical, there was heavy borrowing of Bessie Smith's motifs and lyrics. Alice Pearson, for example, despite being an eyewitness, begins "Greenville Levee Blues" with "I woke up this morning, couldn't even get out of my door," and begins stanza four with "They

was rowing little boats five and ten miles away." Other songs incorporated imagery that was unrelated to the actual events, and a number of songs brought in
the love theme so central to the blues tradition. Blue Belle begins her tune with
this stanza: "The rivers all are rising, ships sinking on the sea (x2) / I wonder do
my baby think of me." Though this stanza links environment to emotion like
Bessie Smith's song, in my mind the linkage is so abrupt as to strain it. Though
the flood could be experienced as simultaneously cosmic and local, and seemed
an implosion of the whole round world into one's smaller sphere, this inclusion
of the love theme in this instance verged on trivializing the epic tableau already
created. Motifs most common across this spate of springtime and summer
flood songs were images of a body caught in water, the movement to higher
ground, looking back down to see either an absent or demolished house, and
place-names associated with affliction. A few of the lyricists also comment critically on the faulty communication network, as when Sippie Wallace sings
"They sent out alarms for everybody to leave town (x2) / But when I got the
news, I was high water bound." As these songs were released and marketed during the spring and summer, they, like Bessie Smith's composition, became a
means to communicate the physical and geographic details and the emotional
and social consequences of this disaster—to foreground it as an event of broad
public concern. Though companies like Columbia, as they promoted their "race
records" in black newspapers, encouraged a kind of intoxicating consumption
of the flood blues, as when they suggested to listeners "let your ears drink in
'Back-Water Blues' as Bessie Smith mixes the notes," the various publics of blues
songs were anything but lulled into a stupor by this music. Indeed, these modern southern eclogues, arising out of abiding transhistoric issues of rural land
sovereignty and the particular modern American condition of Jim Crow, and
finding form in African American musical fusions, became a vital way to communicate, memorialize, and make meaningful the displacement of "southern
people."

FIVE

Catastrophe Comes to Vaudeville

In the spring of 1927, the Lower Mississippi Valley was transformed into an impromptu circus. On display were spectacular distortions, suspenseful scenarios, and bodily metamorphoses—scaled-up versions of the kinds of effects staged, but nonetheless managed, within traveling entertainments. If carnivals typically showcased disturbance so that viewers could experience wonder as that disturbance was brought under control, such conventions had no bearing on the tempestuous outside world that spring. Sometime around the last week of April 1927, storms broke the pole in the big top of the John Robinson Circus, touring Louisville, Kentucky. The cookhouse, horse tent, and pad-room tents were also blown down.[1] In Benham, Kentucky, on May 8, a high wind struck the midway of the Page & Wilson Shows, and, as it struck, "The ferris wheel was moved about five feet off its base"[2]—a sight that must have been terrific to behold. The mechanized thrill of defying gravity had been subjected to the unpredictable properties of weather. In early May, the C. R. Leggette Show, a touring troupe of cabaret dancers, musicians, and minstrel performers, found itself "marooned" for twenty-seven days in McGehee, Arkansas, a town in the Delta County of Kesha, about sixty miles southeast of Pine Bluff. As *Billboard* magazine told it, "Conditions were indescribable while the levees were in danger of breaking." Ultimately, "water rose 18 feet above the rails where the show cars were parked." All the young men in the show apparently pitched in, carrying sand bags and operating motorboats. After their unexpected waylaying, "the show train, the first to move north in four weeks, ran thru two to three feet of water for 20 miles on a roadbed which resembled a roller coaster."[3]

As the typical sites of entertainment had been absorbed into a wider atmosphere of apparently natural spectacle, performers, as the above example suggests, were called upon to perform new roles. A man who styled himself "MARTINELLI [the] Handcuff King and Escape Artist," and who promised theater bookers that he could wriggle out of "Boxes, Straight Jackets, Handcuffs, Leg

5.1. Stationery, Martinelli. John Welsh ("Martinelli") to Charles Douglass. Courtesy of the Middle Georgia Archives, Washington Memorial Library, Macon, Georgia.

Irons, Mail Sacks and Torture Straps," had been "many years with circuses" when he was caught in the Flood of 1927 (Fig. 5.1). "His business here was to put on shows," a Mississippi paper, the *Winona Times*, put it in mid-May. "But the flood-swept Mississippi! Martinelli forgot in a measure the show business. On his own initiative he met trains in the day or in the night. . . . He assisted refugees coming thru the town to find lodgment, something to eat, or secured information for them." Along with these acts of assistance, the escape artist put on a benefit performance at the Dixie Theater while in the flood zone. The *Winona Times* editorial summarized by saying: "All the world is kin."[4] Martinelli, whose real name was John Welsh, a white man of Irish descent who hailed from Georgia and who courted as his patrons both white and black theater owners in the South,[5] did not exactly "forget the show business." It was true that his staged acts of marvelous self-liberation were, at times during the flood, set aside; in their place, he performed works of altruism, getting others out of tight spots and constraining circumstances. Acts of entertainment in which the boundary between performer and audience was secure were temporarily restaged during the emergency. Martinelli did not just display his own virtuosity but came to know, and to remedy, the distress of others with whom he shared the space of catastrophe.

5.2. "Eddie Foy and Eight Little Foys." Hartsook Photo S.F.-L.A. Publicity photograph of Eddie Foy and the Seven Little Foys for the Keystone Company as published in *Moving Picture World*, October 23, 1915. Billy Rose Theatre Division, New York Public Library for the Performing Arts, Astor, Lenox and Tilden Foundations.

On May 4, the *Atlanta Constitution* reported that "many vaudeville performers [are] in town this week whose engagements have taken them into the inundated areas." These Vaudevillians, the paper pointed out, possessed "a first-hand knowledge of the urgent need for relief."[6] Interviewed was Charley Foy, a headliner with the B. F. Keith Circuit, one of the reigning North American consortia of Vaudeville theaters. Foy had been part of a family act begun in 1912 by his father, called "Eddie Foy and the Seven Little Foys" (Fig. 5.2). The *Los Angeles Times* later remembered them as "one of the hottest acts in show business" and suggested that part of what made them popular was their display of "organized chaos."[7] Irish American Eddie Foy Sr. had achieved fame not only for his "droll antics, absurd pantomime, . . . farcical singing and dancing,"[8] whiteface clowning, and drag impersonations but as the one performer in *Bluebeard* who, during Chicago's notorious Iroquois Theatre fire of 1903 in which six hundred people died, stayed onstage—in drag, no less!—trying to calm and direct the audience. Foy finally escaped through a sewer. Foy the father first staged his family as an act in Vaudeville when his youngest child, Irving, was only four. The varying sizes of the bodies and the bits of each performer, especially the misrule of the youngest (or tiny "end-man"), along with the comic exasperation of the father made the group function as a coordinated assemblage in which individuality emerged and receded without disturbing the whole.[9] By 1927, Charley and three other Foy siblings (Madeline, Mary, and Irving, now nineteen) had spun off a smaller family act featuring synchronized tap-dancing punctuated by pratfalls, quickly extinguished "conflicts," and the serial display of virtuoso physicality.[10]

It is this group of four that found itself caught in the flood in the middle of May. "Conditions on the Mississippi are awful," Charley attested. "We staged a flood benefit in Little Rock, Ark., and in Birmingham, Ala., and would gladly stage on[e] a week wherever we go to help those poor souls out there." Foy recounted his and his siblings' experiences in traveling through Arkansas, telling how they had to wade through water and cross broken places in the highway. "Why, in one place where we had to climb up a log to reach a bridge, the man before me fell off and went into mud up to his neck—and we had a hard time saving him with a rope. Dead horses, cows and other livestock floated everywhere."[11] If the Foys provided pleasure to their audiences by letting them experience finely choreographed family commotion, a household hubbub on the brink of chaos but always pulled back through ensemble organization, this must have been a doubly pleasurable routine for those in the disaster zone. The *Atlanta Constitution*, by offering a behind-the-scenes look at these performers in the muck and contingency of disaster, emphasized that the Delta was the "marvelous attraction"[12] of the moment while showing that on-site improvisation had temporarily upstaged and repositioned playhouse routine.

The Flood of 1927 turned theater out of doors. Or, to put it another way, it produced a kind of environmental theater. Scholars of performance and theater will associate that phrase with the work of Richard Schechner. In his dialogues with anthropologist Victor Turner during the 1970s, Schechner became attentive to the ritual saturation of everyday actions. Schechner hailed a new theater that would get outside the playhouse, traverse and animate everyday space, so that "the space of the performance is defined organically by the action" and humanity's distance from its environment can be abrogated, making both more alive.[13] Revising his definition in the 1990s, Schechner then incorporated the natural world into his model, so that "environments ecological or theatrical" could become "co-consciousnesses," or "active players in complex systems of transformation."[14]

Disaster theorists, with their own indebtedness to anthropology, are likewise attuned to the relation between environments and ritual action. It is not to everyday rituals they look but in particular to the ways in which, after a major eco-catastrophe, a society becomes an enormous, metaphorical arena to stage "expiation" and thus "ward off danger and reestablish normality."[15] Such rituals of gift-giving and blaming, as discussed in chapters 2 and 3, occurred in every available medium. Schechner's idea of environmental theater can add concreteness to the metaphor of a world turned into a space of ritual theater. How did actual, brick-and-mortar theaters and people professionally trained to entertain act within this larger realm and moment of theatricality? What was the special function of live theater in a world symbolically saturated by expiating ritual? And what was the role of entertainers who brought their training out of doors into the muck and mire, or who brought their experience of that muck—and its human costs—back onstage?

In the scenes just recounted of Vaudevillians in the disaster zone, "the space of the performance" was "defined organically by the action" as the customary separation between humans and their environment collapsed. Imagine the four Foys, trained from early childhood in concerted and virtuosic motion—having used their bodies as communicative instruments much of their lives—needing to contour those bodies to broken roads, makeshift log ramps, and roping rescues. The flood's unfolding sweep created the unexpected mise-en-scène of the Foys' traveling performance. It produced the set, "the space," and, for that matter, "the action" or imbroglio for which they used their highly trained bodies to articulate a response. Likewise John Welsh, alias "MARTINELLI [the] Handcuff King and Escape Artist," who used his repertoire of self-liberating body acts to assist others, creating a "kin"ship by immersing his stage act into a new scene of action in which the physical line between performer and audience disappeared. Perhaps this was not the scene of transformative "potentiality" Schechner theorized. As Charley Foy said, "conditions . . . were awful"; refugees were without shelter and disoriented, and the mud was home to a legion of decaying animal carcasses. Humans fought a river system they had themselves imbued with uncharacteristic force in a space that felt like one part battle zone, one part senseless circus. Here was a valley-long environmental theater produced by fifty years of improvident everyday actions. Yet these Vaudevillians' rescue acts represented occasions in which "performance" arose as a response to "first-hand knowledge" of others' crucial needs. Seen from this angle, the Delta housed a kind of environmental theater in which professional entertainers followed "the action" to gain understanding and to perform socially meaningful acts.

As this 1927 version of environmental theater was mediated for audiences outside the valley, it did not, however, receive critical praise. A *New York Times* reporter censured the flood for *not* being the kind of drama favored by the Western tradition: "Great news, like great drama, must have unity of time, place and action."[16] Not only did this flood not live up to Aristotle's *Poetics*, it failed even to live up to the word "catastrophe," which signified, beginning in the days of early modern theater, the "change or revolution which produces the conclusion or final event of a dramatic piece."[17] Here was no abrupt overturning that led the way to closure. In this catastrophe, people had to watch a tinkered nature *come apart over time* rather than *go all at once*.[18] It was aesthetically disappointing.

These examples of rescue efforts by individual Vaudevillians, however, present an interesting alternative to the judgment about the mediated flood lacking "great drama." And they point to a different kind of theatrical tradition, arising out of the broad concourse of the everyday, which brings us closer to Schechner's "potentiality." It was not classical or "great drama" that helped the nation better understand what disaster really meant to its victims. Euripides' classical tragedy *Iphigenia*, when it was staged in D.C., offered a plangent rendition of what the flood meant symbolically as part of a saga of nationhood, while the anguish of the common folk appeared as only a minor choral counterpoint. In 1927, for a live audience to participate in a gift-giving rite in which the experiences of dispossession were placed center stage, they had to go to Vaudeville. Here was the theatrical milieu through which this flood could be transformed into rites that disrupted what Dewey called "routine consciousness." Vaudeville's own form—a string of heterogeneous acts lined up with "utter inconsecutiveness"[19]—suited the form of the flood's sequential unpredictability, its surprises of one thing after another. And, as I suggested earlier, the physical contortions and feats of Vaudeville's "dumb acts" staged a version of the extremities of embodiment and material undoing brought on by high water. But it was especially its talent that made Vaudeville the place to encounter "first-hand knowledge" of disaster.

Vaudeville in the United States has been described as "a people's culture," political only in as much as it was "a thumb to the nose at pretension and the people who ruled the roost of business, government and culture."[20] Given that bodies onstage call forth sociohistorical associations or stereotypes, that acts typically played on these stereotypes, that theaters were often racially segregated, and that Vaudeville itself became a mass industry with its own labor disputes, it was, in fact, a politically charged enterprise in any number of ways. In 1926, the theater critic for *The Nation*, Joseph Wood Krutch, averred that these kinds of revues "are to a democracy what troupes of dancing girls were once to Kings."[21] What distinguishes this modern democratic entertainment from its courtly predecessor, though, was how the audience saw a version of itself represented onstage, and could, because of the pleasures and artistry and comic intelligence of that stage, become open to experiencing itself anew.

Beginning in the 1840s, as mixtures of songs, comedy sketches, short drama, recitations, and dance, variety revues brought together, in dance and beer halls, a "series of unrelated acts on a single bill."[22] If there was no overall narrative logic to a given evening, there was, however, a calculated building up, in pacing and intensity, toward the big headliner who appeared after the intermission.[23] Through the entrepreneurial efforts of figures like Tony Pastor, and especially B. F. Keith and E. F. Albee, as well as a ramifying national infrastructure of railroads, telegraphs, and towns, Vaudeville developed by the early twentieth century into a circuit—some would say an "octopus"[24]—of some two thousand big and small theaters around the country, promoting "respectable" entertainment that was nonetheless a combination of "high" and "low" acts, put on by working-class multiethnic and multiracial talent for a socially diverse audience, all of which connected localities into a mass audience.[25] As one historian put it, in the hands of Keith and Albee, Vaudeville could provide "tea for the swanks as well as a dish for the masses."[26]

Coming to prominence in northern cities alongside new waves of immigration from Europe and migration from the U.S. South, Vaudeville became, according to one historian, "an arena for communication" and "genial subversion," for trying on alternate ways of being and thinking, a place of discordant but entertaining "polyphony."[27] Dating back to the nineteenth-century variety traditions, which relied heavily on racial and ethnic "types" for its comedy, Irish, blackface, Dutch (or German), and Jewish acts comprised the typical medley, all creating hybrid, comic, distinctly American personae more than transmitting Old World cultural traits. Also dating back to the 1880s, labor issues and strife were common stage material.[28] Overall, though, "comedy was the essence of American Vaudeville," and this comedy involved "a critical, satirical summation in topical humor of the social, economic, and political trend of the time."[29] For some years, Vaudeville was able to adapt to the rise of cinema by incorporating it into programs. By 1930, though, Vaudeville would be dead, killed by the talking film, network radio, and the stock market crash. Also lethal was Albee's miscalculated over-glossing of its informal, populist elements: "he dressed up Vaudeville fit to kill and it committed suicide."[30]

Vaudeville, though based on a "variety" model drawn from pluralistic society, had no institutional dedication to progressive social reform; Vaudevillians, on the other hand, could be remarkable social workers. Imagine the social and geographical knowledge these performers accumulated through a lifetime of bookings: constantly moving around the country, from small town to city to small town again, never staying in any one place for longer than a day or two. Not only were these performers endlessly mobile, but their geographic reach had to be coupled with social insight for them to be successful. They had to know what would make people laugh—or scream or applaud or hurl bricks—

and how that might differ in various U.S. regions. They needed to turn their bodies—their agile voices, facial expressions, and limbs—into instruments of popular pleasure. Theirs was a life of constant experimentation in which their performing bodies functioned as the medium for making and testing their social expertise. These itinerant performers were anthropologists who made a repertoire out of and for their subjects. Certainly vaudevillians felt themselves trapped at times by what their audiences wanted. But there were also times in which these performers could use their expert social knowledge as a means to puncture or subvert or commandeer those demands.

"Entertainment" represented to its critics the *anti*-medium through which to communicate vital matters to a democratic public in the 1920s. That the world of real events was, to a feckless public, as inconsequential and deceptive as the world of popular theater was Lippmann's great fear: "The booboisie and the civilized minority," he quipped, "are at one in their conviction that the whole world is a vaudeville stage." This "conviction" amounted to an admission that no "public event really matters very much."[31] To Lippmann, the Vaudeville stage kept the populace from seeing not only the gravity of a public event but also what those in power were doing behind the scenes. Political "insiders" used illusion to dull the curiosity of the great mass of people, the "outsiders." And the job of the media "expert" was to struggle against that illusion and rescue some "truth" for the public to see. Lippmann, because of his own wartime experience with presidential advising and diplomacy, imagined "truth" as high-level decision making concentrated in the hands of the powerful. Mainstream historiography, as it was professionally practiced in his time, would have concurred. Popular performers trained in a back and forth with the "modern mass constituency"[32] of Vaudeville would not have seen "truth" in such a limited fashion and would thus have a more populist definition of expertise. During the Flood of 1927, some consequential executive decisions certainly were shrouded from public view. But what the public really needed to understand—if their gift-giving was to rise above a consumeristic act of "charitainment"—were all the diffuse effects of bad social, environmental, and engineering policies and practices. They needed to know what was occurring in the concentration camps and on the levees, where their dollars were being sent. Media studies scholars who focus on contemporary mediated public rituals that follow disasters have argued that these disasters can allow nonelites to act as the "'primary definers' of the story of blame and accountability" as they "direct criticism at power holders in society."[33] In 1927 mainstream journalism, the black nonelites who made up the great majority of the evacuees tended to appear in the form of an "Uncle Eph" or a "Negro Noah." Thus flood victims needed go-betweens to "direct" and voice their "criticism" from the bottomlands upward and outward. These "experts," then, were not in Washington, D.C., for they needed to see the flood up close. It is this ground's-eye knowledge that certain Vaudevillians possessed. As they combined this knowledge with their long-honed awareness of public sensibility, they became its signal live communicators in 1927.[34]

I have discussed how Bessie Smith, brought up in the Vaudeville circuit apprenticing to Ma Rainey, acquired direct knowledge of the super-flood while on tour in the Ohio River Valley. Being an "Empress" did not cordon her off from the evacuee experience; rather, her itinerancy allowed her to traverse and survey flooded territory for a number of weeks. Her lyrics, her singing, and her accompanist's playing let a listener not just hear but also feel how the environment of disaster could sink one into speechlessness.

It is to the comedians of Vaudeville I now turn. As we saw with Harris Dickson's series, using comedy to represent disaster can be ruefully dismissive. An African American cultural critic writing for the *New York Amsterdam News* called Dickson's flood dispatches "Grotesque Journalism" and "newspaper minstrelsy." The *Amsterdam News* author hoped that there would be a time when "white journalists will realize that Negroes have reached the stage where they rightly resent 'end men' stuff in printer's ink" and that there is a more "appropriate style in which to describe either Negro life or Negro death." The writer summarized: "comedy and tragedy never appear together on the same stage."[35] This critic was right in noting that to practice flood comedy in 1927 necessarily involved the performer in the minstrel repertoire, so intimately connected were popular national depictions of Dixie with minstrelsy. A few of the Vaudeville headliners, however, who also happened to be southern men of color, managed to use their foolscap as a feint. Once their audience was pulled in, the real "intelligence work" began.

Underlying my approach to their comic acts is a qualified agreement with Walter Benjamin's assertion that "there is no better starting point for thought than laughter." Laughter is the outward expression of a "spasm" of consciousness.[36] The flood archive suggests that there are, in fact, many starting points for thought—variously initiated by songs, cartoons, novels—but also that when a mass audience gathers in response to disaster, comedy has a particular ability to draw together a wide, heterogeneous audience who wants to "get" the humor. If that audience has to consider the world from the perspective of a different social position in order to get humor—in order to experience the physical and mental pleasure of communal laughter—then comedy does not so much distract its audience from crucial matters as it attracts them.[37] Embodied entertainment modes—rather than modes of disembodied deliberative reason—can offer venues that disrupt a broad public's customary thought patterns. At these Vaudeville flood benefits, an unanticipated moment could cause a spasm of awareness: audience members, while enjoying themselves, could learn to think through the reasons for their donations and their participation in the larger problematic structures of the nation manifest in the disaster. In sum, live comedy had a peculiar ability to make diverse publics think together.

The Benefits of Vaudeville

In the spring of 1927, as Vaudeville was in the process of being simultaneously "dressed up" and being eclipsed by electronic, virtual, and easily reproducible forms of entertainment, it awakened its still considerable network to raise money for the Mississippi flood victims. Its powerful but doomed circuit and its intrinsic form represented the public's signature rite of live response to the social and environmental collapse occurring in the Delta. These benefits took place between May 2 and June 1, that is, after the crevasse at Mounds Landing turned the overflow into "the most staggering disaster this country has ever suffered"[38] and before transatlantic flights had turned the public's heads. Over this month, the flood was transformed from a historically unprecedented spectacle into a politically charged debacle. In Boston, a midnight variety show at the National Theater on Tremont Street was staged to benefit flood sufferers; the National, with 3,800 seats, billed itself as "the largest Vaudeville theater in the world."[39] In Chicago, a benefit was hosted at the Apollo Theater. In New York City, as the *New York Times* reported, "Vaudeville seems to be concerning itself just at present chiefly with a series of six benefit performances which will be given simultaneously next Saturday at midnight to aid the Mississippi flood sufferers. All the circuits [throughout the boroughs] . . . are joining in the project"; "All-star programs are promised at every house."[40] Earl Carroll's *Vanities*, a variety show made risqué by the scantily clad female chorus, put on a midnight flood benefit at its 50th Street theater. The *New York Times* reported that "girls from the chorus . . . will invade the Wall Street district this morning to sell tickets at 'catch-as-catch-can' prices for the benefit."[41]

In numerous venues around the country, blackface minstrelsy was used as part of these appeals for the South. Much as we saw minstrelsy's appearance in print journalism, it worked on the stage as a readily available means of leavening the tragedy of southern white suffering with the somehow inevitably ludic form of black distress. The humor of this disaster minstrelsy shared in the derision of Harris Dickson's remark—that "a negro comes in contact with trouble

5.3. Publicity photograph of the Duncan Sisters as Topsy and Eva, 1923. Witzel Photo. Billy Rose Theatre Division, New York Public Library for the Performing Arts, Astor, Lenox and Tilden Foundations.

because he gets bumped into [it as] a rear-end collision."[42] Charles Mack and George Moran, white comedians who donned burnt cork to become "The Two Black Crows," entertained audience members at Carroll's *Vanities*.[43] The head-lining comedy act at the Shrine "Monster Benefit" in Los Angeles was the Duncan Sisters, doing their signature blackface "Topsy and Eva" routine, which they themselves called a "travesty" of the Louisiana plantation scenes from Harriet Beecher Stowe's *Uncle Tom's Cabin*, a novel with a prodigious afterlife in the nationally popular "Tom Shows" (Fig. 5.3).[44]

Around the country, these variety revues attracted more patronage than did the long-running Broadway shows that offered up a night's proceeds to the Red Cross, in part because in many cases they were cobbled together especially for the benefit performances. Audience members in New York or Boston or Los Angeles could imagine taking part in a motley collective assembled in festive celebration of the larger, more abstract national assemblage. All could participate in the spontaneous staging of democracy in motion. What's more, these revues, often put on at midnight and called "frolics," promised exhilaration, amusement, wonder, and self-abandonment. In each of these Vaudeville flood benefits, though, restraints existed on the transformative potential of an event staged as a response to a major disaster. In the Hollywood and midtown Manhattan venues, the synecdoche for the South was a northern-born white comedian in blackface. For these whites donning the comic mask of blackness, one predicated on the minstrel equation of blackness with clownishness, they used the cork to heighten the comic effect of the act more than to explore the southern black experience.[45] The complex history evident in the flood was not visible onstage. Democracy's theater was in the house, but the catastrophe was missing.[46] There were, however, two Vaudeville benefits in which famous southern comedians of color performed in the northern metropole. And it was in these two venues that a more transformative circuit of exchange likely occurred. They were comedians who, unlike the Duncan Sisters or Moran and Mack, fulfilled the "clowns' traditional function as social critics."[47] Looking at these venues, we will ask: how can entertainment, which has the power to move outside the enclave of the racial counterpublic and create alliances with the broader population, manage to make people laugh and conceptualize problems while they are laughing?

Getting the Drift

At Harlem's Lafayette Theatre "one of the greatest shows presented on a Vaudeville stage in years" appeared on May 10 to a sold-out house of two thousand seats. The *Pittsburgh Courier* announced that "all the leading Race stars of Broadway and New York fame" were there.[48] The *Chicago Defender* touted that "every star within 50 miles of the tall town tried to appear on the program." The Lafayette Theatre itself, at 132nd Street and 7th Avenue, was a landmark in black dramatic achievement—the "best known colored playhouse in America."[49] Its all-black stock company, the Lafayette Players, put on dramatic productions in whiteface and comedy in burnt cork. White taste-makers like the Vanderbilts as well as white Broadway actors attended performances.[50] On the evening of May 10, then, the combination of a blockbuster lineup and the symbolic importance of the Lafayette Theatre locale made it the most significant theatrical "Race" response to the catastrophe and, as such, an event that would have attracted white New Yorkers as well. The *New York Amsterdam News* urged attendance: "The daily accounts of the appalling disaster which is overwhelming both white and colored people in the stricken areas have brought a realization of the absolute necessity of the colored residents of Harlem coming to the rescue of the countless number of their fellow men who are without food and shelter."[51] In the 132nd Street Theatre that night, then, was likely a mixed audience of Harlem professional and working classes, those born in the North as well as those emigrated from the South, as well as some white fans of black Vaudeville.[52]

The roster included Bill "Bojangles" Robinson, Noble Sissle and Eubie Blake, Ethel Waters, Wilbur Sweatman's Revue, Butter Beans and Susie, Marcia Marquez, the Cotton Club Revue, Connies Inn Revue, "Lucky Sambo," "Gay Harlem," and more.[53] Receiving top billing in the advertisement was the two-man comedy act "Miller & Lyles," major stars in their day who had become a crossover success on white Broadway (Figs. 5.4 and 5.5). Flournoy Miller and Aubrey Lyles got their start around 1905 at Chicago's black Pekin Theater, eventu-

5.4. (left) Flournoy E. Miller, 1923. From *Simms' Blue Book and National Negro Business and Professional Directory*, James N. Simms, compiler and publisher. Schomburg Center for Research in Black Culture, New York Public Library. New York Public Library/Art Resource, NY. 5.5. (right) Aubrey L. Lyles, 1923. From *Simms' Blue Book and National Negro Business and Professional Directory*, James N. Simms, compiler and publisher. Schomburg Center for Research in Black Culture, New York Public Library. New York Public Library/Art Resource, NY.

ally touring on the international Vaudeville circuit and entertaining hospitalized soldiers in war-torn London. Returning from Europe, they "heard that Moran and Mack was doing our act even to the comedy boxing," a theft that prompted them to invent new material.[54] They teamed up with Blake and Sissle in 1921 to put on the all-black Broadway hit *Shuffle Along*. Two years later, the pair starred in *Runnin' Wild*, the musical comedy that made the Charleston famous. In brief, they were the 1920s successors to the earlier big-time black comic duo Bert Williams and George Walker.[55] Given their presence at the Lafayette that night, their having grown up in Tennessee near the flood zone, and the fact of their later involvement in musicals that either explicitly or implicitly focused on the flood, Miller and Lyles provide a key source for thinking through how black verbal and physical artists with cross-over appeal communicated the meanings of the 1927 disaster.[56]

To reconstruct how Miller and Lyles would have responded to the news they had been reading in both white and black presses about the situation in the

Delta and how they would have transmuted this information into a comedic act, we need to understand their own history, and especially how they came to understand the group psychology of the color line, in both the South and North, through black performance. Both were raised in professional families in Tennessee and both graduated from Fisk University. Miller, whose father established the first black newspaper in Columbia, Tennessee, the *Nashville Globe*, recalled being seduced away from the "respectable" path his family had designed for him by the dazzling appearance of traveling minstrels. Miller's recollection, in particular, of one episode in turn-of-the-century minstrel history that occurred in the northern extremity of the Delta illustrates his complex sense of black performance as both an explosive stage "trap" and a "divine gift," a precarious force for change contending with a volatile white audience. Miller remembered how some southern whites' "jealousies were heightened when a colored minstrel show came to town. The parade was too much for them[:] the walking gents strutting proudly in their high hats, Prince Albert suits and walking canes." And the way black mistresses of white townsmen would have their eyes turned by the minstrels' fine form could produce serious "trouble for the whole troup [*sic*]." Only the striking up of "Dixie" by the band "change[d] the jeers to cheers."[57]

Miller recalled in particular one "tragedy" inside a theater in the Delta town of New Madrid, Missouri. It was sparked after a white boy had thrown mud at the "well tailored top coat" of the singer Louis Wright, "impeccably attired" and on his way to perform in the Richards and Pringle's Original Georgia Minstrel Show.[58] As one black journalist put it, this particular troupe "reign[ed] supreme in the South"[59] in the 1890s and were treated as "visiting royalty" by black communities wherever they traveled.[60] Wright reacted to this affront with a "spontaneous" curse word. During the show, "every number got tumultuous applause" from the audience.[61] At the time of the finale, though, white men in the audience started "throwing stone bricks and all sort of debris at the Minstrels," who were "trapped" onstage until one fired a revolver at the ceiling, making possible an escape for the troupe, still in their minstrel costumes. Later that night, all were brought to jail and "subjected to the South's special brand of interrogation for Negroes!" Wright was the last one called in for abuse. "An hour later, his uncovered body lay on top of a wagon, and all of the boys were forced to view it through the windows of their cells." Only the troupe's white manager tracking down the "decent white element of the town" secured the release of the rest of the minstrels. The sheriff's wife, outraged by his racist cowardice, shouted "hysterically": "You're not fit to be the father of our children. I'll never spend another night with you." When word of this made it across the Mississippi River to Miller's town, he recalled asking his father, "How could [the minstrels] continue on, following this call to make people happy, and receive so much unhappiness themselves"? His father "smiled sadly" and spoke of these performers' "divine gift." Miller felt that he, and his brother, "had been born with the same inexplicable calling, that regardless of the defeats, the heartbreak, the prejudices that we too later endured, for us, the 'show' was the thing."[62]

As his careful rendition of this scene in New Madrid attests, Miller was as much a mindful delineator of racial tragedy as he was a promulgator of Dixie burlesque. Indeed, for him, the two were inseparable. Miller saw his own work through the scrim of Wright's martyred body, poised as it was, onstage and off, between the "decent white element" and the "angry [white] mob," between the "show" as aesthetic and social good and the "trap" of performing blackness. Miller confirmed Jessie Fauset's 1925 observation that the "colored men who have gained a precarious footing on the stage [use comedy] to conceal the very real dolor raging in their breasts" and yet they somehow manage to communicate "a sort of cosmic gladness," a "superabundant vitality," therein performing a kind of "emotional salvation."[63]

Thus, despite the episode in New Madrid, Miller believed that "Negro personalities on the stage had made m[an]y friends for our race." He explained that "blackface was the bait to draw them in. Once on the inside they would enjoy our fine artist[ry]."[64] He saw white people as capable of both moral action and group savagery. In particular, he saw the southern white audience as a kind of eruptive act in itself: shifting in an instant from "jeers" to "cheers," and back again, from "applause" to violence. The black performers needed simultaneously to *be* the act while carefully monitoring the bigger racial performance that they could not control, except through a delicate playing upon an elusive white patronage system. By slight contrast, the northern audience craved race caricature but could be educated by fine art. That said, Miller explained, in 1926, the potential aesthetic damage all white audiences could inflict on black comic performance: "White people when they go to our plays want a certain amount of hokum, and we gave them hokum alright. . . . But once you begin to use hokum you begin to go down hill, artistically."[65] Contrary to earlier black performers who, as Daphne Brooks argues, produced an effect of Brechtian distanciation through the self-referentiality, opacity, and the exaggeration of these caricatures,[66] Miller sought new avenues toward an art-without-hokum. In the mid-1920s, balancing the popularity of racial self-burlesque against the desire to devise an original comic aesthetics, Miller and Lyles sought to raise capital to open a black theater on Broadway that would present them, as Miller put it, "not as mere cartoons of humanity but in a serious though sometimes a comedy spirit, as human beings created in the image of God." As Lyles put it, this theater would be for "a cosmopolitan audience," "presenting us as we are." Lyles concluded: "We have merely amused long enough."[67] Aesthetic originality and precision, racial revelation, and an audience open to both were the three ingredients simultaneously required for a transformative public black theater. Feeling the distorting force of a white love of "hokum" and the violent potential in the white crowd, devoted to developing an aesthetic form that would emerge from an honest comedic self-presentation, and raised near the Delta disaster zone, it seems likely that on May 10, playing to a cosmopolitan audience of both races, Miller and Lyles would have employed their comedy to do more than "merely amuse."

The routine that Miller and Lyles had developed since their early days at the Pekin Theater involved their assuming the identities of two men from Dixie, "Sam and Steve," constant verbal pugilists whose conflict often flared up into a dancing boxing bout (see Fig. 5.6).[68] Lyles's father had wanted him to be an orchestra leader devising an "expression of a race" "evolve[d]" from jazz and "syncopation,"[69] one in which anticipated rhythms could be creatively disturbed.[70] Though Lyles's music career never took off, the pair created what they called a "syncopated argument" as their signature routine. The back and forth between the interlocutors provides the base rhythm; the comedy enters in through the temporal, and epistemological, disruption in that exchange.[71]

The archive is silent on what Miller and Lyles performed on May 10, but my hunch is that the devastating flood in the Delta, combined with the outcry already resounding in the black press about racial discrimination and violence in the camps, would have made its way into their routine. Specifically, in the ten days leading up to May 10, a National Guardsman had fatally shot one black man in the Vicksburg camp and a mob had lynched another black man in Arkansas (an act denounced by Little Rock's white newspaper). Given that they typically located "Sam" and "Steve's" shenanigans in black Dixie, and given that they were onstage that night to entertain and, in entertaining, to "come to the rescue of . . . their fellow men," how might they have handled that complex imperative of producing a socially engaged—a mindful—kind of laughter? A typical sketch from the 1920s—the kind I suspect they performed at the Lafayette—was this one about Sam working in a dynamite factory. This sketch in particular may have seemed to them a particularly germane routine to stage during a benefit event for those living in Red Cross concentration camps. The skit considers the precarious position of industrial laborers in high-risk situations and the abuses of employers who make workers pay for injuries sustained on the job. What with the explosive bursting of industrial-scale levees in the Delta—

5.6. Publicity photograph of Vaudeville comedy duo Miller and Lyles, performing their prizefighting routine, ca. 1910. Schomburg Center for Research in Black Culture, New York Public Library. New York Public Library/Art Resource, NY.

the cause of most black deaths during the flood—the connections between two highly precarious modern labor scenarios would have presumably been evident to audience members. The back and forth went as follows:

> STEVE: "Ain't you got no better sense than to work where all that powder
>   is?"
> SAM: "Takes a smart man to work in a dynamite factory."
> STEVE: "Then you ain't the man, 'cause if ignorance was a alley, you'd be
>   a boulevard."
> SAM: "What do you know about dynamite?"
> STEVE: ". . . I know enough about it to let it alone. . . ."

[Sam explains that he made $10 a week in salary.]

> STEVE: "Ten dollars a week! That ain't no salary. That's wages."
> SAM: "Well, I got it for ten weeks."
> STEVE: "Didn't your boss raise you?"
> SAM: "Boss didn't have to. The dynamite did. Raised me 'bout a 1000 feet."
>
> . . . .
>
> STEVE: "Didn't nobody try to catch ya'?"
> SAM: "Nobody but Mother Earth."
> STEVE: "Mother Earth, huh? Well, I guess you collected for damages then didn't ya?"
> SAM: "I didn't collect for damages, but I collected many damages."
> STEVE: "Well then how much money did you get?"
> SAM: "Didn't get none."
> STEVE: "None?"
> SAM: "No. My boss even docked me for time out in the air I wasn't workin'."
> STEVE: "He's some mean boss."
> SAM: "Yeah, I hate him. I wish I had a thousand graveyards and he was buried in all of them."

In this scene set in "Jimtown," Sam moves from fulfilling expectations about southern Negro "ignorance" to gradually placing ironic quotes around his own talking cartoon as he partakes in wordplay with his puns on the words "raise" and "damages." It is on these puns that the syncopation, or unexpected stress, occurs.[72] Behind these puns, and this dialogue about low wages, long hours, hazardous working conditions, and employer chicanery, is an oblique critique of abusive labor relations. Its fantastic hyperbole—as it imagines a man soaring up and falling one thousand feet, and another man, in perfect compensation, buried in a thousand graveyards—turns on a fantasy of white abuse and black revenge. Sam's play on the blackface cartoon of "ignorance," his punning, and his visual hyperbole sublimate this scene of abuse and revenge into a syncopated art form. For the audience at the Lafayette Theatre, presumably there was a pleasure in watching the derogatory cartoon be undermined by the artistry of the black performance itself.

Another sketch, one they were working on at this point in 1927, was called "Evolution." Its putative humor stems from Sam not understanding Steve as Steve tries to explain to him about Darwinian theory. Sam keeps mishearing words: the word "forefathers" brings up the impossibility of a man having "four fathers." "Ancestors" gets confused for "aunt's sisters." Sam keeps answering Steve's questions about "*what* did you come from?" as if he's asking "where?": "I come from Georgia. . . . Right out of the cotton fields of Georgia." Sam is all mired in a plantation-circumscribed reality, characterized by cotton fields, a history of sabotaged black paternity (multiple fathers) that results in matrilinearity (kinship defined by the female), and racist epithets of "smokes" and "monkies." So he cannot catch on to the "revolution" in human thinking about origins, one that potentially empties out the category of race, and the exceptionality of the human species, in one stroke.[73] Staged two years after the Scopes "Monkey" Trial took place in Miller and Lyles's home state of Tennessee, in which the South was pilloried for its fundamentalist retreat from modern knowledge, the sting of the routine derives from turning the racist accusation of monkey kinship into a "new style of revolution," one that means that *every* "man comes from a monkey."[74] If the burnt cork that Miller and Lyles applied implicated them in just such a racist circus of "smokes" and clowns, it was, on the other hand, in the substance of their routines that we see the subtle interpolations of and commentary upon contemporary conflicts over labor, racial origins, and intelligence. For black audience members at the Lafayette, who were used to seeing serious drama played in whiteface and comedy in blackface and who, as residents of the northern black metropole, might have been inclined, too, to laugh at caricatures of the impoverished country bumpkin in order to inoculate themselves from just such a stereotype, Miller and Lyles's routine would have provided an encounter with this process of intraracial and cross-regional reckoning. It might also have recapitulated their own daily performance of blackness outside their communities, as intelligence artfully struggled against caricature.

Two months later, on July 12, "Steve" and "Sam" appeared at the Royale Theatre on 45th Street, just west of Broadway, as the comedic stars of a new musical called *Rang Tang* (Fig. 5.7). Between their Lafayette appearance and this one at the Royale, an even more extensive airing in the black press of the flood "debacle" had taken place. Because we know exactly what their lines were on July 12, this musical provides a final, and more concrete, opportunity to watch Miller and Lyles stage their brand of flood comedy. Moreover, because the comedy was put on for a majority white audience, it allows us to see how the African American critique of the flood, mainly limited to the black press, might have "gone public" on Broadway. In the scene that virtually all reviewers of *Rang Tang* singled out for its excellence, Sam and Steve find themselves adrift on a small, downed aircraft somewhere in the middle of the Atlantic Ocean. The object in which the two men sat on the middle of the stage must have been an extravagant pasteboard stand-in for the real machine; one reviewer called the prop a "burlesque airplane,"[75] and another noted that the scenery appeared to be the "work of some delirious Gauguin suddenly gone Ziegfeld."[76] This scene was quite topical, for just six weeks before, on May 21, Lindbergh had made his historic crossing from New York to Paris. On the stage at the Royale, Steve and Sam, sitting in their "burlesque" sea-stranded plane, take in the landless world that surrounds them:

STEVE: "They sure is a whole lot of water in the ocean, ain't it?"
SAM: "They sure is."
STEVE: "Water, water, water. Everywhere you look, you don't see nothin' but water."
SAM: "That's all."
STEVE: "I never seen so much water before in *all* my life."
SAM: "This is the first time I've ever seen anything that there was enough of."

And then the pair commence, as one critic put it, a "fretfull bickering against fate and their own enforced companionship in that unending dialogue that belongs to this embittered pair."[77]

STEVE: "I know you didn' know nothin' about runnin' no airplane. I know that."
SAM: "I *started* it, didn' I?"
STEVE: "You always startin' somethin' you can't stop."
STEVE: "Well . . . didn' it stop?"
SAM: "Look where it stopped!"
[pause]
STEVE: "I know my mistake and you was it."
SAM: "*I* was it?"
STEVE: "Yes sir, you was my mistake. Mr. Lindbergh was smart. He went alone."

Ba-boom. Finally, the two start to reckon with the possibility of their deaths.

STEVE: "Sam?"
SAM: "Yeah?"
STEVE: "I don't think we're going to be able to hold out much longer."
SAM: "I knows we ain't."
STEVE: "I feel like we gwanna drown too."
SAM: "Me too."[78]

5.7. Al Hirschfeld, *Rang Tang, 1927*. Printed in the *Morning Telegraph*, July 24, 1927, 1. © The Al Hirschfeld Foundation. www.AlHirschfeld Foundation.org.

"Final confessions" then ensue, made comedic because what is revealed, yet again, is each man's rascally self-interestedness.

One way to read this dialogue, and its appeal on Broadway in 1927, is as a burlesque of black history and of black modernity. If Lindbergh's solo flight across the Atlantic, one month before, signified a technological maturity of Nordic America, the crash landing of the "Lost Aviators" seems to merely recapitulate, in a self-mocking way, that Africans could never be modern, technologically apt, conquistadors of the Atlantic. We could read the scene then as a clownish version of the critical statement made by the black satirist George Schuyler in a *Nation* article just that March, in which he said: "You have long looked upon the black citizen as a tragic figure—a pathetic figure—a helpless transplanted child of the jungle caught by the cruel meshes of machine civilization."[79] Miller and Lyles seem to fulfill this judgment of mental ineptitude before "machine civilization" as they drift in the Atlantic calling out "Help! Help!" spoofing the very idea of black men becoming Lindberghs. In making the near-drowning of black bodies in the middle of the Atlantic Ocean the stuff of laughter, moreover, the pair could also be accused of desecrating the memorial space of the Middle Passage and of the Atlantic as a contemporaneous vector for pan-African solidarity.

Called "Lost Aviators" when it was recorded onto vinyl in 1928, the scene's original stage title was "Adrift," a title that places the emphasis less on the failed flight and more on the condition of losing oneself within precarious water-borne motion. A few days before the performance of "Adrift," a journalist writing for the *New York Amsterdam News* called the African American refugees caught in the "stricken southland" a "floating population," whose future is "most uncertain." Another black journalist, writing in the *Southern Workman*, worried about the "general mass of the floating population," who might be "exploited," "scattered," or "left to drift," eventually becoming a "menace to themselves."[80] Though these journalists' concerns were enclaved within the black counterpublic, Miller and Lyles, in front of a large, and largely white, Broadway audience, could, as they said, make "friends for [their] race" by turning this "floating population"—invisible to New Yorkers—into a visible, embodied quandary.

Perhaps the "real dolor" of this castaway scene, connected as it was to a population "floating" in the "stricken southland" or, long before that, drowning in the middle of the Atlantic, was not *utterly* concealed. Perhaps, by revealing themselves to be "genuine showmen," to be verbally, temporally, and physically virtuosic comedic artists, they could show up Sam and Steve's incompetence as mere hokum. As Daphne Brooks has argued of the earlier black comic duo Williams and Walker, we could say that Miller and Lyles "critically defamiliariz[ed] their own bodies by way of performance in order to yield alternative racial . . . epistemologies."[81] George Schuyler had gone on in his essay to argue that it was the Anglo-Saxons who were made truly primitive by their worship of racial idols and the "Aframericans," especially those with "a developed sense of humor," who were the real sophisticates.[82] The complexity of Miller and Lyles's performance is that their sophistication emerges as they both burlesque Anglo-Saxon idols of primitivism while simultaneously placing before their audience the real dolors of drifting on the Mississippi, of being adrift in a concentration camp, or being afloat and near death in the middle of the Atlantic Ocean. When Paul Gilroy invented the concept of the Black Atlantic, he wrote that the time was overdue for "the primal history of modernity to be reconstructed from the slaves' points of view."[83] Miller and Lyles, by evoking, in the tableau of their downed and drifting airplane, the Middle Passage, the flooding Mississippi, and modern transatlantic aviation, are prodding their audience to do just what Gilroy suggests: to imagine technological modernity from the perspective of those whose bodies have absorbed its dangers, its risks, and its displacements even while initially igniting its engine. Miller and Lyles used syncopation, a surprising rhythm shift, to interrupt flows of public thought. And, as they generated puns, words acted less like the denotative pointers of Reason and more like a playful arena of reversals and reinventions. We can see "Adrift" as conveying a knowledge of Dixie disaster—and of Black Atlantic history—not readily available in newspapers. Zora Neale Hurston saw precisely this potential in black flood comedy, for, in her flood novel of 1937, *Their Eyes Were Watching God*, it is in the comedic back and forth, or, the "thought pictures," of two "mule-talkers," Sam and Lige, that a prophecy about Nature's cataclysmic potential is entertained.[84]

The Cherokee Cowboy Humorist

Eight days before the Lafayette benefit, and about sixty blocks south, white New Yorkers were witnessing another blockbuster Vaudeville lineup at the Ziegfeld Theater to raise money for Mississippi flood victims. On May 2, the day of the benefit, levees were just beginning to fail in Louisiana. The benefit's headliner was a man who might fairly be considered the most popular man in the entire country at that time, at least until Lindbergh's transatlantic flight a month later.[85] He was, in the words of one cultural historian, "one of the most important molders of opinion in America from 1922 until his untimely death in 1935."[86] To another, he was "the Cherokee voice of America."[87] And another remarks that this entertainer "comes nearer being a *Jogleur de Dieu* than any other world personage," a reference to St. Francis's mirthful spiritual power.[88] Rogers raised more money for the American Red Cross than any other single nongovernmental individual in 1927.[89] Telegrams were sent to Rogers by Red Cross leaders attesting that "You Have Done More than Any One Else in the United States Except Hoover . . . to Bring to Attention American People the Need and Distress Occasioned by the Flood."[90] Rogers raised $20,000 that night as he offered his mixed repertoire of fancy rope tricks, gum-chewing, and humorous political commentary (see Fig 5.8). His was the climactic act anticipated by two hundred other performers in the revue. We know that in his routine that night, Rogers "spoofed" the American penchant for seeing Europe "without seeing this country first" and detailed his visit with the Italian Fascist dictator Benito Mussolini.[91] What he said about the flood itself was not recorded. Clearly the ethics of nationalism was on his mind. But how it achieved a particular shape in response to the current American catastrophe is something we must surmise from his copious print journalistic responses to the flood.

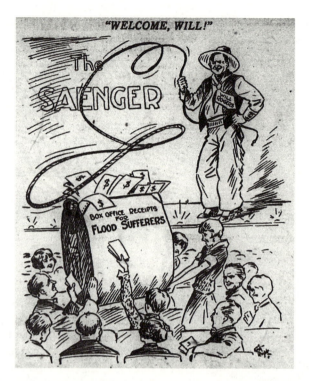

5.8. Advertisement for Will Rogers June 1 flood benefit at the Saenger Theater, New Orleans, in the *Times-Picayune*, June 1, 1927, 10. The Times-Picayune/Landov.

Will Rogers's own inheritance of southernness was a portrait-in-miniature of the nation's conflicts. His father was a prosperous rancher of Cherokee and Scots-Irish descent in Indian Territory (later Oklahoma) who had been part of a hierarchical, slaveholding culture, who fought at the rank of captain with his own regiment for the Confederacy, who was a delegate to the Cherokee Confederate Convention of 1862, and who served four terms in the Cherokee senate beginning in 1879.[92] Rogers the son hated Andrew Jackson for the Indian Removal Act of 1832 and other crimes against his indigenous Georgia ancestors[93] and professed that "there's nothing of which I am more proud than my Cherokee blood."[94] One of the ways he navigated his ancestry and its place in national history was to broker a bodily accord between cowboy and Indian with his fancy roping act as he capitalized on the public's nostalgia for an open frontier. The other was to dramatically appropriate—and hence differentiate himself from—"black" culture, much as Eric Lott describes working-class northern whites doing in antebellum days.[95] As Rogers put it, both mockingly and self-mockingly, in his memoir: "I wasent only raised among Darkies down in the Indian Territory, but I was raised by them," a phrase that addresses the issue of his Indian ancestry in an oddly ambivalent way (was that "I" a "Darkie" as well?) and that marks his affluent Cherokee family's status *above* the African American servants in their household. And yet he spoofs the concept, or fetish, of "whiteness" by associating the category with animal husbandry. He claims that he hadn't been exposed to it until "a white [child] showed up about the same time that Hereford cattle came in. I thought this white child and this bald-faced Hereford was the same breed," a joke that introduces whiteness as an interspecies oddity. The white child/cow is a hybrid "breed," while Rogers, the Anglo-Irish Cherokee, is an "I" somewhat removed from all this racial branding. Not only would he apply burnt cork to his face in films in later years with Bill Robinson, whose tap-dancing he would try to mimic, but as a young man, he began to craft a stage presence by trying on various "black" personae: singing Bert Williams-esque "coon songs"; "putting on white gloves, a swallow-tailed coat, and glasses, blackening his face and imitating a black preacher"; and studying the craft of a talented black roper on his father's ranch, Dan Walker, all the while arguing "with much heat and no humor," as a classmate remembered, that "the two races were wholly different in origin, ideals, characteristics and possibilities."[96]

He toured with Texas Jack's Wild West Show & Circus in South Africa as the "Cherokee Kid" but alternated between playing an Indian and a Black American. He would go on to develop his Vaudeville following as a fancy Cowboy roper among the other "dumb" (or spectacular physical) acts. As his routine evolved, he began to do the thing that made him world famous, which was *to talk* and, specifically, to comment satirically upon the news of the day. From thence forward, his voice became increasingly omnipresent with the American public (see Figs. 5.9 and 5.10). People saw in him someone with an unparalleled ability "to get at the very heart and nub of the matter and split it open with a laugh," to be a "puncturer of self-made balloons," or, as Franklin Roosevelt put it, Rogers, "while seeing facts, could always laugh at fantasy."[97] Rogers could indeed "split . . . open," "puncture," and "laugh at" many aspects of American, and international, politics, history, and culture without ever alienating the public, but he also (despite Roosevelt's comment) embodied and performed a "fantasy" of national concordance. Whether he learned it from southern elite or Cherokee leadership culture, or the Indian Territory's historical combination of the two, Rogers cultivated his prestige specifically as a power to bestow public

5.9. Will Rogers. Courtesy of Will Rogers Memorial Museum.

5.10. Will Rogers. Courtesy of Will Rogers Memorial Museum.

gifts (of humor, of attention, of money) within a hierarchical structure. In Rogers's racial hierarchy, the Indian and the European, and all mixtures thereof, were equally on top while the African American stood on a lower rung.[98]

On issues of Indian history and land—again through a combination of southern and indigenous environmentalism—he was the most critical. He could, for example, not only embody "the frontier" in his acts but also deliver, in one of his radio shows during the 1930s Dust Bowl crisis, a trenchant analysis of the exploitation endemic to a resource frontier: "I think if we just stopped and looked at history in the face, the pioneer wasn't a thing in the world but a guy that wanted something for nothing . . . wanted to live off of everything that nature had done. . . . we're just now learning, you know, that we can rob from nature the same way as we can rob from an individual."[99] In the winter leading up to the Mississippi flood, he castigated the practice of monoculture farming. Referring to any farmer stupid enough to continue planting cotton, corn, or wheat exclusively, "we should," according to Rogers, "take a hammer and hit him twice right between the eyes."[100] Along with the shibboleths of the frontier and the plantation, Rogers took on another iconic American idea: the Pilgrim. In another 1930s radio show, he wondered: "I am sure that it was only the extreme generosity of the Indians that allowed the Pilgrims to land. Suppose we reversed the case. Do you think the Pilgrims would have ever let the Indians land? Yeah, What a chance! What a chance! The Pilgrims wouldn't even allow the Indians to live after the Indians went to the trouble of letting 'em land."[101] And: the Pilgrims "were very religious people that came over here from the old country. They were very human. They would shoot a couple of Indians on the way to every prayer meeting."[102]

In 1927, Rogers was already an international celebrity. He had figured out how to contour his appeal to every medium: the Vaudeville circuit, radio broadcasts, "Daily Telegrams" syndicated to over four hundred papers, weekly articles, books of wit, lecture tours, and motion pictures. As his biographer has put it, by 1925, "Rogers had been disseminated to the country at large by every currently available mechanical means."[103] Rogers not only understood, as had Lippmann and Dewey, that, as he said, "We are living in an age of publicity," but knew how to project his publicity as familiarity and immediacy. Much like Benjamin Franklin, Rogers used the media technologies to manufacture himself as a public personality all the while satirizing the ways in which reality, desire, and subjectivity are themselves media fabrications.

Before the New York benefit, Rogers toured the refugee camps with the Louisiana flood "dictator" and Delta plantation powerhouse John Parker[104] and flew with a Navy Flier "for hundreds of miles over nothing but a sea of water and housetops." He wrote in his syndicated weekly article: "If you have never seen a flood you don't know what horror is."[105] And, "I don't really believe that 80 or 90 per cent of the people realize just what flood disaster means, and what type of people it is that lost most by this particular horror," namely, "the poorest class of people in this country . . . the renter farmer," or share-cropper. "He is in debt from one crop to the other to the storekeeper or the little local bank." He admonished his readers: "City people don't realize the poverty of poor country folks." So that they can see that poverty up close, he prompts: "Look at the thousands and thousands of negroes that never did have much, but now [it's] washed away. You don't want to forget that water is just as high up on them as it is if they were white. The Lord so constituted everybody that no matter what color you are you require about the same amount of nourishment."[106]

Elsewhere he turned this commentary on what "city people don't realize" to a critique of how the media produce public desire for certain narratives at the expense of others: "There's hundreds of thousands of people being driven from their homes. . . . yet Mrs. Snyder's picture has occupied more space in the papers than the whole of Mississippi fighting for its life. / There is more heart interest in one housetop with its little family floating down the river on it than all the corset salesmen in the world."[107] Rogers was referring here, in this *Washington Post* piece, to the murder trial of Queens housewife Ruth Snyder and her accomplice, the so-called corset salesman, Judd Gray, in the strangling death of her husband, the scenario upon which *Double Indemnity* was based. Rogers further diagnosed what he saw as the excessive coverage of that trial by saying: "No, sir, you can't blame that on the Public. It's the papers that causes all interest in these things like this. If it wasent in the papers for you to read you wouldent know or care anything about it."[108] In the *New York Times*, he put it more succinctly: "The camera has made more criminals than bad environment."[109] Rogers is expressing what many believed to be a regrettable turn of the popular media toward manufacturing "sensationalism" under the pretense of providing the public with forensic exposure. As the media broadcast the most lurid scenes of private life, it embodied the public as one in its predatory fascination and enervated responses.

He criticized the misdirection of popular attention not only toward the lurid but also toward distressed nations beyond U.S. borders. Why should Poland, Russia, and Armenia receive our aid, while sharecroppers in our own country none? Of Rogers's appeal to give to flood sufferers "even if they aren't Armenians but only Americans," the *Los Angeles Times* praised the comment for having "the lash and sting of great satire."[110] Rogers summed up his message: "Now we have the greatest chance to help our own that has ever been given us. . . . Give it to them. Never mind . . . Old Lady Snyder and Corsets. One little Coon saved down on the Mississippi is worth more to America than both of them if they lived 100 years."[111] Rogers's inclusive populism is here running up against his own nationalist and paternalist racial hierarchy. On the one hand, he articulates a kind of radical Christian leveling of human value: the Lord "constituted everybody" alike in terms of needs and vulnerability. "Everybody" requires food and shelter, and has a legitimate claim to care. Attention to those in need is a higher and nobler national calling than attention to those who commit private outrages (Mrs. Snyder and her lover Judd Gray) and even to those fellow humans in distant lands who are vulnerable (Poles, Armenians, etc.). He tries to educate whites on the race-blindness of disaster, on a more significant material life than that based on skin color, but then partly undoes that work by offering an almost collectible miniature charity mascot or sentimental fetish— "One little Coon"—in return for white donations. Rogers communicated concern for all sharecroppers' economic and physical precarity but no acknowledgment of the "trap" of blackness as enforced performance and environmental liability.

Given the tenor of his printed remarks, Rogers, in his May 2 Ziegfeld benefit, likely sought to popularize a particularly paternal but also southern environmentalist reading of the flood to his northeastern audience. Like Miller and Lyles, he first drew people in by playing the affable fool. As a *New York Times* reviewer wrote of Rogers's characteristic Ziegfeld tactic:

> When Will Rogers comes on stage at the Follies, with his jaw full of chewing gum and his arms loaded with ropes, he makes you feel sorry for him. You know he is going to get tangled up in the ropes or lose a stroke of his gum. . . . You know you could do it better than he. When he begins to make the ropes writhe like snakes and strike the bullseye again and again with his quaint, homely wit, you are as proud of him as if you had done it yourself. But those seemingly offhand remarks of his are neatly timed to coincide with some spectacular stunt with the ropes. . . . [Later] you realize two things: he put it over in the only language and intonation possible, and he said something keen and penetrating and true. All in the name of gawky, innocent, country-jake, amateurishness. . . . He is an expert satirist masquerading as a helpless, inoffensive, ineffectual zany.[112]

Like Miller and Lyles, he feigns the "country-jake" clown until the temporal art of humor gives a lie to that embodiment. Apparent amateurs are revealed to be experts, and primitives are shown to be sophisticates. For Miller and Lyles, the timing comes in the unexpected stress in the rebuttal, in the syncopated argument; for Rogers, the art is in the precisely timed coincidence of rope and word, of instrument and voice. Seeing him always on the edge of mishap, the audience takes his part, and as it does, digests his commentary.

On May 2, Rogers was at the Ziegfeld Theater to entertain and to make philanthropic gifts flow. As he executed some "spectacular stunt," he perhaps brought his listeners around to the southern states' downriver point of view, by making an accessible analogy: "Even a town where people live on top of a hill they are not allowed to just throw everything out of their doors and let it roll down the hill on to the people that live at the bottom on the level ground." He might have visualized the water flowing over the Delta as the refuse of a broad, national watershed, as "SEWERAGE from Chicago, Kansas City, [and] St. Louis."[113] He may have lampooned Congress's inevitable inability to get beyond talk to formulate constructive policy: "Some will suggest moving the river over in to some other Senator's state." He might have told his audience that the levees-only approach was structurally bankrupt and that new watershed management was "the biggest thing before the country today," but he would have leavened this policy lecture with the aside that to afford the river intervention we'd "have to cut down on ammunition expenditures in Nicaragua and China. But it looks like saving and protecting some of our own is better than trying to shoot somebody else, especially when we have to go so far to get to shoot at 'em."[114] Rogers, like the Vaudevillians stranded in the Delta discussed at the beginning of the chapter, had "first-hand knowledge" of the flood: he had toured camps on foot and achieved an aerial sense of the expanse of devastation; he had spoken with both levee engineers and southern farmers. He understood the environmental justice issues for the South as a region and the economic and physical issues for sharecropper evacuees. His means of rousing national engagement with the catastrophe was through the idea of "protecting our own," with the sense of both obligation and hierarchy that such a phrase suggests. Though he was, in the words of one historian, a "stealth minority with access to a forum," his understanding of Indian dispossession as historically produced did not extend to his conception of African American disadvantage, a blind spot that left him with limited means to critique the current mediatized visibility of black Americans.[115] Given his benign rendition in print of his encounter with Mussolini[116] and his appeal that night for Americans to put their own country first, Rogers likely roused sympathy at the Ziegfeld for the South's regional grievance by appealing to nationalist solidarity; having northerners imagine the South dwelling "at the bottom of the hill" called forth the imaginary space and the affective obligation of a national neighborhood. It also had the effect of "reducing massive, abstract threats in politics and society to manageable proportions."[117]

* * *

That Rogers was ultimately taken to be an expert barometer—and shaper—of public opinion was borne out in the fact that he was called to testify before the congressional subcommittee on flood prevention policy in January 1928. As discussed in chapter 3, the fact that an entertainer was given such intimate access to the levers of legislative action signified to the editor at the *Afro-American* that "the United States is run by propaganda."[118] The editor's concern was that as long as any lobby on a given side of an issue had the money to hire a popular entertainer to represent their position winningly, that lobby would hold sway. And it is certainly true that the major economic players of the Delta—like cotton planter John Parker, who gave Rogers his tour of the flood zone—stood to gain from having the economic burden of flood control shift wholly to the federal government. In other words, the position a popular entertainer espouses is not automatically the people's will. And yet Rogers's commentary on the flood and his vision of social obligation engaged much more with the "horror" of the situation than did virtually all popular messaging disseminated by the Red Cross or Hoover through the mainstream press. He chided the nation for allowing itself to have its attention directed by a sensationalist media and urged the country to think of the actual bodies of the "poorest class" of rural laborer at a time when the suffering of African American flood victims was virtually invisible in the national press. Though he used racial condescension to engender the nation's protectiveness—and to manage his own multiracial lineage—he yet had a vision for a participatory disaster citizenship.

Rogers's power to influence, and to ventriloquize, the vox populi was considerable. He could propagate his own opinion through multiple channels. Power, like Lippmann said, is theatrical; politicians can influence the public through "illusion." But what Lippmann left out of his appraisal is the flip side of this idea, namely, that the theater itself is powerful in its own right and constitutes a legitimate arena of communication. Vaudeville, by offering places of live public convergences, and by arranging a mass of performers into one variegated "bill," also enacted rites of pleasurable "stranger-sociability." The plurality could be held together and be in happy physical unison for a night. Moreover, this motley assemblage could stand in for a nation galvanized into coherence by catastrophe. Here was a group brought together not merely to "frolic" but to "frolic" for the good of others. Pleasure felt was also a gift given. What some of Vaudeville's entertainers understood was that within pleasure could also come understanding. As Walter Benjamin put it in a 1930 Berlin radio address, "Prescriptions for Comedy Writers": when a society is "deluding" itself, the comedy writer must "point the way" while making everything "enjoyable"; the comedy writer's "great consolation," he added, is that "the audience takes its castigation as entertainment."[119] And more castigation is possible because, in a comic artist's hands, it will entertain. By their carefully timed deployments of language, these comedians did not make audience members the object of their ridicule as much as subjects partaking in their knowledge. The knowledge Rogers wanted to communicate involved the social obligations that living together in a watershed, or a nation, demanded. Miller and Lyles sought to subtly undermine the "hokum" of minstrelsy and with it a delusionary picture of a contented Dixie. To quote Lippmann once more: "All the world" was, in many ways, "a vaudeville stage" in 1927. At times, that was a very good thing.

MODERNISM WITHIN
A SECOND NATURE

By the summer of 1927, the Great Flood had largely subsided as a suspenseful mass news phenomenon. Once the flood was, for the general public, "relegated to that hazy limbo peopled by the heroes and villains of old murder trials, popular favorites fallen from grace, and the rest of the great newspaper sensations,"[1] it began to take on a new print life as literature. The flood provided the materials for nonfiction books, autobiographies, poetry, short stories, novellas, and novels in the years between 1927 and World War II. In the wake of the New Orleans levee disaster in 2005 and rising ocean levels, the Great Flood once again has generated novelistic treatment, such as Bill Cheng's *Southern Cross the Dog* and Tom Franklin and Beth Ann Fennelly's *The Tilted World*, both published in 2013. After a brief survey of the literary (and radio narrative) remediation of the flood in the few years immediately following the disaster, I turn in the final chapters to its two most significant literary chroniclers. The representational possibilities and tactics of modernism helped William Faulkner and Richard Wright transform this flood into enduring world literature. And, to flip that statement around, Wright and Faulkner used their unique position, surrounded by rural modernization and Jim Crow, to bring inside the horizon of modernism the emergent global condition of life within a catastrophe-prone "second nature." Wright and Faulkner communicated that a rural environment could be thoroughly fabricated by humans, and fabricated in such a way as to intensify its inherent risks, so that these environments could become—indeed, had become—as political and modern and violent a product as a machine gun or a tank.

In October 1927, Lyle Saxon published a partly fictionalized, partly reportorial "scrapbook" of the river's history, *Father Mississippi*, which culminated in an account of the flood drawn from his summertime *Century Magazine* pieces. Saxon was a *New Orleans Times-Picayune* reporter, self-styled scion of a Louisiana sugar plantation, and short story writer, living in Greenwich Village when the disaster began. He got himself down to the Delta in May and participated in rescue work with the Coast Guard. Nobody then publishing journalistic pieces on the flood, in Saxon's opinion, was "able to get it wet enough or muddy enough to please me"; hopefully his southerner's firsthand account could remedy that.[2] In one "episode," he and one other white man, a civil engineer, spend a night "shelterless" on a levee with a group of African Americans who are "adrift." While his companion claims that "the negroes" "don't mind" the trouble because "they're used to adversity," Saxon disagrees, recording the lamentations of a woman in childbirth (who names her baby "Refugee") and the "moans" that follow the death of an old man, "his head pillowed in the lap of a woman, almost equally old"; and he makes plangent the repeated searching of a young black man for his wife, whom only we know has already drowned in a building collapse. The reader sits vigil with this community, and is asked to taste and see, up close, black charity to white in the form of the sweet "crumbling loaf handed me by black fingers."[3]

Throughout these chapters, moreover, Saxon fashions a new geopolitical "unit," "the Mississippi Valley, a third of the United States," not connected by growing seasons as was the Confederacy, but by its vulnerability to the river and its federal mishandling. This unit speaks as one in its critique of deforestation, drainage, and the levees-only policy, about which he quotes Gifford Pinchot denouncing the policy as the "most colossal blunder in civilized history." Though Saxon judged some of the earlier chapters in his book "moronic,"[4] given his rush to concoct a full-length volume in a number of weeks, the later chapters of *Father Mississippi* were important in representing black distress and resourcefulness with dignity, and in drawing the Deep South into a new north-south geographic imaginary—the Valley—whose own experts were rethinking the modern management of nature. If the collective ideas produced by the Mississippi Valley were heeded, this could be, Saxon said as he invoked H. G. Wells and others on the Great War, the "flood to end floods." His book was also important, we shall soon see, as a resource for William Faulkner.[5]

In the early 1930s, before the Dust Bowl became the key socioenvironmental index of "folk" experience in the liberal imagination, the 1927 disaster was constituted as a landmark—pun intended—of that experience. People became "folk" by being steeped in one particular locale, so the flood was understood as a kind of biocultural authentication of the laborers whose lives it marked.[6] Folklore collector Benjamin Botkin published three volumes of *Folk-Say: A Regional Miscellany* between 1929 and 1931. This *Miscellany* was a key venue for the memorialization of the flood as an event that simultaneously naturalized and culturally valorized "the folk." In its second volume, the African American poet Sterling A. Brown contributed his poem "Ma Rainey" to the section titled "Wide River." Brown was born in the nation's capital, educated at Williams College and Harvard University, and, in 1930, was teaching at Howard University. Other than a few years teaching at a college in Lynchburg, Virginia, he lived in the North. In stanza three of the poem, Rainey—Bessie Smith's early mentor—is singing "Back-Water Blues." Brown has a few stanzas of Smith's song displace his own, after which he records the audience's reactions: "de folks, dey natchally bowed dey heads an' cried" for "She jes gits hold of us, dataway."[7]

Later in the volume, in a section titled "Genres and Media," Brown contributed an essay, "The Blues as Folk Poetry," which was a brief for the blues, produced by a people "living a life close to the earth," to be considered as part of the lyric tradition. Regretting that the blues "are sung on Broadway in nearly unrecognizable disguises" and have been disseminated so far and wide through radio, phonographs, and Vaudeville that "it is becoming more and more difficult to tell which songs are truly folk" and which are "cabaret appetizers," Brown sets out to recover the indigenous elements of the genre. After cataloguing various blues concerns (love loss, incarceration, railroad escape), Brown gets to the category of "sorry tricks played upon these folks by Nature" and especially "the 1927 disaster." He singles out Bessie Smith's "Back-Water Blues" for "authenticity of folk utterance" and for presenting not a "bookish dressing up and sentimentalizing" but instead "the thing seen." Because the very definition of "folk," for Brown, is dependent on "living a life close to the earth," a life that involves experiencing Nature's "tricks" directly, Brown roots "authentic" expression in environmental disaster. What he ignores in doing so is how these "tricks" themselves have been intensified by industrialism, a fact that makes "folk" experience more modern and more affected by distant factors like global capitalism than he discusses. Moreover, he ignores how much Smith herself is a product not only of lowland Chattanooga, but also of the Vaudeville circuit, big cities, and technologies of mass dissemination, facts that make her "utterance[s]" highly mediated by modern mass forms.[8]

What defined "American Folk"—according to an entry by Mary Austin in the same 1930 *Folk-Say* volume—was: "To be shaped in mind and social reaction, and to some extent in character, and so finally in expression, by one given environment, that is to be Folk." This "profound saturation" by one environment whose "pattern and meaning they understand," Austin argues, makes for a "profounder spiritual integrity than is usually found among sophisticates, who are exposed to all the cross-currents of thinking in an amazingly muddled world"; such cosmopolitan sophisticates succeed in "button-pushing mechanisms" but not in "art."[9] And as J. Frank Dobie put it a few pages later, "The folk . . . are those people who have some of the soil of the[ir] region still clinging to their feet, who have not become so standardized."[10]

Brown subscribes to a similar dichotomy between "muddled," "standardized" "sophisticates" and "authentic" "folk," and likewise tries to mend his own sophistication through such "folk." There is not exactly a "spiritual integrity" here; rather, the local spirits of place scour away at received religion. In "Children of the Mississippi," a poem included in his 1932 collection, *Southern Road*, knowledge accrues to folk as they live close to the earth. His poem's folk are indeed, as Austin describes, "profoundly saturated" by their environment: "Blackwater" creeps into their sight, laughter, knowledge, and memory. Their experience with "fear," "grief," "death," and "doubt" forms a "strong undertow" beneath "their dark laughter / Roaring like a flood roars." Their sense "memories" are themselves "dank . . . bracken as the waters." While this saturation ensures accurate seeing and foreknowledge, it does not guarantee a "spiritual integrity." Rather, experience produces doubt, and an awareness of the slippage between biblical narrative and actual history: "These know no Ararat; / No arc of promise bedecking blue skies; / No dove, betokening calm." As his folk speakers say: "*De Lord tole Norah* [Noah] / *Dat de flood was due . . . Wish dat de Lord / Had tole us too.*"[11] If "*De Lord*" is absent, "slow-footed Fate" manages to creep in. Indeed, the "Blackwater" *is* their "Fate" and the Lord of Noah too distant for conversing. Spirituality here is made of the deities, and necessities, of local biology.[12]

One sees a similar rendition of local nature as a hieratic Fate in another piece of flood literature, "Ole Miss," a short story by white Mississippi author Ruth Bass included in the third volume of *Folk-Say*. The story takes place amid the "folk of Charmont Bottom," "high-brown mulattoes [who] owned their own land" on the eastern banks of the Mississippi. Though the townsfolk worship at a Catholic church, the main character, Overlea, a dark-skinned woman who comes from up in the hills, has a more direct relation with her deity, Ole Miss. Because she lives outside the faith and cultural practices of the local community, and because her skin is darker, the people accuse her of being "Jes in from Af'ica!" True to her unchurched relation to nature, she tells her husband one fall day, "Dat river am a witch"; minutes later the river sucks him under. Even after this sacrifice, Overlea still sees the "*gris gris* river" as "touched with something precious and holy." The following spring, presumably in 1927, a flood bursts the town's levees during the holy weekend. Overlea finds a young woman trying to give birth inside the church as waters rise. Though the church does not save the woman, and indeed topples over in the flood and "float[s] away, its cross half-buried in water," the little newborn boy is saved by Overlea. The river has given Overlea a child to make up for the husband it took. "Muddy water laps [Overlea's] feet" in the final moments as she muses about the "spell" that keeps her drawn to the "old witch river."[13]

In this folk genre, for Ruth Bass, as for Sterling Brown and Mary Austin, nature reigns. It is alive, sentient, willful, purposive. It reacts to propitiation and it shapes its people. For these authors, the pressures of a standardizing, muddled, mechanical world sent them looking for a folk made authentic by a purposive environment. Believing in such a nature, authors like Brown and Bass turned a deaf ear to the discussion about humanity's profound alteration of the natural world and, in particular, given the setting of their stories and poems, humanity's degradation and mechanization of the Mississippi watershed. They do not seem to ponder the question: what would a folk be inside a "second nature"? Could such a people still be valorized as "truly folk"? The two authors we are about to discuss, Faulkner and Wright, were, by contrast, keenly aware of how humanly designed their Delta and upland Mississippi environments were. Each in his own way was drawn to recent literary innovations and techniques that accentuated not a people's natural "integrity," spiritual or otherwise, but rather human susceptibility to a rueful modern history of its own creating.

Before turning to Faulkner and Wright, the foray of one other prominent interwar figure onto the terrain of the inundated Lower Mississippi Valley deserves attention. In a little-known radio broadcast for the children of Berlin in 1932—indeed his final broadcast from that city—Walter Benjamin took up the 1927 flood as a means to offer commentary on the politics of nature in America and the nature of contemporary politics in Germany. That Benjamin remains one of the most influential theorists ever to have addressed modern media's capacity to occasion public expertise in the face of autocratic messaging *and* that he actually wrote and broadcast a segment on what he, too, called "the great flood of 1927" gives us a remarkable, if brief, opportunity to see how he turned this event into public knowledge—how he practiced what he would, a few years later, preach.[14] For his own radio listening and broadcasting was, in the early 1930s, allowing him to formulate the idea of the citizen-critic we associate with his famous 1936 essay, "The Work of Art in the Age of Mechanical Reproduction." In a radio address from 1930–31, "Reflections on Radio," for example, Benjamin worried that the radio—being used merely as a one-way transmitter—was creating "dull, inarticulate masses" rather than "develop[ing] the expertise of the listener."[15] How, then, did he take up the internationally relayed dispatches about the flood in order to turn his young audience into critics? Might the Mississippi disaster have contributed to his theorization of the role of media in the modern state?

Benjamin's series of radio broadcasts for adolescent Berliners—"Aufklärung für Kinder" (Enlightenment for Children)—began in 1929 with relatively light fare (toys and puppets) but, with the worsening political atmosphere in Germany in 1930, came to take on increasingly weighty material. Addressing the children directly in the second person, often beginning with questions, and often commenting on his storytelling methods, Benjamin virtually conveyed his middle-class listeners to tenements in their city, described swindles and deceits of various sorts, and told them of political terror in the form of early modern witch trials and the prerevolutionary Bastille prison. In his final broadcasts, from October 1931 to March 1932, he turned to the history of disaster: the destruction of Pompeii, the Lisbon earthquake, a nineteenth-century theater fire in Canton, a railway bridge collapse in Scotland, and, last of all, "The Mississippi Flood of 1927." Such a concentration on these events seems altogether fitting given Benjamin's figure for human historical time—articulated later in his 1940 "Theses on the Philosophy of History"—as an angel, with his back to the future, staring at "one single catastrophe which keeps piling wreckage upon wreckage and hurls it in front of his feet"; that which blows him irresistibly onward is the "storm" that "we call progress." In that essay, he averred that though the "exploitation" of nature and labor tended to happen simultaneously through technological changes, a fair labor situation would instead "deliver" the "potentials" lying in nature's "womb." In other words, he was not opposed to the instrumentalization of nature as long as this "delivery" of nature's immanent powers and goods occurred through fair labor. Benjamin's concern in the interwar years about the appropriation of the benefits of technology by capital or the state (an appropriation that was then championed as "progress") and the foisting of its detriments on an endangered public occasioned him—I would argue—to home in on this group of disasters, spread across world history, as representing "a past charged with the time of the now" and bearing "Messianic" insight.[16] If future disaster was to be averted, his young listeners needed to examine the telling signs of these past calamities.

The few Benjamin scholars who have commented on his flood broadcast have tended to focus on the story within the story, noting how much it uncannily augurs Benjamin's own death by suicide as he lost hope of escaping from Vichy France in March 1940; had he only held out slightly longer, he would have been allowed to travel across the border to Spain. In the firsthand flood account that Benjamin inserts in his text, events are described by "Louis," a survivor from Natchez, Mississippi. We hear of his clinging to a roof amid rising waters with his two brothers; to Louis's horror, he must watch as each of them succumbs to the flood, one after spitting in the river "with angry disdain" and commenting, "It's taking too long."[17] What is so "very moving" about this story in the light of Benjamin's future suicide, remarks Esther Leslie, is that it offers "an alternative" (to Benjamin's own forfeiting of his life) in the person of the surviving brother, who manages to endure and tell the tale.[18] I agree that, knowing how Benjamin's own end will uncannily replay the choice of the lost brother, it *is* intensely moving. What is also true, though, is that this particular story of the three brothers, which Benjamin encourages us to hear as a firsthand account, never actually happened. Or at least it never happened in Mississippi. It did, however, take place in the village of Saint-Jory, France, or in a novella about Saint-Jory called *L'Inondation* written by Émile Zola in 1880. From the narrator's name (Louis), to the brother who spits in the river, to a boat that circles and departs, to far-off voices of survivors from the church steeple, everything in Benjamin's Natchez tale is transported from Zola's French flood story, albeit condensed into a more fable-like scope. As a personal emblem for Benjamin, and of his own life within a rising German fascism, the brothers' story is no less powerful. It is not, however, the part of his broadcast about Mississippi that shows Benjamin genuinely constellating its particulars within a meaningful historical pattern.

Instead, it is in what the 1927 flood tells him—and in turn his young listeners—about the interrelation between nature, labor, technology, capital, and the state that it becomes a luminous world event. The broadcast starts as a lesson in natural unpredictability. Benjamin imagines his listeners opening a virtual map to see "that giant-sized . . . sinuous line" and wants them to notice that not only does the river proceed inevitably from north to south but also, surprisingly, from east to west and west to east. You might think, seeing it on a map, that a river's oceanward directionality makes it as reliable as a railroad line, he says, but locals in the river valley "know this appearance is deceptive"; they see the lagoons and ditches where the river used to run and know that "never is it satisfied with the bed it has made for itself." Added to this, the river has "annual mood changes" that come with the spring inrushes of water from its countless tributaries. Complementing, or opposing, this natural changeability is the human determination to make the physical world predictable. Benjamin stresses the massiveness of individual levees and their 2,500-kilometer-long stretch, which represent one of "the largest public projects in American history"; he also marvels at the massive deployment of ships and airplanes required by the flood's breaches of this levee system.[19]

Benjamin moves quickly on to what he saw as the "most appalling and miserable episode of the great flood," namely the governmental destruction of the levee at Caernarvon that inundated St. Bernard and Plaquemines parishes. The story that Benjamin fashions of this episode is of "bitter civil wars" between poor farmers armed with machine guns and organized into militias to protect their levees—and even to assassinate secretary Hoover—and the wealthy trading metropolis of New Orleans, backed by the federal government, which appointed a "general to act as dictator" and conduct a "state of siege" against the farmers.[20] Much of this account is true: armed men from these parishes were guarding their levees with guns and did fire at any boat perceived to be approaching too close, including a boat carrying Hoover; Hoover did appoint Louisiana planter John Parker as a "dictator" to run recovery efforts in the state;[21] the bankers of New Orleans, eager to protect not only the city but the city's reputation to investors, did willfully (and, it turned out, needlessly) sacrifice the less powerful rural region. Benjamin did not know or note that the Louisiana governor, the secretary of war, and the chief of the Army Corps of Engineers all resisted the appeal of this cadre of powerful bankers on many occasions before each capitulating to their demands, nor did he mark that these parishes were also home to wealthy and corrupt bootleggers.[22]

Benjamin's remediation of the flood as "Die Mississippi-Überschwemmung 1927" gives us a sense of how the U.S. catastrophe traveled internationally: which details were preserved on newsreel or wire dispatches and which obscured by dominant media technologies and socially inflected pathways of information. An explosion that New Orleans potentates wanted to disseminate because it assured the world of the security of their city *did* travel, even if someone like Benjamin would alter its significance in his rebroadcast, while other, especially racial, injustices remained less internationally visible. Though Benjamin did not detect telling truths about race *in* this disaster, he did see the flood as a metaphor for racial and ethnic terror within Mississippi. Benjamin signed off his broadcast with a promise that "On some other occasion we'll return to [the river's] banks" to look into "America's greatest and most dangerous secret society," which represented "raging elements of human cruelty and violence" that legal "dams" have no better contained than "the actual ones made from earth and stone." The very last sentence Benjamin broadcast in Berlin contained the words: "stay tuned for the Ku Klux Klan."[23]

In sum, Benjamin found in this flood a signal emblem of modernity in need of exposure. Nature is not typified by the solidity of rock, for Benjamin, but by "loose ground" and unreliability; though humanity will invariably engage in, as he said in his account of the Scottish catastrophe, a "great struggle" with such a material milieu, humanity will not necessarily progress toward victory.[24] Technology might merely involve us in gestures of mighty building and sublime destruction. Humanity, moreover, is also made up of outwardly explosive as well as secretly "raging elements." The perils of a state able to willfully break down its own protections—and send raging water onto its poor laborers' land—or of a secret society able to go around legal containments needed to be publically broadcast, traveling from Mississippi to Berlin, as a form of enlightenment. Benjamin asked his young listeners to ponder whether other courses, forgotten but still visible beside the main channel of history, might be found.

* * *

According to much recent scholarly summary, European and American modernism was not particularly concerned with environmental degradation as an

historical phenomenon. When scholars set out to explain the social and material origins of modernism, they typically focus on urbanization and population
growth, the acceleration of industrialism, the growth of a mass-consumer economy, mass transportation and mass communications, and the effects of these
changes on embodiment.[25] Moreover, a "crisis of political liberalism," World
War I, the rise of communism and fascism, genocide, women's suffrage, imperial crises, the Depression, and World War II, as well as the rise in immigration
in the United States, are central to accounts of modernism.[26] Developments in
science and philosophy, such as Marx's prediction of inevitable historical revolution, Darwin's theory of evolution, Freud's concept of the unconscious, and
Einstein's special theory of relativity, are enlisted to explain how those certitudes about human reason and agency within a stable world that were a hall-
mark of the Enlightenment were unseated in the late nineteenth and early
twentieth centuries.[27] As a reaction to this newly understood "evanescent flux
of the phenomenal world" and discoveries in psychology, according to Michael
Levenson, writers turned inward, to human consciousness, and the unconscious, to find the world's "pattern and significance."[28] Downplayed in modernist fiction were plots centered on consequential events, a concrete external
world, and an easily imagined rendering of space and time.[29] As a focus on the
factual gave way to an appreciation for—or despaired retrenchment to—subjective experience, the omniscient narrative perspective was typically replaced by
a focus on the subjective and on unreliable or embedded narrators. The new
speed, automation, and scale of industrialism as well as the newly detected role
of chance in the universe also offered stimuli for a formal artistic overthrow of
realist forms of representation. While in the earth and social sciences, vying
models of stability and random dissonance coexisted in this period, in avant-
garde art, "modernist clangour" came to eclipse "Victorian harmony."[30]

Though many aspects of modernization and imperialism had impacts on
the natural world, and on the relation between the human and nonhuman
realms, writers and artists apparently paid little heed to such impacts—according to the dominant definition of modernism. That modernists were rebelling
against either the nature focus of Romanticism or the objective orientation of
Realism has served to explain why changes to the environment were not on
their radar.[31] In a related development, the branch of literary study that puts
the natural world, and human/natural relations, at the center of its inquiry—
"eco-criticism"—has tended not to focus on modernism.[32] Modernism's attraction to subjective experience and its urge to defamiliarize the world likely has
made its authors' and artists' engagements with environmental experience difficult to identify or access.[33] However, if one notes modernism's critiques of

Enlightenment rationality and its engagements with the new twentieth-century sciences emphasizing uncertainty and relativity, one can see that this period in cultural history made important contributions to the history of Western thinking about and representation of the natural world. We have just seen, in the case of Walter Benjamin, that a key European commentator on modernity believed that the human relationship to nature was intimately connected to questions of the state, capital, labor, and communication. Moreover, as I am about to show, two of the most significant modernist authors in North America, Wright and Faulkner, came to reckon with their place in modern experience, and plot their coordinates as writers, by thinking about politicized riverscapes and by committing the 1927 event to paper.

SIX

William Faulkner and the Machine Age Watershed

One of Faulkner's signal contributions to global modernism was his engagement with environmental trauma as a major category of experience and a major symptom of modernization. Though modernist artists responded to the Machine Age in varying degrees of exultation and distress, Faulkner was among those who remarked on the profound, sudden, and uneven changes this period brought to a rural—some would say a colonized—periphery.[1] It could seem to him that he lived in the resource frontier and the fantasy backwater of a northerly empire, one that extracted trees, cotton, sugar, tobacco, and soldiers for overseas wars, while purveying mass media distractions about a charming Dixie tableau arrested in time. Coming of age in the first decades of the twentieth century, Faulkner witnessed up close an intense period of environmental degradation in his region. Accepting—you could even say *relishing*—that "man" was "puny," in fact puny and vainglorious at the same time, ruled by the social shibboleths of blood, section, manhood, and womanhood, and compelled by unconscious proddings, Faulkner also concerned himself with the state humankind would find itself in after it had warped its biological matrix beyond recognition.[2] In particular, the Flood of 1927 seemed to him the South's most all-consuming experience of modernization. If he was to find *his* way to be a modernist in the world, this flood would have something to do with it.

At the time of the 1927 disaster, Faulkner was twenty-nine years old. He had written an unremarkable book of poetry, *Marble Faun* (1924), in which an imaginary pastoral setting is filled with satyrs, shepherds, and fauns, and three novels critics typically consider his "apprentice" books.[3] Both *Soldiers' Pay* (1926) and *Flags in the Dust* (written in part during the flood and published in 1929 as *Sartoris*) showed Faulkner writing on what he must have felt to be the most germane modern topic, and the most fitting threshold to modernist authorship, namely, soldiers returning home damaged from World War I.[4]

As he consumed, throughout 1927, the media coverage of the Great Flood, especially the South's representation of the event as a second War of Northern Aggression and as a symptom of southern colonization at the hands of outside capital, he came to realize that a scenario of modernization—which had not yet become a standard European modernist topic—had occurred just miles from his own town. What's more, the flood would allow him to adapt or contend with urban European models of modern subjectivity (found in Freud or Dada, for example) by giving form to a 1920s rural, multiracial environmental crisis. Before he reckoned, in *Absalom, Absalom!* (1936) and *Go Down, Moses* (1942), then, with how the southern and Caribbean slave-based plantation complex had "outraged the land" beginning in the early modern period,[5] he first mused upon his own period's *national* environmental transgressions in which modern federal engineering, as well as agriculture and silviculture throughout the valley, all coalesced in their misunderstanding and misuse of the continent's major watershed.[6] In this situation, southerners appear not so much as the central culprits but as improvident colonial dependents collaborating with highly capitalized outsiders. For Faulkner the writer, the southern landscape in the years leading up to the flood had been a repository of elegiacally pastoral conventions;[7] this event made unmistakably clear to him that political acts occurred through the medium of nature and that he needed to experiment with new narrative forms to communicate this awareness.

It is not surprising that this eco-catastrophe would have a strong impact on his thinking. In the way that the lives of Henry David Thoreau and George Perkins Marsh were shaped by the deforestation and industrial development of New England, Faulkner's first forty years corresponded with the rapid transformation, and destruction, of his southern environment. Though Faulkner was rather proudly derelict in many matters as a youth, he cared from his early years about the nonhuman world around him. The northern Mississippi woods were where he developed his imaginative life in play with his brothers, where he was instructed in ornithology by his African American caretaker, Caroline Barr,[8] where he was a conscientious scoutmaster, where, though otherwise an oddball aesthete,[9] he hunted for large game in what seemed an immemorial manly rite. What he came to see in the woods were resources that he understood as decidedly southern—as the only possible basis of his region's culture but that had become an opportunity zone for northern and European investors. Such resource extraction seemed another mark of the South's effectively colonial status in relation to outside capital.

The event that brought the catastrophic dimension of the South's environmental situation home to him was what one of his narrators would call "the flood year 1927."[10] He began incorporating the year-long event, along with its history and its reverberations, into his fiction even before returning refugee sharecroppers planted their first new crop of cotton in the spring of 1928. And he continued thinking about the flooding of the Mississippi through three novels and various short stories, even up to a 1954 *Holiday* article on his home state, in which he described how the "Old Man"—the Mississippi River—paid "none of the dykes any heed at all" as he "gather[ed] water all the way from Montana to Pennsylvania . . . and roll[ed] it down the artificial gut of his victims' puny and baseless hoping."[11] Attending to this subject in Faulkner helps us see that historians of modernization and modernism have yet to adequately gauge how much environmental degradation and ensuing disasters were crucial to the period—its thinking, its sense of altered embodiment and perception, its aesthetics and strategies of representation.

Faulkner did his most intense and most creative thinking about the flood, and about the land-use practices that produced it, in the years immediately after the historic event. Because he was, in these late 1920s works, exploring issues of regional and environmental history through the vehicle, or construct, of the family, we have not heretofore understood *The Sound and the Fury* and *As I Lay Dying* as novels that meditate on how subjectivity, knowledge, experience, and ontology itself have all been altered by industrialism's profound environmental reshaping. Moreover, because Faulkner, in keeping with other modernists, chose not to plot these novels around an explicitly named historic event as a realist novel might have, we instead encounter the event in the form of psychological and perceptual traces left on the minds of his first-person narrators—narrators, it should be added, who grow increasingly desperate and apparently insane the more immersed they become in flood experience.[12] While Faulkner uses this modernist device of the non-normative point of view narration, he simultaneously uses the much older form of allegory, such that the house at times operates at the scale of a bioregion, characters' bodies become storehouses of resources, and individual actors typify larger political vectors. In some sense, then, as I resituate his first two major novels in the milieu of environmental trauma in which they were written, I will perforce need to take semiotic lines that Faulkner left oblique, circuitous, or faint and make them bold and straight. In doing so, I mean this straightening process to be only temporary. In other words, I don't contend that the Flood of 1927 somehow *solves* either work. They are novels, after all, and so are never "about" any finite thing. I do contend, though, that the flood changed Faulkner's thinking about the geography of the modern, and about the modernity of the neo-nature surrounding him, and thus that the 1927 event subtly permeates these novels, topically and formally.

When, some ten years later, Faulkner wrote his third flood novel, *The Wild Palms* [*If I Forget Thee, Jerusalem*], he would take an entirely different approach: he made the catastrophe the explicit subject of one of its two storylines, announcing the historical referent in the very first sentence. This rush to realism at the story's opening is a kind of feint, because the novel employs a large wardrobe of literary styles that it wears and then discards, trying to get to a place of "peace" where all media—aside from the body and land—are unnecessary. While the flood in this book is first a sign of the river's alteration under industrialism, it soon becomes, strangely enough, a sign of Nature's rollicking good health, an expression of its normalcy. I would suggest that by 1937–38, when he was writing this, his third flood novel, the 1927 event was no longer a mysterious atmospheric of his imagining but instead had become a curious device.

The Sound and the Fury: The Environmental Unconscious, Race, and Epistemology

When Faulkner sat down to write, in the winter of 1928, "Through the fence, between the curling flower spaces,"[13] the Delta catastrophe bore down on his consciousness mightily, as much as, for example, the New Orleans levee disaster would have a Louisiana author in 2006, or the 9/11 attacks any U.S. author working in 2002. Registering fully, then, that *The Sound and the Fury* was written in the year after the Flood of 1927, all its dispersed and seemingly merely metaphorical references to "water building and building up," "debris on a flood," "bubbles rising in water," bodies "lying in the water," "drowned things floating," "all dat flood-watter," and, finally, a "whelmin flood" (138, 78, 296, 149, 128, 114, 296) suggest a repositioning of Faulkner's first major, and most beloved, work as a post-eco-catastrophe novel. Moreover, as the only one of his three flood novels to include significant African American characters, *The Sound and the Fury* offers us the rather unique opportunity to explore the ways in which Faulkner perceived traumatic environmental experience, and its knowledge, to move across the color line.

Thus far, the dominant interpretative approach toward the novel, other than a formalist one, has been psychoanalytic, appropriately and productively so, given how much psychosexual turmoil is fenced inside the Compson domain: castration anxiety *and* castration, incestuous desire, maternal and paternal dysfunction—the list goes on.[14] With such a family romance, it is not surprising that critics have read the environmental references in the novel as only offering a kind of disposable Ariadne's thread leading us toward the apparently repressed psychic material. Time seems overdue for us to rethink which are the manifest and which the hidden realms of the novel. Brothers having to hunt for dropped knives, or keys kept fast in their mother's pocket, or brothers holding flowers with broken stems, or almost getting hit in the head by other men's balls—these are not exactly hidden, or particularly subtle, occurrences in *The Sound and the Fury*. In other words, these are the manifest, perhaps even operatic elements of the text. The material that Faulkner chose not to address as directly—as he incorporated the modernist technique of subordinating event to consciousness—was the flood event and its linkage to southern, or modern, environmental history.[15] It was not for lack of tracing the complex anthropogenic causes of the catastrophe. As I have detailed, southern newspaper editors and national pundits had done so with gusto throughout the previous year. Instead, Faulkner was finding his narrative zone—a zone somewhere among the familial, historical, environmental, and mythic-apocryphal. At this stage in his career, the human-in-the-family was, to use a narratological term, his *focalizer* for these extrafamilial and nonhuman realms. He would write in 1935, when he turned down a request to author a nonfiction book on the Mississippi River: "I am a novelist, you see: people first, where second."[16] As he saw it, his chosen métier obligated him to bring out the "where" through its sedimentation in the "people," but this is not to say that he saw the environment as in fact secondary. People were made in nature's "implacable and brooding image" even as people transformed nature into the brooding image of their desires.[17] Both consciousness and the unconscious were housed in the broadest kind of geography.[18] What was more, Faulkner understood how much race determined one's placement within southern geography, and hence the ways an individual felt, sensed, knew about, and internalized the land.[19]

When Mr. Compson says to Quentin, "it's nature is hurting you not Caddy" (116), or when he tells Quentin, "you are still blind to what is in yourself to . . . the sequence of natural events and their causes which shadow every mans brow" (177), I take him to be addressing nature not only at the scale of the individual id but also at the scale of a bioregion. Mr. Compson, the character known for demolishing human constructs, raises the novel's important consideration about what "causes" external biogenic "events" and how they "shadow every man's brow" and get inside the "self." In short, he urges Quentin to consider how we are part of causing "events" that in turn permeate our identity. This eco-historicist reading does not jettison those realms of the human mind modeled by psychoanalysis. Instead, I want to argue that we have not heretofore gotten Faulkner's response to Freud quite right.[20] I see Faulkner as signifying upon Freudian theory in order to force Freud out of doors. When Faulkner has Quentin "tak[e] a cut" (77) for missing psychology class on the morning of June 2 so that he can, instead, traverse and inspect the Charles River watershed surrounding him, Faulkner is slyly demonstrating his own sense of the physical *situation* of the psyche and of academic psychology's error in too strictly immuring identity inside the self and the family. In Quentin's section, Faulkner revisits the cultural and linguistic material upon which Freud based his theory of "the 'uncanny'" (1919) and draws out from these sources their broader mapping of subjectivity. In so doing, Faulkner taps into a part of the modern psyche that Freud himself had overlooked.

Freud's essay was translated into English in 1925, at a time when Faulkner was living in New Orleans where, as he said, "everybody talked about Freud."[21] Faulkner is not yet writing the kind of "nature story" in which nonhuman actors share the stage with the human—as, for example, Lion, Old Ben, and the Big Woods do with Ike McCaslin in "The Bear." He writes *The Sound and the Fury* in an anthropocentric narrative mode all the while giving the reader textual clues for sensing how mutually constitutive are the human and environmental realms—for seeing how much a person's "inner weather" is connected to the disturbed intelligence of the "outer."[22] Appreciating how Faulkner wanted to map the human psyche back onto that outer world is one way we can perceive how modernism's interest in the mind does not preclude its interest in that outer material world. Because Freud has been understood as the muse of modernism's inward turn, it is critical for us to see where, and how, Freud cordoned off the mind from its broad environmental matrix and how Faulkner defined his southern, American version of modernism at variance to such a model.

In his 1919 essay, Freud theorizes that "an uncanny experience occurs either when infantile complexes which have been repressed are once more revived by some impression, or when primitive beliefs which have been surmounted seem once more to be confirmed." He first explores the uncanny's odd conflation of the familiar and the terrifying by showing how, in German-language usage, the word *heimlich*, or, "belonging to the house, not strange, familiar, tame, intimate, friendly, etc.," "develops in the direction of ambivalence, until it finally coincides with its opposite, *unheimlich*."[23] To make his case, Freud includes an 1860 German dictionary entry for the term. Although he will draw from this wide usage of the term *heimlich* a narrow sense of the "familiar" as connoting "infantile complexes" and "primitive" modes of thinking, we can see from the entry that the word had a host of environmental associations that were very much alive in nineteenth-century German culture but that Freud ignores. These overlooked associations suggest a sense of the *situation* of consciousness in a more capacious kind of household or environmental matrix. Because I take this understanding of the embeddedness of the psyche in its nonhuman environment to be not only present in this dictionary but also one of the central contributions of Faulkner's—and Bessie Smith's and Richard Wright's—writing on the Flood of 1927, it is important to carefully lay out how Freud willfully constricted this more pervasive notion of environmentally linked subjectivity. Then I will demonstrate how Faulkner uses the physical details of the German dictionary entry, as well as Freud's anecdote about getting turned around in an Italian neighborhood, as a kind of itinerary for Quentin's sojourn.

In the dictionary definition for "heimlich," the category "belonging to the house" moves back and forth between indicating something "within . . . four walls" to something inside the self to something characterizing a broader territory.

> "Is it still *heimlich* to you in your country where strangers are felling your woods?" "She did not feel too *heimlich* with him." "Along a high, *heimlich*, shady path . . . , beside a purling, gushing and babbling woodland brook." "To destroy the *Heimlichkeit* of the home." . . . "The protestant landowners do not feel . . . *heimlich* among their catholic inferiors." "When it grows *heimlich* and still, and the evening quiet alone watches over your cell." . . . "The place was so peaceful, so lonely, so shadily-*heimlich*." "The in- and outflowing waves of the current, dreamy and lullaby-*heimlich*." . . . "That which comes from afar . . . assuredly does not live quite *heimelig*." . . . "The sentinel's horn sounds so *heimelig* from the tower, and his voice invites so hospitably." . . . "*like a buried spring or dried-up pond. One cannot walk over it without always having the feeling that water might come up there again." "Oh, we call it 'unheimlich'; you call it 'heimlich'. Well, what makes you think that there is something secret and untrustworthy about this family?"* [Freud's emphasis].[24]

For the second sense of the word, "Concealed, kept from sight," the entry reads: "To throw into pits or *Heimlichkeiten*"; "'the *Heimlich* art' (magic)"; "I have roots that are most *heimlich*. I am grown in the deep earth."[25] In a time close to Romanticism and the rise of industrialism, this usage attests to how important nature, its ownership, and its alteration were to these subjects' cultural sense of home. Not of much interest to Freud the city-dweller, the environmental associations would not have been lost on Faulkner, the small-town southerner who witnessed profound anthropogenic changes to his region throughout his youth. In sum, Faulkner read Freud as I believe we should read Faulkner—as situated within environmental history. He did not reject Freud but instead, through his character Quentin, redirects our attention to the extended geography of the psyche and of the realms that make and unmake it.

Spring 1927

Recall that Faulkner's nearest metropolitan newspaper, the Memphis *Commercial Appeal*, reported on, and editorialized about, the flood throughout the disaster's long cycle. The *Oxford Eagle*, Faulkner's hometown paper, reported on the crisis throughout the spring and, on May 26, reprinted on its front page this editorial from the *Manufacturers Record*:

> The disaster is an appalling one. It is the direct outcome of the unpardonable failure of the Federal Government to make such a condition impossible. For many years engineers and others have urged the Government to carry out a broad scheme of river improvement which would have turned this tremendous liability into a national asset of enormous value. But the Federal Government has failed to do so. The nation itself is, therefore, responsible for this disaster, for the waters which started in the upper reaches of the Mississippi, the Missouri and the Ohio have been pouring their floods down through the Mississippi from Illinois to the Gulf.[26]

Along with these print sources, Faulkner was well acquainted with southerners in the thick of flood rescue and media activity. William Alexander Percy, whose poetry collection, *In April Once*, Faulkner had reviewed in 1920 and with whom Faulkner spent time in New York City in 1921,[27] was in charge of the Greenville levee and had received much condemnation in the national black press for his flagrant and racist mishandling of the situation, despite priding himself on being a liberal-minded cosmopolitan and a benign paternalist.[28] Faulkner also spent time with Lyle Saxon, author of *Father Mississippi*: they had known one another in New Orleans beginning in 1925 and socialized together there in the summer of 1927 while Saxon was writing *Father Mississippi*; moreover, Faulkner boarded with Saxon in his Greenwich Village apartment briefly during the fall of 1928 while he was consumed with revising *The Sound and the Fury*.[29] The first line of Saxon's coverage of the "Good Friday" storm may sound familiar: "But the day dawned black."[30] Was it in the back of Faulkner's mind as he began his fourth section with "The day dawned bleak and chill"? Saxon would review

The Sound and the Fury in the *New York Herald Tribune* in early October 1929, writing: "I believe simply and sincerely that this is a great book."[31]

Strangers Are Felling Your Woods

Because Faulkner was writing a novel ("people first, where second"), and what's more, an experimental modernist novel in which the appearance of a third-person narrator is deferred, Faulkner had the authorial challenge of representing how environmental trauma had affected characters' emotions and thoughts without wanting to explain the precipitating event. Faulkner does so by situating the river material as the disguised content of Quentin's dreams, flashbacks, and preoccupations. In one of the first scenes that Faulkner wrote for the second section of the novel, Quentin challenges Dalton Ames, his sister's seducer, to a kind of duel. The memory sequence works according to a synecdochal logic to hint at Quentin's submerged awareness of the environmental dimensions of his impotence and of Caddy's downfall. This flashback takes place inside Quentin's head as he is being beaten up in Cambridge, Massachusetts, by a human avatar of the New South's nouveau riche, Gerald Bland. What this scene obliquely suggests is that Quentin feels environmentally outmanned by a leagued maneuver of northern capital and New Southern profiteering.[32] Quentin and Caddy's northern lover meet on a bridge in the woods, and Dalton keeps doing strange things with bits of wood:

> . . . he had a piece of bark in his hands breaking pieces from it and dropping them over the rail into the water
> I came to tell you to leave town
> He broke a piece of bark deliberately dropped it carefully
> into the water watched it float away

After more bootless threats from Quentin:

> Then he laid the bark on the rail and rolled a cigarette with
> Those two swift motions spun the match over the rail
> what will you do if I don't leave
>
> . . .
>
> the smoke flowed in two jets from his nostrils across his
> face
>
> . . .
>
> he raked the cigarette ash carefully off against the rail he
> did it slowly and carefully like sharpening a pencil . . .

Quentin tries unsuccessfully to hit him; Dalton holds both of Quentin's wrists.

> he took the bark from the rail and dropped it into the
> water it bobbed up the current took it floated away . . .

Dalton shoots at the wood in the stream.

> . . . the bark disappeared then pieces of it floated up
> spreading he hit two more of them pieces of bark no bigger
> than silver dollars

Quentin tries again to hit Dalton and is again restrained. Quentin "leaned on the rail looking at the water." Dalton rides off, "and after a while [Quentin] couldnt hear anything but the water." Quentin goes and leans his "head against the tree"; he hears "the water and then everything sort of rolled away and I didnt feel anything at all." Caddy arrives on horseback and, in a kind of fit, keeps "bumping [Quentin's] head against the tree." When Quentin asks her "do you love him Caddy," "she looked at [Quentin] then everything emptied out of her eyes and they looked like the eyes in statues blank and unseeing and serene" (160–63). Later in time, once the dishonored Caddy has been engaged to a cheating banker from Indiana, Herbert Head, Head appears in the Compsons' living room to continue the exploitative procedure practiced by Ames: as his burning cigar threatens three times to "blister" the family's wooden "mantel" (109), Head tries to offer Quentin his "damned money" (110) and equates Caddy's future sexual favors as services to be rendered with "interest" (111).

Quentin mentally replays his standoff with Caddy's consorts as scenes involving the decimation and removal of wood in exchange for payment. The buried logic is this: the northern interloper takes bark (i.e., trees), breaks these into pieces and mills them, sets them on rails (as "smoke flowed in two jets from his nostrils"), then moves them onto rivers for further transport to the world market ("hes crossed all the oceans all around the world" [150]), occasionally dispersing logjams with explosive force. What is left after "everything [was] emptied out" is cut-over land ("The sawdust flowing from what wound in what side" [175]) that has lost its health and commercial value and is in a state of vulnerability to fire ("Caddy you've got fever" [111], "spun the match," "ash," "blister[ed]" "mantel" of woods). Not only is this land susceptible to fire, but it also lies less protected from the "Head" waters of the North; recall, too, that Quentin is increasingly covered in vital bodily fluids during his memory replay. What remains is only the sound of water as "everything sort of rolled away"—as when all things solid roll away in a crevasse and water breaks through. "Blackguards" of the North conspire with southerners willing to exploit their region to translate themselves into a kind of lethal apotheosis ("Bland came out, with the sculls" and "went to the river" [90]). Caddy is not only, as is often assumed, an amorphous nature figure but here is specifically the forested resources of the South that northerners are despoiling; Quentin cannot protect his region's integrity.

Always Having the Feeling That Water Might Come Up

Much has been said about Quentin's preoccupation with his shadow, which before it can take on an association with biraciality and historical time in *Absalom, Absalom!* here marks his obsession with Time as a key index of being. Indeed, once Quentin has mutilated the face of his watch, his body and its accompanying shadow come to function as an inescapable walking sundial. Connected, though, to the transformation of his body into a timepiece is its operation as a divining rod. Quentin's body is acutely tuned to water: he "feel[s]" it (115), and "feels water again" even when it is "mute and unseen" (135–36), feels it "below the path" (140), "smell[s]" it (89, 156, 169, 170), "watch[es] it" (105), and sees a "glint of water" (89), sees "a long way into the motion of the water" (116), and always knows "where the water would be" (112). In a meaningful sense, it is not that Quentin jumps into water after his section ends (in the break between his and Jason's narratives) but that water keeps "building and building up" (138) as his day accomplishes, until, back in his room at day's end, "it would begin to come into the room in waves building and building up until I would have to pant to get any air at all out of it" (173). Finally, still in his dormitory, after the appearance of "Moses rod," water begins to enter "*the long silence of the throat* .... A quarter hour yet. And then I'll not be. .... *Non fui. Sum. Fui. Non sum*" (174). Read this way, the river and its tributaries that Quentin travels over during his narrative (a displaced Mississippi watershed) finally inundate him, choking out air as the water passes down his throat; he anticipates by a sounding—of time and of the water's depth—the moment he will change tenses and be a *was* and not an *is*.[33]

Time and water are initially linked together in Quentin's section when, as a child at school in Jefferson, he is folding down his fingers in an attempt to sync himself with the school's clock. Doing so, he has blotted out a question the teacher has asked about the Mississippi River (88). As Quentin attempts to discipline his own nature—and avoid questions about his region's nature—by a simplifying mechanism in the classroom, so do engineers attempt to order the Mississippi's complex and unpredictable flow with overly basic systems. Scientists trying to understand how smoothly flowing water becomes turbulent began in 1944 to theorize that its onset "represents the piling up of huge numbers of incommensurable frequencies"; as one steady flow curls into multiple eddies, one time signature turns into many. This "complex, apparently random behavior" of turbulence makes it akin "to a clockmaker's shop with a huge number of clocks each ticking at a different, irrational rhythm."[34] Some fifteen years before turbulence was scientifically modeled, Faulkner invents precisely this scenario for Quentin to confront while on the streets of Cambridge when he looks at a shop "with about a dozen watches in the window, a dozen different hours and each with the same assertive and contradictory assurance" (85). Time, for Quentin, is no longer characterized by periodic seconds but instead by incommensurable frequencies. The connection between rivers and this new appearance of multichronic time becomes clearer when Quentin enters the shop. Going inside, Quentin sees the cranium of the man tasked with repairing the "mechanical progression" (83) of time: a "tube tunneled into his face," leaving his head "like a drained marsh in December" (88) and his eye "blurred and rushing" (83). Quentin reads this head, a would-be *cogito* of the mechanical age, through the scrim of his afflicted river environment: tunneled or straightened by machinery, drained of wetlands, and then "rushing" in dangerous tempo. When technologists attempt to simplify a complex phenomenal pattern—whether of time or water—those patterns can become even more "contradictory" and uncontrolled. Both Quentin's and the river's submissions to an overly simple mechanized model will begin to come undone. His own death becomes a harbinger of the flood that will surely come.

That Quentin imagines Moses' rod to appear right before his own drowning suggests that he associates his "people" and their works with the Egyptians. As the 1850s spiritual goes, "The Lord, by Moses, to Pharaoh said: Oh! Let my people go. If not I'll smite your first-born dead—Oh! Let my people go." Quentin, the first-born, is not allowed passage through the waters to elude his people's racial—and environmental—transgressions.

To Throw into Pits

Recall the bundle of associations in the German dictionary definition of that usage of *heimlich* that means "Concealed, kept from sight." The entry reads: "To throw into pits or *Heimlichkeiten*"; "'the *Heimlich* art' (magic)"; "I have roots that are most *heimlich*. I am grown in the deep earth." These topoi of what's hidden—depressions in the earth and the underground—are associated with occulted knowledge. In Faulkner's mind, both are associated specifically with situated black knowledge. A few years earlier, Sherwood Anderson had shared with Faulkner his vision for his novel *Dark Laughter*, in which the African American characters provide a counterpoint to modernity with their "mysterious" "dark, earthy laughter—the Negro, the earth, and the river."[35] Here, of course, are old associations between nonwhites and nature, hidden places and hidden knowledge, deriving, at least in the American South, from a kind of spatial zoning of black and white lives and resulting forms of knowledge. As European and colonial Enlightenment practitioners officially distanced themselves from magical thinking while they sought to survey, catalogue, and exploit American territories for commercial or scientific uses, there existed a lingering sense within white epistemology that the occulted knowledge non-Europeans produced—and which was often associated with "hidden" spaces like swamps, canebrakes, forested interiors, caves, and so on—possessed an ongoing power.[36] Freud describes the uncanny feeling modern men continued to undergo—in his own latter-day imperial era—when gripped by an awareness of this knowledge, a knowledge he disparages by calling it a "primitive" "belief in the omnipotence of thoughts."[37]

In Faulkner's Yoknapatawpha, the temporally progressive phases of animistic-to-rational that Freud outlines in his essay are instead spatially mapped and differentiated as high and low ground, as white neighborhood and "Nigger Hollow," as Compson upstairs and servants' downstairs. Blues songs, including those adapted and performed for white audiences in Oxford and other Mississippi towns by W. C. Handy, also associated "low-down" spaces with black experience. Handy's "The Basement Blues" (1924) includes phrases like: "The man I love's got low-down ways fer true. . . . Well, I am Hinkty and I'm low-down too. . . . I was born low-down, way down in the low-ground. . . . Down in Zero, Mississippi all my folks is at, An' colored folks can't live much lower downer than that."[38] Both Caddy and Quentin, during their childhoods, pass between these alternate epistemological and territorial regimes. And recall that Benjy is down in the cellar on Easter morning listening to Luster trying to make music out of a saw. In the Ur-scene of the novel—"the only thing in literature which would ever move [Faulkner] very much"[39]—seven-year-old Caddy tries out a high-ground way of knowing as she ascends a tree to spy on the adults inside her house. As Benjy tells it: "We watched the muddy bottom of her drawers. Then we couldn't see her. We could hear the tree thrashing. . . . The tree quit thrashing. We looked up into the still branches." This scene might appear at first glance to be Faulkner's insertion of an overdetermined Garden of Eden tableau, as the inevitable "snake crawled out from under the house" and a female "Satan" (as Dilsey calls Caddy [45]), enlisting the help of a reluctant male (Versh), seeks the knowledge of life and death (in the form of Damuddy's funeral) and becomes marked, or soiled, by her infraction. And yet it fails as a replay of the classic Western epistemological fable, for Caddy actually gains no knowledge up in the tree. All she reports of what she sees is: "They're not doing anything in there. . . . Just sitting in chairs and looking" (46). It is actually Frony, the Gibson child, who possesses the knowledge of death, as she says, three times, "I knows what I knows" (36, 38, 39). Caddy greets these oracular statements with mixed emotions ("How do you know. . . . You dont know anything" [39]), unwilling to admit fully that a more insightful knowing must happen otherwise. Caddy has begun to sense that there is a limit to what she can discover through high-ground surveillance. Perhaps she just doesn't possess the charm to make this kind of masterful gaze work, so embodied, as a female, on the wrong side of the Enlightenment divide *as* nature.[40] More to the point, Faulkner is suggesting here that Caddy has already been initiated into another way of seeing so that the product of white observation will be forever unsatisfactory.

For some time, Caddy has been learning to inhabit (what Faulkner took to be) a black way of knowing: embodied, experiential, low-ground divination. We see this initiation in the story begun even before the pear tree scene appeared in Faulkner's mind and continued after *The Sound and the Fury* was finished, called "That Evening Sun," a title borrowed from the first line of W. C. Handy's song "Saint Louis Blues." In it, Nancy, the Compson family's laundress—the anti-Dilsey—introduces a very curious Caddy to a world of southern blues: coercive cross-racial sex, white male abuse of black women, attempted suicide in a jail cell, murder, haunting, possession, and conjuration.[41] What separates the Compson household from Nancy's house in "Nigger Hollow" is a "ditch," the crossing of which Nancy manages with perfect balance until her cuckolded husband, Jesus, lurks there to exact his revenge. In the story, Nancy typically inhabits a lower vantage from which she looks up with nonhuman eyes at the children. Her body becomes a kind of automaton at one point, caught up in a trance-apprehension of the death that "belong to" her (96). Caddy takes it all in, asking questions at every turn: "Slit whose belly, Nancy?" (83), "What did you see down there in the kitchen?" (84), "What ditch? . . . Why did a queen want to go into a ditch?" (91), and, moving through the ditch: "If Jesus is hid here, he can see us, can't he?" (98). The ditch where Nancy's bones ultimately lie appears a number of times in *The Sound and the Fury*. "Nancy" now refers to an animal whose carcass buzzards are undressing: Benjy sees them (33), and, just after Caddy and Quentin's failed murder-suicide scene at the branch, they come to "the ditch [that] was a black scar on the grey grass . . . lets see if you can see Nancys bones" (153). This story represents Caddy's initiation into low-ground perception.

Up in the pear tree then, Caddy is already marked with bottomland ways of knowing. Quentin wonders: "Why must you do like nigger women do in the pasture the ditches the dark woods" (92). The term associated with Caddy, "Muddy Bottom," suggests the bottomland hardwood forests that enriched the South and slowed the floodwaters before the era of deforestation. It also describes, for Faulkner, a bodily, experiential, low-ground, and magical way of knowing he associated with black people. He gave that phrase to Caddy as a kind of blues moniker. Through the mediations of Benjy and Quentin, Faulkner equated her body with the timbered resources of this bottom that northerners, in league with New South opportunists, were exploiting. Faulkner saw the knowledge she gains through physical experience and exploitation as the form black knowledge took in Mississippi. Caddy had an immersive blues knowledge of the Muddy Bottom, wherein embodying and knowing are indivisible.

The Sentinel's Horn

It is important to remember that Quentin was there, too, in "That Evening Sun." Odder still, Faulkner has Quentin narrate the story posthumously, much like Addie does in *As I Lay Dying*. He comes back from the grave to give witness to his and his siblings' initiation into a blues world, a world his father had termed (three times) "Nonsense" (96). Quentin, too, passes through the ditch and into the Hollow—encounters the space and episteme of the black environmental *heimlich*. When he looks down from his bed at Nancy on a pallet on the floor—the title of another Handy blues song[42]—"it was like Nancy was not there at all; that I had looked so hard at her eyes on the stairs that they had got printed on my eyeballs" (84). Quentin's second sight is that of an abused and possessed woman of African descent; it is the idea of a blues perspective that Faulkner derived from W. C. Handy's lyrics. Quentin learns about life in the low ground again when Versh tells him of a man who "mutilated himself. He went into the woods and did it with a razor, sitting in a ditch. A broken razor flinging them backward over his shoulder" (115–16). Quentin comes to read his own sense of environmental gelding into and through the black experience: the black male labor of deforestation appears in the form of black self-mutilation, such that what he's flinging backward over his shoulder are pieces of trees, the reproductive organs of the forest. In "Pantaloon in Black," Faulkner would forge the link in this substitution in the person of Rider, the conjured sawmill worker, when "the log seemed to leap suddenly backward over his head of its own volition."[43]

If Nancy gave Quentin the eyes to see his own life through the black environmental *heimlich*, it is Louis Hatcher who shows Quentin how to augur the environmental history of the South with a black second sight. Hunting with Louis, Quentin asks him: "when was the last time you cleaned that lantern?"

> "You member when all dat flood-watter wash dem folks away up yonder? I cleant hit dat ve'y day. Old woman and me settin fo de fire dat night and she say 'Louis, whut you gwine do ef dat flood git out dis fur?' And I say 'Dat's a fack. I reckon I had better clean dat lantun up.' So I cleant hit dat night."
>
> "That flood was way up in Pennsylvania," I said. "It couldn't ever have got down this far."
>
> "Dat's whut you says," Louis said. "Watter kin git des ez high en wet in Jefferson ez hit kin in Pennsylvaney, I reckon. Hit's de folks dat says de high watter cant git dis fur dat comes floatin out on de ridge-pole, too."
>
> . . . .
>
> "And you haven't cleaned that lantern since then."
>
> "Whut I want to clean hit when dey aint no need?"
>
> "You mean, until another flood comes along?"
>
> "Hit kep us outen dat un."
>
> "Oh, come on, Uncle Louis," I said.
>
> "Yes, suh. You do yo way en I do mine. Ef all I got to do to keep outen de high watter is to clean dis yere lantun, I wont quoil wid no man."

Quentin's recollection ends with the thought that when Louis "called the dogs in he sounded just like the horn he carried slung on his shoulder and never used, but clearer, mellower, as though his voice were a part of darkness and silence, coiling out of it, coiling into it again" (114–15).

The flood Louis and Quentin are referring to was the Johnstown Flood of 1889: though deemed an "Act of God" by the courts, over two thousand lives were lost in this ironworkers' town, made up of German and Welsh immigrants, when a dam, perched above their valley and improperly maintained by wealthy Pittsburgh steel magnates, collapsed. Two things are striking about its inclusion in Quentin's section. One, it was the first major anthropogenic flood in U.S. history. That Faulkner was drawing a genealogical line between it and the 1927 flood that runs through this novel is significant for our understanding of how Faulkner was sketching out a bigger, national pattern of class-based environmental injustice of which 1927 is a part. Second, Louis contends that floodwater originating in Pennsylvania could indeed get out as far as Jefferson. Much of the newspaper coverage of the Mississippi flood was at pains to make precisely this point that the Mississippi River drained the continent's waters "from the Rockies to the Alleghanies [sic],"[44] the latter being a range that extends into north-central Pennsylvania. When the Mississippi was severely flooded, as it was in 1927, it forced its lower tributaries to run in reverse, including the Yazoo River, to produce backwater flooding. Oxford (a.k.a. "Jefferson") makes up part of the Yazoo Drainage Basin.[45] In a very real, hydrogeological sense, then, Louis Hatcher was right when he hypothesized that floodwater from Pennsylvania *could* get as far as inland Mississippi. If it had been to escape the 1927 flood that he had climbed to the "top o dat knoll back de graveyard" (114) with a readied lantern, he would have been vindicated.[46]

Faulkner pairs this canniness on Louis's part with the kind of trust in illogical causation that Freud would have diagnosed as a trust in "the omnipotence of thoughts" that modern white men had "surmounted" and hence found to be uncanny. Louis thinks that if cleaning the lantern got him out of the first flood, that same act will save him and Martha from all future floods. The act of preparing a lantern, of course, is a way the gospel of Matthew imagines, in the Parable of the Ten Virgins (25:1–13), the anticipatory state of those wise enough to be always ready for the second coming of Christ. Hatcher trusts in ritual efficacy, but he also does not underestimate the physical breadth of the Mississippi River floodplain; he attributes causation to both physical and nonphysical forces. Faulkner casts this way of knowing as "coiling out of . . . and into" the atmosphere, as indistinguishable from its site of making. As such, it "sounds" environmental truth without pressing a "quoil." Even the word "quarrel"—or logocentric knowledge more broadly—starts to curve and flow into nature. Faulkner placed this scene here to suggest how this complex black environmental sensibility better augurs the Flood of 1927 than did white engineering.[47]

Faulkner imagined that what he considered to be black ways of seeing and knowing—of sounding and fathoming truth—coiled in and out of the Compson children: out of the ditch, the "Hollow," the bottom of the stairwell, the pallet on the floor, the "wet flo" of the cellar, all the lowland spaces. Caddy, as a figure for the rich bottomland hardwood forests of the South—the trees of the Muddy Bottom that "northern capital would convert into dollars in Ohio and Indiana and Illinois banks"—comes to share Nancy's state of being possessed ("everything emptied out of her eyes and they looked like the eyes in statues blank and unseeing and serene") and shares her sad foreknowledge of the environmental death that "belong" to her.[48] Quentin, powerless to stop this exploitation, and unable to husband these resources in regional isolation, comes to turn his body into a kind of divining rod—a figure who can feel the rising waters even when to others they are mute and unseen—and whose death can act as a "sign" (as Roskus said) of the floods to come. Jason, the narrator who turns the plangent subjective experience of others into merciless fact, who turns lyrical "discourse" into vindictive "story," is fittingly the first narrator explicitly to reveal the Flood of 1927 as a major historical signified of the text. Brooding, in his present moment of April 1928, on how "these damn jews" in New York bet on cotton futures and make a "killing" every time the price of cotton goes up in flood times, he spits:

> With the whole dam delta about to be flooded again and the cotton washed right out of the ground like it was last year. Let it wash a man's crop out of the ground year after year, and them up there in Washington spending fifty thousand dollars a day keeping an army in Nicarauga [*sic*] or some place. Of course it'll overflow again, and then cotton'll be worth thirty cents a pound. (234)

In other words, the politicians in Washington don't formulate a flood prevention program so that the bankers in New York can profit while the suckers in Mississippi get flooded and lose their crops. Jason's thoughts resemble the editorial comments appearing in the southern press during the flood; he's doing something like an unsavory version of a Will Rogers routine in stream of consciousness.[49]

It is left to the fourth narrator in *The Sound and the Fury* to traverse the "black scar" in the earth into the space of the African American community, where the narrator allows the reader to witness a "whelmin' flood." The Holy Weekend of 1928 marked the year's anniversary of the week when the high water passed the Delta, between the "Good Friday Storm" and the Mounds Landing crevasse six days later. As Dilsey, Frony, Luster, and Benjy head toward Easter service, the "street turned off at right angles, descending, and became a dirt road. On either hand the land dropped more sharply; a broad flat dotted with cabins whose weathered roofs were on a level with the crown of the road"; "broken things," "rank weeds," and "foul desiccation . . . surrounded the houses" below the "shaling [or gravel] levee" (290–91). To get to the black community from the white section of town, one descends and drops sharply to a flat plain below a levee; though it seems as if what is on top of this incline is just a road leading to the church, Faulkner places the word "levee" here to suggest the vulnerable lowlands running alongside and, during flood time, *below* the height of a swollen river—the land first to be flooded in the case of a crevasse. Inside the church, the preacher, a figure described as "long immured in striving with the implacable earth," takes up the sentinel's sound (begun by Louis Hatcher many years before) as his voice takes on the "sad, timbrous quality" of "an alto horn" (294). That note of warning ceases and his voice turns into "successive waves" that "whelm" the "worn small rock" of his body. Faulkner makes reference here to the same W. C. Handy song from which he took the title of "That Evening Sun." The line goes: "Dat man got a heart lak a rock cast in the sea / Or else he wouldn't have gone so far from me." But we are in a church on Easter Sunday, so the meaning of the blues line has been inverted. The preacher's body may be an overwhelmed rock, but not his heart. Songs have been made up throughout the year about the flood: from Bessie Smith's "Back-Water Blues" to Blind Lemon Jefferson's "Rising High Water Blues" and Barbecue Bob's "Mississippi Heavy Water Blues." In this liturgical commemoration of the Great Flood, though, Reverend Shegog reenacts it as a kind of passion play, using his voice to plummet his very body "beneath the successive waves" until they "consumed him" and then "took [the congregation] into" the waters as well. As the congregants go under, voices "without words" ascend like "bubbles arising in water." Finally, the "whelmin flood roll between." Because this is Dilsey's space on Easter Sunday—not the blues space of Nancy's conjured lowland hollow—Jesus here signifies the possibility of resurrection for those who "sees en believes" that the blood of sacrifice is meaningful. Louis's sentinel horn reappears as "de golden horns shoutin down de glory" and his wisely prepared lantern as "de resurrection en de light" (294–96).

Christianity, then, offered the only viable version of magical thinking for Faulkner's black environmental *Heimlich*. An immersive way of knowing, in which the mind and voice are "whelmed" by or "coiled out of" the very elements themselves, is terminal (as for Nancy, Quentin, and Caddy) unless one has the spiritual exhumation of Christianity to cast you as the last ruin standing. Recall how Bessie Smith described flood displacement as catastrophic in "Back-Water Blues": her protagonist is stuck between not being able to stay and not having any place to go, and sinks downward into a moan after her buoyant attempts to recover from the high water fail. And yet, according to Ralph Ellison, "within the tighter Negro community where the blues were a part of a total way of life . . . she was a priestess, a celebrant who affirmed the values of the group and man's ability to deal with chaos."[50] As cultural respondents to the flood, African American lyricists and blues preachers did not only forbear and "endure" like Dilsey or become tragic scars on the memory like Nancy. They became a major public voice of the southern region.

"The Mind(s) of the South" and Environmental Trauma in *As I Lay Dying*

The flood provided the environmental unconscious of Faulkner's first major novel, *The Sound and the Fury*.[51] In slyly performing a kind of "cut" to Freudian theory by bringing the unconscious back where Faulkner thought it belonged—

out of doors, that is—he wrote a novel in which his characters' lives, psyches, and ways of knowing were profoundly shaped by the environmental history of their region.[52] Because the Compsons are townsfolk who entitle themselves, through their racial and economic standing, to a certain distance from bottom-land experience, the children come to know about or symbolically suffer through the flood through black intermediaries. *As I Lay Dying*, written a year later, transforms the flood from an oblique referent (that is racially mediated from unconscious to conscious material) into a plot occurrence that is experienced by its main characters. Focusing in this novel on the Bundrens, Faulkner affords himself the opportunity to imagine how a family of small-scale cotton farmers might have physically encountered backwater inundation from the 1927 Mississippi flood. He places the river scenes at the very center of the novel, in a cluster of chapters that comprise one-sixth of the book. Though the flooding is at the experiential core of the novel, it is nevertheless not an event realistically or directly rendered. We rely on minor narrators to let us know that this high water is an historically unprecedented flood while each of our major narrators gives us a variant, emotionally and perceptually shocked rendering of the strange cosmos before them.

Though Faulkner saw the 1927 flood as the South's most catastrophic collision with modernization to date, he also understood the flood's place in a looping series of crises brought on by the Machine Age, reckless resource extraction, and speculative capitalism. Casting Darl as a returning veteran of the Great War, on the one hand, and dating his manuscript October 25, 1929, the day after the Wall Street panic erupted, Faulkner signals that these two crises are the bookend occurrences of the book's modern world. Critics have thus understandably read *As I Lay Dying* as both a World War I novel and a novel that inaugurates the fiction of the Great Depression.[53] I concur that Faulkner deeply interested himself in how—as John Dewey put it—"forces so vast, so remote in initiation, so far-reaching in scope and so complexly indirect in operation" could be "felt" and "suffered" by people in apparent peripheries but not fully "known."[54] To critic John Limon's claim, though, that "the Great War explains *As I Lay Dying*," I would answer: only in part. And to his rhetorical question, what else is "the reason for the sheer muddiness of [the novel], which is perhaps the muddiest book in all literature?" I would answer that, while the mud in the novel recalls that of French and Belgian trench warfare, it is more certainly and substantially the mud of the estranged Mississippi watershed. It represents the mud made when water, mechanistically shunted from northern soils and corralled into four-story-high levees, broke like a cataract onto the Delta. If, as Limon argues, Faulkner began his career writing war fiction with

Soldiers' Pay "on the assumption that coming to terms with the Great War was the first obligation of the novelist," I would argue that Faulkner arrived at his great fiction once he decided that coming to terms with the land-use practices of global capitalism—and how they were locally felt—was an even greater obligation for him.[55] *As I Lay Dying*, narrated mainly by a character who experiences the flood through a visual, psychic, and epistemological apparatus deeply affected by the war and its art forms, gives us a singular opportunity to watch Faulkner connect the Great Flood with the Great War, while also adapting European avant-garde representational techniques to his region's crisis.

Though there are many similarities between *The Sound and the Fury* and *As I Lay Dying*—each operates at the scale of the family, and in each family is a single daughter, multiple brothers, a bedridden mother, and a wounded or weak patriarch—the 1930 novel uses to different effect the family's role as a focalizer of larger patterns of social history. While character names like Candace, Jason, and Benjamin allude to biblical or Greco-Roman mythological figures, allusions that loosely suggest the imperial dimensions of 1920s North-South relations, the character names in *As I Lay Dying* instead draw into the novel's orbit a world of southern, and especially Mississippi, politics.[56] Any reader paying attention to recent southern culture and politics would have recognized the names Cash, Anse, Whitfield, and Vardaman. Residents of Faulkner's home county may have heard in the name "Lafe" a suggestion of their locale, Lafayette County. And citizens of Oxford would also have known the name Bundren. Faulkner enlists this recent regional history as a means of producing a satirical political portrait of the South's ongoing experiment in modernization. Coiled together with this satirical strand, though, is a plangent exploration of scientific and aesthetic responses to the crises that coalesced in 1927. While *The Sound and the Fury* buckled with Freud to propose a psychogeographic foundation of self, *As I Lay Dying* puts both the science of equilibrium and the practices of revolutionary art to the test as means by which to grapple with the calamities of the modern age.

Slanted Names

The names locate the Bundren family in political time and space. They suggest to readers that what may seem like an eccentric remote kin-world poised on top of a "damn mountain" (43) can also be read at the scale of a broader political and geographic unit. J. B. Bundren was elected the supervisor of Beat Four in Lafayette County in 1911.[57] Anselm (or Anse) McLaurin was both U.S. senator from and governor of Mississippi intermittently in the 1890s and 1910s. A rather scandalous public figure, he was associated with nepotism, open drunkenness, the nefarious pardoning of convicted murderers, vote rigging, and vindictiveness against his enemies; he ruffled big-time Delta planters, including LeRoy Percy, but "sensed more than any other Mississippian of his time the growing political consciousness of the small farmer."[58] James K. Vardaman was Mississippi's governor in 1904 and its senator in 1913, defeating Percy. He was "the political champion of the hill-county whites"[59] and a reformer of institutions (including insane asylums) as he opposed the planter oligarchy, banks, railroads, the lumber trust, and all other "'predatory' corporate interests."[60] His populist advocacy of poorer whites was coupled with fierce racist pronouncements, ranting that "we would be justified in slaughtering every Ethiop on the earth to preserve unsullied the honor of one Caucasian home" and alleging that the Negro had cost the country more than "all the wars it has waged, added to the ruin wrought by flood and fire."[61] In 1924, Henry L. Whitfield, a former superintendent of education, was elected governor of Mississippi, defeating another key race-baiting demagogue, Theodor Bilbo.[62] These names—Whitfield, Vardaman, Anse, and Bundren—once brought into the world of Faulkner's novel, call forth the genuine hardship of hill-country whites within a national economic milieu as well as the political conflicts in Mississippi having to do with intrawhite class antagonism and its invocation of "the Negro" as a hysterical lever in that debate.

The name "Cash" moves us outside of Mississippi. Just months before Faulkner started writing his novel in October 1929, Wilbur J. Cash had thrown down a rather contemptuous gauntlet at the region of his birth in the form of his *American Mercury* article "The Mind of the South." Heavily influenced by the verbal style and past efforts at southern critique by the magazine's editor, H. L. Mencken, Cash attempted to hang up in print, for the world to see, a picture of the dopey intransigence of the region's "group mind." Here was a mind that "begins and ends with God"; sees evolution as "the overthrow of Heaven"; "cannot retain or contemplate hard facts"; swears by John Locke's "private rights" philosophy and Adam Smith's realpolitik of individualist self-interest without perceiving that the factories of the New South were turning the Machine Age worker into nothing but "an atom among atoms," a mote who had placed his rights "within the hands of a steadily decreasing few." He closes his piece by predicting that, despite this antimodern mentality unknowingly caught in the meshes of industrial modernization, a change would surely come: "For, undeniably, there is a stir, a rustling upon the land, a vague, formless, intangible thing which may or may not be the adumbration of coming upheaval."[63] Cash's high-visibility critique of the South—and what it borrowed from Mencken's own fulminations—certainly represented a prominent tactic that Faulkner deployed in the book's more contemptuous moments, in Peabody's diatribes, for example, or in the book's devastatingly smirky conclusion.

The naming process, however, does not work in the straightforward way that it might if *As I Lay Dying* were a simple allegory. Though the corrupt behaviors of Anse Bundren and Anselm McLaurin do correspond in telling ways, the naming otherwise falters as a key to character. If, for example, the nationally known political name "Vardaman" was meant to operate as a sign for a race-baiting demagogue, why would Faulkner give that name to a child character whom the author associates not with political rhetoric or action but with imaginative processes of cross-species substitutions in the wake of his mother's death? Vardaman, moreover, is much more under the spell of Darl, the brother Faulkner associates with a very different kind of (aesthetic) radicalism than the politician's radical racism. And why would Faulkner give the name "Cash" to the brother least given to criticizing his family's failings? Faulkner brings these names to the Bundren farm not to make his characters exact stand-ins for political figures but rather as a kind of heavily squatting political ambience or cloud. The reader will be stumped if she tries to impose Wilbur Cash onto Cash Bundren. The reader, instead, has to observe what Cash Bundren actually does and says to infer an historical echo. Thus the names work as a both heavy-handed and mischievous invitation to understand contemporaneous southern mentalities and materialities through an alert study of the characters' modes of perception and histories. As such, Faulkner not only was undertaking a family saga that could stand on its own internal dynamics but was simultaneously crafting a work of experimental southern historiography.

The central female characters—when read at the regional scale I am suggesting Faulkner invites us to do—embody the southern land and its resources. Addie, as many have noted, is associated with "new earth," "water bubbling up and away," trees, the "quiet smelling of damp and rotting leaves" (169), "wild geese" and "wild darkness," being "planted" (170), and "the red bitter flood boiling through the land" (174). She is, lying under humanity's, and especially patriarchy's, errant constructions, "the dark land talking the voiceless speech" (175).[64] In short, she is the wild, violated, and "harsh" environmental matrix of the South. Dewey Dell, her daughter, is associated likewise with the land at large—"the horizons and the valleys of the earth" (164)—but also quite specifically with cotton, or what becomes of wild land once it is turned into a mono-culture. The burden she carries with her to town, trying to unload with various double-dealing middlemen along the way, is associated with a scene of cotton picking. Dewey Dell decides that if her sack is full by the time she finishes picking a row of cotton then she "could not help" but have sex with Lafe; Lafe, rather unscrupulously, "pick[s] into [her] sack" (27) to make it full. Though the new pregnancy she carries in July could not have been the result of this specific sexual encounter, the connection between her procreation and the cotton field's harvest is hard to miss.[65] What is suggested is that Lafayette County coerces its fields into reproduction, and the market forces subject that yield to new forms of coercion. The female Bundrens, when read allegorically, represent the environmental matrix of a land that has been domesticated to the point of a strange enfolding of death within life.

Darl's Spy-Glass

Darl and Cash are the most prominent characters through whom Faulkner muses upon, and tests out, potential aesthetic and scientific responses to this crisis in human-environmental relations. Darl dominates the narration of the novel with nineteen chapters (as opposed to his brother Jewel's one, for example). Early on, as soon as Darl describes what Jewel is doing in a far pasture (12), we realize that Faulkner has crafted this "Darl" as an experimental hybrid, for Darl is both a character intimately sharing his own thoughts and a third-person omniscient narrator. It is as if, having tried both techniques in separate sections of *The Sound and the Fury*, Faulkner wonders how it will work to combine the subjective and (putatively) objective into one. Part of Darl's strangeness derives from his being simultaneously fleshed and unfleshed, intradiegetic and extradiegetic, one susceptible brain and the authoritative cogito of this fiction. That Faulkner chose to pair Darl's narrative weirdness with Darl's exposure to war—and eventually flood—suggests that the author wanted us to consider, and closely feel, the links between traumatic experience and strangely unbounded epistemology. We depend on Darl more than on anyone else because of the frequency of his narration and because he is given an extraordinary access to the storytelling machinery. That Faulkner allows Darl into his own extradiegetic space, moreover, invests Darl's fate, and the imploding of his sanity, with something of Faulkner's own position. When Darl rides the train to Jackson, then, at the novel's end and has drawn that third-person objectifying gaze perilously inside his brain, our loss of Darl as a subject is remarkably disturbing. It strands us.

To better understand how Faulkner uses the odd configuration of Darl's narration to communicate the historical crises of war and flood, let us first explore his optical disposition. Faulkner's shorthand for describing the mental apparatus Darl got "in France at the War" is to say that he acquired a certain "spyglass" (254). When Darl was a boy, Anse tells us, his eyes were "full of the land all the time." Darl "was alright" because "the land laid up-and-down ways then," but once "that ere road come and switched the land around longways" and the law "threaten[ed] me out of him," Darl acquired a pair of eyes that nature had "run out of" (36–37). Ever after Darl would be distinguished by "them queer eyes of hisn that makes folks talk" (125). In other words, Darl was sane before he was drafted and sent to Europe. Importantly though, Anse also ties his son's loss of sanity to shifts in land use from a local subsistence economy to one controlled by global commodity and financial markets.

Once he possesses the "spy-glass," nature doesn't rule his mode of seeing, for Darl has abandoned the viewing habits fostered by painterly naturalism for the visual estrangements of the avant-garde. As Watson Branch and others have noted, Darl turns his surroundings into startling art objects.[66] He sees cotton fields as a collection of geometric shapes viewed simultaneously from multiple perspectives. He visually penetrates the clothing of his adolescent sister and spies out her hidden sexual acts. Like others in the Dada and Surrealist circles, he is a shocking monteur, who combines human bodies with inanimate materials, with animal heads and legs and wings, and with violating tools. He dwells on nocturnal dream sights of an "orifice in nothingness" (11) and "surreptitious" worms that shock one awake (103). He sees art in chance occurrences (as in wood chips whose pattern on the ground becomes "random smears of paint"). Finally, Darl's ability to see in two geographically distant places at once speaks to the uncanny aspect of the various modern optical technologies—like film and photography—in which "the real" is both extended and undermined by mechanical reproducibility.[67] Darl sees "queer" because he wears the glasses of modernization and modernist art. Moreover, by allowing Darl to be both first- and third-person narrators, Faulkner brings these modern visual technologies of "distance" seeing into the novel, thereby disturbing it.

Faulkner himself when in Paris in 1925 had viewed the work of Cubist painter André Lhote, but he had also visited a "very, very modernist exhibition . . . futurist and vorticist" as well as other galleries exhibiting "numberless young and struggling moderns."[68] The Vorticists, in their heyday just before the war, had emulated the designs of machines as a way to perceive the fundamentals of matter—in order, as Wyndham Lewis said, "to get deeply enough immersed in material life to experience the shaping power amongst its vibrations."[69] Faulkner came to interest himself not so much in mechanization's "shaping power" but in how natural things had been turned into odd, colossal machines capable less of "shaping" than of violently disintegrating and recombining their own biology.

During and just after wartime, it was especially the Dadaists, developing in the separate metropoles of Zurich, Berlin, Cologne, New York, and Paris, who, witnessing a machine, war, and consumer age that had brought on a kind of disastrous "exploded mimicry"[70] of familiar forms, drew attention to this process by cognate acts of representational shock.[71] I imagine Darl, when in France, being drawn to such a movement. Indeed the "little spy-glass" he acquires there—loaded inside with a scene of "a woman and a pig with two backs and no face" (254)—sounds like the description of a Dada montage, its shocking combination revealing the mind's uncanny thoughts and desires. Darl must have been reminded a decade later, once he tumbles into floodwaters, that no other way of seeing makes quite so much sense. In one manifesto, Tristan Tzara pronounced that Dada was "a furious Wind, tearing the dirty linen of clouds and prayers, preparing the great spectacle of disaster, fire, decomposition."[72] Dadaists responded in an "*occasional*" (or occasion-based) and spontaneous manner to use art to redirect the world toward "*something else*."[73] The practitioners' visual tactics included abstraction, collage, and montage as well as processes involving chance and automatization.[74] Naturalism, or "any imitation of nature, however concealed," was, in the words of Dadaist Richard Huelsenbeck, "a lie" that linked itself with bourgeois morality and tired art traditions.[75] Though Dada, in mimicking the war's splicing of "the human" with so much considered un-human, sought to expose that "Nature" was just an Enlightenment invention that policed its own fondest polarities (human/animal, human/machine, man/woman, reason/unreason), it rarely addressed the environmental effects of modernization as such. Faulkner, to the contrary, makes apparent in *As I Lay Dying* that an "imitation of nature" would not be "a lie" as long as it acknowledged how strange nature had become. For Faulkner, being a Modernist of the rural South meant that his "exploded mimicry" would first and foremost take its cue from imitating the neo-nature around him. He would call *As I Lay Dying* a deliberate "tour-de-force" because, as he said, he "took this family and subjected them to the two greatest catastrophes which man can suffer—flood and fire."[76] Darl, possessed of that Tzara-like, "furious" mode of seeing, has the "queer eyes" to connect Dada's "disaster, fire, decomposition" with what lies before him in Mississippi. Darl has the consciousness of the postwar avant-garde artist. He is the novel's internal modernist who can also access and alter the book's narrative machinery.

Cash's Tools

What the spy-glass is to Darl, the carpenter's tools are to Cash. They are the materializations of his consciousness. And what these tools are meant to do is design and build the world into perfect composure and "balance." Cash does not show himself to be particularly aggrieved by his mother's deteriorating health. In some ways, it does not matter to Cash whether she is alive or dead, as long as she is framed by a secure structure. As Addie looks out her window at him building her coffin, Cash "slants" two boards "into their final juxtaposition, gesturing toward the ones yet on the ground, shaping with his empty hand in pantomime the finished box" (48). In the window, she is turned into a "composite picture" by his glance; this temporary framing anticipates his ultimate composition of her body in the box. Cash constructs a careful "clock-shape" (88) design, made to "balance" according to Addie's "measure and weight" (90). Cash defends, in an enumerated list, the thesis behind the coffin's design. Though these reasons start out with a physical logic to them (beveled seams give nails more surface to grip), they quickly become strained, reaching, speculative, dead-pan nonsensical (6. is "Except"), and vitalist (8. is "Animal magnetism") (83). The form of the methodological abstract, or manifesto, is strictly adhered to, but the content becomes unknowingly auto-parodic. There is something slightly quackish in Cash's science. Despite his strangely doctrinaire design, it is foiled when the womenfolk put Addie in her coffin upside down. Over the ensuing days, when Addie's decomposing body tilts off kilter, Cash will come to be identified with the utterances: "It wont balance" (96), "it aint balanced now" (98), "It aint on a balance" (144, 145), and "It wasn't on a balance" (165).[77] Having fallen off a church, "balance" is Cash's true God.

When *As I Lay Dying* is viewed as a work of regional historiography, Cash becomes suggestive of contemporaneous southern social scientists. In their mixture of ardor for and obsessive analysis of the South, and the way they created word portraits that seemed to function like immuring boxes, these practitioners must have made Faulkner muse about the best way to "*Tell about the South*"[78] in print to a curious world. Take, for example, Howard W. Odum, a South Carolinian by birth with a Columbia PhD, chair of the South's first sociology department at the University of North Carolina, founder of the Institute for Research in Social Science, and editor of the influential *Journal of Social Forces*.[79] During the 1920s, Odum developed an "all-embracing portraiture approach" to his subject, one that, through the inclusion of a mass of data poised between the negative and positive, would render the South "a visual, almost palpable entity" and stress its inherent "balance."[80] Social science would provide him with the tools, or the "artificial mechanical extension of man's senses," to carry out "exact quantitative, mechanistic measurement of relationships."[81] Through his training in sociology at Clark University and Columbia, Odum had imbibed the organicist model[82] developed earlier by Herbert Spencer, which saw society as a kind of organism that grew increasingly complex, specialized, and stable as it evolved, ultimately achieving a long-term equilibrium. Odum saw that the South was bedeviled by problems—racial conflict, industrial labor issues, and a lack of healthy institutions—but he trusted that equilibrium was the state it would ultimately achieve, especially with the help of social scientists. His composite pictures argued for an inchoate but evolving balance.[83]

Faulkner's Cash, like these southern-born social analysts, is a believer in quantification, measurement, classification, and the "artificial mechanical extension of man's senses." Like Odum, and his compulsion to insert "balance" into all of his data fields because balance held a transcendental truth for him, Cash is trying to assure "balance" by placing Addie (or the southern matrix) in its carefully measured frames exactly so. Cash continues to assert, in a weary echo of himself, that if only "balance" can be achieved, the social organism will progress without disturbance. Faulkner satirically reveals the way in which quantitative science can become its own God by having Cash insert in his rationalist list a vitalist category.[84]

Land Use

What moves at the center of this family saga is, of course, Addie's corpse, the storm it raises up, and the flood it brings on. When we approach the novel as a work of modernist historiography, we see that Faulkner is exploring how segments of southern society—the academic social critics and scientists, and the avant-garde artists—address the fundamental issue for a rural region, namely land use, and in this case its catastrophic consequences. In short, he explores how white southern publics relate to their material ground. Doctor Peabody, the expert diagnostician who arrives from town too late to do any good, doesn't ever tell us much about Addie's body but does give us discomfiting information about the topography of the Bundrens' land and the area's history of logging. With Peabody's arrival, we come to see the terrain as dramatically vertical: the house perches atop a "bluff," a "damn wall" (42), indeed, a "damn mountain" that can't be scaled without a rope to "haul" a body up and down it (43). That Anse offers a "plowline" (42) to do the hauling makes the connection between the practice of plowing and the perilous verticality of the topography. The environing, apocalyptic weather also makes Peabody see the "black cloud" on high as a "topheavy mountain range, like a load of cinders dumped" (42). This image of a mountain range reduced to cinders then leads Peabody to reflect on "a worry about this country being deforested someday" (42). What Peabody has conjured before our eyes is a vision of the Bundren land as a nearly tree-less and overplowed terrain in which the soil has been subjected to ever more dramatic gullying and a vulnerability to extreme weather events.

In the early twentieth century, "the hill lands of the north Mississippi Loess Plains . . . were among the most severely eroded in the United States," explains Charles S. Aiken, due in part to "careless tillage practices," practices that led one commentator as early as 1860, only thirty years after white settlement, to comment that this land was "in danger of going, in the most literal sense, '*down hill.*'"[85] Peabody sees the supine body before him, already "dead these ten days" (43), not as a human but as a "tenement or a town" (44), "a bundle of rotten sticks," a rubber "hose," "lamps" nearly empty of oil, and a "pack-horse" (45). In other words, he sees the cadaver before him as a humanly settled, severely worked, commodified, and "wor[n] out" (41) place.[86] Again, it's not a woman all this causes him to muse on but instead "our rivers, our land: shaping and creating the life of man in its implacable and brooding image" (45). Having catalogued the human power to harm the land, with this statement he completes the thought, attesting to the ongoing power of an altered nature to "shap[e]" the "life of man." Indeed, though the object of his diagnosis is already "dead," it still has the power to express itself "harsh and strong" (46). The ensuing flood is testimony, in this story, to how a deadened nature speaks. Moreover, Faulkner's placement of Addie's section in the midst of the river scenes connects her utterances to the river's own vocalizations.

This scene of a doctor who brings a diagnosis but no relief to the suffering patient appeared in newspapers during the Flood of 1927. Recall the cartoon "After the Diagnosis" that was printed in the *Philadelphia Ledger* during May, depicting the Mississippi River as an ailing, supine patient ineffectively ministered to by Secretary Hoover and Army Corps of Engineers chief Edgar Jadwin (see Fig. 3.7). The Memphis *Commercial Appeal* produced its own version of this cartoon on June 1, called "Saying It with Flowers," that visualized President Coolidge presenting a pathetic potted flower as "the Government's Official Sympathy" for "The Crippled South," bedridden and bandaged (Fig. 6.1). Addie, likewise, has a bioregional body. Though many visit her bedside, none—not even those with expert knowledge of the origin of her disease—can provide a cure.

More information about local logging practices emerges the closer we draw to the flooded river. As Darl, Cash, and Jewel are looking for the old ford to get over the high water, the older two brothers share thoughts about the fact that Vernon Tull, their neighbor, has been logging down by the river: "cut a sight of timber outen here" to pay off his mortgage, one says. Indeed, because Tull "cut them two big whiteoaks" by which folks had in "the old days . . . line[d] up the

SAYING IT WITH FLOWERS!

6.1. J. P. Alley, "Saying It with Flowers," *Commercial Appeal*, June 1, 1927, 1. Commercial Appeal/Landov.

ford," the brothers cannot locate a path across the water (142). Another feature of the deforested riverscape is that, because an "old road" had been "cleaned out" of vegetation by Tull to transport his lumber, the road seems to Darl to be "soaked free of earth and floated upward, to leave in its spectral tracing a monument to a still more profound desolation than this above which we now sit" (143).

Tull, a name associated with the modernization of husbandry, is suggestive of a New South agriculturalist.[87] Unlike the younger Bundrens, who hire themselves out as wage laborers (transporting timber and clearing fields) even though Pa owns his small farm, Tull uses his property's surplus resources (trees) to operate in wider mercantile and credit markets. As such, Tull also represents the postbellum practice of southern states that handled their straightened economies by selling off the region's forests, and other resources, to external financiers. Tull distinguishes himself from Darl, who, he says, "thinks by himself too much" (71), by averring that a brain should be "like a piece of machinery. . . . best when it all runs along the same, doing the day's work and not no one part used no more than needful" (71). Like Darl, he too sees through "one of these here spy-glasses," but instead of the pig-woman copula inside Darl's French optical apparatus, he sees his own prosaic mule, and in him "all the broad land and my house sweated outen it like it was the more the sweat, the broader the land" (139). In other words, Tull sees the surplus value created by his animal laborer and the various forms this surplus value will assume. Though Tull's mechanistic brain processes this input from his "spy-glasses" with assurance, Darl and Cash look out at the logged riverscape and, instead of seeing surplus, feel perilously disoriented. And while a human corpse lies in their cart ("above which we now sit"), it is especially how that body indicates the overall "specter" of earthly things being "soaked free of earth" that betokens for Darl "a still more profound desolation."

In the Water

What lies before and under the two brothers is not just a swollen river. It is a "flood" (157). As Tull explained, "a fellow" looking at it "couldn't tell where was the river and where the land. It was just a tangle of yellow and the levee not less wider than a knife back" (124). Armstid reported a tremendously long crevasse where "the levee through Haley bottom had gone down for two miles" (185). At Samson's, they "hadn't never see the river so high" and the old men there "hadn't never see nor hear of it being so in the memory of man" (111).[88] Though the river crossing is rich with biblical and classical echoes, Faulkner has clearly taken pains to link this scene of high water on the Yoknapatawpha River with the historical referent of the 1927 flood, when water reached unprecedented levels "in the memory of man" and made numerous tributaries run in reverse, producing extensive backwater flooding in the Yazoo River Basin. Faulkner described, in a 1954 article titled "Mississippi," how the overflowing big river would push the little ones backward "as far upstream as Wylie's Crossing above Jefferson."[89] We've discussed, too, how Louis Hatcher had informed Quentin of similar backwater flooding. Though the first high waters receded in Mississippi during May, a second episode of flooding occurred in June, meaning that waters did not finally recede until August. Faulkner is therefore tying the Bundrens' July crossing of a flooded Yoknapatawpha River to events in the spring and summer of 1927.

Because Faulkner has provided, through Peabody, Darl, and Cash, information about the deforestation of this watershed, as well as descriptions of the monoculture planting of cotton—effectively providing much of the contemporaneous environmentalist explanation for flooding—it is no surprise that midriver what upends Addie's coffin—or a reified, wasted territory—is a log, surging "*for an instant upright . . . like Christ*" or like "an old man or a goat" (148). It is as if "something huge and alive" that lives "just beneath the surface" of the water, coming into "alertness" (141) only an instant at a time, has jetted out this log as its satyr-like agent of revenge.[90] Unlike all the journalistic commentators who, during the spring of 1927, personified the flooding river as something monstrous—a "giant, bloated snake," a "mighty old dragon"[91]—Faulkner's choice of an animated agent of destruction incorporates an environmental critique as he links the commodification and destruction of forests with flooding through the figure of the crucified tree.

Faulkner arranges the figures on the riverbank with great deliberation. While he shows some getting safely to the other side on a bridge, he places Cash, Darl, and Jewel, along with Addie and three animals, *in* the flood itself. Having associated Darl and Cash with contemporary art and science, this spatial positioning allows him to move them through the flood and examine their mentalities and behaviors in the urgency of a particular historical and environmental crisis. The flood will have the plastic power to test the fate of modern science and art under the most extreme duress. Because Jewel is represented frequently as a physical actor but seldom opened to us as a thinker, it is hard to know what Jewel imagines will solve the problems before him. Despite his relatively closed-off consciousness, his bodily dramaturgy—as when Jewel's head is surrounded by a "glittering maze of hooves" that seem like "an illusion of wings" (12)—is, in its part-mythical, part-biblical fantasia, suggestive of repurposed religious iconography. Given that he is inseparable from his horse and associated with a violent and isolationist love of Addie (15), Jewel brings to mind a long tradition of southern chivalry, memorials to Confederate cavalry, and, more specifically, a "Lost Cause" regional defensiveness.[92]

As the three brothers, bearing Addie, prepare to enter the flood, they link themselves together by a rope. The rope begins in Darl's hands and coils around Cash's seat stanchion until it coils around Jewel's saddle horn and into his hand. This configuration, followed as it is by scenes of one or another brother riding on the coffin, seems to gesture toward the novel Faulkner said in 1927 he most wished he had written: *Moby Dick*.[93] In Melville's novel, the "monkey rope" literalizes the bonds of homosocial obligation and fellowship; in the *Pequod*'s motherless world, it is a kind of fraternal umbilical cord.[94] In Faulkner's novel, the rope seems likewise to offer the guarantee of fraternal solidarity in a time of crisis. But when the satyr-god "rocket[s]" out of the water to upend Addie's coffin (inverting *Moby Dick*'s closing scenario),[95] Cash quickly unloops the rope from around his seat, tells Darl to let it go, and urges Jewel onward, even as he

makes Jewel believe he is still tethered to his brothers. Liberated from the burden, Jewel and his horse move "unbelievably fast" (148). Meanwhile, the team
of mules, who have "already seen in the thick water the shape of the disaster
which they could not speak" (147) and who cannot sever their "taut" connection to the wagon, for an instant "shine black out of water" until "the downstream one vanishes, dragging the other with him" (148); a moment later, the
"head of one mule appears, its eyes wide," looking "back at us for an instant,
making a sound almost human" before vanishing again (149). As Cash tries to
brace the coffin and his tools, Darl "jump[s]" (149) into the water. And soon
enough, despite Cash's "leaning more and more" to provide counterbalance, the
wagon is "tilted" (153) beyond recall. The log, after completing its "job," moves
on and the box is set "loose" (154).

Cash, having broken his leg once when he "fell off that church," breaks it
again. His public devotion to the science of "balance" has been violently dis-
proven. In a profound, ontological sense, this flood experience has intimated to
him that the universe is not characterized by equilibrium but by "risk" (127),
fluidity, and disturbance. Having put "balance" to the test and watched it fail,
Cash is "sick on the box" (195). The object of his exact design ("the box") has
become an exhibition platform for the "exploded mimicry" of his methodology.
Cash now wears a "profound questioning look" (209), with eyes "interrogatory,
intent, and sad" (207). His toolbox overturned, each of his tools has spilled out
into the water. Carefully recovered by Tull and Jewel, the tools henceforth perform no work but instead are treated by Cash as a kind of holy relic.[96] Darl now
sees his older brother not as a "piston" (77) of modern energy but as a container
of "sawdust . . . running out" (207). Cash's balance will never be restored; as
Peabody says: "don't tell me it aint going to bother you to have to limp around
on one short leg for the balance of your life—if you walk at all again" (240).
"Balance" now indicates a remainder of time rather than an inherent quality of
the universe. Nor will Cash himself define balance the same way going forward.
When he muses about Darl's incarceration, he uses "balance" to mean a kind of
tyranny of the majority or a way to talk about ideology: "Sometimes I think it
aint none of us pure crazy and aint none of us pure sane until the balance of us
talks him that-a-way. It's like it aint so much what a fellow does, but it's the way
the majority of folks is looking at him when he does it." But, he concludes, "I
don't know" (233–34).[97]

Jewel was not so much harmed in the flood as he was intensified. That motion lost to Cash seems almost to have been transferred to his more adamant
brother, whose motto is "Just so we do something" (146). The whiteness in his
eyes turns to a "bone-white" (187) and his face begins to shake as if he had "a

aguer" (188). Associated as Jewel is with Lost Cause iconography, one could say that catastrophe makes him more possessed by the idea of whiteness, a possession that gives him a sickly, even cadaverous intensity. Jewel has not reassessed anything in the flood; rather, the crisis has hardened his determination to achieve a vision of southern advancement as an enactment of white homecoming. Recall that it is especially after the flood, and its degradations, that Jewel takes his shame out on African American strangers. For days leading up to their arrival in Jefferson, the family has had to subject itself to the outraged scrutiny of townsfolk. During the Flood of 1927, like the Scopes Trial two years before it, a northern media circus came to squat on the South. As I detailed in chapter 3, the press produced coverage for the rest of the nation that was by turns paternalizing, gothic, outraged, and acidic. The *Chicago Daily News*, for example, quoted one outside official involved in recovery work as saying, "If we can get these people to clean up physically and socially, we can save them."[98] In the novel, the Bundren family is exposed throughout their travails to the external gaze and touch of "healers" (doctors, pharmacists, and preachers) who appear to offer aid but in fact only extract more resources from family members. Faulkner's treatment of bloated and acid-tongued Dr. Peabody, in fact, operates like an amusing send-up of Mencken the self-serving social diagnostician.[99] But it is particularly when Jewel sees "shock and instinctive outrage" in the faces of three "negroes" that Jewel spits out "Sons of a bitches" (229). Faulkner depicts, by having characters continuously note Jewel's darker and then ultimately black skin, the fury white southerners felt when the flood seemed to place rural whites below the caste of cosmopolitan blacks.[100]

What happens to Darl in the waters? Even before the flood, Darl has been made apparently "queer" in the head by his exposure to war, modernization, and modernist art in France (125). It is a mark of the traumatic psychological and epistemological force of the flood that, comparatively speaking, it is this event that causes the "majority" to see Darl as "crazy" (233). Indeed, Faulkner seems to give some substance to this diagnosis as he puts Darl through a transformation: while passing through the flood, Darl comes in contact with an intense vitalism. Below the water's surface is "something huge and alive" (144). Underneath the "false blandness the true force of it leans lazily against us" (158). This force is radically creative, working "like hands molding and prodding at the very bones" (158) and turning the ford's "flat surface" into "troughs and hillocks" (147). While underwater, Darl seems to have been "dissolved into" this "myriad original motion," such that "seeing and hearing" become "blind and deaf" (164). Two key organs of the human perceptual sensoria, those channels for data through which the Lockean mind is filled and energized toward higher activities, have been terminated. Moreover, the Cartesian distinction between subject and object has been obviated. Before the flood, Darl had been a prodigy of super-sensory knowing, functioning much like the latest modern visual technologies as he saw at great distances and through solid matter. After the flood, though, his senses no longer provide a pathway to information. Like Cash, he now responds to his family's expectation of his seer-like perception with the phrase "I don't know" (162).

Cora thinks that "it was the hand of God" (153) that caused the flood and that Darl, in particular, was "touched by God Himself" (168). Though the log avenger, really a composite of log-goat-Christ-old man, suggests that a much more syncretic divinity than Cora has in mind is at work here, Darl is "touched"—indeed, molded, prodded as well as blinded and deafened by its force.[101] Running through the river's "myriad original motion" are other, stranger, more latter-day velocities and forces. Darl feels in the river the "motion of the wasted world accelerat[ing] just before the final precipice" (146). With the words "accelerating" and "precipice," Faulkner makes this "wasted world" seem more apocalyptic engine than cyclical *bios*. This is the motion of an engine that has worn itself out in a kind of suicidal love of hyper-celerity. Elsewhere, Darl feels the river's altered motion to be like that of "machinery" (163) capable of "sever[ing] . . . at a single blow, the two torsos" of Jewel and Tull. These two dismembered torsos then appear to "mov[e] with infinitesimal and ludicrous care upon the surface" (163). Blind Darl, unclotted and dissolved into water, watches two other half-men glide atop the river.

Though there has, up until this scene, been an ambient doom in the sulfurous, world's-end landscape atop the Bundrens' "mountain," it is only now, as the adulterated river shows its machine-like destructive capacity, that the trauma of Europe's Machine Age war comes back to Darl. Looking at the flood, he recalls, and superimposes, the trenches. In Mississippi mud is the doubled presence of the muddy battlefield. Thus all the abstract pictures Darl has been making with his mind since he returned from France have, in the flooding river, at last found a fully stimulating, or radicalizing, objective correlative.[102] If the war made him see "queer" but not quite as "queer" as a Dadaist, the flood at his doorstep afflicted "Darl" with the most profound kind of un-homing and un-selfing possible.[103] Seeing in the flood a déjà vu of the European war zone was a commonplace of journalistic coverage, as when Harris Dickson saw in the Delta's "water-conquered country" a scene "far lonelier than the hell-swept fields of France."[104] And, in the years leading up to the flood, others compared the severely deforested region to "the shell torn area of France."[105]

Consider the similarity in tone, then, between Darl's riverscape, in which a

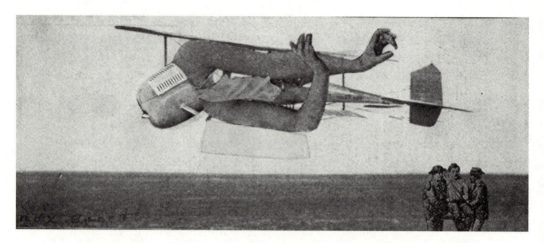

6.2. Max Ernst, *Untitled*, ca. 1920, Collage of cut, printed, and photographic reproductions with pencil on photograph, reproduction mounted on paperboard. Overall: 2 3/8 × 5 3/4 in. Menil Collection, Houston.

strange bearded satyr creature has left behind him the wreckage of gliding torsos and an earless, eyeless, unclotted man, with an untitled 1920 photomontage produced by German Dadaist Max Ernst (Fig. 6.2). Playing with the reality-effects of photojournalism, Ernst turns a World War I bomber, which should be a prosthesis of a masculine technological will, into a silken, almost self-caressing dominatrix who brings about male disintegration. Faulkner likewise turns the river from a mechanized canal of human wishes into a mockingly alive, weird goat-tree-man montage who cuts men in half and drowns their tools. The river has become as uncanny a contrivance as Max Ernst's silken-armed bomber.

In the river, Darl's vision for the destination of Addie's wasted body—his vision for how the South will be reincorporated into the nation—is radicalized. Rather than belonging to the nation as a kind of dependent but vulnerable periphery, with its poverty, backwardness, and radical racism—in short, its degeneracy from apparently foundational national ideals—flouted in a time of disaster, Darl comes to doubt the legitimacy of "property" itself (233).[106] If the land throughout the Mississippi watershed has been transformed into highly capitalized zones where deforestation, industrial farming, and immured water have made the earth "spectral," then both property and the social underpinnings of its distribution needed radical rethinking. Note that a politician as conservative as Herbert Hoover publicized, in the midst of the 1927 flood, his thoughts on a major redistribution of property to small farmers in the Delta, a plan he only seems to have abandoned because of his run for the presidency.[107]

Darl's vision is bigger, it seems, because he doesn't see the problems to be only southern. His vision is bolder, too, than that of the anti–industrial age southern artists and writers known as the Nashville Agrarians, who, in their protests against northern factory encroachment, wanted to maintain their region's agrarian traditions, along with its race-based labor system.[108] Darl, "insane" as "the majority" saw him, wanted to burn the whole structure down.

Having been unable to help the river divinity finish its work in the flood, Darl takes up what he perceives to be a new call to "lay down [the] life" (215) of the South, that is, as Tzara put it, in the "the great spectacle of . . . fire" he has staged in Gillespie's barn. Like a Dadaist, "he cultivates the curiosity of one who experiences delight even in the most questionable forms of insubordination," for he "knows that this world of systems has gone to pieces."[109] That he sees his incendiary act as an aesthetic performance is emphasized again when Darl relates that "we watch through the dissolving proscenium of the doorway" (221). If the barn door is a "proscenium," the barn is Darl's stage, his incendiary cabaret, and his words to the actors over the course of this scene have essentially been stage directions.

Interestingly, what he hears in Gillespie's barn, in the midst of the performance, is a "quite peaceful" sound, "like the sound of the river" (221). This comment indicates that Darl, having been dissolved into those strange currents, is trying, through his art, to reproduce the destructive vitalism he found to be at the core of modernized matter and to turn it against itself. Darl may have succeeded in re-creating, through a work of art, the trauma of anthropogenic flood, but he ultimately fails to produce a political act of transformation. For in the barn, Jewel upstages Darl as, "enclosed in a thin nimbus of fire" (222), he achieves his own apotheosis, rescuing "the South" for its return to Jefferson, or a return to a Jeffersonian agrarian ideal foundational to the nation.

At the novel's end, the law of property, and the use of others' labor to produce surplus value for accumulation and trade, is upheld. The view of "the majority," that anyone threatening these southern, and indeed broadly capitalist, tenets must be incarcerated, is likewise sustained. Of the three brothers, then, it is only Jewel's pantomime of the South's modern destiny that is executed. Cash is "sick on the box" with his sawdust innards "running out." His bodily balance is gone, as is his impetus to produce balance through his designs. Instead he will become a consumer of a kind of commodified portraiture, for, as he says of the family's newly acquired graphophone: it is "all shut up as pretty as a picture" (261).[110] Darl's absorption into the apparatus of the state as an insane criminal not only terminates his anarchic activities and cuts off his access to those creative/destructive forces of modern turbulence but also reifies him *to himself* as an absurdist character. Any opportunity that the trauma of flood may have provided for reassessing environmental practices, as well as labor and race relations, has been lost. Fierce race hatred presents itself in Jewel even as it becomes increasingly evident that the position of the poor white farmer in the southern plantation zone has much in common with the darker races of the Global South. Participation in distant networks of capitalism only provides the family with darkened bodies, double-dealing, consumer trinkets, and a kind of false belonging in this bigger world.[111] Indeed, as they sit in their wagon eating bananas, consuming a staple from some "Banana Republic"[112] in the nation's tropical imperium not very different from Mississippi in its economic and political weakness, Darl watches from the train, convulsing in laughter because what the family thinks of as marks of their cosmopolitan arrival are to Darl actually marks of their peripheral subordination.[113] The final scene, of the Bundrens freshly accoutered with their new commodity blandishments, seems to fulfill Wilbur J. Cash's 1929 prophecy, namely, that after a great "upheaval," "the South will merely repeat the dismal history of Yankeedom, [so] that we shall have the hog apotheosized—and nothing else."[114]

When Faulkner wrote this novel in the last, nervous weeks of the 1920s, he could foresee neither the Great Depression nor the environmental disaster of the Dust Bowl. He is not anticipating the decade of tribulations to come, even if the Bundrens seem so aptly to embody them. Rather, he was meditating on the preceding decades of drastic environmental changes to the state of Mississippi and to the Mississippi Valley—*"deswamped and denuded and derivered in two generations"*[115]—whose consequences washed over the doors of southerners in 1927.[116] As in his two prior war novels, Faulkner shaped his dominant narrator, Darl, as someone who has been profoundly changed by the Great War; he has brought back not a physical wound on the exterior of his body but instead the perceptual apparatus engendered out of that conflict. Wearing those "queer" European spy-glasses makes Darl uniquely able to sense the cognate modern convulsion at home, allows him to feel that precipitate machine that the Mississippi River had become. Like the radical artists in European urban centers who used art as an occasion to redirect the public to *"something else"* through their acts of representational shock, Darl tries to help drown, or burn, the current, and strangely decomposing, life of the South. Taking a wholly different approach, the oldest Bundren son, Cash, believes that, with the help of tools, measurement, and sound structures, the southern body politic can be made to balance. Crisis, he trusts, provides an ideal opportunity for human social engineers to enter in and redesign the social order along the lines of nature's own "patient self-rectification." When Cash's design encounters the flood, though, where there is no natural touchstone of equilibrium, his carefully built structure "wont balance," his tools are toppled, his own body broken, and his methodology defeated; worse still, he must be paraded throughout the countryside lying prostrate on top of his failed design. The flood does not allow southerners to recalibrate the social order or destroy its unsustainable foundations. The South will be an internal Banana Republic—giving up its natural resources in exchange for modern trinkets—while disguising its dependency through fiery enactments of chivalry.

1920s Flooding, 1930s Form: *If I Forget Thee, Jerusalem*

In the year of the tenth anniversary of the Great Flood, Faulkner sat down on September 15 to begin a new novel. Since the publication of *As I Lay Dying* in 1930, he had written two other major works, *Light in August* (1932) and *Absalom, Absalom!* (1936).[117] In the first, Faulkner continued to think about the destructive practices of southern logging: one of the book's main female characters, Lena Grove, is seduced and abandoned by a mill worker, a "sawdust Casanova," among hills "devastated" by clear-cutting and likewise abandoned by the industry, which had left behind only rusting machinery amid "a stump-pocked scene of profound and peaceful desolation."[118] In the 1936 novel, the "demon" Thomas Sutpen, who is the repeated obsession of the storytellers, perpetrates analogous outrages against both land and family; as he "tore violently a plantation" from the Mississippi hinterlands of the 1830s, so he inaugurated a chain of family violence worthy of Agamemnon's bloody household.[119] Faulkner had moved, then, from a consideration—both political and environmental—of the South as a postbellum U.S. internal colony to a reckoning with the brutalities—again, both political and environmental—of the antebellum southern plantation.

Between the end of 1929 and the summer of 1937, the country and the world had entered a different historical era characterized by financial collapse and the Great Depression, ecosystem collapse on the American grasslands resulting in the Dust Bowl, growing national sympathy for the southern sharecropper, New Deal policies meant to address poverties of soil and citizenry, and the portentous rise of fascism in Europe. In many respects, the economic and political crises faced by poor, displaced southern laborers, especially those subjected to racial subordination and even terror, in the 1920s were harbingers of problems that would become national and international in the 1930s. New fiats about form, subject matter, audience, and the sociopolitical purposes of literature emerged from left-wing critics in organs such as *New Masses* and the *Partisan Review*.[120] Who could write proletarian literature, whether it was reaching the targeted reader, and whether it was meaningful or aesthetically worthy were key literary questions taken up during the decade. Faulkner paid close attention to these developments and debates and responded to them in the fiction he wrote in the 1930s in ways that were characteristically complex and interrogatory.[121] His third and final flood novel shows Faulkner reenlisting the 1927 disaster a decade later as a vehicle through which to think through the interlinked issues of aesthetic practice and environmental belonging. During the first stages of composition, though, this novel had nothing to do with dramatic rivers.

In September 1937, after typing six pages of his new story, Faulkner stroked two characters more, "a" "r," hit the dash key, and then caught a train from Oxford, Mississippi, to Manhattan. While there, he indulged in the rather exquisite torture of socializing with his ex-lover, Meta Carpenter, and her new husband; this led invariably to too much drink, to a run-in with an exposed hot water pipe, to a third-degree burn on his back, and, finally, to his being bundled by a friend into an automobile for the more than thousand-mile trip back to Oxford where, finally, on November 23, bandaged and in pain, he would finish that word: "c" "h" "a" "i" "c" ("archaic").[122] In a suggestive coincidence of literary history, two other southern authors were in New York City at the same time, seeing flood stories into publication. In August, having recently moved from Chicago to Harlem, Richard Wright welcomed the appearance in print of his eight-page Mississippi flood narrative, "Silt," in *New Masses*. Zora Neale Hurston arrived in New York City on September 22, on a steamship from Haiti; once on shore, she made her way to the Manhattan office of J. B. Lippincott to behold her newly released book, *Their Eyes Were Watching God*.[123] She must have been impressed as she took in the image of tilted fury on its cover (Fig. 6.3). It wasn't but ten days more when Hurston would read the dismissive review of her novel in *New Masses* by Richard Wright, who, accusing her of peddling a "quaint," minstrel rendition of black life in the South, somehow missed the devastating critique in the novel of the Jim Crow practices of the National Guard during the hurricane and Lake Okeechobee (Florida) flood of 1928.[124] In December, Wright won a prize from *Story* magazine: his manuscript collection of stories, containing the long flood narrative "Down by the Riverside," would be published by Harper and Brothers the following March as *Uncle Tom's Children*.

We cannot know whether Faulkner was aware, while in Manhattan, of Hurston's and Wright's 1937 literary output on the topic of southern flooding. Hurston's previous books had received mainstream acclaim, and *Their Eyes Were*

6.3. Book cover of the J. B. Lippincott 1937 edition of *Their Eyes Were Watching God* by Zora Neale Hurston. © 1937 by Zora Neale Hurston. Renewed © 1965 by John C. Hurston and Joel Hurston. Foreword © 2000 by Edwidge Danticat. Reprinted by permission of HarperCollins Publishers.

Watching God was quickly reviewed not only by Wright but also in *The Nation* (by Sterling Brown), the *New York Times*, and the *Saturday Review of Literature* while Faulkner was in the city. They had a mutual friend in Carl Van Vechten and both published stories under H. L. Mencken's editorship. It would have been unlikely that he didn't hear of Hurston's new novel and surprising if he wasn't curious about what *New York Times* reviewer Lucy Tompkins called "a well-nigh perfect story" on southern Negro life.[125] We know that Faulkner would later read Wright's *Native Son* and *Black Boy* because he wrote his fellow Mississippi author a letter around 1940 to argue to Wright that for an "artist" to write "the good lasting stuff," he must concentrate his energies on fiction; autobiography, Faulkner cautioned, merely recorded the "memory of [one's] own grief" while fiction comes out of the author's "sensitivity to and comprehension of the suffering of Everyman, Anyman."[126] It is certainly possible that Faulkner read "Silt" in the early fall of 1937 and Wright's longer Mississippi flood story when it appeared in the spring. And it is certainly possible that both authors made him think about how to write a southern flood story for a new historical moment.

Beyond Wright and Hurston, the topic of humanly altered rivers was every-where in the public eye that year. In the winter months of 1937, tremendous flooding occurred on the Ohio River.[127] A multivolume series, The Rivers of America, was inaugurated with the volume Kennebec: Cradle of Americans; its initial editor, Constance Annie Skinner, envisioned that a folk history of the United States would emerge as creative artists reckoned with how rivers and citizens had made each other. Also published in 1937 was Emil Ludwig's The Nile: The Life-Story of a River, a book Faulkner kept in his library. A biographer of humans who had always imagined his subjects' lives in the shape of rivers, Ludwig had, once he encountered the Nile, "beheld in a river the image of man and his fate"; the river had shifted from a metaphor to a medium of human his-tory. In particular, Ludwig called his book a "history written from below . . . as the fellah saw [it]."[128] Finally, the filmmaker Pare Lorentz, who had made a documentary on the Dust Bowl commissioned by President Roosevelt, wrote and directed a Farm Security Administration documentary on the Mississippi called The River, which considered "Where it comes from, where it goes; What it has meant to us—And what it has cost us."[129] Archival footage and narration link the industrial development of the valley with cut-over and eroded hills, floods, and widespread tenantry and poverty; the film ends with a celebratory sequence describing how the Tennessee Valley Authority will repair these prob-lems in one part of the watershed. Faulkner, having put aside the topic of flood-ing rivers for the previous eight years, must have felt prodded to address it once again.

The story Faulkner began to type on September 15 and took back up in late November was called "Wild Palms." In its early stages, he wrote it—as he would later say—"to stave off what I thought was heartbreak."[130] It showed Faulkner troubling over precisely that thing he would warn Wright to avoid, namely, the "memory of his own grief" over the dissolution of his adulterous liaison with Meta Carpenter and, before that, the unrequited longing he experienced as a younger man for Helen Baird.[131] Taking his own advice to a certain extent, Faulkner turned his "heartbreak" into an elaborate work of cautionary roman-tic metafiction. If the reader is never convinced by the love of the two protago-nists, Charlotte Rittenmeyer and Harry Wilbourne, it is because what they con-tract when they first meet at a New Orleans artists' soiree is not so much passion or affection as it is a bug for living out literary scripts of amorous fatalism. As Thomas L. McHaney has detailed, Faulkner's lovers were his means of signifying upon the literary romances—and the literature-addled romances—in Anderson's *Dark Laughter*, Hemingway's *Farewell to Arms*, Dante's *Divine Comedy*, and *Tristan and Isolde*, as well as contemporary pulp fiction romances, with detours into the philosophy of Arthur Schopenhauer and Frederic Nietzsche.[132] That the love story in "Wild Palms" ends badly—Charlotte dies of septicemia from a botched abortion performed by Harry, who is then incarcerated—is meant to make clear, says McHaney, that "when real people copy characters in books they suffer real pangs."[133] The tradition of Western romance, in both its high-culture origins and its 1930s mass-market forms, was, for the female protagonist of "Wild Palms," and perhaps for her creator, a dangerous toxin, a readerly disease.

Charlotte remarks, just as the couple is about to commit adultery, and in a phrase that establishes from the outset the terminal course of their relationship, that she "love[s] water" because "That's where to die. . . . The water, the cool, to cool you quick so you can sleep, to wash out of your brain and out of your eyes and out of your blood all you ever saw and thought and felt and wanted and denied" (49–50). This is a familiar Faulknerian motif: we've encountered it in Quentin, whose love of death/water Faulkner gave an eco-historical resonance by associating it with the 1927 flood. Ten years later, as he is using the waters of 1927 again, he does so to different ends: Faulkner introduces water—propulsive, overcharged, unpredictable, manic water—into this novel as a means by which to "wash out" of his consciousness, and out of the novel form, these historically accumulated and culturally contagious toxins of the Western love plot. Instead of having the Mississippi flood burble underneath the surface of the text as he did in *The Sound and the Fury* or be the unstable poly-referent of multiple narrators in *As I Lay Dying*, he would now call up the flood to act as a purgative narrative instrument—which is to say, he seems to have felt, when he began composing this novel, that he had learned all he needed to know about the flood in the writing of those two earlier novels, so that now he could use it as a device.

As he enjoins the flood to perform a certain therapeutic job, though, it invariably starts to multiply in meaning and to mean something different than it had eight or nine years before. By its completion, *If I Forget Thee, Jerusalem* was not merely the expression of his personal grief but had become the "good lasting stuff." Faulkner had written a novel not only about a doomed extramarital romance but about something on another order entirely: how cultural consumption and production, both proletarian and popular, can exile moderns from the environmentally situated natal inheritance of their species. Traumatic as the flood is for the character who encounters it in "Old Man," the contrapuntal story interspersed with "Wild Palms," it nonetheless functions as a raucous initiation for him into Nature's resurgent power—not its obsolescence through modernization. The tenor of damnation in which the novel ends—two protagonists are incarcerated and the third is dead—shows Faulkner brooding over the human tendency to either flee from or let go of meaningful ecological situation, or, in his biblical shorthand, to "forget Jerusalem."[134] Though he wrote the novel in the 1930s, he does not convey these musings through a consistent mode of the social realism that typified the decade; rather, the novel shows him, in a series of metafictional gestures, trying on and casting off multiple literary conventions: romantic, social realist, comedic. It is only when ink sinks into water, when it is mazed into liquid channels, that Faulkner's protagonist locates a homeland in which nature and culture exist in mutual adjustment.[135]

The flood story, "Old Man," begins by introducing this protagonist, a "tall convict" incarcerated at Parchman Prison Farm in the Delta, as someone who hopelessly misreads fiction and its rhetorical condition of mutual pretending, expecting instead a complete "verisimilitude" (20) of page and world. He does not understand that true-crime stories and dime-novel westerns are written according to a convention for entertainment but insists to his detriment on reading them as how-to manuals for real crime. Imaginative culture to this "pine-hill" (22) country naïf is a kind of Gorgon's head, a dangerous and outrageous adversary, as it is also for the provincial, or "yokel," Harry Wilbourne, who early in "Wild Palms" stares at a wall of paintings that the narrator describes as "the monster itself" (33). While Harry is absorbed utterly by this Gorgon's stare, turned into a will-less and petrified convert to the art (of love) pursued through an antibourgeois life, the convict by contrast is absorbed into culture's apparent opposite—literality or materiality or Nature—with a vengeance. Faulkner hurls him bodily into a physical event so engulfing and undeniable that "even an illiterate should be able to read" it (25).

Beginning this tale with an "outraged" critic of popular literary enterprise who seeks greater "verisimilitude and authenticity" (20) is not only a kind of deadpan satire of the Mississippi hillbilly but also a satirical commentary on the literary mandates of the left during the mid-1930s.[136] One such mandate, *A Note on Literary Criticism* (1936), written by James T. Farrell, defined proletarian literature as that which was written by and for the working class, to whom it must "[reveal] some phase of [their] experience" and which "enforce[d] . . . the views of the proletarian vanguard."[137] Its political efficacy lay in its combination of empirical grounding, direct revelation, and martial enforcement. Critics of proletarian writing, who found a venue in the *Saturday Review of Literature* in the mid-1930s, were quick to point out that the American working-class reader was much more likely to read daily papers and "True Stories, Wild West Tales, or Screen Romances." These genres represented "the *real* proletarian literature"; it was, one argued, actually "middle-class romantics" who "gobble[d] up" working-class fiction.[138] Faulkner's "tall convict" and his characters Charlotte and Harry seem to reside at the crux of these matters: while the convict is a member of the rural proletariat who reads precisely these pulp genres but cannot understand their conventionality, Charlotte and Harry are the "middle-class romantics" who, as Charlotte jibes, go "slumming" (34). They abjure their white-collar professions or affluent households in order to live close to the bone; and Charlotte uses her artistic ability, at one point, to let a group of miners in Utah know that they have been cheated out of their pay by drawing a kind of proletarian cartoon that is "unmistakable" (169) in its meaning. Harry, in fact, has given up his moneymaking pastime of writing mass-market romances so that he can be a doctor to these miners. Their own "middle-class romantic[ ]" sojourn among the working class ends when biology kicks in (Charlotte is pregnant) and the only job Harry can find (and rejects) is as a "rankless W.P.A. school crossing guard" (185).

In the way Faulkner designs his main characters' reading and writing tastes, then, his novel seems to agree with the assessment of the critics of proletarian writing: it's the middle class who romantically traffic in working-class plots and representations while the working class reads paperback fantasies. That these patterns of cultural involvement lead to criminal scenarios (robbing a train and committing abortion) shows Faulkner taking his own implicit critique of both left-wing literary doctrine and conventional pulp a step further. More curious still is that in the second chapter of "Old Man," Faulkner has his narrator employ a social realist mode to describe the convicts' first contact with the flooding Mississippi in a way that "unmistakabl[y]" condemns the modern industrial state. He practices this social realist art not to monumentalize the laborer as much as to show laborers' effacement and dehumanization: "Inside the high, stall-like topless body the convicts stood, packed like matches in an upright box or like pencil-shaped ranks of cordite in a shell, shackled by the ankles to a single chain which . . . was riveted by both ends to the steel body of the truck" (52). The state—or the Mississippi State Penitentiary, to be exact—"pack[s]" these human bodies into its container like a factory producing explosives; the convicts' undifferentiated, fungible forms are absorbed into the "steel body" of the industrial, penal, war-formed state. Public media during this scene, moreover, take on a unidirectional, authoritarian cast: the *Commercial Appeal* is described as "the warden's newspaper" that talks in "black staccato slashes of ink" (25).[139]

The natural body of the river has likewise been recast into an industrial mold: as the water spreads in the bottom of plow furrows, it appears "in the gray light like the bars of a prone and enormous grating" until, the furrows gone, there is only "a single perfectly flat and motionless steel-colored sheet in which the telephone poles and the straight hedgerows which marked section lines seemed to be fixed and rigid as though set in concrete" (53). The audible "rumble" reminds the narrator of "a subway train passing far beneath the street" at "a terrific and secret speed" (53). The rural world of planted soil, running water, and hedgerows has "vanished" (53) only to be replaced by a new "fixed" steel and concrete system, linked together by telecommunications and mass transportation. Hello New York City; farewell, Mississippi. The urban industrial takeover that the Agrarians saw in the modernizing program of New South apologists and in the encroachment of northern capital happens here at "nightmare" (55) speed, as quick as the unconscious imagination might work to substitute one scene for another or a cosmic factory worker might fill a mold. The flood is the medium of this swift transformation.

In *The Sound and the Fury* and *As I Lay Dying*, Quentin and Darl supply us, unconsciously or consciously, with the environmental history behind this disastrous loss; both, moreover, point to the northern and global speculators as well as southern collaborators involved. We watch each of them experience an immersion in this knowledge as a form of psychic and physical drowning. Here, in this "Old Man" scene, we do not inhabit the consciousness of a character undergoing a loss of world; rather, an urbane social realist narrator describes the scene filtered through the perspective of the collective convict gaze, strangers to this place who are also inured to strangeness. There is certainly a grim notation of the conjoined forces of modernization, urbanization, and state power but told as a fait accompli rather than an unfolding tragedy.[140]

The tone of this scene is an anomaly within the tale, though. Faulkner employs it and then sloughs it off. Once we are hitched, narratively, to the tall convict and his crazily mobile physical experience, social realism gives way to slapstick. Faulkner asks us, as we watch the individual convict encountering an outrageous river, mainly to see the collision as physical farce. For example, as the convict is, for the second time, wrong about where he is in relation to the flood crest (as he says, "I aint never knowed, where I aimed to go or where I was going either" [129]) and is thus again surprised by its assault, the narrator describes the scene thus: "As the wave boiled down and the skiff rose bodily . . . on a welter of tossing trees and houses and bridges and fences, [the convict was] still paddling even while the paddle found no purchase save air" (148). We see the convict's body, riding the crest and paddling nothing but air, at a moment in which its indefatigability—its unceasing and beyond-human effort—has be-come detached from purpose; this aquatic "medium" (149) ridicules human embodiment, even at its most tenacious. Moreover, we experience this scene, and the ensuing scenes, as a tale within a tale, putatively told by the convict who has made it back to prison but really told by our narrator, who has rather wicked fun with the process. When the convict speaks, "despite the fury of the element which climaxed it, it (the telling) became quite simple . . . as though he had passed . . . into a bourne beyond any amazement" (147). Our narrator talks over and orally eclipses the convict, not believing him qualified to do justice to what seems to be the narrator's fundamental tenet, namely that humanity's "in-finite capacity for folly and pain . . . seems to be its only immortality" (146). We worry not, therefore, about the convict's ultimate safety but instead experience the tale for its own aesthetic, philosophical, and darkly comedic sake.

This flood comedy is different from that produced during the 1927 disaster by purveyors of minstrel or Vaudevillean routines. As discussed in chapter 5, a steady stream of minstrel comedy was produced and disseminated nationally, staging the Red Cross tents as tent-show entertainment. These minstrel sce-narios, appearing in the *Commercial Appeal*'s Hambone cartoons, in the *Los Angeles Times*' "Negro Noah Gets Wet Feet" (see Figs. 2.6 and 2.7), and in Har-ris Dickson's nationally syndicated column, used the apparently jolly antics of African Americans coming in contact with flood trouble as, in Dickson's words, a "rear-end collision" to act as a comic interlude for the media's presentation of white suffering.[141] Will Rogers and Miller and Lyles, by contrast, used comedy in the first case to satirize congressional inaction and the public's distraction and, in the second case, to encourage a popular audience to get the drift of black abandonment. Because Miller and Lyles, moreover, were the monteurs of their own bodily predicaments, the audience could perceive the designing mind in the body—could see the hapless body as a virtuoso instrument. Faulkner produces a different kind of flood comedy here. First, he does not segregate white tragedy from black comedy but fashions his hapless naïf into the shape of a Mississippi hill boy (like the Bundrens), who is nonetheless eth-nically and racially multivalent, associated as he is with "Indian-black hair" and "china-colored" eyes (20), and later likened to the Cajun he hunts with; he is the folly-prone "Everyman, Anyman." Having established the convict's cultural simplicity—his inability to navigate the codes of a playful, multivalent cultural landscape—Faulkner's narrator takes over the explication of the convict's expe-rience especially to show it as a pantomime of human bafflement.[142]

It is not only the convict's body that the narrator employs to act out this dictum about "folly and pain" but also the river. In the chapter in which we encounter the river turning into a sheet of metal, the river is denaturalized, created in industrialism's planetary foundry; in this part of the tale, by contrast, the river is imagined to have regained its lusty health. It occurs to the convict that the river's motion was not an aberration—a catastrophe—but rather "the norm"; the river may have "waited patiently" for many years, abiding the "frail mechanicals of man's clumsy contriving," but "the river was now doing what it liked to do" (135) in its "viciousness and innate inventiveness" (138), "kicking" (135) and "chuckling" (143) all the while at man, his "toy and pawn" (137).[143] Much flood reportage likewise personified the river as lustily or diabolically rebelling against human technology. While, in the earlier scene, humanity's conquest of nature through modernization comes back full circle to make humans seemingly "dead" (55), nature's normal, immemorial, and now renewed toying with frail and clumsy men reveals—ironically—"man's" capacity for "immortality" in a minor key. It is in a state of humble awkwardness that man begins to find his ecological and spiritual niche.

Nature is ultimately invented in this novel to discipline humanity, to return humans to the "Jerusalem," or the cosmic homeland, which is their inheritance and their circumference. Faulkner's desired title, *If I Forget Thee, Jerusalem*, is taken from Psalm 137, which is sung by Jewish exiles during the Babylonian captivity. These exiles weep by the riverside as they think on Zion; they resist their captors' insistence on singing and mirth; and they are so assured of Jerusalem's place in their heart that they ask God to afflict their hands and mute their speech if they ever forget their homeland. Because the three main characters of the novel hail from Oklahoma, Louisiana, and Mississippi, "Jerusalem" in their case seems to refer specifically to the Mississippi River and its valley. The narrator of "Old Man" explains of the river that "the course of [Man's] destiny and his actual physical appearance [were] rigidly coerced and postulated by it" (131): it was the river who thought up and shaped its humans and their histories, not the other way around. Charlotte, in fact, seems especially to be a physical cognate of the yellow, muddy river: she loves "the water, the cool" (49); she is unpredictably willful and creative; she sculpts things in the medium of clay; and Harry seems "to be drowning, volition and will, in the yellow stare" of her eyes (34). Despite this affinity—this having been made in the river's image— Charlotte and Harry exile themselves from its reach. Though they meet in New Orleans, their entire experiment in the culturally contagious western love plot, and in the romance of proletarian relinquishment, occurs just beyond the Mississippi's watershed: in Chicago, in northern Wisconsin, in Utah, in San Antonio, and, finally, on the Gulf Coast east of the river's mouth.[144] In the "Wild Palms" story, Faulkner posits, then, an opposition between the dangerous fatality of humanly invented romance as set against the integrity, and the inevitability, of regional land features. He uses the geography of the Mississippi River and its watershed as a natural boundary against which to measure their errancy. This couple has fled the human ecology that is their destiny. In arriving at this cautionary point, "Wild Palms" seems to show Faulkner identifying with the writers of "folk" fiction I mentioned earlier. Recall that Mary Austin defined "American Folk" as people "shaped in mind and social reaction, and to some extent in character, and so finally in expression, by one given environment."[145] This "profound saturation" (287) by one environment makes for a "profounder spiritual integrity than is usually found among sophisticates, who are exposed to all the cross-currents of thinking in an amazingly muddled world" (288). Charlotte and Harry seem to typify just such sophisticates who lose their spiritual and physical integrity as they abjure contact with the environment that shaped them.

While the trajectory of Charlotte and Harry's journey skirts the Mississippi watershed, the tall convict's unwitting escape from prison immerses him in the Lower Mississippi Valley: he moves from Parchman prison situated one county east of the river, to the levee south of Mounds Landing, through the flooded Yazoo-Mississippi Delta to the Yazoo River (a tributary running in reverse), and eventually past Vicksburg onto the "Old Man" itself, at which point he (and his pregnant charge) are taken west to the Atchafalaya basin in Louisiana, then far southeast to Caernarvon, Louisiana, back up the river to New Orleans, then upriver further to a sorghum farm, upriver still more to Baton Rouge where he works in a sawmill, back to a cotton plantation in Mississippi, and finally, completing the circuit, turns himself in at Parchman. Quentin's day-long, zigzagging inspection of the Charles River watershed in *The Sound and the Fury* and Darl's relatively quick, if intense, river dunking seem brief in comparison with this character's riverine education. Perhaps Faulkner needed more time to affect this "Everyman" than he did with Quentin and Darl, whose inner disturbances made them quick studies of river distress.

If the convict mistakenly sought "authenticity" in pulp fiction only to find it a "fraud" (21), on the river and its shores, tributaries, and wetlands, he eventually finds something approaching integrity. If at first he was baffled by the "concentrated power of water" (209), he eventually comes to earn something like dignity from the archaic labor he performs as a hunter of alligators in the "secret inky channels which writhed the flat brass-colored land" (214). Here he feels a "pure rapport" with the Cajun coworker he cannot verbally comprehend, because both embrace the philosophy in which life is simply the "permission to endure and endure to buy air to feel and sun to drink for each's little while"

(214). The previous seven years of incarceration sink away "like so many trivial pebbles into a pool" as he thinks: "*I reckon I had done forgot how good making money was. Being let to make it*" (219). At Parchman, by contrast, given the convicts' forced labor, they felt that "it could have been pebbles they put into the ground" (26). Thus, despite Faulkner's seeming to agree—in the initial shaping of his hillbilly convict—with the critics of proletarian fiction that the working class only wanted escapist dime novels, Faulkner initiates his member of the rural proletariat through an experience of humility before nature's power and then rewards him with a sense of profound "peace and hope" (219) in a wetlands ecology where labor relations, bodily cunning, animal being, and horizoning earth are all (for a time) secure.[146] The media that were earlier a mark of his bafflement or alienation—ink spent on pulp, social realism, comedy—now spill out into the "secret inky channels" of this "teeming and myriad desolation" (214); the newspaper wraps up his prison clothes and is put out of sight (212); no "written and witnessed contract" (218) is needed because of the gestural rapport and trust of the two men.

The story, of course, does not end there. The convict is soon exiled from the "magic" of this "lost land" (219)—from this newfound Jerusalem. The achievement of a "folk" ideal of "profound saturation" in place is only temporary. As in the historical record, the federal government, prevailed upon by powerful interests in New Orleans, blows up the levee at Caernarvon, flooding the bayous of St. Bernard and Plaquemines parishes and displacing its politically marginal Cajun population. Though the convict tries other rural labor regimes in the Lower Valley—working with cane, cotton, and lumber for pay—he ultimately returns to the uncompensated, thoroughly alienated labor at Parchman farm, to a prison sentence extended by ten years by corrupt state officials, and to his own culturally vicious final epigram. His last words, in the final sentence of the entire novel, are: "women, shit" (287). Given that the anonymous woman who accompanied him throughout his river travels—a woman who was variously pregnant, giving birth, and nursing—was a perpetual, on-board analogue of the "teeming" biology all around them, the convict's final repudiation and denigration of womankind indicates a kindred repudiation of that environing biology and a retraction of the convict back into his, and his nation's, debased cultural shell. Nature that was kicking, chuckling, secret, and myriad will resume its degradation, within the industrial penal farm, as mere "papier-mache" (26): a dire coda for Faulkner's flood trilogy!

Faulkner claimed that the title he wanted for the book, *If I Forget Thee, Jerusalem*, "invented itself as a title for the chapter in which Charlotte died and where Wilbourne said 'Between grief and nothing I will take grief' and which is the theme of the whole book."[147] Given Charlotte's likeness to the Mississippi, which not only crashes through the convict's story but is voluble as a contrapuntal tempo that breaks up hers, and given the fact that the captive exiles in Psalm 137 weep by a river, it seems warranted to assume that this "grief" is not only romantic but also environmental. Grief over a lost homeland was, to put it mildly, a major theme in the postbellum South, reanimated by the Agrarians in the 1920s as an anti-industrial, green stance. In its association with diaspora, the lost homeland motif had resonance with both the African and Jewish diasporas so undeniably topical in the 1920s and 1930s. And Faulkner's initiation of his alienated captive into the goodness of environmental belonging was consonant with 1930s theories of "folk" formation, theories that were co-opted in Germany to naturalize a racially "pure" folk as the foundation of nationhood. All of that is to say that the ideas of territorial belonging and exile were highly charged political issues as Faulkner wrote his novel. That Faulkner uses corrupt prison officials caught up in an emergency as a synecdoche of "the state," that the plantation is dramatically imagined as a denatured place of incarceration, and that the convict laborer only comes to feel the goodness of work once he owns the means of production—his skilled body—in the Louisiana bayou all point to Faulkner's effort to distinguish his version of environmental belonging from that of the Lost Cause, the Agrarians, or German fascists. In this novel, he imagines an oasis, a "Jerusalem," that is outside of and vulnerable to the state, accidentally found and soon lost, in which alliance is cross-ethnic and language is embodied.[148] In the late 1930s, writing "Old Man," Faulkner seemed to want to imagine that Nature was not a mechanical colossus as much as an enduring "norm" that could discipline us back into its rapport.

* * *

On December 10, 1950, at the City Hall in Stockholm, Sweden, William Faulkner addressed the assembly gathered to award him the Nobel Prize for Literature. In his speech, he voiced worry about the state of writing in a nuclear age. The "problems of the human heart in conflict with itself" had for millennia distinguished us as a worthy species and provided storytellers with their only meaningful materials, Faulkner said. Our distinctive and age-old human qualities, consisting of "love and honor and pity and pride and compassion and sacrifice," now risked being deflated into a single, anxious question: "When will I be blown up?" In the midst of the Cold War, this "general and universal physical fear" had left humankind in a downgraded condition. Our spiritual and emotional organs were now mere "glands."

Ulrich Beck likewise imagined a break in human history with the advent of the nuclear age in 1945. Beck contended that risk, which had up until then been felt most by those at the bottom of society, was now so generally shared and geographically dispersed that it would bring about a new and productive skepticism toward science. As humans came to associate science with risk—as opposed to with increased human security—science itself would be transformed by public scrutiny. If Faulkner saw the bankrupting of the human soul, Beck hoped for the arrival of a saving skepticism.

Neither Faulkner nor Beck, it turns out, got the future of the psychology and the experience of eco-risk quite right. Though nuclear arsenals, nuclear waste, and damage from nuclear explosions are very much still with us, the most pressing question in the early twenty-first century is not an equally shared planetary one ("When will I be blown up?"). Instead, questions about biosecurity now have to do with the ability of earth to support human life as we are living it. It is not the possibility of one single fatal human decision that haunts humanity but the reality of increased heat, droughts, storms, floods, fires, mass displacement, and associated public health crises that plague especially those who live in vulnerable geographies without the resources to relocate or to protect themselves in place. As long as certain nations, and classes within those nations, can buffer themselves from the strange new energies of global climate change, the consequences of our contemporary risk society remain unshared. It was not Faulkner's nuclear-age jeremiad that has proved the most prophetic of the current physical and psychological conditions facing an increasing number on the planet but instead his 1920s and 1930s books on the "low-ground" experience of poor whites and blacks facing anthropogenic flood in the Deep South.

SEVEN

Richard Wright: Environment, Media, and Race

When Richard Wright was eighteen years old, living, working, and avidly read-ing both black and white papers in Memphis, the Mississippi Flood of 1927 spilled across his life and his consciousness. Though the city, with its relatively high elevation, was protected from direct inundation, it was a central hub in rescue and relief organization, and it was only some 150 miles away from the most notorious Red Cross camp at Greenville.[1] Wright's constant migrations as a child and his work as a young man for an insurance agent had brought him familiarity with both the Arkansas and Mississippi deltas and with life on the levee. Indeed, a particularly terrifying childhood memory involved his uncle driving him, on a horse-drawn buggy, from a Helena levee *into* the Mississippi River.[2] If he did not have direct experience as an evacuee in 1927—as did Bessie Smith during her ten-day holdover in Nashville—he did have knowledge of the social and physical terrain of a great part of the flood zone. What is more, as a consumer of the Memphis *Commercial Appeal* and major national black papers and magazines—the *Chicago Defender*, the NAACP's *Crisis*, the National Urban League's *Opportunity*, the *Pittsburgh Courier*, the *Baltimore Afro-American*, among others—Wright had the chance to see how the flood was taking on meaning across American public spheres. Not only did he come into contact with minstrel renditions of black refugees and with Red Cross promotional ico-nography, but he was exposed to H. L. Mencken's anti-Dixie editorial and its southern rebuttal, as well as the protest journalism and exposés of the likes of Walter White, Ida B. Wells, Jesse O. Thomas, and W.E.B. Du Bois. Given its popularity, its topicality in the spring of 1927, and the frequent airing of her songs on Memphis radio stations, Smith's "Back-Water Blues" no doubt reached his ears as well. Through this exposure to both black and white flood culture, he came to see that something apparently natural and catastrophic could actually be produced by human agency and that it could be highly political. And he saw that an event in the Delta could command the nation's attention, a nation which, in its fractiousness, attributed utterly contrary meanings to that event. Out of this exposure to a catastrophe that was both anthropogenic and polysemous, Wright produced a short story, "Silt" (1937), a novella-length story, "Down by the Riverside" (1938), and his first piece of life writing, "The Ethics of Living Jim Crow" (1936), the last two brought together in 1940 in a revised version of *Uncle Tom's Children*.

Wright drafted and revised these texts over a number of years in the 1930s, after he had moved north to Chicago in November 1927. While doing so, Wright engaged with the dominant theories about social organisms, and especially how these organisms stabilize after disaster, produced by the Chicago School, many of whose practitioners he came to know during these years. Wright parted ways with the Chicago School sociologists, for whom the social organism was patterned much like the apparently self-stabilizing ecology of the natural world. Instead, he used more individual-centered fictional and nonfictional genres that would allow him to plot the accidents of an individual negotiating an uncertain world. Wright also drew upon his new exposure to Marxist theory, gained through his involvement with the Communist Party while in Chicago.[3] For Marx, alienation occurred as the rural or industrial laborer under capitalism "sinks to the level of a commodity"[4] as he gives his self to the things he produces; for Wright, alienation for people of African descent in the South, facing not only the alienations of labor but also the visual and spatial encoding of race, occurred as a still more profound break between the human and his or her omnipresent bodily and cosmic envelopes. Wright's adaptation of Marx to consider politicized space anticipated the late twentieth-century work of Henri Lefebvre; Wright, forty years before Lefebvre, drew attention to how a "second nature" can be constructed as the strategic bulwarks of those in power.[5]

It was Wright's reading of a now obscure apostate to Freudianism, Trigant Burrow, and his thesis about humanity's "biological recoil," as well as its "substitutive image-production," that helped Wright shape a kind of critique that was a better fit for the Jim Crow South than that provided by the Chicago School or by Marx.[6] Moreover, in order to explode what he considered the many false "image-production[s]" concerning the flood, he made use of a repertoire of jarring representational tactics he learned from European avant-garde artists who developed them in response to the history, and the propaganda, surrounding World War I and the rise of European fascism. The Dadaist and German Communist Party agitprop graphic artist John Heartfield, in particular, provided him with a political aesthetics for critiquing the mass mediation of the flood. The critical journalism produced during the flood lingered in his mind as a model of verbal protest. Clues to these influences appear in the extant records of Wright's life, but Wright also tagged various characters in his fiction with the names of writers and artists he was engaging with. Characters in his flood fiction—"Heartfield," "Mann," "Burgess," and "Burrows"—draw into the orbit of the story the wider intellectual and geographic worlds of the Dadaist Heartfield, the sociologists Delbert Mann and Ernest Burgess, and the psychologist Trigant Burrow.

In recovering the extent and the nature of the flood's influence on Wright, and on his development as a thinker and writer, I intend to shift our understanding of the author. As critics have examined his connections with the Chicago School, with the Communist Party, and with the genre of naturalism, they have tended to see the environmental and political theories guiding those movements as "intellectual[ly] graft[ed]"[7] onto Wright, so that the self in Wright is essentially a product of a social environment that operates according to ineluctable patterns. Yet Wright saw the social and physical environments as not only shaping but also politically—that is, humanly—shaped. This insight—which he drew from the protest literature surrounding the flood—allowed Wright to anticipate much work that has come out of the Environmental Justice Movement in recent years.[8] Moreover, the canonical status of *Native Son* has led to an association between Wright and the northern urban "street." Once we better appreciate that Wright's critical edge came not only from the city street but also from the South's "second nature," we see that for an author to place black characters in the southern countryside in this period is not necessarily a nostalgic gesture. The famous schism between Wright's work and Hurston's—as one example—thus comes to appear less substantial. As I mentioned in chapter 6, Wright himself called the rural setting for *Their Eyes Were Watching God* "quaint" and minstrel-inflected;[9] Hurston called the violent plots in *Uncle Tom's Children* derivative.[10] Though this conflict attests to important differences in representation, it can obscure the fact that *both* authors in these works concerned themselves with major historical eco-catastrophes—the Mississippi Flood of 1927 and the Okeechobee Flood of 1928—as they depicted the chance and violence inherent in rural life but exacerbated in the Jim Crow South by anthropogenic environmental change and racialized space.

Reading the Press

When Wright attests in *Black Boy* to learning how to use "words as a weapon" from reading H. L. Mencken in 1927 (248),[11] readers seldom realize that his exposure to Mencken occurred in the midst of the flood and in the context of a wider print culture having to do with the catastrophe.[12] Indeed, in the months between the flood and Wright's departure north in November, a "new knowledge," as he put it, "was dawning within me" (251), a knowledge he carried within him like "a secret, criminal burden" (252) and that created a "vast sense of distance between me and the world in which I lived" (253). This knowledge had partly to do with his commencing to read notable American authors, but it also had to do with the ways in which the flood became a flashpoint in American interracial and interregional relations.

On May 28, 1927, Wright read "Another Mencken Absurdity," an editorial in the Memphis *Commercial Appeal* that was a response to Mencken's own Baltimore *Evening Sun* editorial of five days earlier, "The Mississippi Flood." In his editorial, Mencken rather blithely put salt in the wounds of the flooded region, declaring that "New Yorkers [would] refrain from sobbing" for the suffering of "the least advanced white people now living in the United States." Southerners, whom he saw as fundamentalist "yokels" and "Ku Kluxers," were not fellow Americans, but rather a "hostile tribe on our borders."[13] The editors of the *Appeal*, turning the tables, accused Mencken of "ignorance" and of "pl[ying] the trade of the most credulous of the revivalists who see in every cataclysm of nature, God's visitation for sin."[14] Wright was struck, when reading the *Appeal*'s response, by the "scorn" (244) flowing between northern and southern whites, prodding him to wonder: "Were there, then, people other than Negroes who criticized the South?" (244). As Wright recalled, this discord within American whiteness opened up for him a rhetorical space and allowed him to begin to imagine belonging to a larger world of print. If mainstream print culture could provoke within itself a public discord, rather than merely project a single ideology, then perhaps he could enter into its fray. Moreover, realizing that there were whites who fiercely opposed the South made what was a private, unspoken revolt against his region feel legitimate.

Beyond this rhetorical model for an anti-southern stance, Wright would have seen, as a frequent reader of the *Commercial Appeal*, an active, white verbal and visual culture of satire, and specifically a surprising kind of minority satire.[15] That Wright encountered a public discourse of minority resistance in the shape of white southern editorials must have produced in him a strange dissonance: after all, how could his oppressors see themselves as oppressed? As an adolescent, Wright had been mentored in the practice of decoding visual caricature by a "soft spoken black man" (129), thus his critical viewing skills were presumably honed by the time he was eighteen.[16] The white South saw the recurrence of devastating Mississippi floods as a supreme indicator of their region's continuous suffering "for no offence it committed and because of no fault of its own."[17] The flood made manifest to the South its existence as a kind of internal colony, denigrated "tribe," or perpetually disabled white minority within the nation. Wright would have absorbed white southerners' contention that this flood was not an "unprecedented visitation of nature's wrath" but rather a sign of land-use negligence on the part of "the whole nation" and poor engineering design by federal planners.[18] The critique of Washington's fake and scanty "SYMPATHY" in relation to a South "crippled" by such negligent assault (see Fig. 6.1) would no doubt not only have made Wright think about print satire and of an intrawhite resentment he believed to have ended with the Civil War (244) but also have made him wonder about how the white South understood and represented its region's suffering within a national realm. In particular, the *Appeal*'s tactic of representing flood suffering through a disabled white male body must have jarred against awareness within the black community that it was they who comprised the majority of the flood's bodily victims.

Along with resentment about federal negligence, a major element of white flood print culture—as I explained in chapter 2—involved a racialized drama in which whites tended to take center stage as romantic and heroic protagonists while blacks appeared as entr'acte minstrel figures of comic relief. For this black figure, the flood was a godsend, freeing him from work and allowing him to bask in the federal munificence. It was precisely this division of performative labor that Wright would reverse in his flood stories. In a Memphis *Commercial Appeal* front-page cartoon of April 26, for example, the gender inversion of the *Pietà* assemblage tells a story of chivalric rescue (Fig. 7.1). As the white woman lies collapsed and Christlike, with her left arm dangling limply at her side, her bearer becomes not a maternal Mary figure but rather a virile Christian avatar of salvation: a Red Cross knight in the body of a modern athletic icon. And a front-page cartoon from April 21 would have made painfully clear to Wright how a mainstream white southern public saw the participation of African Americans within the conversation about catastrophe (Fig. 7.2). While the "[white] Public," "Trade," "Farming," "General Business," and "Transportation" huddle under a large, sheltering umbrella to strategize and to come up with "Relief Plans," "Hambone," a regular comic presence in the daily, has no place in what Queen and Mann called "a better organized community working more effectively toward the solution of its various problems."[19] Though the cartoon notes Hambone's exclusion from this process, it also justifies his exclusion as it vocalizes his thinking as a form of subrational folk animism: "Uh! Ef de ole

THE NATION'S LIFE-GUARD.

7.1. J. P. Alley, "The Nation's Life-guard," *Commercial Appeal*, April 26, 1927, 1. Commercial Appeal/Landov.

Mis'sippi is de 'Father O' Waters,' den Pappy sho done rolled outen he bed!!!" Picturing black incompetence and dependence serves to publicize white organizational mastery and paternalistic munificence.

The writer who during the flood produced the most pervasive narratives of minstrel comedy and white derring-do was Wright's fellow Mississippian Harris Dickson. One of his stories, in particular, seems to have provided a narrative template that Wright undid and reversed in "Down by the Riverside."[20] In "One Tiny Tragedy Tells Horrors of Flood Area," Dickson weaves a suspenseful tale of Jim Massey, a poor white farmer from the Sunflower River area who is trying to protect his wife and newborn child, both of whom are in bad shape. A discussion ensues between the father and a neighbor woman, Mrs. Pullen, who has helped at the birthing, about how to get the mother and baby to help. Word comes that the levee has broken at Greenville, and they know they'll need to board their old bateau and head to higher ground until a steamboat can carry them to Vicksburg, but even on higher ground, the baby and mother will be exposed to the elements. The third-person perspective penetrates the protago-

7.2. J. P. Alley, "Let's Pray for a Drouth!" *Commercial Appeal*, April 21, 1927, 1. Commercial Appeal/Landov.

nist's thoughts as waters rise: "Another matter worried Jim. Instead of falling with a thud, the snake had fallen with a splash. / Water. So near his house." The scene cuts to Vicksburg, where seven white men and one "red-headed Boy Scout" receive word of the Masseys being stranded; one of the men says to the scout, "Red, listen. A friend of mine, Jim Massey, has got his sick wife and newborn baby on Barton's Ridge. In the rain. No shelter. Mother and child may die." A rollicking tale then ensues of Red's plucky and successful adventure with his "gang," "De Dirty Dozen," who, in order to shelter the Masseys, filch tents off of a railroad car because, as Red says: "Couldn't let that baby die in the rain." It is a Tom Sawyer–like tale of lawbreaking undertaken for a higher social good. The reader sympathizes with the pluck of the young white scofflaw.[21]

Unlike the white print culture Wright conspicuously engaged with, black print culture during the flood, according to Wright's telling in *Black Boy*, had little influence upon him: "When I read a Negro newspaper" in the months comprising the disaster, "I never caught the faintest echo of my preoccupation in its pages" (252). Given that local black papers perhaps could not afford to be critical of Jim Crow southern politics, this attitude about the local press is not surprising.[22] It is a strange omission, though, that Wright mentions being enlightened by Mencken's anti-southern polemic during the spring and summer of 1927 but says nothing of the constant barrage of flood exposés written by nationally known African American pundits and activists.[23] As I explained in chapter 3, African American reporters, and white reporters writing for the black press, told of how, in one *Defender* reporter's words, "The ugly specter of Race hate has reared its head above the angry waters."[24] And the likes of Ida B. Wells insisted that "the only way to bring public opinion to action is for those whose race is suffering to cry aloud, and keep on crying aloud until something is done."[25] It seems well-nigh impossible for Wright to have been unaware of this and other protest literature, whether he read it hot off the press in the summer of 1927 in Memphis or via faded copies in Chicago in the ensuing years. Indeed, while Wright was working on the drafts of his flood stories and "Ethics" in the mid-1930s, he lived at 3743 Indiana Avenue in Chicago.[26] The Associated Negro Press, headed by Claude Barnett, a member of the Colored Advisory Commission who had toured the Red Cross camps, stood just down the street at 3423 Indiana Avenue[27] and presumably would have housed some of the journalistic materials, both black and white, connected with the flood. In writing these stories, then, Wright was, without giving any specific credit to black journalism, belatedly fulfilling Wells's injunction to the race to "protest" and "cry aloud."

Rethinking the Ecological Approach

How, when Wright sat down to write his flood fiction in the early 1930s, did he represent the relationship between humans and their environment?[28] One prominent model for conceiving of this relationship belonged to the Chicago School. The story of Wright's immersion in its scholarship, and his connections to individual scholars in that community, is well-known.[29] Most famously, Wright claimed that "I did not know what my story was . . . until I stumbled upon science," after which "I discovered some of the meanings of the environment that battered and taunted me."[30] And in *Black Boy*, he explained that sociology's "tables of figures relating population density to insanity, relating housing to disease, relating school and recreational activities to crime" all helped explain "the causes of my conduct and the conduct of my family" (278). From this research, Wright, as he put it, "absorbed some of that quota of inspiration necessary for me to write *Uncle Tom's Children* and *Black Boy*."[31] It is certainly true that Wright encountered sociology at a critical juncture in his maturation when its linkages between social conditions and behavior gave scientific validation to his intuition that African American misery ("insanity," "disease," "crime") was not racially inherent but socially and historically produced; and, as he tells it, sociologists provided for him, in Chicago in the 1930s, one of his first intellectual communities.[32] Hearing such testament from Wright about sociology's heuristic powers, we have tended to let it stand as a simple fact of his own development and a definition of the prime "science" behind all his designs of autobiographical and fictional characters. Wright's attitude about the institutions of the academic sciences and the extent of their applicability to him were in fact more equivocal. To appreciate Wright's transformation of the journalistic critique written during the flood into a prescient form of environmental justice literature, we must first understand where he parted ways with the Chicago School's environmental theories.[33]

Two anecdotes suggest Wright's discomfort with the reification that seemed to accompany institutionalized empiricism. In the early 1930s, Wright first met Horace Cayton, the PhD student of sociology who, along with St. Clair Drake, would in 1945 write *Black Metropolis: A Study of Negro Life in a Northern City*. According to Cayton, when Wright saw the files Cayton and his advisor Louis Wirth were accumulating on "every facet of the city. . . . the vast complex of human beings who make up the monster of Chicago," Wright observed, "You've got all your facts pointed, pinned to the wall like a collector would pin butterflies,"[34] a remark that suggests Wright's sense that much was sacrificed as mobile life became "pinned" "facts." Indeed, Robert Park had proudly avowed this disposition of sociology to dispassionately "dissect" when he told graduate students inclined toward racial activism that "their role was to be that of the calm, detached scientist who investigates race relations with the same objectivity and detachment with which the zoologist dissects the potato bug."[35]

At the time of his interchange with Cayton, Wright was working as a laboratory assistant in a medical research institute at a prestigious Chicago hospital. As he describes it in *Black Boy*, he and three other African Americans occupied an "underworld position" (303) in the basement, keeping watch over the animal research subjects. The dogs whose vocal cords he helped slit and who "gape[d] in a silent wail" seemed to him a recognizable "symbol of silent suffering" (305). One day, when two of his fellow employees got into a brawl, all the cages holding the carefully separated rats, mice, guinea pigs, rabbits, and dogs clattered down and opened. Amid the ensuing chaos, the four men held "a strange scientific conference" (312) about how to restore order to the mayhem of data, for, having been kept intentionally blind to "the meaning of the experiments" (312), they did not know the researchers' principles of categorization. Largely "at random" (312), then, the four reclassified the animal specimens. The white doctors, suspecting nothing, continued to work with these randomized subjects as they painstakingly recorded "findings" (314) on their charts, perhaps giving to "some tested principle . . . a new and strange refinement" as a result of this "fresh, remarkable evidence" (314). Wright tells the story of this "secret disaster" (314) as an American epistemological and racial allegory, asking: since we were seen as "close kin to the animals we tended" (314)—like them "locked in the dark underworld of American life" (314)—and kept ignorant of the ordering principles and experimental goals of the laboratory work, how could we muster a commitment to producing or safeguarding a knowledge that was so socially and ethically contaminated?

To be sure, a different scene presented itself at the University of Chicago, where a number of African American sociologists were trained in the 1920s and 1930s and mentored by Park, who had worked as Booker T. Washington's secretary for seven years.[36] And certainly W.E.B. Du Bois's work in sociology (at Atlanta University) helped make it a symbolically significant field for black investigators. And yet Wright's sense of being—like those "facts," dead butterflies, and other animal subjects—"pinned" and "locked" in America by his racial and class position gave him a mixed view of the empirical social sciences. "Science" made manifest to him the truth that social, physical, and mental anguish often resulted from concrete and quantifiable external causes, yet he knew from experience that the "havoc" (310) and "helter-skelter" (312) of life in the "underworld" was not as reducible to "facts," and to theory, as social scientists believed. He knew that "scientific truth" (314) could "devocalize" (305) subjects; that subjects could "shrewdly . . . cover up . . . evidence" (311); and that "guesswork" (311) entered in, especially when a "vast . . . distance" (314) separated knower from known.

Apart from these issues involving what we would today call the sociology of science, Wright also demurred from certain assumptions then underpinning the science of sociology. In a paradigmatic study, *The City* (1925), leading practitioners Robert Park, Ernest Burgess, and Roderick McKenzie devised the term "human ecology" to indicate the study of "the spatial relationships of human beings" that are produced by "competition and selection" and that evolve over time. Though humans might believe they are consciously designing their habitats and selecting their own positions within these habitats, they are in fact responding to spatial conditions in an inevitably recurring pattern of "disorganization, reorganization, and increasing differentiation."[37] Directing this methodology was the assumption that neither individuals nor small groups of men willfully created institutions and communities ex nihilo but that human collectives, like plant groupings, operated according to fairly predictable laws of behavior and change. In particular, as they implemented their "ecological approach,"[38] these sociologists called frequently upon the work of leading American ecologist F. E. Clements, whose 1916 *Plant Succession* had argued that species in a given area over time evolve progressively toward a climax stage, at which stage they represent a superorganism, a community interconnected and self-balancing enough to be understood as having achieved an integral identity.[39] Though Park and Burgess in their *Introduction to the Science of Sociology* (1921) defined their method as a "science of society" and distinguished it from August Comte's and Herbert Spencer's nineteenth-century philosophies of history *as progress*, they nevertheless, in seeking predictive social laws, trusted in Clements's notion of detectable and stabilizing patterns. For, as they argued, "society is an immense co-operative concern of mutual services."[40]

While one might assume that the preponderance of disasters in the early twentieth century would have caused the field to doubt its thesis of ineluctable stabilization, these crises—as I explained in chapter 1—did not upset but instead reinforced the prevailing sociological model.[41] Or, to put it another way, this trust was so strong that it could incorporate, and neutralize, evidence of human error writ on a tremendous scale. Along with Samuel Henry Prince, who argued in his study of the Halifax disaster that it was *because of* the explosion that "the City of Halifax [was] galvanized into life. . . . [and] has caught the spirit of the social age," sociologists Stuart Queen and Delbert Mann wrote in their disaster study, *Social Pathology*, that cataclysm invariably brings about a "realignment of social forces which will make for a better organized community working more effectively toward the solution of its various problems." Disasters act as overdue social heuristics, making needs "apparent" and "open[ing] the way for rendering long-needed services."[42] According to Prince and Queen and Mann, the superorganism comes to know, and to fix, itself under stress. Equilibrium is the key feature of the universe, of ecology, and thus of human ecology; periodic disturbance exists mainly to adjust and deepen that equilibrium. Wright's experiences of rural life, his direct observations of the 1927 flood, and his reading of its press coverage all gave him reasons to be skeptical of such a model.

At the same time that Wright was reading sociology in the 1930s, he was reading psychologist Trigant Burrow's 1927 *The Social Basis of Consciousness*, which analyzed in particular the problem of human alienation from an internal and ambient biology.[43] Burrow's model got at Wright's sense of the problems of modernity more accurately than did the sociologists of the Chicago School. An analysand of Carl Jung's who had practiced psychoanalysis for some years, Burrow became increasingly dissatisfied with the individualist orientation of psychoanalysis, as well as its therapeutic goal of a "normality" he viewed as fully implicated in a "disease process" of repression—a process that parents, education, and culture all tended to substantiate. The problem, as Burrow saw it, was that humans as a species had acquired consciousness wrongly. Viewed phylogenetically, consciousness in humanity appeared as an unfortunate *self-consciousness*, as a "biological recoil," or a recoil away from the continuous biology of life. The human self was constituted upon a fiction of biological transcendence, and hence a repression of the biology within. Thus humanity stood "irresistibly arrested before the mirror of his own likeness." In that mirror, humanity did not see a self seamlessly integrated into and made out of a biological process but rather perceived as real his or her own "substitutive image-production." Burrow sought to redirect "consciousness" so that humans could experience life as "integral members of an original organic matrix." He rejected not only Cartesian theories of cognition but also Hobbesian theories of appetite, averring that the "instinct of tribal preservation is by far the dominant urge in us." To illustrate that humans are essentially allocentric rather than egocentric, he tells the story of a female companion of his who, upon seeing capsized sailors struggling for their lives far out in a lake, "dashed toward the water" because she "just couldn't let them drown like that!" Humanity needed to respond to "the organic behests of our common societal instinct" to broaden its conception of biological entanglement and debt. Otherwise, he warned, a crisis that has been gathering steam for centuries "will descend upon the world with inevitable fatality." It would be through a social application of both Darwin's theory of evolution and Freud's evolutionary theory of mind that humans would find "the entire repudiation of man's image-production and a re-uniting of his organic and conscious life into a single constructive whole."[44]

Much in Burrow's book must have suggested to Wright ways to diagnose his experience: how "image-production" tied in with a visual logic of racial hierarchy and black stigmatization; how socialization via family, education, and culture could merely set up eidolons of self-interest or pain avoidance; how history, with the rising fascism of the 1930s, was gathering toward a "fatality" unless a new "social mind" could be collectively brought into being; how revolutionary art *could* be a "repudiation" of man's dominant "image-production" and a "re-uniting of his organic and conscious life." And yet as he wrote "Down by the Riverside," he tested—or he had his protagonist "Mann" test—the limits of one individual's enactment of a "social mind."

The Green Ethics of the White South

"The Ethics of Living Jim Crow" is the fifteen-page "Autobiographical Sketch," originally published in 1936, that Wright attached as an introduction to the five novellas that comprise *Uncle Tom's Children* when the 1938 publication was expanded two years later.[45] Thematically, the particular relationship between "Ethics" and the second novella of the collection, "Down by the Riverside," is that between learning to remember the southern rules of embodied space and hazarding to forget these rules. Wright presents his own story as a case study in the internalization of Jim Crow violence.[46] In the novella, Wright then tests out through his protagonist, Mann—whose thoughts and feelings we are intimately privy to and who provides our only vantage onto the world—what happens to a black man in the Delta who, in an emergency, lets go of this chronically internalized racial "education."[47] One of the central features of this education involved learning to read the tactical quality of white land-use practices. Wright's very "first lesson in how to live as a Negro," as he tells it, involved seeing how Jim Crow environmental design masked itself as nature, even as a picturesque nature. "Down by the Riverside," in turn, tells the story of how that design, as it succumbs to disintegration in the flood, assaults, again and again, the "head"— the epistemological processor of space and history—of Mann. If *Uncle Tom's Children* represented at the time of its publication, as Richard Yarborough has argued, "the most unrelenting and rage-fueled critique of white racism ever to surface in fiction written by blacks directed toward a mainstream American readership,"[48] this landmark text also delineated how such racism operated through a tactical management of the rural built environment and of "green growing things" (1). That Wright chose to open the 1940 revised collection with "Ethics"—after he was dismayed by the uptake of the stories in 1938 as sentimental tear-jerkers[49]—suggests that he was trying to not only give his fiction "the documentary solidity of firsthand personal testimony"[50] but also insert commentary upon the episodes in his young life as a guiding primer in racialized geography, a primer that might promote in his readership the capacity for critical distance. That way, when readers, later in the volume, encountered Big Boy's or Mann's fatal run-ins with white domination, they would know how to approach the plots analytically.

In the opening paragraph of "Ethics," Wright describes the "cinder environment" of the house he lived in for a time in Arkansas: "Nothing green ever grew in that yard. The only touch of green we could see was far away, beyond the tracks where the white folks lived." He "never missed the green growing things" because he believed the cinders paving his yard made excellent combat material for the "nice hot war" boys in the neighborhood were continuously waging among themselves (1). One day, though, when his gang found itself "engaged in a war" with white boys from that green space across the tracks, he came to see the "appalling disadvantages" of his own environment. The white boys threw broken bottles from behind "fortifications" and "trench[es]" much superior to Wright and his gang's, that is, from behind "trees, hedges, and the sloping embankments of their lawns" (1–2). Badly cut in the neck, Wright had to be taken to a doctor for stitches by a neighbor woman. When Wright's mother returned home, rather than offer balms and sympathy, she took this as an opportunity to be an intermediary for Jim Crow discipline: she beat him until he had a fever of one hundred and two. That Wright tells the incident differently in *Black Boy* (both sides had broken bottles, and it's his mother who takes him to the doctor before she punishes him [83]) suggests the symbolic contraction of the anecdote. What he wants readers to perceive is not only how black parents are forced to become unwilling administrators of racist violence but also how the green landscape of the South is not natural and is by no means picturesque. Rather, it was strategically designed by whites to maintain superiority in an unceasing race war. "The green trees, the trimmed hedges, the cropped lawns grew very meaningful" in the wake of his first decisive battle, and "through the years they grew into an overreaching symbol of fear" (3). As signs, "white" and "green" became coiled together.[51]

The ensuing episodes that comprise "Ethics" serve to reinforce this initial "lesson," namely that if you attempted to "exceed [your] boundaries" (7)—spatially and epistemologically—you would be physically violated. The stringent social hierarchy of the Delta was enforced through divisions of space and of knowledge. To be in a white neighborhood after dark was as dangerous as trying visibly to "git smart" (4). As Wright represents it, southern black boys learned early that not only was the green environment tactically fabricated by whites but virtually all inhabitations of space and knowledge were performed to support what Burrow would call the "substitutive image-production" of whiteness. Because of the South's own particular "biological recoil" represented by its creation and dogged retention of the race-based plantation complex over three hundred years, the "original organic matrix" was almost impossible to glint or to feel within. More blocked still were the "organic behests of our common societal instinct." What Wright's introduction to the spatial protocols of the South also establishes is an exception to the thesis of Park, Burgess, and McKenzie in *The City* that spatial allocation of humans has to do with "processes of competition and accommodation" so that "human communities are not so much the products of artifact or design" as many suppose.[52] "Ethics" asserts, by contrast, that in a post-plantation, post-slavery milieu this model of multiple groups interacting in "competition and accommodation" does not pertain; moreover, a dominant group can, to a certain extent, "design" space and can design it so that all its advantages accrue to this group. Park, in his chapter titled "The Mind of the Hobo," goes on to assert that while locomotion—wandering, travel, itinerancy—does increase knowledge, and social knowledge in particular, "in order that there may be permanence and progress in society the individuals who compose it must be located"; they must stay long enough in one place to establish relationships, "for it is only through communication that the moving equilibrium which we call society can be maintained."[53] For Park, location, or coming to rest, fosters a stabilizing social dialogue. In "Ethics," by contrast, locomotion is full of the dangers of finding oneself in the wrong place at the wrong time and hence mainly produces the knowledge of where *not* to go, while being in "place" (7) requires stanching one's thoughts and trimming one's tongue. For Wright, "communication" does not result from established settlement patterns. Society is not an organism characterized by "equilibrium" but is rather a just-suppressed "uproar" (15).

The black male subject Wright produces in "Ethics" has been conditioned by his social environment to be alienated from and mistrustful of the green world. That which is green is neither within nor closely around him but far away, commandeered by his white foes to produce tactical advantages and to make those advantages appear natural. Green has become the environmental skin of white property. By contrast, he feels at home with cinders, those waste products of human interventions in nature, and can turn these into tools of attempted resistance. He repurposes this biological analogue of himself into what appeared to be a "fine weapon" (1) but that ultimately can't compete with the cultural bulwarks of "green growing things."

For Marx, within the industrial capitalism that engulfed both city and country in the nineteenth century, the laborer loses life by investing it in the commodity he produces but does not own. As he works, he feels alien from his body and from that which his body makes as it replaces him.[54] And yet this alienation is not only quarantined to the time and place of his work, for, in as much as the laborer must appropriate "the *sensuous external world*" to produce for others, he likewise severs himself from "*nature*." Before his labor becomes alienated by capital, "Man *lives* on nature—[which] means that nature is his *body*," and through nature, "man really proves himself to be a *species being*." But, Marx concludes: "estranged labor tears from him his *species life*," and hence "his inorganic body, nature, is taken away from him."[55]

In "Ethics," Wright describes a similar alienation from "*species-being*" and from "*nature*" brought about by the historical and social relations of labor in the Jim Crow South. Indeed, though it hardly seems possible to imagine an alienation more total than the one Marx describes, Wright suggests that when a segment of the population is spatially sorted and visually stigmatized as "labor," then the severance from one's natural body and the body of nature occurs not only in acts of labor but all the time and in all space. Because whiteness reproduced its privileges by inscribing itself on the skin of nature, appropriating green as white, an African American not only had to experience nature's estrangement when her labor turned cotton plants into a bale for her landlord's weighing but also experienced the "second nature" Jim Crow built as an unavoidable space of "fear."

And yet Wright, in the early pages of *Black Boy*, recalls a time in his childhood *before* such estrangements—while being in nature still offered the experience of, in Marx's words, "life-engendering life."[56] Indeed, in these pages, Wright describes the rural landscape as the very source of his aesthetic and emotional reserves and the origin of his future authorship. In his country environs, he feels "wonder" looking at "spotted, black-and-white horses" and "delight" seeing "long straight rows of red and green vegetables"; experiences a "faint, cool kiss of sensuality when dew came on to my cheeks and shins as I ran down the wet green garden paths in the early morning"; and acquires a "vague sense of the infinite" while looking down upon the "yellow, dreaming waters of the Mississippi River" (7–8). And the list goes on at some length, as Wright shows his acquisition of a complex emotional lexicon—including "disdain," "nostalgia," "melancholy," "desire," "hot panic," "astonishment," "quiet terror," and "love" (8–9). He links each emotion to a rural glyph: landscapes, cultivars, the built environment of the farm, and especially animals (ants, wild geese, sparrows, crawfish, snakes, beheaded chickens, and slaughtered hogs). He ends this catalogue of his rurally inscribed interiority with an ellipsis and an abrupt transition to his city life in Memphis where, he remembered, the "absence of green, growing things made the city seem dead" (10). He describes his coming into a varied emotional repertoire via the "coded meanings" (7) of a countryside he internalizes to decipher. In short, rural nature presented him with his first semiotic puzzles, and his varied emotions arose in the process of puzzling them out. By representing this early experience, Wright suggests that coming

into the construct of race as an older boy entailed for him a simultaneous rip-
ping from the fabric of nature, at the level of both his body and his environment. In *Black Boy*, then, unlike in "Ethics," "green" and "white" had not yet
become synonymous.[57]

Rather than an "intellectual grafting" of the Chicago School, then, Wright,
in coming to understand how space is socially created and inhabited, instead
engages with and modifies those theorists while he simultaneously considers
the work of Burrow and Marx. In synthesizing and modifying these theorists,
Wright anticipates the influential 1970s work of Henri Lefebvre, who understood space as a kind of dynamic "social morphology."[58] Lefebvre, a French contemporary of Wright's, who was likewise influenced by Marx, sought to shift
what he considered the too-exclusive emphasis in Marxist thought on dialectical change *in time* to an awareness of how dialectical change occurs, or might
occur, *in space*. He describes how, increasingly with modernity, "nature's space
has been replaced by a space-*qua*-product," a "second nature." He describes
how "hegemony" establishes itself in space by using a "variety of brutal techniques and an extreme emphasis on visualization." In particular, the dominant
authority designs space to separate class divisions: "the *social relations of reproduction*" from "the *relations of production*." Such a division is authenticated by
being symbolically "displaced onto" the "backdrop of nature." In this scenario,
"Nature is imitated . . . but only *seemingly* reproduced: what are produced are
the *signs* of nature or of the natural realm—a tree, perhaps, or a shrub." When
the fact that this space has been sorted in such a way is "obscured," so that this
"second nature" seems natural and "absolute," its "'users' spontaneously turn
themselves, their presence, their 'lived experience' and their bodies into ab-
stractions too" such that they cannot "recognize themselves" or "adopt a critical
stance." Spatial protocols are internalized as corporeal alienations. Lefebvre
avers that despite the ways in which hegemony sorts space, the system that is
made is "decidedly open—so open, indeed, that it must rely on violence to
endure."[59]

Wright's "Ethics" is an autobiographical telling of processes much like these.
It is an auto-ethnography of spatiality composed some forty years before Lefebvre. Wright notes how nature has been transformed into look-alike "symbols"
of itself—hedges, trees, sloping embankments—that become a fortification
from behind which Wright's young body is cut open and marked. Nature's im-
partial and undirected behavior has been reformulated to give partisan support
to white victory (in an everyday trench warfare enacted across neighborhood
color lines). If, for Lefebvre, class is what is primarily enforced in space, for
Wright's Delta, whiteness reproduces itself by marking itself off from black

production; labor and blackness are yoked together and differentiated from biological reproduction within the white family "through an extreme emphasis on visualization." As Wright put it, describing the peril of being caught—even while laboring—in a white neighborhood after dark: "the color of a Negro's skin makes him easily recognizable, makes him suspect, converts him into a defenseless target" (10). Per Lefebvre, Wright, as a "user" of the streets, was trained to see his body as the "abstraction" that white viewers would affix to him as a kind of optic target.[60]

Yet for Wright, inhabiting this "abstraction" did not comprise a total bodily and cognitive alienation but was instead the ongoing performance of a "role which every Negro must play if he wants to eat and live" (13). Wright put on a blank face in the presence of white prostitutes while working in a hotel, looked "as unbookish as possible" (14) in the Memphis library, and generally "exercised a great deal of ingenuity" (15) to pass as this abstraction. Wright could only continue to "recognize," or re-cognize, himself as human by articulating to himself that this behavior in white-dominated space was a "role." Writing "Ethics," then, offered him the opportunity to commit to the public page this previously silent "critical stance" he had adopted in relation to the southern mise-en-scène of race. He opens up his performance to a much broader audience than the one for whom it was originally staged and, by doing so, turns his autobiographical sketch into a kind of Brechtian theatrical space in which Wright the "role" player moves in and out of embodying the "southern Negro" abstraction and analyzing how that abstraction was devised and enforced. "Ethics" was meant to bring public distance to the "social morphology" of the Jim Crow South and prepare readers to critically approach the novellas that followed it.

Mann's Risk

"Down by the Riverside" is not about everyday Jim Crow. It is about the Delta during a major flood. Though Wright does not specify a date for the disaster in the novella, his self-described "dawning" of "new knowledge" during the spring and summer of the Great Flood and his signifying on its white print culture suggest that Wright's novella performs nothing less than a critical retrospective of the Flood of 1927 and especially of its public mediation. In the novella, the carefully constructed "fortification" that is white-designed space has been compromised and is made increasingly illegible by the "tricky" (70) floodwater as the story progresses. That the familiar built environment disappears in the flood does not, however, mean that the mandatory racial divisions that have been so thoroughly incorporated into that environment will also disappear. Though invisible beneath the dark water or behind the "walls of solid darkness" (74) hemming in the black protagonist during his nighttime travails, the apparent disappearance of the old customary world belies the continuing presence of the South's social structure. The story is about how the black protagonist fatefully "tak[es] out of the intense pain" of the disaster "a sort of forgetfulness" (89) of this fact. He assumes that a "relief machine" has replaced the old structure, not admitting that the emergency has actually heightened Jim Crow's customary violence. And even when Mann realizes his mistake in geographic and social perception, he fails meaningfully to adjust his own survival tactics.

When we first encounter Mann, his wife, Lulu, has been in labor for four days. They, along with their first child and Lulu's mother, are stranded in one of the last standing structures in the vicinity. Water is six feet high and rising, and the family has no boat. It is established right away that Mann is a "fool" (63), for even the cows fled to higher ground days before while Mann thought waiting it out would mean he'd be the first to get his seeds in the ground. Rather than responding as part and parcel of a diffuse biological intelligence, he thinks only about his position in the market. To get his wife to the Red Cross hospital in town, Mann accepts a white boat that's been stolen by his friend from the postmaster, a man named Heartfield. That the boat is taken from the postmaster, a man at the hub of the town's communications network, and an ardent racist, suggests that Wright wants the theft to work symbolically as a kind of black appropriation of the white-controlled communications infrastructure. Rowing in darkness, and disoriented, Mann, aiming for the hospital, instead literally bumps up against none other than Heartfield's house. The postmaster shoots at him; Mann shoots back in self-defense, killing his target. When they arrive at the Red Cross, he finds that his wife and unborn child have died en route, presumably while National Guardsmen detained them for precious minutes in the driving rain. Immediately conscripted into a work gang, Mann helps save numerous patients from the flood, is taken to the levee just in time to see it break, and then is asked to take a motorboat—along with another black man named Brinkley—to rescue the remaining Heartfields, which, after contemplating murdering them but relenting because of Brinkley's gaze, he does. Recognized by the son as the murderer of his father, though, Mann, once they all arrive at the Red Cross camp in the green hills, is taken away by National Guardsmen to be shot. His final gesture—running away from his captors toward the river and its alluring white boats—does not interrupt his fate, for they shoot and kill him, but it at least allows him to feel that he plays a dynamic part in its enactment.[61]

In constructing his plot, and his third-person narrator's tight and penetrating attention to the imperiled family's father thus, Wright closely parallels Harris Dickson's syndicated newspaper vignette. The *New York Amsterdam News* had printed a scathing, syndicated review of Dickson's "Grotesque Journalism" and his "newspaper minstrelsy." This review had expressed hope that "some time, perhaps, white journalists will realize that Negroes have reached the stage where they rightly resent 'end men' stuff in printer's ink. Times are too serious nowadays," the writer concluded, to proffer this improper mixture of "comedy and tragedy."[62] In this same critical vein, but working in fiction rather than editorial commentary, Wright likewise sets out to disprove Dickson's "newspaper minstrelsy." In both Dickson's and Wright's narratives, a family is trapped in its house by floodwater around the time of the pregnant woman's troubled labor. In Dickson's story, the family possesses a boat and makes it to a ridge where the stolen tents will provide them necessary shelter; in Wright's story, the family's lack of a boat triggers a theft that leads to lethal confrontations. While the white volunteer network's tactical law-breaking saves the Massey family, the black network's illegal act attaches itself to and destroys the Mann family.

Wright fashions his protagonist as a human produced by the same "education" as he had experienced, albeit without the ability to see and critique his resulting consciousness as the mis-creation of the South's "social mind." Wright keeps us inside Mann's head throughout the entire story, but unlike in "Ethics," where we watched Wright put words, and words with ironic barbs, around his own past predicaments, we experience Mann's head as a more inchoate organ, as an organ processing information in something like real, effluent time. Feverish, intruded upon by a "dull ache" (62), assaulted by stimuli but blocked off from recognition, Mann's brain is an embattled epistemological zone that readers are conscripted inside. Wright does not relate Mann's thoughts in seemingly unmediated stream of consciousness in which sensory triggers might send thoughts randomly careering into other times and spaces. Rather, he opts for a third-person narrator who provides atmospheric, material information, Mann's physical and emotional responses, and his mental reactions (in free indirect discourse), all the while restricting Mann's awareness to a physically immediate present tense. We are caught inside a tight empirical feedback loop, watching ideas form out of their contact with matter and chance.

We do not view this flood as a distant panorama; it is not rendered as a "survey graphic," to quote the title of the social work magazine. Instead, we perceive the disaster in the way that it suddenly and intimately keeps bumping up against a very mobile but disoriented Mann. Because of this narrative technique, something like full, wide-angle, neutral, and comprehensive knowledge of this event seems impossible. More than being in a world characterized by Park's triad of communication, equilibrium, and security of place, we seem to have been cast, in medias res, into a world of risk and coincidence. Whether Wright arrived at this cosmology because he is describing a disaster or because, from his perspective, even everyday life in the South is one of just-suppressed "uproar" (15), he comes to fashion a milieu much like that envisioned by other leading philosophers of risk working in his day. John Dewey contended in his 1925 *Experience and Nature*, "Man finds himself living in an aleatory world; his existence involves, to put it baldly, a gamble." Ecologist Henry Gleason described biological life as full of "*coincidence*." And economist Frank Knight, in his 1921 *Risk, Uncertainty and Profit*, expressed a particularly pessimistic diagnosis for human empiricism: because the world is characterized by unpredictable change, we do not build accurate knowledge out of "a direct communication from the nerve terminal organs" but instead merely create "an imaginative construct" out of "what we *infer*."[63] Mann's story is so bleak in part because he creates the wrong "imaginative construct[s]" out of "what [he] *infer[s]*" from his "nerve terminal organs." In a world of "*coincidence*," he makes the wrong "gamble."

The first incorrect thought that Mann puts together is, of course, that nature will remain constant and not produce an erratic high water. He is like many others in 1927 who did not foresee that the "sinister rhythm"[64] of simultaneous tributary overflows, the watershed soil's diminished storage capacity, and the levee's structural weaknesses would create a massive flood in the Lower Mississippi. The second mistaken inference has to do with his process of reconstructing the layout of the town once the flood has "hid" (75) many of its old landmarks. Looking out his window, what he sees doesn't resemble a habitation built slowly out of history. Rather, it seems that "Mabbe somebody jus *dropped* them houses n trees down inter tha watah" (64). The random assemblage before him seems stripped of its social design. Though Mann is urged not to take the stolen boat to the hospital—he's told "theres trouble a-startin in town," men being driven "like slaves," and "nothing but white men wid guns" (69)—Mann disregards black eyewitnessing, trusting instead in the abstract tenet that "white folks. . . . would not let a woman die just because she was black" (66), and opts to hazard the journey. While Mann is rowing his family toward the Red Cross, managing the exigencies of the "strong n tricky" river (70), he has trouble orienting himself. Structures are "hidden" by "walls of solid darkness" (74) so that he does not encounter objects until he is right upon them. Once he touches something familiar—as Knight would say, attaches his "nerve terminal organs" to matter—his "mind weave[s] about" each "clue" a "quick image" (74) of remembered geography. As he moves along, he fabricates tentative structures in his mind, "yearning for something to come out of the darkness to match an inner vision" (75). Mann is trying to produce, in a quasi-artistic, quasi-forensic fashion, a series of images by the use of his hands, his eyes, and his mind's eye.

This matching of an inner vision of the remembered town to an estranged outer vision of an inundated geography works for a while. Through trial and error and using his sense of touch to conjure the material clues into full landscapes, his creative empirical process is working. Where he goes wrong is when he sees "two squares of dim, yellow light." These "puzzle[ ]" him (77) because he could not "associate them" with anything; or, to put it slightly differently, he could not read them *socially*. He begins to attribute to "their soft, yellow glow" a symbolic property and an agential power. "They helped him, those lights" (77), so toward them he moved. And though his mind "groped frantically in the past" to remember the human source of these lights, "the past would tell him nothing" (78). His internalized territorial map—or his memory of the ways that human history has occupied space—has been eclipsed by an illusory ethical geography.[65]

The "imaginative construct" of this geography is not just the random creation of Mann's solitary brain. Mann pulls it out of the messaging of the "huge relief machine," the biopolitical culture of the State and its journalistic propagation, which co-opts Christian iconography and which seemed to address a total southern public. Recall that in the many promotional images for the Red Cross, the agency's iconic crucifix appears over the waters as a glowing beacon of relief, a torch in the darkness, to "The Distressed Southland" (see, for example, Fig. 2.4).[66] Mann puts trust in this public iconography and forgets his truer, more historically based "education." He lets slip from cognition his experiential knowledge that, as the *Pittsburgh Courier* put it: "Farms, cattle, furniture and houses may be washed away by the disastrous Mississippi flood, but race prejudice remains as prominent as a butte on a Western plain. So deeply is the philosophy ingrained in the soul of the white South, that even a major calamity cannot eradicate it."[67] Consumption of white mass media, combined with his physical pain, shuts off Mann's access to memory, unlike, as Ralph Ellison would describe it, the medium of the blues, which represents "an impulse to keep the painful details and episodes of a brutal experience alive in one's aching consciousness."[68] Mann fails to create worlds in his mind out of the darkness—fails to practice a vernacular, forensic art of living—once he allows publicly produced white visual culture to supersede or obscure his own image-making and world-constructing powers. Wright has used the flood to turn the making of black art into a do-or-die proposition or, rather, to show that it already is such a proposition.

Soon enough, out of those softly enticing "square yellow lights," to which Mann prayerfully turns "his face . . . upward" (78), issues a more alarming visual signal. Mann sees emerge out of one of the squares a "white man with a hard, red face. . . . playing the yellow flare over the black water" (80). It is Heartfield the postmaster, who transforms that "soft glow" of incandescent yellow into a "shot" of his flashlight that "blinded" Mann and "caught the boat" (79). The postmaster's son exclaims, "That's our boat, Father! Its *white*!" just as Heartfield hails Mann as a "Nigger" (79).[69] What has occurred in these moments is that the designed world—the "past" accreted as space—that Mann believed to have been washed away in the flood, leaving him absent of coordinates, and full of prayerful hope, has reclaimed the blankness of night with a supercharged and violent visual field. In this field, white signifies danger and possession; black signifies nonhumanity; and light is the streaming weapon that projects such a schema onto the dark screen. Mann's attempt to turn white visuality and media control (represented by the postmaster's framed and lit window) into a picture of universal "help" is the fatal error that lures him into its actually violent, race-producing, projectile range. Attached to a house at the center of the white communication network, mediation becomes a "shot" that captures and "blinds."[70]

Wright's giving to the violent postmaster the name of "Heartfield" at first seems merely a piece of irony. In fact, though, with this name, Wright continues to offer clues that link his stories from the Mississippi Delta with the global intellectual circuits and social ills of his time. Here, specifically, Wright links up his own exploding representation of the human symbol of Jim Crow image-making with the work and methods of the German artist John Heartfield (b. Helmut Herzfeld). We have proof of the connection between Wright and Heartfield in the fact that Heartfield designed the cover of the London edition of Wright's 1941 *Twelve Million Black Voices: A Folk History of the Negro in the United States of America* (Fig. 7.3).[71]

The work of Heartfield was, I feel sure, familiar to Wright before the 1940s. The artist was an internationally known figure in the Berlin Dada movement during World War I, was "world famous"[72] during the interwar period especially for his photomontage work as a parodist of Hitler and other Nazi leaders in *Arbeiter-Illustrierte Zeitung* (*The Workers' Illustrated Newspaper*), or A-I-Z, and was an agitational image-maker for not only Germany's Communist Party but increasingly the global Communist movement. It would not only have been Wright who saw the connections between fascist propaganda and the white control of mediation in the United States; Heartfield too made the reverse connection, visible in one of his photomontages called "Black or White: In Struggle

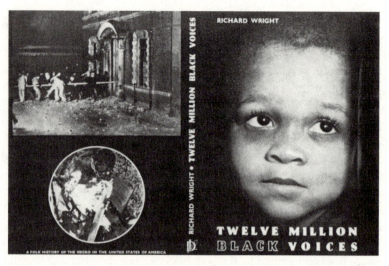

7.3. John Heartfield, cover art for Richard Wright, *Twelve Million Black Voices* (London, 1941). © Artists Rights Society (ARS), New York/VG ild-Kunst, Bonn.

United" (Fig. 7.4), designed for a 1931 issue of *A-I-Z* devoted to racial injustice and produced in the context of the Scottsboro trial in Alabama.[73] His cognizance of race as an important factor in proletarian struggle is also evident in the book jacket he designed for the 1923 Berlin edition of Upton Sinclair's *100%: The Story of a Patriot*, a cover that argues for the link between Wall Street's pernicious control over labor-derived capital and the Ku Klux Klan's spectral control over southern black labor (Fig. 7.5).

Wright would have been drawn to Heartfield's politically radical visual messaging, but especially to the German's "parodic photojournalism," his aesthetic objective to be both artist *and* media critic simultaneously.[74] Heartfield did his most important work in the medium of photomontage, in which—through calculated cutting, strange scaling, startling juxtaposition, and re-captioning—he tried to violently interrupt German military and political rulers' use of photographic "authenticity" to accredit themselves. As art historian Andres Zervigón has written, in Germany's early postwar years Heartfield "reached for any mass-reproduced image or text whose evisceration and reordering could duplicate the [general social] din of nervous breakdown."[75] His scissors would not only duplicate upheaval but also, as Douglas Kahn has said, get below "the static surface of photographic appearance, where deals are struck, meaning unfolds and actual history resides." Photomontage did not just represent a new

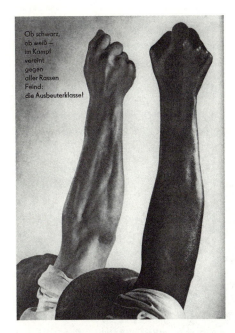

Ob schwarz,
ob weiß —
im Kampf
vereint
gegen
aller Rassen
Feind:
die Ausbeuterklasse!

7.4. John Heartfield, "Black or White: In Struggle United," *Arbeiter-Illustrierte Zeitung* [*The Workers' Illustrated Newspaper*], 1931. © Artists Rights Society (ARS), New York/VG ild-Kunst, Bonn.

7.5. John Heartfield, cover art for Upton Sinclair, *100%: The Story of a Patriot* (Berlin: Malik, 1923). © Artists Rights Society (ARS), New York/VG ild-Kunst, Bonn.

ADOLF – DER ÜBERMENSCH

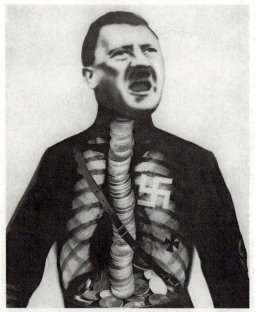

SCHLUCKT GOLD UND REDET BLECH

7.6. John Heartfield, "Adolf, der Übermensch: Schluckt Gold und redet Blech" ["Adolf the Superman: Swallows Gold and Spouts Tin"]. © Artists Rights Society (ARS), New York/VG ild-Kunst, Bonn.

style, as Devin Fore observes, but a new "instrument of thought itself," nudging the viewer along an inductive process from awareness of visual data to a "synthetic judgement" about meaning.[76] For example, "Adolf, der Übermensch: Schluckt Gold und redet Blech" ["Adolf the Superman: Swallows Gold and Spouts Tin"] (Fig. 7.6) literalizes this aesthetic tendency to peel away mendacious surface by shifting from photography to x-ray, as it "reveals" Hitler to be not a representative of the people but rather a capitalist piggy-bank automaton.[77]

Wright imported the work of John Heartfield at precisely this moment in "Down by the Riverside" as a means to explode the delusion of white institutional aid and comfortable black dependence that had been delivered by the national media and that had so dangerously magnetized Mann. Through words, rather than through photomontage, Wright makes the scene of darkness, relieved only by soft yellow lights, instantly explode into an angry red face, a gun, a lancing beam, and virulent hate speech. Recognizing this as a Heartfieldian moment, we watch as this house, standing at the center of a communications network and appearing to be a citadel of white Christian luminosity, effectively breaks its own surface appearance. In this instant, Wright has borrowed from John Heartfield the idea, and the tactics, for how to turn the artist into a media critic. While *Mann's* art-making—as he uses his hands to turn memory into a world—becomes overwhelmed by the more powerful tug of mass media imagery, *Wright* here performs a more revolutionary kind of art, pressuring the manufactory of illusion-making to reveal its contents.

Another image of hope that is revealed to be a lure of death is that attached to the National Guard and Red Cross. After killing Heartfield in self-defense, Mann rows toward the "barely shining" (82) lights of town, thinking that "he would have to tell the truth and trust God." Once again, "a glare of light shot"[78] at him from two rifle-bearing soldiers whose white faces present to him as "square blocks of red" (83). They stall Mann with caustic questions, oblivious to his wife's medical emergency. When Mann and his family finally enter the Red Cross hospital, they are met by a "sign," which, unlike the glowing lights, is unmistakable; it reads "FOR COLORED." Mann stretches Lulu's "soaking wet" body out on a white marble examination table, where her "left arm fell from the table and hung limp" (87); she, and their unborn child, lie dead on the sacrificial slab. In the ensuing hours, Mann returns mentally to Lulu's limp arm three more times (88, 94, 95) and finally, at his own death, answers her gesture as his own "black palm sprawled limply outward, trailing in the brown current" (124). Recall that in the Memphis *Commercial Appeal* front-page cartoon of April 26 (see Fig. 7.1), the swooning white woman who stands in for all the "FLOOD VICTIMS" is saved by the Knute Rockne-esque "LIFE-GUARD." Observe how the woman's left arm hangs limp. Wright positioned both Mann's and Lulu's dead bodies in exactly the same manner as did the illustrator here. By doing so, he offers more violently parodic commentary on the unfulfilled—indeed the mendacious—quality of such promotional iconography. If, in this cartoon, we see a rearranged *Pietà* in which, happily, the Christic figure's resurrection will happen in *this* life, in Wright's story, we apprehend two sacrificial figures whose earthly salvation is past hope and whose ultimate resurrection is uncertain. No human form supports them that might prefigure eternal life's second embrace. Only the minerals of marble and earth lie beneath them to suggest a bare, biological reincorporation.

It is Mann who acts throughout the crisis as the community's "LIFE-GUARD" as he carries white hospital patients to safety and rescues the remaining Heartfields from their unmoored house. He is the figure who, as Burrow put it, seems to "subordinate[ ]" his "self-instinct . . . to the organic behests of our common societal instinct."[79] Because Wright goes to the trouble to show that Mann's extraordinary physical feats are, when associated with whites in distress, socially compelled more than organically occurring, Wright seems conspicuously to adjust Burrow's claim. Wright implicitly theorizes that when a system of racial domination is deeply entrenched in a culture, it conditions humans even at the core behavioral zone of what Burrow calls "common societal instinct." Wright shows that the self-protective drive in black southerners is merely "subordinated" to the *social* behests of a hierarchical mandate. Mann was disciplined to be allocentric. To put it another way: white authority figures in the story, by and large, use discipline to enforce black altruism. Only if there could be, as Burrow hoped, an "entire repudiation of man's image-production and a re-uniting of his organic and conscious life into a single constructive whole" could humans undo the "biological recoil" and be a part once more of the living continuum. Only if the visual regime of race, the anti-biology of race, could be dismantled, Wright seems to imply, could humans move beyond an "instinct of [visually coded] tribal preservation" and cultivate a broader "common societal instinct" in a modern heterogeneous world.[80]

In Mann's final resting place, Wright signifies upon the African American spiritual after which the story is named. In the spiritual "Down by the Riverside," which Mann's extended family sings as the flood rises, the riverside is incanted as a place of "peace," where one can lay down one's "sword and shield." Like the numerous instances during the 1927 flood in which African American crowds refused to consent to white requests that they sing spirituals, and thus perform the choral balm to white woe, Wright, by scripting this plot irony, by making the riverside a place of fatal assault, likewise refuses to have his flood novella restoratively exorcise sorrow. That Mann dies within sight of "boats, white boats, free boats, leaping and jumping like fish" (122), suggests that Wright was engaging not only with the black tradition of the spiritual but also the slave emancipation narrative. During a key moment in his *Narrative*, Frederick Douglass apprehends sailing freely on the Chesapeake Bay "beautiful vessels, robed in purest white" as symbols of his own, relative, bondage but also as harbingers of his ultimate liberation as they provoke him to determine: "I had as well be killed running as die standing."[81] Unlike Douglass, of course, who reaches freedom, Mann is "killed running" by the National Guard. The boats merely recapitulate the original stolen property—Heartfield's white boat—that ensnared Mann in a fatal sequence of events. Their liveliness and freedom "shout" (123) in acidic commentary upon his captivity and death. By dying, Mann has finally reached that "far away" "touch of green" (1) associated, in "Ethics," with white property and with Jim Crow "trench" (2) warfare. If, in "Ethics," the green landscape was a "symbol of fear" (3), here, as Mann lies, with "his face buried in the wet, blurred green" (123), the symbol is realized.

Gothic Mud

Wright wrote his much shorter flood story, a sketch of seven pages called "Silt," at the same time that he was drafting his flood novella. "Silt" was published first, in August 1937, in the U.S. left-wing weekly magazine *The New Masses*, edited by Marxist critic Granville Hicks.[82] If "Down by the Riverside" is about how media construction trumps sensory encounter in the midst of a flood when landmarks are hidden, "Silt" is about how the flood's deposit of mud, after the waters recede, estranges the known world in yet another way. High water—and relief propaganda—made Mann mistakenly believe that his Jim Crow environment had been washed clean of its undergirding mentality; "Silt" offers no such temporary illusion. Instead, the layer of mud clinging to the black family's domestic terrain and possessions serves to defamiliarize consumer ownership itself and to reveal the post-slavery relation of landlord to laborer to be one of ongoing ownership. The mud shows plantation-linked consumption to be spectral and entrapping. The river's replenishing disturbance regime—as it bears silt from the upper to lower watershed and creates the Delta's fertility—seems here to not so much make wealth as reveal the forms of economic dependence and predation that produce wealth. Playing with the Gothic genre, Wright discerns and displays the essentially Gothic logic of Marx's proposition that capitalism deadens humans while it enlivens commodities.

"Silt" describes one afternoon in the life of a black family who has just returned to their "mud-caked cabin" (102) and small crop-lien farm after a great flood has receded. What occurs is not much more than an inventorying of damage to their landlord's farm buildings and to their own movable possessions. After repeated acts of frozen "looking," the father, mother, and daughter then begin the slow process of reestablishing their human presence. They pump water and boil it; discover a little tobacco stashed on a shelf above the "flood mark" (103); and begin to clean and disinfect their home. As darkness falls, their landlord, Mr. Burgess, comes by in his buggy, warns the father, Tom, not to try to flee, and thereby slip clear of his eight hundred dollars of debt, and then takes the father to the plantation commissary to get more farming supplies and hence increase his indebtedness to Burgess. As the buggy pulls away, the mother calls out a request to "Bring some 'lasses" (108) for their daughter, Sal. Given Wright's habit of naming characters after the theorists whose suppositions he is fictionally testing, it is no surprise that Burgess the landlord is given the name of the prominent Chicago sociologist Ernest Burgess who coauthored *The City* and *Introduction to the Science of Sociology*. Burgess's assertion that "society is an immense co-operative concern of mutual services" and his theory that calamity is followed by social stabilization through an "increasing differen-tiation" of social functions are handily refuted through the behavior of the Delta planter.

The narrator of "Silt," by contrast with that of the novella, does not enter the consciousness of any of the three family members. He shows them in frozen postures of looking—standing with "bewildered eyes," "without moving a mus-cle" or with one lifted finger (102)—but he doesn't really seem to describe their version of what they see. Each character remains opaque and generic. The nar-rator, however, is quite sophisticated, using words like "scalloped" and "depres-sion" (103), and quite literary, conjuring out of bare matter a Gothic atmo-sphere full of strangely animated things, full of "weird" objects and "ghost[s]" (104) that are much more expressive of emotion than are the returning humans. "Over all," the narrator explains, "hung a first-day strangeness" (103). While it seems to be the first day of creation—a day when the maker surveys his first act of drawing light from darkness, or when Noah first contemplated a purified, post-diluvian world from atop Ararat—it is in fact a day made strange by the slowly appearing signs of old objects smeared totally away: henhouse, pigpen, chickens, Miz Flora's house that stood next door, the very road itself.

The objects that remain are, at one and the same time, animated and spec-tral. The gatepost, for example, only "half buried," calls attention to itself as it rises out of the ground: its "rusty hinge stood stiff, like a lonely finger," which the father pried loose and "caught . . . firmly in his hand" (103). While the daughter's finger was described as "skinny" (102) and Tom's as "thick" (103), this "lonely" defunct hinge, once tasked with the job of connecting one object to another, *feels* the loss of its companionate objects. The father's grasping it suggests an attempt to draw from the hinge its promise of and desire for con-nection, for hinging thing to thing, and thing to feeling. The water pump, once awoken, issues a "dry, hollow cough" (105). As they move toward the house, they find that the cabin, its bottom half painted yellow by the silt, "looked weird, as though its ghost were standing beside it" (104). The door is not closed, as they left it, but "half-opened" (104), as if a visitation has occurred, a visita-tion that "somehow . . . seemed natural" (104). Indeed, nature—or muddy water "eight feet high" (102)—has been the visitor here, or the intruder, mark-ing, opening, drowning, warping, sweeping (103–4). It has awoken objects into a grotesque life. Thus, when the family steps inside their house, they encounter something like a murder scene: a "smell" assaults their nostrils; a dresser ap-peared, "its drawers and sides bulging like a bloated corpse"; the bed "was like a giant casket forged of mud"; the only things to escape this lively death are "two smashed chairs" that "huddled together for protection" (104).

Just two objects are completely untouched by the silt: a box of matches and "a half-full sack of Bull Durham tobacco" (106). Tom quickly rolls a cigarette. This, and the fact that the one thing Sal later requests from the commissary is some molasses, suggests that while objects from their private sanctum—beds, chairs, dressers—have been made "weird," the commodities produced by plantation monoculture are somehow invulnerable. In other words, the sharecropping system, despite the eight-foot flood marauder, remains intact. The system of plantation monoculture, based on producing addictive stimulants like sugar and tobacco, and in more tropical regions, coffee and tea, somehow even knows how to perpetuate itself through generating a human dependence on and desire for its cultivars. Tom and Sal show that they are human—that they desire—mainly through their attachment to the very thing that enthralls them.

The human face of their thralldom is the planter, Mr. Burgess. Because they are in debt to him for eight hundred dollars, they cannot leave his land lest they be arrested. And, because they now need new supplies, their debt will only increase. As Tom says: "Ef we keeps on like this tha white man'll own us body n soul" (106). As Mr. Burgess threatens "the sheriff" if Tom tries to "dodge" his debts, Tom seems to be accepting a kind of fatal sentence. The narrator mentions twice that Tom "stood with his back against a post" and says "nothing." He then "pull[s] himself into" Burgess's horse-drawn buggy, and the last description reads, "Tom's head came out of the side of the buggy" (108). Something about this finale has the quality of a beheading. To be absorbed into this plantation vehicle, into a deeper debt arrangement, into ownership "body and soul," is to lose his status as head of the family and to lose his power of independent cognition. Now Tom is merely a body incorporated into his master's engine.

Richard Wright had experimented with the Gothic form before and was by this time a reader of Edgar Allen Poe, Henry James, and Faulkner. The quasi-aristocratic or *haute bourgeoisie* status of the cursed families in stories like "The Fall of the House of Usher" or "The Turn of the Screw" or *Absalom, Absalom!* implied that the doom settling onto each domicile involved the stewing fetor of a wealth that wished to isolate itself from its extramural sources. These are stories, in other words, of imploding dynasties—of houses burned up or caved under by the force of their repressions. In "Silt," Wright uses the genre to a different end. It is not the master's house put under surveillance by a curious, external narrator but rather the servants' quarters. The destruction does not arise from within this house but from without, coming in the form of a marauding, eight-foot visitor. And what this "natural" visitor does is leave "marks" the next, unembodied, narratorial visitor can read. Silt and water is the medium of this communicative signage. And by its smashing, warping, and caking, it remakes the built environment of the plantation laborer "back of the big house."[83] It signifies to the narrator, by giving the utilitarian materials a "weird" ghostly life while arresting the humans in frozen postures of bewilderment, that the plantation reifies its laborers more utterly than it does its ostensible "things," its pumps and hinges and floors. Reminiscent of Wright's own teenage role as a literate, relatively well-educated insurance claims processor visiting the houses of impoverished and uneducated residents in the Delta, this narrator surveys and records the damage in a mode that is inaccessible to the inhabitants.

The flood in this story by no means liberates the black inhabitants of the plantation lowlands. Because of the labor and credit system to which they are beholden, the flood makes them more captive to that system's economic protocols. If the flood becomes an instrument of more intense domination by the planter who now owns his workers "body and soul," it is also a kind of marking instrument that makes this Gothic captivity more visible to the eyes of the literary narrator and his readers. The Gothic was typically used, beginning with its eighteenth-century English origins, to defamiliarize wealth and to make dynastic power seem really creepy. In "Silt," the same sociopolitical critique is achieved, but this time by dwelling on the weird situation *behind* the big house where people lose their heads and objects possess a sad consciousness. In "Silt," Wright continued to draw out the spatial and environmental implications of Marxist theory, and to add to Marx's European critique of class, a critique of race called for by a century, and a world, defined by the "color-line."[84] In Marx's observation that both the laborer's "*species life*" as well as his "inorganic body, nature, is taken away from him"[85] as the laborer produces an enlivened commodity, Wright saw the Gothic syntax in which categories of life and death switch places. Wright represents nature being turned into a catastrophic "second nature" as a Gothic horror story.

* * *

In "Ethics," "Down by the Riverside," and "Silt," Richard Wright shapes a new form of black environmental writing. Addressing southern rural and town locales, he undercuts and modifies a number of the presiding sociological and psychological theories of the 1920s and 1930s. The world of Jim Crow, its everyday and its exceptional disasters, required a different kind of modeling. Wright suggested that spatial design, and human habitation within that design, was here not a happenstance outcome of competition and selection among sparring human groups that stabilized over time. In the plantation and post-plantation South, once this racial and land-use design took hold in its early decades and was codified into law and naturalized over time, it became impossible to eradicate. Even the biggest flood in recorded history could not wash away its "CUSS-EDNESS." And the flood certainly did not, according to Wright, act as a social tonic. Wright's environmentalist critique is not, as with white southern editorials, directed at federal engineering negligence and upriver land-use practices. Rather, he seeks to show that what appears to be natural in the South—"green growing things," embankments, tobacco, sugar—are in fact human cultivars and products that entrench and perpetuate the labor and racial system by which they are produced. For Wright, as opposed to Faulkner's 1920s flood narratives, it is not the flood itself that is man-made but rather the environment through which the flood moves. For Wright, white print mediation, both verbal and visual, along with the more diffuse visual regime of Jim Crow, was a key source of this perpetuation. Carefully signifying upon the promotional and minstrel cartoons associated with the Flood of 1927, and demonstrating how white visual devices (flashlights, signs) sustain Jim Crow logic even in disaster, Wright, drawing on John Heartfield, posited a role for the black artist who sought to represent catastrophe. That artist must, out of the darkness, create a world in his mind and with his hands. Unlike Mann, that artist must not abdicate his powers of creation to distant visions he imagines will help him. Because those beguiling representations of social solidarity will explode with aggression, the black artist must give in to neither promised "help" nor fabled hope but must hold fast to his painful memory—like a Dadaist or a blues singer—and work from within his cognitive "ache." Plots that turn on subjects navigating risk, losing gambles, and meeting improbably unlucky coincidence would communicate to readers the aleatory world black citizens daily confronted in the South, a world whose aptest synecdoche was a disaster.

Though Wright and Zora Neale Hurston squared off as they reviewed each other's fiction in 1937–38, the way each represented major historical floods in these works shows their commonality. In *Their Eyes Were Watching God*, Hurston addressed the 1928 flooding of Florida's Lake Okeechobee that was responsible for more deaths to people of African descent than occurred in any other day in U.S. history.[86] She critiqued the black "folk," who, as disaster neared, abdicated their long-ingrained knowledge of risk, trusting instead the assurances of nature's stability and manageability offered by white authority figures.[87] Like Hurston, Wright calls readers' attentions to the racial, media, and physical landscapes of a disaster zone during an historic flood. And he, too, showed the dire consequences of abdicating your head, your knowledge, your senses, your memory, to white regimes of truth. Wright accused Hurston, in his review of her novel, of using "the minstrel technique that makes the 'white folks' laugh";[88] he could not hear the environmental prophecies spoken by her "end-men" when they talked of a "monster" capable of eating up people's homes.[89] Hurston, in her subsequent review of *Uncle Tom's Children*, likewise accused Wright of having produced in the character Mann "a stupid, blundering character. . . . elemental and brutish."[90] She did not see that Wright had fashioned in Mann an experiment, acted out in something like real time, in letting knowledge of risk slip out of your hands and your memory. Though neither could see beyond their differences in technique—with her indebtedness to black comedy and his to communist and antifascist agitprop—both authors produced some of the most important fictional memorializations of early twentieth-century Jim Crow environmental disasters.

Conclusion: Noah's Kin

In the year that Richard Wright published *Uncle Tom's Children*, a quite different representation of the Mississippi Flood of 1927 appeared in the popular press. Readers who opened their copies of the May 6, 1940, issue of *Life* magazine saw a two-page color reproduction of John Steuart Curry's painting *Hoover and the Flood* (Fig. C.1). The painting had been commissioned by the magazine's editor, Henry R. Luce, as part of a series that memorialized "dramatic scenes" in recent American history.[1] The publishing titan was hoping for a Republican presidential victory later that year and, along with it, a suspension of New Deal restrictions on free enterprise. Rehabilitating Herbert Hoover, the last—and defeated—Republican president, by picturing him in a supreme moment of managerial control, fit well into Luce's agenda.[2] Beyond the coming presidential race, Luce had a vision, articulated months later in his "American Century" editorial, of a new international world order with the United States at its helm. This vision for the future likely affected how Luce curated the recent national past in his *Life* pictorial series. Though the United States had become "the most vital nation in the world," Luce argued, Americans could not "accommodate themselves spiritually and practically to that fact" and had therefore disastrously "failed to play their part as a world power." Revolution, the rise of fascism, and now war in the eastern hemisphere all showed that the planet needed the United States to be both a leader and a Good Samaritan. Citing Hoover, Luce urged Americans to become a "powerhouse" that disseminated its vision of civilization to lift mankind from "the level of the beasts" to that level a "little lower than the angels."[3]

The moment Curry chose to depict is one of dramatic rescue: as Hoover and his aides arrive on the right, the sun breaks forth out of the clouds in a divine pronouncement of heroism. Encircling the group of refugees, we see a series of rock-solid tents; a mighty steamboat chugging ever nearer; sailors poling their raft in commanding but graceful unison; Red Cross personnel

C.1. John Steuart Curry, *Hoover and the Flood*, 1940. Oil on panel, 37 1/2 × 63 in. Morris Museum of Art, Augusta, Georgia.

bravely encountering death and protecting life; and, finally, a moving picture camera that stores this event for future retrieval. The central figure of a woman and nursing infant, echoed by other maternal acts of care before and behind her, would have reminded viewers of an iconic Associated Press photograph of a nursing woman caught in the 1937 flood that became famously known as the "Memphis Madonna."[4] It also evokes the grouping of white mother and children that dramatized "The Distressed Southland" in the *Columbus Dispatch*'s 1927 lithograph (see Fig. 2.4). In that image, however, the mother desperately beckoned for the Red Cross; here, the mother is enwrapped in the surety of its care. Out of the black mass of bodies stretch three kinetic gestures: the gamboling boy motors his arms in excitement at Hoover's arrival while the more mature woman on the raft and the hoary elder in the center lift their arms up to the sky in an expression of praise and thanksgiving for God's having sent His emissary at last. In the context of 1940 geopolitics, the 1927 catastrophe offers a dense tableau of the turmoil then besetting what Luce called the "world-environment."[5] Hoover, the well-organized patriarch and Good Samaritan, enlists modern science and technology to help the global masses gain a foothold on Christian civilization.

The archive of the 1927 flood we have explored throughout this book gives us a critical purchase on Curry's representation and, behind Curry, Luce's act of politically savvy historical memorialization. Hoover's "relief machine" did rescue thousands of people in the Delta that spring, using modern transportation and communications technologies and complex organizational networks to do so; African Americans did gather to ceremonially praise Hoover; and much of the public media at the time supported Hoover, accrediting and amplifying his message. The full historical experience, however, is much more complex. A rescue barge was sent *away* from the Greenville levee empty because planters insisted that their laborers remain in place. Throughout the Delta, homeless blacks did not so much await rescue as provide the labor that buffered whites and white property from inundation. Red Cross officials and workers were complicit with racially prejudicial delivery of relief. The media did not project a single, unifying stream of information but engaged in interregional and interracial cross talk. African Americans did not simply praise Hoover, but also lobbied to help direct his rescue efforts or denounced those efforts entirely. Industrial technology not only enabled the "huge relief machine" but also destabilized the environmental integrity of the Mississippi Valley. God had not sent the flood to purify His people and draw forth a modern Noah to save the world, as Curry's *Life* image suggests. Powerful humans had trusted too much in the ability of industrial technology to control biological behavior and in the power of the state, business, and an allied publicity machine to control the behavior and the expression of Delta laborers, dissenters, and artists.

In the twenty-first century, we are no longer living in the American century as much as we are living on the American planet—or, on the planet where the particular environmental experience of North America has been exported. From the early modern period, as European nations became imperial powers, they swelled their biological and monetary funds by extracting natural resources from colonial territory, much of which was in the Western Hemisphere. Race was invented to putatively single out European American, or "white," bodies from those who labored in but were seldom entitled to own land. Once the United States achieved independence, it gradually shifted its former (exotic and slightly degraded) status as an extended British plantation onto one particular region: the South.[6] And as the nation expanded westward, it inherited its former colonizers' sense of an imperial relation to a western wilderness that offered itself up providentially to be "improved" by a new master. Though the extreme alteration of nature, imperialism, and industrialism represent geographically broad features of modernity, it was particularly in the Western

Hemisphere that Europeans and Euro-Americans derived a combination of technological trust, missionary purpose, and a belief in both resource plenitude and racial superiority. The United States became an exporter of this western eco-political history and mentality at the beginning of what Luce called the American Century.[7] As an exporter of prodigal environmental behavior and, at the same time, a "powerhouse" and "Good Samaritan," the United States is in a quite contradictory world position.

Given the U.S. ascent to sole superpower after the end of the Cold War, its role in overseas wars as a purported protector rather than an aggressor, and its self-conception as a polity both founded upon equality and blessed by God, the nation was not prepared for what happened in New Orleans and the Mississippi Gulf Coast in August 2005. To be an "emergency world leader" fighting the War on Terror abroad but so visibly unprepared for a furious "act of God" at home called into question many features of America's providentialist global narrative. Though Luce had commissioned a portrait of *Hoover and the Flood* as part of a push to help Americans "accommodate themselves spiritually and practically" to their world eminence, it was another Jim Crow disaster, uncannily replaying so many features of the 1927 flood, that threatened to call the bluff on that eminence. How could a publicity giant like Luce derive from the 1927 flood a promise of U.S. global leadership while the public news about the 2005 flooding called that leadership into question? In short, what was it that made the recent disaster we have come to call Katrina, and its mediation, distinct from its 1927 forerunner?

The 1927 and the 2005 cases both involved a faultily designed federal levee system;[8] a degraded riparian or coastal wetlands environment that could no longer protect the terra firma from storm surge or inundation; underresourced people and especially people of color living in the most susceptible, lowest ground without means of evacuation; and events that turned quickly into a real-time global media spectacle in which false information and racist imagery skewed public perception and official responses. Though Hoover's 1927 "relief machine" actually *did* operate with considerably more "smoothness" than did rescue and relief efforts in 2005, its mandate to restore the Jim Crow social and physical plantation structure of the region, and to save wealthy New Orleans, made federal agencies complicit in enforcing conditions akin to slavery for African Americans and causing the displacement and land loss of the Acadian minority. In the wake of Katrina, there was a rush to privatize public goods, a symptom of what Naomi Klein calls "disaster capitalism,"[9] a process that she argues has reversed many social gains won during and since the 1930s. While the U.S. Congress, in the wake of the 1927 flood, did assume greater financial responsibility for managing the Mississippi watershed, this increased public shouldering of infrastructure maintenance (which seemed to anticipate the New Deal) did not necessarily help the small farmer or sharecropper as much as it did the large-scale landholder typical of the Delta. Even though risk became more nationally shared after the 1927 flood, landholding was still private and majority-white in majority-black communities. The power of private interests, therefore, was considerable after both catastrophes.[10] Finally, the same way in which the earlier flood made clear that African Americans in the Delta lived in conditions conforming to slavery in all but name, the 2005 disaster brought to public perception that, despite the legislative advances brought about by the civil rights movement, and despite the technically equal access of minorities to positions of power, the geographic separation of people by race and income—and hence their vulnerability to danger—characteristic of Jim Crow still prevailed. Each disaster made it undeniable that all the progress on racial discrimination and standards of living believed to have been made, or sustained, throughout the United States had not actually been made or sustained. It was Katrina that brought to mainstream attention the ongoing—or worsening—crises in education, housing, transportation, health, and environmental safety for the least-resourced citizens of the United States.

What was most different about the two events, I would argue, is that artists and commentators in 2005 could be more openly critical of the racial and class dimensions of their disaster before a multiracial mass audience. That the first flood took place in the midst of the Harlem Renaissance and at a time when performers of color in Vaudeville had access to big audiences on both sides of the color line meant that artists conscious of the racial and class dimensions of the disaster had a potentially broad opportunity to affect the nation's thinking and imagining about the flood. It was necessary, though, in the late 1920s for these public figures to be indirectly—or, to create an oxymoron—appealingly critical. Miller and Lyles had to lure in their audience slowly and carefully through clowning and then lay down their explosive thought bombs just right, on the off-tempo beat, to surprise their listeners into enjoying an uncomfortable awareness. Miller and Lyles had to trust that the people laughing were beginning to understand the real existential and historical plight layered within their act. Will Rogers made his appeal for black and white sharecroppers in ways compatible with his own complex southern persona but also in a manner that would sell to a mass audience, namely in sentimental, paternalistic terms. Bessie Smith brought distant listeners of all races close to black pain but told of her evacuee's suffering without defining its human source. Du Bois, Wells, Pickens, and others wrote very explicit critiques of the Red Cross, the National

Guard, and Hoover but did so in the more enclaved venue of the black press. While Walter White's critical report on relief efforts appeared in the liberal white organ *The Nation*, he opted to bury its lead—about the "crystalliz[ation]" of a "new slavery" in the Delta—so as not to put off his readers. Faulkner memorialized the black community's submersion in water only through metaphor in 1928 and did so within the context of a Christian rite of resurrection; in 1929, he did diagnose the catastrophic dimensions of rural modernization for poor white farmers but made the regional scale of his assessment allegorical rather than explicit. It took eleven years, and the intervening New Deal mood and aesthetic, for Wright's bleak indictment of the racial dimensions of the 1927 flood to appear in print with Harper publishers. And, as I have just detailed, a more widely disseminated, highly paternalistic, and propagandistic counterrepresentation, *Hoover and the Flood*, appeared in the same year.

By contrast, in the months surrounding and years following Katrina, American artists and documentarians who had access to mainstream media outlets and elite cultural institutions and who wanted the nation to confront the social injustices of the event did so in a media and cultural climate more able to sustain open controversy. During the disaster, the nation saw the entertainment industry superstar Kanye West going off-script on NBC's "Concert for Hurricane Relief" to critique the media's racial double standards when reporting looting and, more famously, to proclaim that "George Bush does not care about Black people," a remark that provoked Bush's later response on NBC News. Ida B. Wells had shown similar temerity with Commerce Secretary Hoover in 1927, but it was not printed in the mainstream media. Spike Lee's documentary *When the Levees Broke: A Requiem in Four Acts* was aired on HBO a year after the disaster, intercutting interviews with people caught in the high water who had direct empirical knowledge of the disaster with public relations scenes staged for the news media by government figures eager to project an impression of concern and competence. You could say that Lee used the documentary genre to reveal what sociologist Lars Clausen has described as the danger when too great a distance grows between the so-called problem-solvers and problem-laymen.[11] Lee democratically redefined expertise.

Within months of Katrina, the artist Kara Walker—known for her visual explorations of the idea that "slavery is a nightmare from which no American has yet awakened"[12]—was commissioned to create an exhibit at the Metropolitan Museum of Art. "After the Deluge" placed side by side Walker's own work with paintings in the museum's holdings like J.M.W. Turner's 1840 *The Slave Ship* and Winslow Homer's 1899 *The Gulf Stream*, both of which depict the plight of Africa-descended people in a world of fatal water. Walker's image,

C.2. Kara Walker, "Post Katrina, Adrift," *New Yorker*, August 27, 2007, cover. Kara Walker/The New Yorker. © Conde Nast.

"Post Katrina, Adrift," appeared a year later on the cover of the *New Yorker* (Fig. C.2). Alluding to Théodore Géricault's "Raft of the Medusa" (1818–19), which used the genre of monumental history painting to bring attention to a politically inflected shipwreck, Walker creates a more spare and abstract monument to the problem of a republic "adrift." The beholder of this cover, accustomed to the magazine's visual brand of light, urbane humor, is instead the bystander to an unheeded, otherwise unwatched choreography of distress. In 2010, Natasha Trethewey published *Beyond Katrina: A Meditation on the Mississippi Gulf Coast*, a creative nonfiction mix of poetry and autobiography that chronicles the ways in which her family and their hometown of Gulfport, Mississippi, struggled to retain their integrity when, for example, the insurance and gaming industries out-resourced longtime locals.[13] Soon thereafter, Trethewey was simultaneously named poet laureate of Mississippi and of the United States. In 2011 Jesmyn Ward's novel *Salvage the Bones*, about a black family in coastal Mississippi in the days surrounding Katrina, won the National Book Award. In *Treme*, the HBO television drama about life in New Orleans in the wake of Katrina (2010–13), it is, in a reversal of popular flood representations in 1927, a white character (Davis McAlary) who plays the jester, offering comic relief, while a black character (Albert Lambreaux) has the gravitas and lineage of a regal patriarch. Historians, reporters, and scientists also produced books in the year or two after the disaster for an audience open to, and even eager for, critical assessments of so much: coastal wetlands and levee mismanagement; city, state, and federal incompetence among elected and appointed officials; poor communications networks; and structures of racism and classism with historical roots that go deeper than individual malfeasance.[14] It is an alarming fact that there could have been such a startling replay in 2005 of the 1927 Jim Crow–era disaster. The challenge is to turn the more open and exploratory national conversation about Katrina into consequential policy changes.[15]

In saying that the public conversation about the ways that race and poverty inflect vulnerability to disaster has become more searching, I do not mean to imply that overtness of critique is the only measure of a work of art's significance or its subtly and slowly generative powers of suggestion. In 1927, Vaudeville comedians, blues singers, satirical cartoonists, folk poets, and modernist fiction writers all experimented with their chosen medium to show that a physical catastrophe of massive dimensions was also an index of social crisis, of the universe's unpredictability, and of the new kind of human who must wager her life in such a universe. The 1927 flood, despite—and even in some cases because of—the constraints I have mentioned on overt communication at the time, occasioned the innovation of these forms of art. It is the ways in which capacious art places something we might call decisive meaning ever beyond the verge of our captious grasp that keeps us returning to it and, in returning to it, making it matter for each historical era anew.

If the future brings more frequent and disastrous weather events, rising sea levels, and mass human displacement, as many scientists predict, how will the journalists and artists who chronicle disaster and the environmental vulnerability of the underresourced stir public consciousness and perhaps shift consumer habits, everyday behavior, and political will? How will communication work if, as Rob Nixon has put it, the violence connected to these events can often be slow to fully materialize while the public's attention is quickly lost? Because we seem as a planet to be at point in time when the consequences of our environmental decisions and habits seem terrifyingly permanent—because we seem as a species to have afflicted ourselves with a new kind of unwitting and unwanted power—how can we find modes of communication commensurate with this present and future condition? Although message creation and dissemination are arguably in the hands of a "democratic multiple" more than ever before, it remains to be seen exactly how these new forms of participatory mediation will translate into a new carbon future.

In 1927, the year that anticipated our contemporary disaster-prone time, John Dewey worried, in his *Public and Its Problems*, how scattered publics could make informed decisions in a world characterized by "forces so vast, so remote in initiation, so far-reaching in scope and so complexly indirect in operation" that these forces could not be traced back to their beginnings and thus understood or controlled.[16]

After his diagnosis of these problems, Dewey recommended to his readers a reinvestment in embodied local publics whose face-to-face connections could provide a way to sort out and confront these mysterious forces. He also welcomed "Poetry, the drama, the novel." Reading these imaginative forms could potentially interrupt "routine consciousness," help the reader conduct "the highest and most difficult kind of inquiry," and adopt "a subtle, delicate, vivid and responsive art of communication." Underlying this need to repair public communication, for Dewey, was the imperative to rethink the relation between the mind, the body, and nature. In 1925 he had written that "Man finds himself living in an aleatory world; his existence involves, to put it baldly, a gamble."[17] Nature, he argued, is contingent and unpredictable. The dominant tradition of Western philosophy, from Plato to Descartes, denied humanity's immersion in such a chancy cosmos. Philosophy needed to put the mind *back* in the body, and hence back into a communicative circuit with the universe's aleatory processes. Such deliberate recognition of our unavoidable immersion in the world's body was, to Dewey, science. Thus, "to be intelligently experimental," to be scientific in the proper sense, is "to be conscious of this intersection of natural conditions so as to profit by it instead of being at its mercy."[18]

Reading *Experience and Nature* alongside *The Public and Its Problems* in our own moment is salutary since together they address how to adjust science, philosophy, art, and communication to contingent biological processes of which our bodies and brains are a part.[19] Though human activity since the beginning of the industrial era has used technology with special intensity "to profit by" natural conditions, humans with exceptional access to capital and political power today need to redefine their relation to scientific knowledge. We must value not only the scientific developments we can capitalize upon but also the sciences that assess the healthily dynamic functioning of natural systems. At the very least, the gamble needs to be longer, the "profit" on a different scale of time. And the risks inherent in the stresses we place on biology should not be sequestered among the least powerful. These bodies in the United States or in the Global South should not be made to absorb risk and thus void that risk from the calculations of those with power. Embodied local publics by themselves, I would argue, will not necessarily create intelligent change. Indeed, connecting a local group or physically proximate "community of danger" to other communities and to a broader virtual public can be essential to investigative and reformative processes.[20] Artists need to interrupt the ways our routinizing minds make comfort out of unsustainable risk. Art must help science in this "most difficult kind of inquiry."

* * *

In April 1927, a poem appeared in print that must have seemed to many readers a providential coincidence. The poem was called "Noah Built the Ark." It was one of many included in *God's Trombones: Seven Negro Sermons in Verse*, a poetic adaptation of the "folk sermons" given by the old-time preachers whom the author James Weldon Johnson had heard while growing up in Florida and whose cultural vitality and oratorical genius he wanted to honor.[21] Instead of dialect, Johnson tried to approximate the "fusion of Negro idioms with Bible English" characterizing these preachers. Next to the poem was an illustration by Aaron Douglas (Fig. C.3). Douglas was a midwestern artist by birth who had risen to prominence in New York City during the Harlem Renaissance, becoming the movement's most important visual artist. His illustrations appeared in Alain Locke's *The New Negro* (1925), in the NAACP's *Crisis* and the Urban League's *Opportunity*, and in books by Claude McKay and Langston Hughes.[22]

The poem moves quickly from the halcyon days in Eden to the point at which "God got sorry that he ever made man." We hear God thinking:

I'll bring down judgment on him with a flood.
I'll destroy ev'rything on the face of the earth,
Man, beasts and birds, and creeping things.

Noah, of course, won favor in the eyes of God and was saved as a remnant of God's first try at making people. God gave him measurements for building an ark. It takes Noah a hundred years, and, through it all, he endures the scorn of the unbelieving rabble. Before that rabble is destroyed, he preaches to them:

Repent, for the time is drawing nigh.
God's wrath is gathering in the sky.

C.3. Aaron Douglas, illustration for James Weldon Johnson, "Noah Built the Ark," *God's Trombones: Seven Negro Sermons in Verse* (New York: Viking, 1927), 30b.

God's a-going to rain down rain on rain.
God's a-going to loosen up the bottom of the deep,
And drown this wicked world.
Sinners, repent while yet there's time
For God to change his mind.

But the rabble doesn't listen. When the time is ready, God tells Noah to get in the ark and "Bar the door!" A tiny black spot in the distance begins to spread, "Like a bottle of ink spilling over the sky." Soon those unbelievers and "the trees and the hills and the mountain tops / Slipped underneath the waters." The ark was sailing over "A sea without a shore."[23]

Aaron Douglas selected one particular moment of this sermon to imagine. Here, Noah is not wizened by work or ridiculed by the many. The strong diagonal lines—of the gangplank, buttresses, thunderbolts, and animal bodies—focus our eye on the ark's magnetic promise of sanctuary amid the approaching storm. Noah and his son, in pared-down profile, rim and ballast the ship with their surety of purpose. God's spotlight has made a banner for their work. Yet, as we can see, night and thunder will soon have their way.

Readers in 1927 must have viewed this image and read this poem with a whole range of reactions. Like other works of the Harlem Renaissance, the poem called upon the currency of folk form to create a public awareness of traditions within African American culture. Douglas mixes the two-dimensional figural representations of Egypt with the complex planes of Cubism as he gives black life a foothold in both the ancient and the modern. If readers in the spring of 1927 had been paying attention to the coverage of the flood then moving down the Lower Mississippi Valley, they might have associated this poem and this image with many other discussions of Noah, and God's angry waters, that appeared that spring. They might have remembered that a preacher who read the flood as God's revenge on southern whites had been upbraided by William Pickens in the *Amsterdam News*: "God is not 'on the Negro's side,'" Pickens averred. "He thinks just as well, to say the least, of white people."[24] Because God had not singled out the American Negro as his new Noah, Pickens urged President Coolidge, in a letter printed in the black press, to appoint a "Negro officer" to be a "right hand help" to whoever was put in charge of relief operations. "It would prevent a great deal of suffering and avoid much American scandal," he added.[25] Americans may have heard the disparaging tale—circulated by Red Cross publicists—of the "Negro Noah" who tried to build his own river-worthy rescue boat. The *Los Angeles Times'* cartoon version of the story, "Negro Noah Gets Wet Feet," showed Noah and his "flock" in blackface, frowning as they bail out their impossible boat (see Fig. 2.6). The ease with which the mainstream press enlisted the minstrel scenario during the flood helps explain why African Americans faced an unsurmountable challenge in 1927 convincing the public, and public officials, that their experience in the Delta prepared them to assume just the kind of purposeful leadership imagined in Douglas's image.

We have encountered many rafts, or floating objects haphazardly put to emergency use, in this history: from the drifting roof of the Currier and Ives image to the drifting roof in Kara Walker's Katrina memorial, from Miller and Lyles's downed airplane to the swimming horse Cash grabs onto in the midst of the flood, from Mann's purloined boat to that battered vessel of the tall convict's unwanted flood odyssey. All of these are examples of floating materials adapted or expropriated, in the midst of unexpected crisis, to work as devices of hoped-for transit or temporary salvation. In a biosphere characterized by uncertainty, and in a "second nature" where uncertainty is exacerbated, such rafts represent an uncanny feature of modern life. They show us that modernity did not outwit chance. They also show us that an intimacy with this kind of biological uncertainty, or indeed catastrophism, has not been distributed by the modern state across its population, as it would be in a fully democratic biopolitics, but has been and still is unequally allotted to poor people and people of color.

Aaron Douglas's image points to an alternate possibility. To me, "Noah Built the Ark" offers a grand revision of Atlantic history in order to imagine an alternate vision of black American life and its future. In the late sixteenth century, when the English were lagging behind other European nations in the colonization of distant tropical latitudes, in part because they worried that their own bodies would be altered and degraded by moving closer to the equator, one of their countrymen, George Best, enlisted the well-known story of Noah and his sons to allay that fear. In his 1578 *True Discourse of the Late Voyages of Discoverie*, Best argued that darkness of skin was not the result of how close to the equator one lived but was instead created by God as a curse for one of Noah's sons, Ham, who dared to gaze upon Noah in his drunken nakedness. Henceforth, all of Ham's progeny would be marked by this "curse and natural infection of the bloud." Englishmen, by contrast, should feel "assured" that the equatorial region is "the most pleasant and delectable place of the world to dwell in."[26] Here we see an early concept of race as a divinely decreed separation of a bad lineage (or "bloud") from a good one. Moreover, these races are invented and separated as a means to buffer the white bodies from the bodily risks of overseas expansion. To encounter and change a new environment, a certain immunity to that environment needed to be invented through the concept of divinely ordained racial difference. Dark bodies, even then, buffered white ones from American environmental risks.

Aaron Douglas reappropriates Noah and his sons to make visible another version of the movement from antiquity to modernity. This version does not involve a curse on African blood that legitimates subjugation; nor does it imagine "Negro Noah" as disqualified for modernity by heredity or by a slave past; nor does it imagine that Noah relies on God to do his work for him. As Best used Noah to imagine a European Atlantic, Douglas here enlists Noah to envision an Atlantic past that did not degrade or defeat its African travelers, and hence to picture a future in which a different kind of Black Noah might exist.

This modern Noah does not assume that he has somehow outgrown his enmeshment in biological life. He doesn't assume that nature is obsolescent, replaced by a more tractable technology. Instead he enjoins technology to fashion a structure that can sustain species other than his own. This Noah assumes that his relationship with divinity requires him to care for all the species of life in a turbulent world. Today, as humans around the planet struggle to understand the new risks and new obligations within the epoch of the Anthropocene, this image of Noah and his kin is one to remember.

ACKNOWLEDGMENTS

I want first to thank my students for their invaluable presence in the collective laboratory in which this book took on substance. The idea for this project came out of a longstanding interest in the history of American plantations as well as a need to reckon with our current environmental moment by fathoming one of its key antecedents; every step of the way, the classroom has been an important place for me to pursue these interests, try out arguments, take in ideas, and confirm the worth of the undertaking. The PhD and MFA students who participated in the three seminars I've given at the University of Michigan on southern literature and South-North-Atlantic world cultural circuits have been a key intellectual community for me. One MFA student in particular, Max Henderson, has been a sustaining interlocutor for a number of years. The first time I met Max was when he came to my office for a quick rundown on grading papers; we got to talking about the Flood of 1927, also an interest of his, and I think the lights in the building went off before we stopped our exuberant exchange. And that was just the beginning of a long conversation, including his extremely helpful comments on chapter 6, and his sharing his adoptive New Orleans with me and my husband a few years later. Three undergraduate honors students wrote theses on Faulkner with me in recent years; what fun to spend time together trying to pick the lock on those lush mysteries. Thank you Jo Adams, Emily Boudreau, and Julianna Restivo. I've appreciated having students from across the university—including, especially, the Program in the Environment and the School of Engineering—bring their own fluencies and methods of thinking to discussions of southern environmental history and its legacies. Student researchers provided much-needed help tracking down newspapers, learning GIS to make initial maps, and figuring out the intricacies of image copyrights. Thank you Emilye Rogel, Cat Kartwright, Kristin Fraser, and Lazarus Belle. I am also grateful for funding from the Undergraduate Research Opportunity Program and the English Department. Finally, a few former undergraduate students have become lifelong friends and have become an integral part of my thinking over recent years; thank you Daphna Atias, Nick Nuechter-lein, and Elizabeth Lalley.

Colleagues and friends at the University of Michigan have offered support at every turn. I recall in particular a lunch with Adela Pinch a decade ago when I was feeling sheepish about redirecting my scholarship to the twentieth century; what I remember her saying is that we don't get to write that many books in our short lives, so write the one that you really want to. That advice really helped! John Knott introduced me to the field of eco-criticism, quietly guided me away from rhetorical excesses and intellectual mistakes (as he read all of my early chapters), and modeled for me the kind of ethical and civil life I will always aspire to. John Whittier-Ferguson carefully read a number of chapters; along with his never-flagging humor and warmth, he shared his deep expertise on modernism and modernity as well as his practice of meticulous writing. Good friends in a writing group, Anne Curzan, Cathy Sanok, Xiomara Santamarina, Meg Sweeney, Jennifer Wenzel, and Andrea Zemgulys, read much of this book in its roughest shape and made it better. Larry Goldstein read an early draft of my analysis of *The Sound and the Fury*; his poet's and editor's ear and his pro-found knowledge of Faulkner were a vital help. The irreplaceable Patsy Yaeger guided me along, as I turned toward twentieth-century southern studies, with characteristic flare and generosity, even though I was slow in appreciating Pat-sy's own galvanic effect on that field; she had a way of simultaneously stretching taller, brightening her eyes and pursing her lips when she liked an idea—it made you want to come up with good ideas as often as you could. Michael Awkward took time for a number of conversations as this project was getting off the ground; Gregg Crane has helped me out on Pragmatist philosophy and been a welcome leader here in the Environmental Humanities; I've benefited from numerous talks with Petra Kuppers on the intersection of performance and the environment; Kerry Larson has shared his capacious knowledge of American literature and intellectual history over a number of key conversa-tions; Marjorie Levinson has gone as far as to share her notes on Marx with me, as well as her interest in the New Materialism, and generally takes any idea she hears and makes it more incisive; and Jonathan Freedman, David Gold, Van Jordan, Sean Silver, Keith Taylor, and Valerie Traub have all offered critical sug-gestions on the project. My department chairs, Sid Smith and Mike Schoen-feldt, helped me secure support from the University of Michigan for time off to write. American Culture and History colleagues at the university—especially Jay Cook and Phil Deloria—have made me stretch to think credibly in their discipline. John Vandermeer in Ecology and Evolutionary Biology generously tried to explain current principles of ecology (I still have the scraps of paper with his diagrams) and is a model of someone who bridges the "two cultures" of the university. Scott Ellsworth and I often found ourselves in intense conversations about Faulkner, and about southern history, and he was an early enthusiast about this book project. And finally, during a year spent at the Institute for the Humanities with a John Rich Fellowship, the other fellows (and its director, Daniel Herwitz) were wonderfully emboldening as I began the research for this book; talks that year with Paul Johnson on the history of anthropology and the African diaspora were especially fruitful.

I have had the real pleasure to make new scholar-friends—and to strengthen ties with old friends—across the country through this book. Jack Matthews graciously welcomed me as a fellow Faulknerian, reading through some pretty scary early work of mine on *As I Lay Dying* without losing hope. Gordon Hutner gave my first twenty-five pages of this project an initial life in print in *American Literary History*; his steadfast faith in the enterprise meant a great deal to me. Jay Watson read the entire manuscript and offered detailed suggestions; the care he took shows his generosity but also his immense dedication to the cultural history represented here. Elizabeth Dillon has shared her knowledge of modern cultural and intellectual legacies of the colonial Atlantic world and her gifts at precise theoretical explication with me over many years. Stephanie LeMenager, along with being a model of path-breaking environmental/cultural studies scholarship, read a draft of the entire manuscript, offering excellent advice. Elizabeth Steeby shared her terrific work on the 1927 flood, Katrina, and biopolitics. I got to talking with Russ Castronovo at the start of this book, and his own work on propaganda, media networks, and aesthetics across U.S. history has been an inspiration. Conversations with Tim Sweet—especially on the long lineage of human-induced catastrophe—were crucial. Hester Blum, through sharing her work on polar exploration lit, taught me that there is a word to describe what I seem invariably to study: "ecomedia." Fredrika Teute, the editor of my first book, generously continued to counsel me throughout this entire project. Joni Adamson's and Kim Ruffin's editorial suggestions on a related piece of the project were very generative. Talking through this book in its early stages with environmental historians John McNeill and Donald Worster was also extremely helpful.

Being able to present versions of many of the arguments in this book has transformed them for the better. I got a chance to participate in Pennsylvania State University's Center for American Literary Study Symposium "Circuit, Current, Connection" in 2014; I'm grateful to Sean Goudie for hosting me. Glenn Adelson invited me on the most fun teaching junket ever—to join his Lake Forest Environmental Studies Program seniors on their capstone trip down the Mississippi to New Orleans and beyond; sharing parts of chapters 2 and 3 by campfire and flashlight on the beach at Grand Isle State Park, with the Gulf of Mexico in my ear, was heart-stopping. Glenn's dual expertise in conservation biology and American literature has made him a remarkable resource for me these past few years. I want to thank Matti Bunzel for inviting me to present at the Chicago Humanities Festival in 2013 and Eric Slauter for connecting up that visit with a seminar at the Karla Scherer Center for the Study of American Culture; fellow panelists Wai-Chee Dimock and Peter Mancall offered terrific suggestions during the seminar. Eric, a close friend from graduate school days, also provided bracing support at a low moment. Scholars at the University of Wisconsin, where I gave a talk in 2012, helped me put more shape around what was still a fairly formless archival excitement; thanks especially to Monique Allewaert, Leslie Bow, Rob Nixon, and Julia Dauer. And the Program in American Civilization at Harvard University invited me out in 2010 to talk about some of the intellectual history behind this project; a sit-down with Lawrence Buell while I was there allowed me to sketch out the emerging shape of the book to pretty much the best audience member one could hope for.

The first person who made me realize that disasters could have aesthetic, philosophical, and spiritual dimensions was the photographer Emmet Gowin, with whom I studied for a number of years in college. In the early 1980s, he was making aerial images of Mount St. Helen's after its eruption; he later went on to document industrially altered landscapes around the world. It was by listening to Emmet talk about images, his own and those of others, that got me to see that form has flesh and history and soul. He made me think about beauty's ethical depth.

A number of brick-and-mortar archives were essential to the growth of this project. I found generous and knowledgeable curatorial staff at the Beinecke Library, the Herbert Hoover Presidential Library and Museum, the Houghton Library, the Schomburg Center for Research in Black Culture and the Billy Rose Theatre Division at the New York Public Library, the Tulane University Library, the University of Maryland, Baltimore County Albin O. Kuhn Library, and the University of Mississippi Archives and Special Collections Libraries. While archive hunting online, I had the unprecedented experience—when I was trying to track down information on "Martinelli, the Handcuff King"—of finding myself on what I came, belatedly, to recognize as a bondage forum! Oops. Less antic experiences included making connections with Martinelli's descendants and the blogger Dan Conaway, grandson of the *Commercial Appeal* editorial cartoonist J. P. Alley. The owner of Venerable Music, Malcolm Vidrine, was extraordinarily helpful to me in tracking down old 78s of Miller and Lyles's comedy skits, as well as extant copies of a number of 1927 flood blues and gospels.

My editor at Princeton University Press, Anne Savarese, has made me thoughtful about my reader and about the book's conceptual design in so many ways for what is now many years; I appreciate her being able to imagine—from the start—a stronger book. Also at the press, Juliana Fidler, an editorial associate, and Ali Parrington, a production editor, have kept complex matters in order; and Jenn Backer, the copyeditor, helped the manuscript at its final stages with her careful eye. Dimitri Karetnikov designed wonderful maps and ensured the quality of the illustrations.

Two extracurricular activities contributed to the making of this book. Whenever I jammed myself into a mental alleyway, too tight for any movement of ideas, the best relief came through taking walks in the University of Michigan's Nichols Arboretum with one of my dogs: first Posey and then, after her loss, Eleanor. Watching each of them become most herself while on the trail of a good scent reminded me what it meant to be wildly curious; I came to feel that I had to be with one of them for the best ideas to fall out of the sky and grace me. Second, I took up the piano for a year so that I'd have an embodied way to imagine the musical responses to the Flood of 1927. I want to thank my teacher, Rodger Devine, for his sweet tolerance of my very unmusical hands.

The most important environment for the creation of this book was the one I found every day with my husband, Bruce, and our three children, Alexander, Grace, and Louisa. All of them traveled on multiple southern trips with me: to Memphis, northeastern Arkansas and Oxford, Mississippi, for starters but also to caves in Kentucky, former rice plantations in South Carolina, a family burial ground in Virginia, and the old sugar capital of the Everglades, Clewiston, Florida. Thank you for knowing how much I needed you to be there on the journey. Though I wish each of you were still little, I am so proud of the adults you have become. Bruce has made me think that there should be a special place in heaven for companions of writers who, by definition, spend many—perhaps too many—hours alone. How often have you let me talk, and talk, and talk about my latest discoveries as if they were glorious to you, too.

NOTES

Introduction

1. Mr. Taylor, untitled 12 pp. manuscript, 6 June 1927, 7, National Archives and Records Administration (hereafter NARA), 4B-224.72.
2. "Sinking Dike Traps 2,000," *Chicago Daily Tribune*, 23 April 1927, 1, AP reporter quoting a public statement by M. L. Kaufman, former member of Mississippi levee board, *ProQuest Historical Newspapers*, 12 March 2011.
3. Editorial, "The Burden of Floods: Who Should Bear It?" *Commercial Appeal*, 24 April 1927, n.p.
4. M. W. Fisher, editorial, *New Iberia Enterprise*, 28 May 1927, qtd. in Glenn R. Conrad and Carl A. Brasseaux, *Crevasse! The 1927 Flood in Acadiana* (Lafayette: Center for Louisiana Studies, University of Southwest Louisiana, 1994), 1.
5. J. Winston Harrington, "Rush Food and Clothing to Flood Victims," *Chicago Defender*, 30 April 1927, 1–1, *ProQuest Historical Newspapers*.
6. J. Winston Harrington, "Use Troops in Flood Area to Imprison Farm Hands," *Chicago Defender*, 7 May 1927, 1–1, *ProQuest Historical Newspapers*.
7. Taylor, untitled ms., 1, 7.
8. Ibid., 7, 8.
9. John M. Barry, *Rising Tide: The Great Mississippi Flood of 1927 and How It Changed America* (New York: Simon and Schuster, 1997), 305, 312. While the crown was only eight feet across, the whole of the levee was between ten and forty feet wider than that.
10. Harrington, "Rush Food and Clothing to Flood Victims."
11. Taylor, untitled ms., 3, 8.
12. Ibid., 9.
13. Pinchot made this statement at the Chicago Flood Control Conference, June 1927, qtd. in Lyle Saxon, *Father Mississippi: The Story of the Great Flood of 1927* (Gretna, LA: Pelican, 1927 [2006]), 408. Pinchot was then governor of Pennsylvania and hence governing part of the watershed; he had been the first chief of the U.S. Forest Service (1905–10) and is associated with the concept of conservation.
14. Barry's *Rising Tide* is especially thorough in its archival explorations of hidden political and scientific decision making.
15. Kenneth Hewitt, introduction to *Interpretations of Calamity: From the Viewpoint of Human Ecology*, ed. K[enneth] Hewitt (Boston: Allen & Unwin, 1983). 13. Atten-

tion, he argued in 1983, is given only to the event that is seen as a violation of the normal (11).

16. Donna Haraway, *When Species Meet* (Minneapolis: University of Minnesota Press, 2007), 7.

17. This term is from Arjun Appadurai, "Disjuncture and Difference in the Global Cultural Economy," *Public Culture* 2.2 (1990): 9. It points to both the technological forms and geographically expressed webs of mediation as well as the images produced through these means; these mediascapes provide "large and complex repertoires of images, narratives and ethnoscapes to viewers throughout the world, in which the world of commodities and the world of news and politics are profoundly mixed"; he also claims that "the further away these audiences are from direct experiences of metropolitan life, the more likely they are to construct imagined worlds which are chimerical, aesthetic, even fantastic objects, particularly if assessed by the criteria of some other perspective" (9). While I agree with the former statement, I believe that this characterization of provincialism within twentieth-century mediascapes does not appreciate the ways in which "facts," scientific insight, and skepticism can originate in rural spaces.

18. Lowell Juilliard Carr, "Disaster and the Sequence-Pattern Concept of Social Change," *American Journal of Sociology* 38 (1932): 207–18, figures and quotes on 209. Ted Steinberg, in *Acts of God: The Unnatural History of Natural Disaster in America* (New York: Oxford University Press, 2000), contends that 1880–1930 period was the most deadly and that after 1930 disaster tended to damage property more than persons (69).

19. In 2000, Paul Crutzen and Eugene Stoermer first used the term in print ("The 'Anthropocene,'" *Global Change Newsletter* 41 [2000]: 17–18) to contend that the humanly induced changes to the planet—in terms of, for example, climate and the chemical composition of the biosphere, biodiversity loss, and species invasions—had reached such a scope that it deserved the designation of a new geological epoch, one that would replace the Holocene. See "The Anthropocene: A New Epoch of Geological Time?" a theme issue of *Philosophical Transactions of the Royal Society A* 369 (January 2011): 1938. Geologists are in the process of debating whether these changes are fundamentally geological in character; others continue to debate whether this epoch began with widespread agriculture thousands of years ago, ca. 1800 with industrialism, or in the 1950s with the invention of nuclear technology. See the web page produced by the "Working Group on the 'Anthropocene,'" quaternary.stratigraphy.org/workinggroups/anthropocene/.

20. My phrase is, of course, an allusion to Bruno Latour's *We Have Never Been Modern*, trans. Catherine Porter (Cambridge, MA: Harvard University Press, 1993), which argued that Western humanity's bid, beginning in the seventeenth century, to wall off nature and culture from each other and thus become "modern" never actually *took*. Along with Latour, scholars across many fields have, in the last generation, taken up this question of human/thing or human/biotic mutual entanglement. Fields and approaches like post-humanism, animal studies, actor-network theory, the new materialism, and environmental history all extend the concept of agency beyond the human and try to take apart the West's inheritance of Cartesian dualism. For an excellent overview of this scholarship, see Michael Ziser's introduction,

"More-than-Human Literary History," in his *Environmental Practice and Early American Literature* (New York: Cambridge University Press, 2013), 1–22. For an introduction to new materialism, in particular, see Rick Dolphijn and Iris van der Tuin, eds., *New Materialism: Interviews & Cartographies* (London: Open Humanities Press, 2012); interviewed in the text, Manuel DeLanda explains that new materialism "is based on the idea that matter has morphogenetic capacities of its own and does not need to be commanded into generating form" by a transcendent brain, God, or command (n.p., answer to Question 5).

21. Francis Bacon, *Novum Organum* (1620), trans. R[obert] Ellis and James Spedding (London, 1905), 59. The scholarship on the change from a European worldview based on a fluxional cosmos (vulnerable to divine interventions) to one based on the idea of a rule-bound, predictable Nature created by a providential God is extensive; for an overview of historiographic debates, see Lorraine Daston, "The Nature of Nature in Early Modern Europe," *Configurations* 6.2 (1998): 149–72.

22. One need only think of Thomas Jefferson, in the Declaration of Independence, invoking "nature and nature's God"—a conjoined deity Enlightenment science had invented—along with the new human capacity to discern the "self evident," in order to sanction the liberation of the former American colonies from British "tyranny," in Merrill D. Peterson, ed., *The Portable Thomas Jefferson* (New York: Penguin, 1975), 235–36.

23. As Niklas Luhmann puts it in *Risk: A Sociological Theory* (Berlin: Walter de Gruyter, 1993), "technology and the concomitant awareness of capability has occupied nature's territory" (xii). See also Carolyn Merchant, *The Death of Nature: Women, Ecology and the Scientific Revolution* (New York: Harper, 1980) on this transformation in Europe in the seventeenth and eighteenth centuries.

24. In *The Production of Space*, trans. Donald Nicholson-Smith (Malden, MA: Blackwell, 1991 [1974]), Henri Lefebvre described how, increasingly with modernity, "nature's space has been replaced by a space-*qua*-product" (90), comprising a "second nature" (345).

25. Ulrich Beck, *Risk Society: Towards a New Modernity*, trans. Mark Ritter (London: Sage, 1992), 35, 155; italics original.

26. For a review of how most U.S.-based sociological work on risk differs from both Beck's position (that modern risk transcends social power differentials, inducing broad skepticism about science) and Anthony Giddens's position (on growing trust in scientific expertise), see Margarita Alario and William Freudenburg, "The Paradoxes of Modernity: Scientific Advances, Environmental Problems, and Risks to the Social Fabric?" *Sociological Forum* 18.2 (June 2003): 193–214; these authors also argue that in the late twentieth-century nuclear industry, risk has not been universally dispersed but rather "socially concentrated" (208).

27. Dipesh Chakrabarty, "The Climate of History: Four Theses," *Critical Inquiry* 35.2 (Winter 2009): 197–222.

28. Alain Locke, "The New Negro" (1925), in *The New Negro: Readings on Race, Representation, and African American Culture, 1892–1938*, ed. Henry Louis Gates Jr. and Gene Andrew Jarrett (Princeton: Princeton University Press, 2007), 114.

29. H. L. Mencken, *The Evening Sun*, 23 May 1927, n.p.

30. Georg Simmel, "The Metropolis and Mental Life" (1903), 12. www.blackwellpub

lishing.com/content/BPL_Images/Content_store/Sample_chapter/0631225137
/Bridge.pdf.

31. See Richard H. Grove, *Green Imperialism: Colonial Expansion, Tropical Island Edens and the Origins of Environmentalism, 1600–1860* (Cambridge: Cambridge University Press, 1995).

32. C.L.R. James, in *Black Jacobins: Toussaint L'Ouverture and the San Domingo Revolution*, 2nd ed., rev. (New York: Vintage, 1989 [1963]), points out that the sugar plantation, involving factory production, an elaborate export-import trade, and crowded living conditions, comprised the first "modern system," one in which people of African descent lived a "modern life" (392); Eric Williams, *Capitalism and Slavery* (Chapel Hill: University of North Carolina Press, 1944).

33. J. M. Albala-Bertrand, *The Political Economy of Large Natural Disasters: With Special Reference to Developing Countries* (Oxford: Clarendon Press, 1993). Thought of this way, plantation laborers producing cultivars like sugar and cotton had been "modern" since the seventeenth century.

34. Cecelia Tichi points out, moreover, that during the early twentieth century, the machine orientation of industrialization penetrated conceptions of nature so that there was "no escape from, say, the mechanized city to the bucolic countryside. Perception itself has abolished the distinction between them." *Shifting Gears: Technology, Literature, Culture in Modernist America* (Chapel Hill: University of North Carolina Press, 1987), 40.

35. Taylor, untitled ms., 10.

36. Giorgio Agamben, *Homo Sacer: Sovereign Power and Bare Life*, trans. Daniel Heller-Roazen (Stanford: Stanford University Press, 1998), 95.

37. Ibid., 73; see also Henry A. Giroux, "Reading Hurricane Katrina: Race, Class, and the Biopolitics of Disposability," *College Literature* 33.3 (Summer 2006), 171–96, who writes that the "regime of the camp has increasingly become a key index of modernity" (180). On the controversy around Agamben's contentions about concentration camps, see Leland de la Durantaye, *Giorgio Agamben: A Critical Introduction* (Stanford: Stanford University Press, 2009); see also Agamben, *State of Exception*, trans. Kevin Attell (Chicago: University of Chicago Press, 2005), 7.

38. Michel Foucault, *Society Must Be Defended: Lectures at the College de France, 1975–1976*, trans. David Macey, ed. Mauro Bertani and Alessandro Fontana (New York: Macmillan, 2003), 259, 249–50, 240, 255. As Timothy Campbell and Adam Sitze describe this historical juncture: "death's slight withdrawal for living opens up the space for a knowledge of life that is irreducibly probabilistic in form. . . . collective life . . . assumed the form of a massive bet—a deadly serious game of chance in which the population is at once *the central player* and *the main prize*." "Introduction," *Biopolitics: A Reader* (Durham: Duke University Press, 2013), 12. In a slave and postslavery society like the U.S. South, the "population" cannot be understood so unitarily.

39. Foucault, *Society Must Be Defended*, 256. As Eric Williams observed in the midst of World War II, trying to understand the connections and distinctions between American and European history, "racism" directed at people of African descent in the Americas was not the cause but rather "the consequence of slavery." In other words, a construct of inheritable inferiority, not based on lineage or rank but on

one's continent of origin, had to be invented to naturalize the contingent fact that African laborers had come to be the most reliable supply of manpower on the plantation (*Capitalism & Slavery*, 7).

40. The thesis I am propounding—about how the black body absorbs inherent, and industrially exacerbated, biological risk—is meant to augment, not contradict, Achille Mbembe's definition of the plantation's "terror formation." Arguing, contra Foucault, that slavery needs to be accounted for in the historical invention of biopolitics, Mbembe states that slavery represented "one of the first instances of biopolitical experimentation," but one that is unique in intensity and paradoxes; "biopower, the state of exception, and the state of siege" all coexisted in the race-based plantation. In other words, plantation elites simultaneously controlled and maintained the "health" of laborers, permanently suspended rules of law because slaves were seen as property not persons, and carried on a perpetual war with the enslaved. "Necropolitics," *Public Culture* 15.1 (2003): 21–22, trans. Libby Meintjes.

41. It was not only biological chance that the enslaved protected his or her master from but other forms of chance as well. Think, for example, of sales of enslaved persons to provide the liquidity to pay off masters' gambling debts, the most notorious of which was slaveholder Pierce Mease Butler's 1859 sale of 436 persons from his Georgia rice and cotton plantations to settle extensive gambling debts he had incurred in Philadelphia. On this sale, see Kwesi DeGraft-Hanson, "Unearthing the Weeping Time: Savannah's Ten Broeck Race Course and 1859 Slave Sale," *Southern Spaces* (18 February 2010), http://southernspaces.org/2010/unearthing-weeping-time-savannahs-ten-broeck-race-course-and-1859-slave-sale.

42. My project of recovering the knowledge belonging to people of African descent who transformed nature and experienced its ensuing crises finds important commonality with Thadious M. Davis, *Southscapes: Geographies of Race, Region, and Literature* (Chapel Hill: University of North Carolina Press, 2011), in which Davis attends generally to the artistry that emerged from African American spatial experience in the Deep South in the twentieth century; it is not only the spatial "exclusion" of Jim Crow that signals this experience, she argues, but also the "diffusion" of "words, concepts, ideas, and practices that may flow" across the black community and redefine that space (16).

43. Paul Gilroy, *The Black Atlantic: Modernity and Double Consciousness* (Cambridge, MA: Harvard University Press, 1993), 15, 53–54.

44. Jace Weaver, *The Red Atlantic: American Indigenes and the Making of the Modern World, 1000–1927* (Chapel Hill: University of North Carolina Press, 2014). See also Kate Flint, *The Transatlantic Indian, 1776–1930* (Princeton: Princeton University Press, 2009).

45. While in *The Red Atlantic*, Weaver is more interested in tracing how "Native ingenuity gave Europeans material culture and technologies" (268) rather than showing how Natives perceived and recorded deleterious environmental effects of colonization, Weaver's earlier collection, *Defending Mother Earth: Native American Perspectives on Environmental Justice* (Maryknoll, NY: Orbis Books, 1996), shows how intertwined European and U.S. colonization and conquest have been with environmental despoliation.

46. Gilroy, *Black Atlantic*, 71.

47. Gilroy borrows this term from Mikhail Bakhtin's exploration in *The Dialogic Imagination* of how distinct space-time configurations are translated into literary form; for Gilroy, the ship is a cultural form that indexes the Middle Passage, the African diaspora, and dreams of return while also being a carrier of ideas, arts, and activists (*Black Atlantic*, 4).

48. The "New Southern Studies" is determined to remove the South conceptually from an exceptionalist geographic isolation—and from the defensive apologetics such isolation engendered—and place the region within its historically significant national and international linkages (with the Caribbean, Mexico, Africa, the U.S. West, etc.), as well as address the region's complex multiracial history that complicates a black-white binary. See, for example, the special issues of *American Literature* 73.2 (2001), "Violence, the Body and 'The South,'" ed. Houston A. Baker and Dana D. Nelson, and *American Literature* 78.4 (December 2006), "Global Contexts, Local Literatures: The New Southern Studies," ed. Kathryn McKee and Annette Trefzer. Despite this important headway, there can still be a tendency on the part of non-southernists to assume a merely regional peculiarity and relevance of the field's contributions.

49. The Fine Cotton Spinners' and Doublers' Association Ltd. of Manchester, England, owned the Delta and Pine Land Company (D&PL), headquartered as of 1927 in Scott, Mississippi. It was sixty thousand acres large. Barry, in *Rising Tide*, claims that it was the world's largest cotton plantation (180).

50. For example, the chairman of Spinners', Mr. Lee, attested: "We probably feel a greater sympathy" with inhabitants of the Delta, "since we are to a certain extent involved in the disaster. . . . one of the first breaks in the levees occurred actually on our big plantation." "Fine Spinners Chairman on Financial and Labour Questions," *Manchester Guardian*, 28 May 1927, *ProQuest Historical Newspapers*.

51. Harris Dickson, "Planter Thought in March," *Atlanta Constitution*, 6 June 1927, 7, *ProQuest Historical Newspapers*.

52. Kevin Rosario refers to this type of phenomenon as the "catastrophic logic of modernity," in which the "quest to make the world more secure" paradoxically produces "myriad social conflicts as well as technological and environmental hazards." *The Culture of Calamity: Disaster and the Making of Modern America* (Chicago: University of Chicago Press, 2007), 10.

53. William Faulkner, *Wild Palms* [*If I Forget Thee, Jerusalem*] (New York: Vintage, 1995 [1939]), 20.

54. Taylor, untitled ms., 1.

55. Vaclav Smil, *Creating the Twentieth Century: Technical Innovations of 1867–1914 and Their Lasting Impact* (New York: Oxford University Press, 2005), 201; Taylor, untitled ms., 2.

56. Douglas Griesemer, cover letter for "final report of Red Cross relief operations" in the 1927 flood, 28 February 1930, NARA archives, GB-224.72.

57. This is Herbert Hoover's term to describe the entire 1926–27 cycle of interconnected flooding throughout the Mississippi watershed. Qtd. in T. H. Alexander, "Herbert Hoover Wins Hearts of Folks in Flood District; 'He'd Make a Fine President,' Both White and Black Declare," *Atlanta Constitution*, 31 July 1927, p. E3.

58. Rob Nixon, *Slow Violence and the Environmentalism of the Poor* (Cambridge, MA: Harvard University Press, 2011), 2.

59. For an earlier sociological study of disaster arguing that *"chronic conditions"* can be as catastrophic as *"acute events,"* see Kai T. Erikson, *Everything in Its Path: The Destruction of Community in the Buffalo Creek Flood* (New York: Simon and Schuster, 1976), 255.
60. "Flood and Flight as News," *New York Times*, 29 May 1927, n.p., *ProQuest Historical Newspapers*.
61. Nixon, *Slow Violence*, 21, 18.
62. Wilbur J. Cash, "The Mind of the South," *American Mercury* 18.70 (October 1929): 189.
63. Editorial, "Withstanding the Flood," *Pittsburgh Courier*, 28 May 1927, 20, *ProQuest Historical Newspapers*.
64. "Big New Crevasse Opens in Louisiana Levees," *New York Times*, 4 May 1927, *ProQuest Historical Newspapers*.
65. Herbert Hoover, Typescript of "Appeal to the American People for Support of Mississippi Flood Sufferers—Address by Radio over National Broadcasting Company Chain and Associated Stations from WMC, Memphis, Tennessee," 30 April 1927, 5, 6, 9, in Herbert Hoover Secretary of Commerce Period Papers, Materials Related to Mississippi Flood, 1927, Herbert Hoover Presidential Library, West Branch, Iowa.
66. Pete Daniel discusses, in *Breaking the Land: The Transformation of Cotton, Tobacco, and Rice Cultures since 1880* (Urbana: University of Illinois Press, 1985), how—in addition to the Flood of 1927—the boll weevil infestation, fluctuating cotton prices, and the drought of 1930 "broke the stubborn southern pride that had rejected aid. Hardship in the 20s and early 30s laid open the South for a Federal invasion" of "agency troops" (65) and Extension service workers who sought to introduce "the regularity of machines and federal guidelines" about scientific farming (xiii); see also 3–22.
67. In the 1970s, Richard Schechner hailed a new theater that would get outside the playhouse, traverse and animate everyday space, so that "the space of the performance is defined organically by the action" and the "separation between man and his environment [is] transcended," making both more alive. *Environmental Theater: An Expanded New Edition* (New York: Applause, 1994 [1973]), xxviii, 17.
68. John Dickie and John Foot, introduction to *Disastro! Disasters in Italy since 1860: Culture, Politics, Society*, ed. Dickie, Foot, and Frank M. Snowden (London: Palgrave, 2002), 11–12.
69. Herbert Spencer, "A Theory of Population, Deduced from the General Law of Animal Fertility," *Westminster Review* 57 (112), n.s., vol. 1 (January and April 1852): 469, qtd. in Mark Francis, *Herbert Spencer and the Invention of Modern Life* (Durham, UK: Acumen, 2007), 194.
70. I borrow the phrase from the title of Perry Miller's book, *Nature's Nation* (Cambridge, MA: Harvard University Press, 1967), and from that of John Opie, *Nature's Nation: An Environmental History of the United States* (New York: Harcourt Brace, 1998).
71. John Dewey, "Common Sense and Science," in *Knowing and the Known* (coauthored with Arthur F. Bentley, but Dewey solely authored the chapter "Common Sense and Science"), collected in *The Later Works, 1925–1953*, vol. 16, ed. Jo Ann Boydston (Carbondale: Southern Illinois University Press, 1989), 244. Dewey continues: "a *medium* is *inter*mediate in the execution or carrying *out* of human activi-

ties, as well as being the channel *through* which they move and the vehicle *by* which they go on."

72. Karen Barad, "Posthumanist Performativity: Toward an Understanding of How Matter Comes to Matter," *Signs: Journal of Women in Culture and Society* 28.3 (2003): 810. See also Dolphijn and Van der Tuin, *New Materialism*, who write that new materialist philosophy "does not capture matter-as-opposed-to-signification, but captures *mattering* as simultaneously material and representational." Contemporary media studies has likewise come to stretch its definition of media to include human interactions with environments; as W.J.T. Mitchell and Mark B. N. Hansen put it in their introduction to Mitchell and Hansen, eds., *Critical Terms for Media Studies* (Chicago: University of Chicago Press, 2010), a new "conceptualization of media as an environment for the living differs from [former] conceptions of the medium/media as a narrowly technical entity or system" (xiii).

73. Donna Haraway describes this methodology as a "webbed account" of "situated knowledges" in her essay "Situated Knowledges: The Science Question in Feminism and the Privilege of Partial Perspective," *Feminist Studies* 14.3 (Autumn 1988): 581, 585, 588. Though modernists mined the multiperspectival method in the early twentieth century, it should be noted that creative writers have been practicing a similar methodology/ontology/epistemology at least since the first epistolary novels came into print.

74. As Robert A. Stallings points out, disaster within the sociological subfield has primarily acted as a "laboratory for the study of basic social processes" ("Disaster and the Theory of Social Order," in *What Is a Disaster? Perspectives on the Question*, ed. E. L. Quarantelli [London: Routledge, 1998], 134). Before the 1970s, the focus was on the disaster as an external agent. In this model, "human communities have been seen as organized bodies that have to react organically against aggression" from without (Claude Gilbert, "Studying Disaster: Changes in the Main Conceptual Tools," in *What Is a Disaster?* 12). Scholars therefore studied how external attacks destabilized communities and what communities did in order to achieve a new stability.

75. Lars Clausen theorized in "Social Differentiation and the Long-Term Origin of Disasters," *Natural Hazards* 6 (1992): 181–90: "Disasters are the long-term outcome of certain destructive elements of divided labour" (181), specifically the "social differentiation between problem-solvers and problem-laymen" (182).

76. Beck, *Risk Society*, 29, 46 (quote on 46; italics original).

77. T. H. Alexander (special correspondent of the *Nashville Tennesseean*), "Hoover Now Hero of Flooded South," *New York Times*, 31 July 1927, 2, *ProQuest Historical Newspapers*. Though Will Rogers had a close relationship with President Coolidge, he was not close to Hoover.

Chapter 1

1. Herschel Brickell, "Again the Old Dragon Mississippi Fumes," *New York Times*, 1 May 1927, p. SM9, *ProQuest Historical Newspapers*.

2. See Leigh Ann Duck, *The Nation's Region: Southern Modernism, Segregation, and U.S. Nationalism* (Athens: University of Georgia Press, 2006) on the "trope of the

backward South" (6), its "frenetic production" (9), and how southern modernists navigated and represented a more complex reality; and Jennifer Rae Greeson, *Our South: Geographic Fantasy and the Rise of National Literature* (Cambridge, MA: Harvard University Press, 2010) on how the young nation shifted its old status as England's plantation onto the South.

3. Stuart Chase, *Rich Land, Poor Land* (New York: Whittlesey House, 1936), 55, 130, 15.

4. Hewitt, introduction to *Interpretations of Calamity*, 25.

5. Maurice R. Reddy to F. A. Winfrey, 18 August 1927, copy, "DR-224/72 Mississippi River Valley Flood 3/30/27 Newspapers, Clippings, Etc.," Central File, 1917–1934, box 742, Collection ANRC—130/77/17/01, NARA.

6. In the field of disaster studies after the 1970s, disasters have increasingly been understood as socially produced, making it impossible to categorize an event as a "natural disaster." As J. M. Albala-Bertrand put it in *The Political Economy of Large Natural Disasters: With Special Reference to Developing Countries* (Oxford: Clarendon Press, 1993): "It is society rather than nature that determines disaster effects and thereby people's vulnerability to disaster"(102); moreover, "Vulnerability is primarily a socio-political issue rather than a question of protective technology or engineering works" (204). To me, the categories sociopolitical and technological seem difficult to pry apart and consider separately. It also seems going too far to remove nature utterly as a factor. I agree with Anthony Oliver-Smith, who has said in "Global Changes and the Definition of Disaster" (in *What Is a Disaster?*), "disasters do not inhere in societies; they inhere in societal-environmental relations" "unfolding . . . over time" (186, 187). As there is no separating humanity and nature's mutual imbrication and alteration, disaster, it follows, is neither purely external nor internal to human society.

7. Robert W. Harrison, *Alluvial Empire: A Study of State and Local Efforts toward Land Development in the Alluvial Valley of the Lower Mississippi River, Including Flood Control, Land Drainage, Land Clearing, Land Forming* (Little Rock, AR: Pioneer, 1961), 4; Mikko Saikku, *This Delta, This Land: An Environmental History of the Yazoo-Mississippi Floodplain* (Athens: University of Georgia Press, 2005), 27.

8. As Saikku puts it, "Ecological units characteristically maintain their structure not only despite but also because of external disturbances"; when these occur with "characteristic" but not necessarily predictable frequency, they create a disturbance regime (*This Delta, This Land*, 23). As Roger Del Moral and Lawrence R. Walker note in *Environmental Disasters, Natural Recovery and Human Responses* (New York: Cambridge University Press, 2007), "annual patterns of high and low water, combined with occasional large floods, constitute the disturbance regime of a floodplain" (123). Contemporary ecologists distinguish between "physical disturbances," such as fires, floods, droughts, windstorms, and hurricanes; "biogenic disturbances," such as the impacts of herbivorous insects, mammals, and pathogens; and "anthropogenic disturbances," in the form of such human activities as logging, drainage of wetlands, clearing for farming, introduction of alien species, and chemical pollution. The first two can be advantageous to an ecosystem because they eventually promote diversity of species. Too much disturbance—and this can

often be anthropogenic—can make it impossible for the ecosystem to recover through diversification (9–11).

9. "Why the Mississippi Goes on a Rampage," *Atlanta Constitution*, 8 May 1927, C2-c2, *ProQuest Historical Newspapers*. Though the word "Delta" suggests the river's outlet area, it actually comprises the strip of counties in Illinois, Missouri, Arkansas, Kentucky, Tennessee, Louisiana, and Mississippi bordering the river.

10. Richard T. T. Forman also notes, in *Land Mosaics: The Ecology of Landscapes and Regions* (New York: Cambridge University Press, 1995), that "the lateral migration of curvilinear streams and rivers produces much of the heterogeneity of habitat and vegetation across a floodplain" (219); "a channelized stream or river causes a reduction in lateral channel migration, habitat heterogeneity . . . and variability in water level" (224).

11. Barry, *Rising Tide*, 38–40, 177.

12. Charles Ellet Jr., qtd. in Barry, *Rising Tide*, 197.

13. See Stephen H. Kellert, *In the Wake of Chaos: Unpredictable Order in Dynamical Systems* (Chicago: University of Chicago Press, 1993), 9.

14. Saikku, *This Delta, This Land*, 36–38; Barry, *Rising Tide*, 40.

15. William Alexander Percy, *Lanterns on the Levee: Recollections of a Planter's Son* (Baton Rouge: Louisiana State University Press, 1973 [1941]), 4.

16. Chase, *Rich Land, Poor Land*, 21.

17. Michael Williams, *Americans and Their Forests: A Historical Geography* (Cambridge: Cambridge University Press, 1989), 186–88, quote on 186.

18. Indeed, 90 percent of central and northern Wisconsin's trees moved to market via that route (Williams, *Americans and Their Forests*, 188). On related developments in nineteenth-century Michigan, see John Knott, *Imagining the Forest: Narratives of Michigan and the Upper Midwest* (Ann Arbor: University of Michigan Press, 2012), especially chapter 3, "The Culture of Logging," 59–92.

19. Agnes M. Larson, *The White Pine Industry in Minnesota: A History* (Minneapolis: University of Minnesota Press, 2007 [1949]), 4, 7, 11.

20. Thomas R. Cox, Robert S. Maxwell, Phillip Drennon Thomas, and Joseph J. Malone, *This Well-Wooded Land: Americans and Their Forests from Colonial Times to the Present* (Lincoln: University of Nebraska Press, 1985), 2, 10.

21. The Johnstown flood resulted in part from deforestation of the Allegheny Mountains, along with river narrowing and foolhardy engineering. In this process, as David McCullough puts it, humans had "failed—out of indifference mostly—to comprehend the possible consequences . . . should nature happen to behave in anything but the normal fashion, which, of course, was exactly what was to be expected of nature," especially when humanity "drastically alters the natural order." *The Johnstown Flood* (New York: Simon and Schuster, 1968), 262.

22. Williams, *Americans and Their Forests*, 238, 243. Though the term "semicolonial" is Williams's, there is a deep tradition in southern history of understanding their economic, and at times political, relation to outsiders—whether they be British or U.S. northerners—as a colonial one. See Joseph J. Persky, *The Burden of Dependency: Colonial Themes in Southern Economic Thought* (Baltimore: Johns Hopkins University Press, 1992).

23. Qtd. in Saikku, *This Delta, This Land*, 180; qtd. in Williams, *Americans and Their Forests*, 279; Cox et al., *This Well-Wooded Land*, 164.

24. Qtd. in Williams, *Americans and Their Forests*, 252.

25. John Solomon Otto, *The Final Frontiers, 1880–1930: Settling the Southern Bottomlands* (Westport, CT: Greenwood Press, 1999), 35. On the environmental changes to the Mississippi River and its Lower Valley brought by cotton and the levee system, see Christopher Morris, *The Big Muddy: An Environmental History of the Mississippi and Its Peoples from Hernando de Soto to Hurricane Katrina* (Oxford: Oxford University Press, 2012), 108–68.

26. In fact, 80 percent of fires nationwide in the years 1917 to 1927 were located in the South. Cox et al., *This Well-Wooded Land*, 164, 210–11; see also Saikku, *This Delta, This Land*, chap. 6, 165–219. See also Gerald W. Johnson's description of this phase of timber extraction in *The Wasted Land* (Chapel Hill: University of North Carolina Press, 1938), 39–41.

27. Thomas D. Clark, *The Greening of the South: The Recovery of Land and Forest* (Lexington: University Press of Kentucky, 1984), 73.

28. Donald Worster, *Dust Bowl: The Southern Plains in the 1930s* (Oxford: Oxford University Press, 2004 [1979]), 71, 82–87, 89–90, 93–94.

29. Chase, *Rich Land, Poor Land*, 36–37. Chase, primarily concerned with his decade's environmental crisis, the "Dust Bowl" in the plains states, and stupendous gullying in the South, saw in flooding its own dangers but also the removal of soil and mineral health that had been building for centuries. Moreover, as soil erosion worsened throughout the watershed in the early twentieth century, the silting made rivers in the watershed "increasingly unmanageable"(168) because subject to "more and more violent interruptions and alterations of stream flow" (qtd. from H. H. Bennett of the Soil Conservation Service, 68).

30. Monoculture is defined by Saikku as "the extensive cultivation of certain, agricultural products over vast areas solely for the emerging world market" (begun as early as the fifteenth century) and in which "local economic development soon became dictated by the supralocal needs of the world economy" (*This Delta, This Land*, 17–18).

31. Hugh Prince, *Wetlands of the American Midwest: A Historical Geography of Changing Attitudes* (Chicago: University of Chicago Press, 1997), 206, 210, 220, 224, 225, 231; quotes on 220, 224, 231. One example of a promotional tract of this period is John Klippart, *The Principles and Practice of Land Drainage: Embracing a Brief History of Underdraining*, 3rd ed. (Cincinnati: R. Clarke & Co., 1888).

32. Barry, *Rising Tide*, 91, 158. In 1913, the Mississippi River Levee Association was founded in Memphis, which lobbied for federal flood control; such federal involvement was forthcoming, via the flood control acts of 1917 and 1923 in a 2:1 ratio of federal to state investment; see Otto, *Final Frontiers*, 50. As Chase summarized: the engineering policy was to "get the water off the land by drain, channel, levee or culvert. In big streams, dredge the channel and hustle it faster" (*Rich Land, Poor Land*, 172). He continued: "The policy is vicious, stupid and wrong. The only intelligent program is to *hold* the water in the soil" or a reservoir (172). See also Saxon, *Father Mississippi*, 274–75, 308.

33. Saikku, *This Delta, This Land*, 161–62.
34. Del Moral and Walker, *Environmental Disasters, Natural Recovery and Human Responses*, 115. Barry notes, "if a levee towering as high as a four-story building gave way, the river could explode upon the land with the power and suddenness of a dam bursting" (*Rising Tide*, 40).
35. James C. Cobb, *The Most Southern Place on Earth: The Mississippi Delta and the Roots of Regional Identity* (New York: Oxford University Press, 1992), 97, 112. This modernization process means that Mississippi being the "most southern place on earth" does not imply that it was an historically retrograde place.
36. Otto, *Final Frontiers*, 81; John C. Willis, *Forgotten Time: The Yazoo-Mississippi Delta after the Civil War* (Charlottesville: University Press of Virginia, 2000), 171.
37. On various forms of peonage in the postbellum South, see Pete Daniel, *The Shadow of Slavery: Peonage in the United States, 1901–1969* (Urbana: University of Illinois Press, 1990 [1972]), 10–11; of the 1920s, Daniel writes that peonage was "deeply rooted," involving "the power of the masters, the corruption of local law-enforcement officials, the ignorance of black victims, the apathy of the Justice Department, and the terrorism aimed at potential witnesses" (132).
38. Cobb, *The Most Southern Place on Earth*, 113–14. Along with lynchings, reprisals against labor unrest occurred; on the Leflore massacre of 1889, see Steven Hahn, *A Nation under Our Feet: Black Political Struggles in the Rural South from Slavery to the Great Migration* (Cambridge, MA: Harvard University Press, 2003), 422.
39. Jane Adams and D. Gorton, "Revisiting Caste and Class in the Mississippi Delta," *American Anthropologist* 106.2 (June 2004): 337–43.
40. Willis, *Forgotten Time*, 152; postbellum racial violence in the Yazoo-Mississippi Delta was provoked by "honor," labor disputes, and politics, and became a gesture more specifically of enforcing white supremacy after 1900 (157). Hahn points out that, despite constraints on black suffrage across the Deep South, in Mississippi, the number of registered black voters actually grew in the 1890s: 8,615 in 1892 to 18,170 in 1899 (*Nation under Our Feet*, 449). Industrial, globally traded, cotton monoculture would transform not only the lower south, socially and environmentally, in the nineteenth century but also parts of India, Egypt, and Brazil, once northern Europeans sought alternate suppliers during the "cotton famine" produced by the U.S. Civil War: Sven Beckert, "Emancipation and Empire: Reconstructing the Worldwide Web of Cotton Production in the Age of the American Civil War," *American Historical Review* 109.5 (2004): 1405–38, quote on 1411.
41. Otto, *Final Frontiers*, 79–81; Jeannie Whayne, in *Delta Empire: Lee Wilson and the Transformation of Agriculture in the New South* (Baton Rouge: Louisiana State University Press, 2011), points out that the number of tenant farmers in the Arkansas Delta increased from 1,204 to 9,561 from 1900 to 1930 (70, 86); see Jarod Roll, *Spirit of Rebellion: Labor and Religion in the New Cotton South* (Urbana: University of Illinois Press, 2010), 12–16, on the Missouri Delta transformation.
42. Hahn, *Nation under Our Feet*, 415, 418, 425, quote on 418. Labor organizing linked farmers and tenants with lumber, sawmill, and railroad workers; African Americans in these organizations were interested in citizenship, social services, education, voting, and protection for labor and crops (417). Violence against labor pro-

testers was exemplified in the killing of fifteen striking cotton pickers in Lee County in 1891.

43. Donald H. Grubbs, *Cry from the Cotton: The Southern Tenant Farmers' Union and the New Deal* (Fayetteville: University of Arkansas Press, 1971), 15.

44. Otto, *Final Frontiers*, 57.

45. Rebecca J. Scott, "'Stubborn and Disposed to Stand Their Ground': Black Militia, Sugar Workers and the Dynamics of Collective Action in the Louisiana Sugar Bowl, 1863–87," in *From Slavery to Emancipation in the Atlantic World*, ed. Sylvia R. Frey and Betty Wood (Portland: Frank Cass, 1999), 107, 116, 118, quote on 121; see also Scott, *Degrees of Freedom: Louisiana and Cuba after Slavery* (Cambridge, MA: Harvard University Press, 2005), 77, 81, 85, 90–93, 257–65; and Hahn, *Nation under Our Feet*, 420–21.

46. Scott, *Degrees of Freedom*, 93.

47. John B. Rehder, *Delta Sugar: Louisiana's Vanishing Plantation Landscape* (Baltimore: Johns Hopkins University Press, 1999), 24, 18. For the broader, hemispheric and transatlantic, history of sugar, see Richard S. Dunn, *Sugar and Slaves: The Rise of the Planter Class in the English West Indies, 1624–1713* (Chapel Hill: University of North Carolina Press, 1972); and Sidney Mintz, *Sweetness and Power: The Place of Sugar in Modern History* (New York: Penguin, 1985).

48. C. Vann Woodward, *The Strange Career of Jim Crow* (New York: Oxford University Press, 1955), Watson quoted on 44–45. See also Woodward, *Tom Watson: Agrarian Rebel* (New York: Oxford University Press, 1963).

49. Matthew Hild, in *Greenbackers, Knights of Labor & Populists: Farmer-Labor Insurgency in the Late-Nineteenth-Century South* (Athens: University of Georgia Press, 2007), argues that "the door to social justice for the region's have-nots, which had seemed partially open . . . appeared to slam shut as the nineteenth century ended" (201). Though Populist efforts moved forward in other parts of the country, disfranchisement of blacks and some poor whites in the South was the stumbling block to real southern reform after 1890s, making impossible a laborers' challenge to a Democratic elite; Democrats could thus ignore social problems afflicting poor blacks and whites: bad public schools, regressive taxes, and lack of social services (217).

50. W. Fitzhugh Brundage, in *Lynching in the New South: Georgia and Virginia, 1880–1930* (Urbana: University of Illinois Press, 1993), summarizes these explanations on p. 11, but then argues for the importance of regional variation vis-à-vis lynching; for Georgia, it was the combination of single-crop agriculture, a black majority, and a stark color line that made conditions ripe for mob violence (120, 138).

51. Joel Williamson, *The Crucible of Race: Black-White Relations in the American South since Emancipation* (New York: Oxford University Press, 1984), 117. On disfranchisement, see 225–34; on segregation, see 249–56. Of the 1892 lynching apex, Brundage lists 155 black deaths and 71 white (*Lynching*, 7).

52. David W. Blight, *Race and Reunion: The Civil War in American Memory* (Cambridge, MA: Harvard University Press, 2001), 3. Walter White, *Rope and Faggot: A Biography of Judge Lynch* (1929; Notre Dame: University of Notre Dame Press, 2001); 105. Woodward, *Strange Career*, 53–54; Williamson, *The Crucible of Race*, 337–40. On religion's role in this postbellum reunification of whites within an ex-

panding, imperial nation, see Edward J. Blum, *Reforging the White Republic: Race, Religion and American Nationalism, 1865–1898* (Baton Rouge: Louisiana State University Press, 2005).

53. Hahn, *Nation under Our Feet*, 452–54, 461; in Mississippi, between 1890 and 1910, African Americans published close to 150 newspapers and journals—14 in Washington County in the Delta (462).

54. Williamson, *The Crucible of Race*, 478, 479, 222, 462–63, 457.

55. Williamson also points out that the Spanish-American War seemed, ritualistically, to mend the breach between northern and southern whites, who seemed key actors in reunion, "while the black actor was shuffled from stage-center to the wings" (*The Crucible of Race*, 336); I would slightly amend this characterization to say that the black actor, both north and south, became the entre-acte comedian to lighten the mood of white drama.

56. Grif Stockley, *Blood in Their Eyes: The Elaine Massacres of 1919* (Fayetteville: University of Arkansas Press, 2001), xiii–xiv. Whayne, in *Delta Empire*, points out that laboring whites may have coveted the tenancies held by the black farmers in and around Elaine (121–22). Hahn, *Nation under Our Feet*, 474, notes the history of labor and Liberian exodus organizing in and around Phillips County dating back to 1891.

57. White, *Rope and Faggot*. To White, not only was the black "buffoon" a stereotype but so—even after the end of the Radical era—was the "habitual criminal of unrestrained appetite" (11, 10). On southern liberalism of this period, see Morton Sosna, *In Search of the Silent South: Southern Liberals and the Race Issue* (New York: Columbia University Press, 1977), 20–59.

58. Natalie J. Ring, *The Problem South: Region, Empire, and the New Liberal State, 1880–1930* (Athens: University of Georgia Press, 2012), 11, 4, Project MUSE.

59. Fred C. Hobson, *Tell about the South: The Southern Rage to Explain* (Baton Rouge: Louisiana State University Press, 1983), 183, 184; in the second quote, Hobson is drawing from the Nashville Agrarian Donald Davidson's *The Attack on Leviathan: Regionalism and Nationalism in the United States* (Chapel Hill: University of North Carolina Press, 1938), 315.

60. Qtd. in Hobson, *Tell about the South*, 192.

61. George B. Tindall, "The Benighted South: Origins of a Modern Image," *Virginia Quarterly Review* 40 (Spring 1964): 281–82.

62. Hild, *Greenbackers, Knights of Labor & Populists*, 215.

63. Arthur Kellogg, "Behind the Levees," *Survey Graphic* 58.5 (July 1927). Beginning on 9 September 1926, just as the Red Cross was about to tackle the Florida hurricane, fourteen cities in southern Illinois were flooded (281).

64. Barry, *Rising Tide*, 173–76, 182–86, 195.

65. According to Kellogg in "Behind the Levees," 4,200 miles of the St. Francis basin flooded beginning 19 April (282).

66. Pete Daniel, *Deep'n as It Come: The 1927 Mississippi Flood* (Oxford University Press, 1977), 9; Barry, *Rising Tide*, 202, 206; Saikku, *This Delta, This Land*, 157; Seguine Allen, qtd. in Barry, *Rising Tide*, 205.

67. Frederick Simpich, "The Great Mississippi Flood of 1927," *National Geographic Magazine* 52.3 (1 September 1927): 248.

68. Barry, *Rising Tide*, 235, 255, 285.

69. Helen Murphy, "Overflow Notes," *Atlantic Monthly* 140.2 (August 1927): 225, 223, 229, 228, 224, 226, 227.

70. This sense of divine abandonment to northern assault echoed, or reanimated, a Lost Cause discourse that wondered aloud about how God could have let the South lose the Civil War.

71. Charles Reagan Wilson, *Baptized in Blood: The Religion of the Lost Cause, 1865–1920* (Athens: University of Georgia Press, 2009 [1980]), explains that the Lost Cause myth and civic rituals "enacted the story of Christ's suffering and death, with the Confederacy at the sacred center"; however, "the Christian drama of suffering and salvation was incomplete: the Confederacy lost a holy war, and there was no resurrection" (24).

72. Murphy, "Overflow Notes," 227.

73. "Sinking Dike Traps 2,000," *Chicago Daily Tribune*, 23 April 1927, 2.

74. Lyle Saxon, "Flood Journal," Tulane Library, folder 4-1-44, "Correspondence, 1927 Jan–June, 20 pieces."

75. "Acadians, Driven into New Exile by Crevasse Waters, Mourn over Loss of Homesteads in Disaster," *New Orleans Times-Picayune*, 18 May 1927, 2. For a study of the hydrogeological features and human conditions in south-central Louisiana during the flood, see Glenn R. Conrad and Carl A. Brasseaux, *Crevasse! The 1927 Flood in Acadiana* (Lafayette: Center for Louisiana Studies, University of Southwest Louisiana, 1994).

76. Murphy, "Overflow Notes," 227, 226.

77. Alexander, "Herbert Hoover Wins Hearts of Folks," p. E3.

78. Harris Dickson, "Free Meals Avidly Eaten at Flood Relief Camps," *Los Angeles Times*, 17 June 1927, 3, *ProQuest Historical Newspapers*.

79. Conrad and Brasseaux, *Crevasse!* 56. They also point out that many evacuees were forced to change concentration camps more than once, increasing their sense of disorientation.

80. "Hoover Speeds Up Flood Restoration," *New York Times*, 20 June 1927, *ProQuest Historical Newspapers*.

81. Simpich, "The Great Mississippi Flood of 1927," 250.

82. Kellogg, "Behind the Levees," 282.

83. Will Irwin, "Can We Tame the Mississippi?" *World's Work* 54 (August 1927): 407, *ProQuest Historical Newspapers*.

84. See Tichi, *Shifting Gears*, on how the figure of the engineer became "a vital American symbol between the 1890s and the 1920s"; he signified "stability in a changing world," as well as "ethical *and* utilitarian power" (99). Hoover, she argues, came to public recognition by walking into an already existing, fictionally created persona (169–70).

85. "Hoover Appeals in Nationwide Call for Relief," *New Orleans Times-Picayune*, 29 May 1927, sec 1A, p. 4.

86. Barry, *Rising Tide*, 406.

87. Taylor, untitled ms., 1,3.

88. Cox et al., *This Well-Wooded Land*, 236; Barry, *Rising Tide*, 285–86, 363; Saikku, *This Delta, This Land*, 156–59.

89. Harrington, "Rush Food and Clothing to Flood Victims."
90. Murphy, "Overflow Notes," 223. Murphy, who lived in Tallulah, Louisiana, had spent years living in New York City. Watching black men conveyed to the levees reminded her "of the colored troops I had seen, nine years ago, quartered overnight in the Armory at Broadway and Sixty-seventh Street, New York" (224).
91. Maneous Williams, 1993 oral interview, quoted in Betty Jo Harris, "The Flood of 1927 and the Great Depression: Two Delta Disasters," www.louisianafolklife.org/LT/Articles_Essays/DeltaDepression.html.
92. Ida Wells-Barnett, "South Backs Down after Probe Looms," *Chicago Defender* (25 June 1927): 1–1, *ProQuest Historical Newspapers*.
93. According to Barry, a friend of Hoover's—Will Irwin of the *World's Work*—told Hoover that he had managed to suppress from publication much of the black anger he found in the flood zone. He cautioned Hoover, though, against Walter White, whom he characterized as a "fanatic" and as "the nigger in the woodpile" who needed toning down by "some of the big negroes" (qtd. in *Rising Tide*, 321), a warning that seems to have propelled Hoover into appointing the Colored Advisory Commission.
94. "Minutes" of Colored Advisory Committee Meeting, 10 and 11 June 1927, 9, "DR-224.91/08 Mississippi River Valley Flood 3/30/27, Negro Commission June 1927 Survey," Central File, 1917–1934, box 744, Collection ANRC—130/77/17/01, NARA.
95. Hoover quoted in Arthur Kellogg, "Up from the Bottom Lands," *Survey Graphic* 58.5 (July 1927): 364.
96. "Report of the Colored Advisory Commission," 3.
97. This conflict between restorationist and liberationist/reformist positions was a continuation of older debates during Reconstruction between southerners and radical Republicans; it is important to note that in 1927, it was a federal bureaucracy, in consultation with southern planters and politicians, that was implementing the restorationist vision and almost exclusively African American political activists who were voicing the older radical Republican position.
98. Alexander, "Herbert Hoover Wins Hearts of Folks," p. E3.
99. Barry, *Rising Tide*, 390–92.
100. "Du Bois Thinks 'Al' Muffed Chance for Race Vote," *Afro-American* (20 October 1928): n.p., *ProQuest Historical Newspapers*. The article expresses anti-Hoover feeling in October 1928 and is especially irate about his stuffing the Colored Advisory Commission with his friends but then being unwilling to publish its restrained criticisms. Hoover "has said not a single public word against lynching or disenfranchisement or for Negro education and uplift." He has "joined openly with the 'Lily Whites' of the South."
101. In *Abraham Lincoln and the Second American Revolution* (New York: Oxford University Press, 1991), James M. McPherson uses this phrase to describe James Garfield, the former Union soldier and then congressman from Ohio, who, in an 1864 speech, urged the House to confiscate Confederate land and redistribute it to emancipated slaves and poor whites (4); abolitionist Wendell Phillips had said that "The whole social system of the Gulf States must be taken to pieces" (qtd. on 6).
102. "Report of the Colored Advisory Commission," 44.

103. Ibid., 50; this pay imbalance was corrected by Father Wrenn, the white priest in charge of the camp. When National Guardsmen were "rough with the refugees" (54), Wrenn likewise interceded.

104. "Report of the Colored Advisory Commission," 20, 21, 25–26. Claude Barnett and Jesse O. Thomas authored this section of the "Report."

105. "Report of the Colored Advisory Commission," 27.

106. Ibid., 28, 29.

107. Ibid., 34; *Crisis* (January 1928): 5.

108. "Report of the Colored Advisory Commission," 69, 71.

109. *The Crisis* (November 1927): n.p., quoting the Jackson, Mississippi, *Daily News*, 30 April 1927, which was in support of this Red Cross practice.

110. "Report of the Colored Advisory Commission," 38, 79; Colored Advisory Commission cover letter to Herbert Hoover, 13 June 1927, 2, "DR-224.91/08 Mississippi River Valley Flood 3/30/27, Negro Commission June 1927 Survey," Central File, 1917–1934, box 744, Collection ANRC—130/77/17/01, NARA.

111. "Report of the Colored Advisory Commission," 62; *Crisis* (January 1928): 27; MS report, 4.

112. MS report, 5; "Report of the Colored Advisory Commission," 35–36, 38–39; T. M. Campbell Report to Moton, included as "Appendix" to the commission's "Report," 82.

113. William Alexander Percy, "Labor Notice," quoted in J. Winston Harrington, "Work or Go Hungry Edict Perils Race," *Chicago Defender* (11 June 1927): 1–1, *ProQuest Historical Newspapers*.

114. Ida B. Wells, "Brand Ministers in Flood Area as Betrayers," *Chicago Defender* (16 July 1927), *ProQuest Historical Newspapers*. Summarizing this situation, flood historian Pete Daniel, also an expert on twentieth-century southern peonage, avers that it "was often the case" that "camps served in effect as prisons where debt-ridden workers were held against their will" (*Deep'n as It Come*, 106).

115. Walter White, "The Negro and the Flood," *The Nation* 124.3233 (22 June 1927): 688–89, quote on 689. Reprinted in the *Chicago Defender* (2 July 1927): A1 and excerpted in "Walter White Finds Peonage Rife in Refugee Camps, Bayonets Bar Flood Victims Refugees Get Out Only When Plantation Agents Pick Out 'Their Negroes,'" *Afro-American* (4 June 1927), *ProQuest Historical Newspapers*.

116. *Crisis* (January 1928): 5.

117. "Correspondence to Dr. Moton . . . Mississippi Flood 1927," Papers of 1927 Flood Information, box 1, folder 1, Archives, Tuskegee University, Tuskegee, AL, 3.

118. "Red Cross Worker Ordered Fired," *Afro-American* (24 December 1927): 1, *ProQuest Historical Newspapers*.

119. "Report of the Colored Advisory Commission," 69, 71.

120. "Correspondence to Dr. Moton . . . Mississippi Flood 1927," 3.

121. Colored Advisory Commission, "Letter of Transmittal" to Hoover, 25 June 1927, 1, "DR-224.91/08 Mississippi River Valley Flood 3/30/27, Negro Commission June 1927 Survey," Central File, 1917–1934, box 744, Collection ANRC—130/77/17/01, NARA.

122. "Withstanding the Flood," 20.

123. Harrington, "Use Troops in Flood Area to Imprison Farm Hands," 1–1.

124. J. Winston Harrington, "Mob Burns Two at Stake," *Chicago Defender*, 18 June 1927, 1–1, *ProQuest Historical Newspapers*.

125. "Mississippi Mob Stages Lynching Bee," *Chicago Defender*, 28 May 1927, 2–2, *ProQuest Historical Newspapers*.

126. Qtd. in "Dixie Women Out to Break Up Lynchings," *Chicago Defender*, 2 July 1927, 4–4, *ProQuest Historical Newspapers*.

127. "How They Do It in Arkansas," *Chicago Defender*, 21 May 1927, 1-A1, *ProQuest Historical Newspapers*.

128. "Withstanding the Flood," 20.

129. "Thousands Leave Little Rock after Lynching," *Chicago Defender*, 28 May 1927, 1–1, *ProQuest Historical Newspapers*. For a few more violent incidents, see Barry, *Rising Tide*, 330, 332.

130. White, "The Negro and the Flood," 689.

131. Achille Mbembe has argued that "the very structure of the plantation system and its aftermath manifests the emblematic and paradoxical figure of the state of exception" in which "the normal" is an ongoing extralegal emergency ("Necropolitics," 21). The flood, then, exacerbated but did not create this extreme situation. It should be underlined that whites in Mississippi and Arkansas did not act as a united force of terror.

132. "City and State Demand Federal Flood Control," *New Orleans Times-Picayune*, 27 May 27, 1927, 4, 2.

133. "Mayor Thompson Breakfasts with President Today," *Washington Post*, 8 November 1927, *ProQuest Historical Newspapers*.

134. Barry, *Rising Tide*, 406–7.

135. Ibid., 423–25.

136. The central thrust of Naomi Klein's *Shock Doctrine: The Rise of Disaster Capitalism* (Toronto: Vintage, 2007) is that, amid the chaos of more recent disasters, parts of the state (schools, the military, infrastructure management, etc.) have been sold off to the private sector, transforming public goods into laissez-faire profit zones. With this 1928 legislation, one sees, to the contrary, the federal government assuming responsibility for levee management that had been historically controlled by either private interests or individual states. One could argue, though, that the timber industry and industrial farming throughout the watershed disproportionately benefited by having the costs of continuing their business shared by the national public.

137. "The Flood Refugees," *Manchester Guardian*, 19 July 1927, *ProQuest Historical Newspapers*.

138. "Red Cross Feeding 71,000 Mississippi Flood Victims," *Pittsburgh Courier*, 10 March 1928, *ProQuest Historical Newspapers*. See also Barry, *Rising Tide*, 415.

139. Editorial note in Simpich, "The Great Mississippi Flood of 1927," 244, 243.

140. *The Odes and Epodes of Horace: A Modern English Verse Translation by Joseph P. Clancy* (Chicago: University of Chicago Press, 1960), Ode 1.2: 25.

141. Reading my colleague Sean Silver's unpublished essay, "Global Storming," on how news of an Atlantic storm of 1703 traveled along lines recently established by British imperial postal networks—and hence how events acquire meaning in part because of the infrastructure and geography of communication in a given moment—

was very helpful to my thinking through the intersection of media, geography, and disaster.

142. See my chapter "Science, Nature, Race," in *The Oxford Handbook of the Atlantic World, 1450–1850*, ed. Nicholas Canny and Philip D. Morgan (New York: Oxford University Press, 2013).

143. According to Frederic L. Clements, who studied successions of plant communities, and who was the leading figure in American ecology from the publication of *Plant Succession* in 1916 through World War II, species in a given area over time evolve progressively toward a climax stage, at which stage they represent a "superorganism," a community interconnected and self-balancing enough to be understood as having achieved an integral identity. See Donald Worster, "The Ecology of Order and Chaos," *Environmental History Review* 14 (1990): 3, 4. As Frank Golley explains in *A Primer for Environmental Literacy* (New Haven: Yale University Press, 1998), 119, it was only after such successional stages failed to appear after the grassland droughts of the 1930s that the majority of ecologists came to think twice about Clements's theory.

144. Herbert Spencer, "A Theory of Population, Deduced from the General Law of Animal Fertility," *Westminster Review* 57.112, n.s., vol. 1 (January and April 1852): 469, qtd. in Mark Francis, *Herbert Spencer and the Invention of Modern Life* (Durham, UK: Acumen, 2007), 193, 195. See also Sharon E. Kingsland, *Modeling Nature: Episodes in the History of Population Ecology*, 2nd ed. (Chicago: University of Chicago Press, 1995), 14–17.

145. "The March of Events," *World's Work* (November 1900): 3. See also Robert J. Rusnak, *Walter Hines Page and "The World's Work," 1900–1913* (Washington, D.C.: University Press of America, 1982) on how the magazine's editor, Page, a Progressive southerner, advocated for U.S. imperialism, Nordic mental and cultural superiority, the industrial education of poor white southerners, who would theoretically pull up the black population in their rise, and the careful absorption of non-Nordic immigrant groups.

146. Thorstein Veblen qtd. in Kingsland, *Modeling Nature*, 21.

147. Daniel B. Botkin, *Discordant Harmonies: A New Ecology for the Twenty-first Century* (New York: Oxford University Press, 1990), 33.

148. Alfred James Lotka, undated manuscript, quoted in Kingsland, *Modeling Nature*, 45; for a general discussion of this trend, see 18–45. On this era of intellectual history in the United States, including a treatment of Herbert Hoover, see Tichi, *Shifting Gears*.

149. Samuel Henry Prince, *Catastrophe and Social Change: Based upon a Sociological Study of the Halifax Disaster* (New York: Columbia University Press, 1920), 19, 139. In 1917, two ships, one carrying more than two thousand tons of explosives and destined to supply the European Front and the other en route to pick up supplies for Hoover's relief efforts in Belgium, collided in "The Narrows" of the Halifax Harbor. The first ship caught on fire and exploded, sending its shards nearly one thousand feet in the air, causing massive tidal and sonic waves, killing nearly two thousand people, wounding nine thousand, and blinding hundreds who had collected at windows to watch the collision. Samuel Prince, a young scholar looking for a

thesis topic, found in this event the ready-made data for a kind of unintended sociological experiment.

150. Stuart Alfred Queen and Delbert Martin Mann, *Social Pathology* (New York: Thomas Y. Crowell Company, 1925), 435–36. See also Carr, "Disaster and the Sequence-Pattern Concept of Social Change," 208, 207. For an earlier example of a Progressive perception of disaster as a supreme canvas for human organization, see "The Rebuilding of Galveston," *World's Work* 1.1 (November 1900): "The efficiency and swiftness of modern organization were never more happily demonstrated than by the almost instant relief of the suffering at Galveston" (6).

151. James C. Scott, *Seeing Like a State: How Certain Schemes to Improve the Human Condition Have Failed* (New Haven: Yale University Press, 1998), 4, 5.

152. Charles Ellet Jr., qtd. in Barry, *Rising Tide*, 197.

Disaster's Public

1. John Fiske, *Media Matters: Race and Gender in the U.S. Politics* (Minneapolis: University of Minnesota Press, 1996), 4, 2.

2. Recent scholarship gives a very broad definition to "media," so that the word suggests an entire environment in which we live, use, and experience our bodies and minds, and make meaning; it denotes a kind of multidirectional circuitry between our bodies and the world, and all prosthetic means through which the human exerts her- or himself onto the world and is constituted in turn; see Mitchell and Hansen, introduction to *Critical Terms for Media Studies*, vii–xxii. Though in later chapters I will address how built space, for example, shapes embodiment and consciousness (along the lines of LeFebvre), and how labor is a medium that alters nature (Marx's concept), in this part of the book, I am concerned specifically—and traditionally—with the forms of mass media technologies available in 1927 that communicated the material experience of the flood to live and virtual publics.

3. In seeing in entertainment the possibility of a widely disseminated or shared critique, I am parting ways with Kevin Rosario's argument that twentieth-century disasters "fueled a mass culture oriented toward entertainment and commodity consumption rather than improvement, social justice, and democracy" (*Culture of Calamity*, 106). All of these civic goods can be deployed through media meant to entertain.

4. H. G. Wells, *The War That Would End War*, qtd. in David Welch, "War Aims and the 'Big Ideas' of 1914," in *Justifying War: Propaganda, Politics and the Modern Age*, ed. Welch and Jo Fox (Hampshire: Palgrave Macmillan, 2012), 72.

5. Ibid., 73–89. See also Harold D. Laswell, *Propaganda Technique in the World War* (New York: Peter Smith, 1938 [1927]), on how propaganda was an "offensive weapon . . . present on both sides of every hotly-contested sector" (219). For a recent recovery of the deployment of "propaganda" as revolutionary propagation, see Russ Castronovo, *Propaganda 1776* (New York: Oxford University Press, 2014), who also discusses the early twentieth-century discussion of propaganda (3–28).

6. Mark Crispin Miller, introduction to Edward Bernays, *Propaganda* (Brooklyn: Ig, 2005 [1928]), 11.

7. Robert H. Zieger, *America's Great War: World War I and the American Experience*

(Oxford: Rowman & Littlefield), 79–80. One of the CPI's signature modes of disseminating the prowar message was through the 75,000-person strong network of "Four-Minute Men," individuals who would, in short speeches, often while reels were being changed in movie theaters, try to convince the country to involve themselves in the war effort.

8. George Creel, *How We Advertised America* (New York: Harper & Bros., 1920), 4, 5.

9. Thomas Fleming, *The Illusion of Victory: America in World War I* (New York: Basic Books, 2003), 98, 119, 120, 173.

10. *Dada: Zurich, Berlin, Hanover, Cologne, New York, Paris*, ed. Leah Dickerman (New York: Distributed Art Publishers, 2005), 8; Brigid Doherty, "'See: We Are All Neurasthenics!' or the Trauma of Dada Montage," *Critical Inquiry* 24.1 (Autumn 1997): 129.

11. Walter Benjamin, "The Work of Art in the Age of Mechanical Reproduction," in *Illuminations: Essays and Reflections*, ed. Hannah Arendt, trans. Harry Zohn (New York: Schocken, 1969), 238.

12. Brett Gary, *The Nervous Liberals: Propaganda Anxieties from World War I to the Cold War* (New York: Columbia University Press, 1999), 1.

13. Ibid., 2.

14. Miller, introduction, 12.

15. Bernays, *Propaganda*, 37. Bernays's first chapter is titled "Organizing Chaos" (37–46).

16. Laswell, *Propaganda Technique in the World War*, 220, 221, 222; Guy Debord, *Comments on Society of the Spectacle*, trans. Malcolm Imrie (London: Verso, 1998).

17. Walter Lippmann, *Public Opinion* (New York: Macmillan, 1922), 320, Hathi Trust Digital Library; on Lippmann and his disillusioning involvement in World War I, see Ronald Steel, *Walter Lippmann and the American Century* (Boston: Little, Brown, 1980), chaps. 8–14.

18. Dewey was on the board of socially reformative institutions like Hull House and the NAACP. According to one panegyrist writing in the *New York Herald Tribune* in 1929, Dewey was so influential that even those who had never heard of him "must live unwittingly in the light or shadow which his mind has cast on practically all phases of American life" (Herbert W. Schneider, "He Modernized Our Schools," *New York Herald Tribune*, 13 October 1929, 8).

19. Lippmann, *Public Opinion*, 71–72, 9, 113, 65.

20. Walter Lippmann, *The Phantom Public* (New York: Harcourt, 1925), 1, 53.

21. Lippmann, *Public Opinion*, 383; Lippmann, *Phantom Public*, 52, 57, 107; Walter Lippmann, *American Inquisitors: A Commentary on Dayton and Chicago* (New Brunswick, NJ: Transaction, 1993 [1928]), 4, 5.

22. John Dewey, *The Public and Its Problems* (New York: Henry Holt, 1927), 146, 175, 131, 158, 184, 183, 109. 219.

23. Johanna Drucker, "Art," in *Critical Terms for Media Studies*, 11.

24. Benjamin, "The Work of Art in the Age of Mechanical Reproduction," 228, 237, 231, 229, 239, 240, 232. The title of the essay is also translated as "The Work of Art in the Age of Its Technical Reproducibility."

25. Ibid., 232, 241.

26. Jürgen Habermas, *The Structural Transformation of the Public Sphere*, trans.

Thomas Burger with the assistance of Frederick Lawrence (Cambridge, MA: MIT Press, 1989 [1962]), 158, 178, 206, 170.

27. Daniel Bell, *The Cultural Contradictions of Capitalism* (New York: Basic Books, 1996 [1976]), 108.

28. See Benedict Anderson, *Imagined Communities: Reflections on the Origin and Spread of Nationalism* (London: Verso, 1983).

29. Olivier Driessens, Stijn Joye, and Daniel Biltereyst, "The X-Factor of Charity: A Critical Analysis of Celebrities' Involvement in the 2010 Flemish and Dutch Haiti Relief Shows," *Media, Culture & Society* 34.6 (September 2012): 710, 712, 719, 721.

30. Corinne Lysandra Mason, "Foreign Aid as Gift: The Canadian Broadcasting Corporation's Response to the Haitian Earthquake," *Critical Studies in Media Communication* 28.2 (2011): 98.

31. Murali Balaji, "Racializing Pity: The Haiti Earthquake and the Plight of 'Others,'" *Critical Studies in Media Communication* 28.1 (March 2011): 61.

32. Simon Cottle, "Mediatized Rituals: Beyond Manufacturing Consent," Media, Culture and Society 28.3 (2006): 422.

33. Mervi Katriina Pantti and Karin Wahl-Jorgensen, "'Not an Act of God': Anger and Citizenship in Press Coverage of British Man-made Disasters," *Media, Culture & Society* 33.1 (January 2011): 118. Focusing on the audience of disaster rather than its direct witnesses, Kevin Gotham argues that even if coverage often comes in the form of an "entertainment" "spectacle," these spectacles are nevertheless "multidimensional, polyvalent and open" so that their reception amounts to "an active process of social construction and negotiation." "Critical Theory and Katrina: Disaster, Spectacle, and Imminent Critique," *City* 11 (2007): 86.

34. Gordon Coonfield and John Huxford, "News Images as Lived Images: Media Ritual, Cultural Performance, and Public Trauma," *Critical Studies in Media Communication* 26 (2009): 459–61.

35. Victor Turner, *The Drums of Affliction* (Oxford: Clarendon Press, 1968), 6, quoted in ibid., 459.

36. Tamar Liebes, "Television's Disaster Marathons: A Danger for Democratic Processes?" in *Media Ritual and Identity*, ed. Liebes and James Curran (London: Routledge, 1998), 74, 75.

37. Cottle, "Mediatized Rituals," 415.

38. Gerard A. Hauser, "Civil Society and the Principle of the Public Sphere," *Philosophy and Rhetoric* 31 (1998): 32. See Rita Felski, *Beyond Feminist Aesthetics: Feminist Literature and Social Change* (Cambridge, MA: Harvard University Press, 1989); Nancy Fraser, "Rethinking the Public Sphere: A Contribution to the Critique of Actually Existing Democracy" (originally a 1992 article), in *The Cultural Studies Reader*, 2nd ed., ed. Simon During (London: Routledge, 1999 [1993]); Todd Gitlin, "Public Sphere or Public Sphericules," in *Media Ritual and Identity*, ed. Liebes and Curran; Michael Warner, "Publics and Counterpublics," *Public Culture* 14.1 (Winter 2002): 49–90; and Catherine R. Squires, "Rethinking the Black Public Sphere: An Alternative Vocabulary for Multiple Public Spheres," *Communication Theory* 12.4 (2002): 446–68.

39. Fraser, "Rethinking the Public Sphere," 527.

40. Squires, "Rethinking the Black Public Sphere," 448, 458.

41. Warner, "Publics and Counterpublics," 56n3, 57.
42. Elizabeth Butler Breese, "Mapping the Variety of Public Spheres," *Communication Theory* 21.2 (May 2011): 130–49.
43. Warner, "Publics and Counterpublics," 86.

Chapter 2

1. "Advertisement," *Billboard*, 28 May 1927, 100–100, *ProQuest Historical Newspapers*. First ad was 14 May in *Billboard*, 86.
2. Although the army had already spent $1 million in funds even before Red Cross fund-raising began; Barry, *Rising Tide*, 273.
3. Griesemer, cover letter of report of American Red Cross relief operations, 28 February 1930, NARA.
4. Walter Lippmann, "The Great Decision," *New Republic*, 7 April 1917, qtd. in Steel, *Walter Lippmann*, 113.
5. Creel, *How We Advertised America*, 4, 5.
6. Fieser qtd. in Barry, *Rising Tide*, 273.
7. Barry, *Rising Tide*, 288.
8. "Red Cross in New Appeal," *Los Angeles Times*, 10 May 1927, *ProQuest Historical Newspapers*.
9. Carl F. Kaestle and Janice A. Radway, "A Framework for the History of Publishing and Reading in the United States, 1880–1940," in *Print in Motion: The Expansion of Publishing and Reading in the United States, 1880–1940*, ed. Kaestle and Radway (Chapel Hill: University of North Carolina Press, 2008), 15.
10. Richard L. Kaplan, "From Partisanship to Professionalism: The Transformation of the Daily Press," in *Print in Motion*, ed. Kaestle and Radway, 127.
11. Associated Press, 1 June 1926; self-published brochure, 3.
12. *Associated Press: The Story behind the (AP) Story*, 1933; self-published brochure, 13.
13. Lawrence D. Hogan, *A Black National News Service: The Associated Negro Press and Claude Barnett, 1919–1945* (Cranbury: Associated University Presses, 1984), 11, 57.
14. Audit Bureau of Circulations statement in *American Newspaper Annual and Directory: A Catalogue of American Newspapers and Periodicals* (Philadelphia: N. W. Ayer & Son, 1927), 257, 763, 98.
15. Ibid., 46.
16. James P. Danky, "Reading, Writing, and Resisting: African American Print Culture," in *Print in Motion*, ed. Kaestle and Radway, 342.
17. Kaplan, "From Partisanship to Professionalism," 123. College-educated readers tended to spread their reading across media, spending more time reading books than did less well-educated Americans.
18. Quoted in Rusnak, *Walter Hines Page and "The World's Work," 1900–1913*, 13. Page himself was quoting Burton J. Hendrick, *The Training of an American: The Earlier Life and Letters of Walter H. Page, 1855–1913* (Boston: Houghton Mifflin, 1928), 205.
19. Richard Ohmann, *Politics of Letters* (Middletown, CT: Wesleyan University Press, 1987), 150. By the 1890s, "monthly magazines had become the major form of re-

peated cultural experience" for Americans (141). By 1905, there were three magazines for every four people, but readership did not extend to the entire population (141–42); this medium "admit[s] ideas and feelings into the arena of the discussable" (151).

20. Armistead S. Pride and Clint C. Wilson II, *A History of the Black Press* (Washington, DC: Howard University Press, 1997), 128. In the South, there were black dailies like the Savannah, Georgia, *Colored Tribune* for example, but the white-owned dailies and weeklies often cornered the entire news market because of their better access to advertising and their ownership of printing facilities (127).

21. This is surmised by George S. Schuyler in "The Negro-Art Hokum," *Nation* 122 (16 June 1926): 662.

22. Maurice R. Reddy, of the national Red Cross, to William M. Baxter Jr. (St. Louis), 10 September 1927, NARA Archive, speaks of Dale's articles having "caused such a rumpus in the South."

23. Danky, "Reading, Writing, and Resisting," 354.

24. "No News Here," *Chicago Defender*, 10 September 1927, 1-A2, *ProQuest Historical Newspapers*. The article stated: "Little Rock spent money buying and burning copies of the Defender sent into that city."

25. Jill Lane, "Black/face Publics: The Social Bodies of *Fraternidad*," in *Critical Theory and Performance*, ed. Janelle G. Reinelt and Joseph R. Roach, revised and enlarged ed. (Ann Arbor: University of Michigan Press, 2007), 145. Lane also points out that the putative promises of body-blindness in the Enlightenment public spheres were gainsaid by the fact that only white male bodies had these privileges "safeguard[ed]" (145).

26. Michele Hilmes, *Radio Voices: American Broadcasting, 1922–1952* (Minneapolis: University of Minnesota Press, 1997), 11.

27. Queen and Mann, *Social Pathology*, 435–36; Prince, *Catastrophe and Social Change*, 139.

28. Queen and Mann, *Social Pathology*, 435–36.

29. "Nation Swift to Aid," *New York Times*, 25 April 1927, n.p., *ProQuest Historical Newspapers*. The *newspaper* made this comment about Coolidge's radio appeal on 24 April, but I believe it characterized Hoover's appeal as well.

30. Hoover, typescript of "Appeal to the American People for Support of Mississippi Flood Sufferers," 30 April 1927, 1, 5, broadcast from the *Commercial Appeal*'s AM radio station, WMC (standing for "We're the Memphis *Commercial Appeal*"), Hoover Archive, West Branch, IA.

31. Hoover speech, 23 May 1927, qtd. in Barry, *Rising Tide*, 365.

32. Hoover, typescript of "Appeal to the American People for Support of Mississippi Flood Sufferers," 30 April 1927, 6, 9, 1. On 3 May, an AP reporter out of Boston explained that "at least 70 per cent. of the power transmitters of the country sent out appeals at half-hour intervals on Saturday night"; listeners were asked at 250 stations to contribute one dollar each. "Success in Radio Appeal," *New York Times*, 3 May 1927, *ProQuest Historical Newspapers*. In Hoover's second appeal, made on 28 May from New Orleans, his voice was "transmitted over the ether to ears of millions of listeners in all parts of the country." "Hoover Appeals in Nationwide Call for Relief."

33. See B. Myerhoff, "A Death in Time: Construction of Self and Culture in Ritual Drama," in *Rite, Drama, Festival, Spectacle*, ed. J. MacAloon (Philadelphia: Institute for the Study of Human Issues, 1984), 150, qtd. in Coonfield and Huxford, "News Images," 460. As Coonfield and Huxford put it, "the news coverage—and the news media—become sites for enacting civil religion" and "consolidat[ing] . . . communal identity" (461, 460).

34. "Cotton and Floods," *Wall Street Journal*, 27 April 1927, *ProQuest Historical Newspapers*.

35. Alfred P. Reck, "Utter Desolation Rules Flood Stricken Regions," *Atlanta Constitution*, 2 May 1927, 12–12, *ProQuest Historical Newspapers*.

36. Brickell, "Again the Old Dragon Mississippi Fumes."

37. Murphy, "Overflow Notes," 226.

38. Irwin, "Can We Tame the Mississippi?" 405–6.

39. Simpich, "The Great Mississippi Flood of 1927," 243–89.

40. "Let the Nation Take Control," *Washington Post*, 26 December 1927, *ProQuest Historical Newspapers*.

41. "Hoover Speeds Up Flood Restoration," *New York Times*, 20 June 1927, n.p., *ProQuest Historical Newspapers*.

42. Hoover qtd. in ibid.

43. "Hoover Urges North to Help Flood Sufferers," *Atlanta Constitution*, 29 May 1927, 1–1, *ProQuest Historical Newspapers*. A subheading reads: "Reconstruction 'Should Be Task of Generous North to Courageous South,' Says Secretary [Hoover]."

44. "Red Cross in New Appeal," *Los Angeles Times*, 10 May 1927, *ProQuest Historical Newspapers*.

45. *Commercial Appeal*, 29 May 1927, front page, AP report from New Orleans quoting Hoover.

46. Abraham Lincoln, "Second Inaugural Address," 4 March 1865, printed in Ronald C. White Jr., *Lincoln's Greatest Speech: The Second Inaugural* (New York: Simon and Schuster, 2006), 19.

47. "Vastness of Flood Devastation Brought Home," *Los Angeles Times*, 26 May 1927, 2, *ProQuest Historical Newspapers*.

48. "Boats for Refugees," *Los Angeles Times*, 26 May 1927, 2, *ProQuest Historical Newspapers*.

49. See Lippmann, *American Inquisitors*, 8–9, 66–72. This anti-British campaign occurred in the wake of propagandist pro-British historiography written leading up to U.S. involvement in World War I.

50. Raphael Kaufman, "Money Available for Use Abroad, but None for Flood Sufferers," *New York Times*, 12 May 1927, n.p., *ProQuest Historical Newspapers*. The United States landed Marines in Nicaragua in 1910 to prop up conservative pro-U.S. leadership; major U.S. banks then extended loans to Nicaragua in exchange for majority ownership of the nation's own banks and railroads; a twenty-year occupation by U.S. forces ensued, often anti-Mexican and anti-"Bolshevik" in character; and a particularly "bloody battle" between the Marines and a resistant Nicaraguan officer occurred in the spring of 1927. The United States was, during these decades of occupation, roundly criticized for its hypocritically imperial behavior. See Walter LaFeber, *Inevitable Revolutions: The United States in Central America* (New

York: Norton, 1993), 47–56, 66–76. As for China, there was a serious famine in north China in 1920–21 to which the American Red Cross administered aid; see *American Red Cross Famine Relief in China, 1920–1921: From the Report of the China Famine Relief, American Red Cross* (New York: Russell Sage Foundation, 1943).

51. See Art Winslow, introduction to H. L. Mencken, *A Religious Orgy in Tennessee: A Reporter's Account of the Scopes Monkey Trial* (New York: Melville, 2006), for an account of how certain Tennesseans responded to ACLU advertisements recruiting teachers to challenge the Butler Act; "Generation of publicity was the primary motivation" (xiii).

52. See the write-up of this same event in the *Chicago Defender*, 2 July 1927, 7, which makes clear the presence of the local black elite who sponsored the meeting.

53. Alexander, "Herbert Hoover Wins Hearts of Folks," p. E3.

54. The relation between Hoover and such minor spirits is something like that between *Moby Dick's* Ahab and Pip, except that Hoover's modernizing drive (also running on rails of steel in this interview) is not here seen as monomaniacal but rather a good blend of the paternalistic and the functionalistic; he is an impersonal system-designer, a cosmopolitan fix-it man moving, without ego or conquest, from job to job around the globe (Russia, Belgium, Mississippi).

55. As an urban Tennessean, Alexander might be expected to believe that the day of the big planter, most typified in the 1920s by the Delta region, was over. It should also be noted that the Scopes case was originally staged by entrepreneurial Tennesseans themselves, not as a grand stand for fundamentalism but as a tourism ploy.

56. *Los Angeles Times*, 14 May 1927, *ProQuest Historical Newspapers*.

57. See Draper Hill, *The Lively Art of J. P. Alley, 1885–1934* (Memphis: Brooks Memorial Art Gallery, 1973).

58. A. G. Whidden to James Feiser, 31 October 1927, NARA Archives, 4B-224.72 "Cartoons" (Ark.).

59. Editorial subtitle in Harris Dickson, "Southerners Calm as Flood Gods Threaten," *Los Angeles Times*, 6 June 1927, 6, *ProQuest Historical Newspapers*.

60. Dickson hailed from Yazoo City, Mississippi; had studied law at the University of Virginia and what is now George Washington University; and became a municipal court judge in Vicksburg in 1905. Two collections of these stories, *Old Reliable* (Indianapolis: Bobbs-Merrill, 1911) and *Old Reliable in Africa* (New York: Frederick A. Stokes, 1920), were published. See biographical heading of Dickson at the Mississippi Department of Archives and History, http://mdah.state.ms.us/manuscripts/z0124.html. Old Reliable was in actuality a shiftless, henpecked, dissembling "Uncle" figure who "had much curiosity and no permanent prejudice against work if somebody else were doing it" (13). The first novel climaxed in a Mississippi flood, the surprise of which is that it is actually Old Reliable who saves the day when his gun inadvertently fires on a timber thief trying to cut the Mississippi side of the levee.

61. Brickell, "Again the Old Dragon Mississippi Fumes."

62. Harris Dickson, "Flood Changes Region into Valley of Sorrow," *Los Angeles Times*, 5 June 1927, 1, 3, *ProQuest Historical Newspapers*.

63. Harris Dickson, "Negroes Sacrifice All to Rescue Flood Victims," *Los Angeles*

Times, 8 June 1927, 8, *ProQuest Historical Newspapers*. Though this is construed as a noble gesture, this couple are deemed "unusual negroes," and the real hero is the tenants' "boss . . . the farthest-sighted planter in the delta" who called for the rescue skiff in the first place.

64. Harris Dickson, "Negroes Real Heroes of Mississippi's Rampage," *Los Angeles Times*, 16 June 1927, 3, *ProQuest Historical Newspapers*.

65. Harris Dickson, "Cry for Boats Rises High above Swirling Flood," *Los Angeles Times*, 9 June 1927, 3, *ProQuest Historical Newspapers*.

66. Harris Dickson, "Flood Refugee Camps Reveal Human Failing," *Los Angeles Times*, 14 June 1927, 8, *ProQuest Historical Newspapers*. On the nineteenth-century minstrel character, who "dressed to the nines in top hat and bright blue tails," see John Strausbaugh, *Black Like You: Blackface, Whiteface, Insult & Imitation in American Popular Culture* (New York: Penguin, 2006), 78.

67. Harris Dickson, "Free Meals Avidly Eaten at Flood Relief Camps," *Los Angeles Times*, 17 June 1927, 3, *ProQuest Historical Newspapers*.

68. Dickson, "Negroes Real Heroes of Mississippi's Rampage," 3.

69. Harris Dickson, "Flood Havoc Still Defies Attempts at Estimate," *Los Angeles Times*, 18 June 1927, 3, *ProQuest Historical Newspapers*.

70. Harris Dickson, "America, Its Dander Up, Vows Revenge on River," *Los Angeles Times*, 19 June 1927, 3, *ProQuest Historical Newspapers*.

71. Dickson, "Negroes Real Heroes of Mississippi's Rampage," 3.

72. See Coonfield and Huxford, "News Images as Lived Images," 465.

73. "To Aid Flood Sufferers," *New York Times*, 27 June 1927, 23, *ProQuest Historical Newspapers*.

74. "Charity Work Told by Russian Woman," *New York Times*, 21 December 1927, 16–16, *ProQuest Historical Newspapers*. The immigration commissioner at Ellis Island had "received instructions from Washington" to "request her to leave the country within a reasonable period." De Petschenko defied the order to leave the country.

75. "Dance Aids Flood Relief: Southern Touch Lent to Affair Given by Mme. de Petschenko," *New York Times*, 30 June 1927, *ProQuest Historical Newspapers*.

76. "To Aid Flood Sufferers."

77. See *The Crisis Advertiser* 6.1 (May 1913): 49, *ProQuest Historical Newspapers*; "Deacon Johnson Cabaret Genius," *New York Age*, 21 May 1921, *ProQuest Historical Newspapers*.

78. B. J. Bearden, "Musicians Owe Start to Deacon," *Chicago Defender*, 3 December 1932, 10–10, *ProQuest Historical Newspapers*.

79. Coonfield and Huxford, "News Images as Lived Images," 465.

80. Gilbert Murray, preface to *The Iphigenia in Tauris of Euripides*, translated into English rhyming verse by Gilbert Murray (New York: Oxford University Press, 1910), v, xi. From the 1880s on, it became very popular in the United States for schools and colleges to stage the classical dramatic canon.

81. www.washingtonart.com/beltway/hughes2.html. The reading was given on 15 January 1926.

82. See, for example, "Display Ad 15—No Title," *Washington Post*, 23 February 1924, 11–11, *ProQuest Historical Newspapers*.

83. "Coming to the Theaters," *Washington Post*, 19 May 1927, 11, *ProQuest Historical Newspapers*. St. Margaret's Boarding and Day School, founded in 1887, no longer exists but used to occupy a building at 2115 California Avenue, at Connecticut Avenue.

84. "St. Margaret's School under New Control," *Washington Post*, 15 March 1924, *ProQuest Historical Newspapers*.

85. http://articles.baltimoresun.com/1993–07–14/news/1993195066_1_mount-st -mary-school-eymard.

86. See Robert Jackson, "The Southern Disaster Complex," *Mississippi Quarterly* 63.3/4 (Summer/Fall 2010): 555–70, on how, particularly in the white southern embrace of classical tragedy from the Civil War onward, that form explains why disaster has struck "in defiance of human agency"; moreover, the "richness of catharsis here depends . . . upon the importance of *not* fixing blame on any specific persons or decisions" (557).

87. *The Iphigenia in Tauris of Euripides*, trans. Murray, 5, 20.

88. Ibid., 23, 32.

89. Ibid., 48, 50, 56, 10.

90. Marcel Mauss, *The Gift: Forms and Functions of Exchange in Archaic Societies*, trans. Ian Cunnison (London: Cohen and West, 1966 [French first ed. 1923–24]), 1, 2, 72, 10, Open library.org. Anthropologist Mary Douglas, commenting on Mauss's work, added that gifts "are more visible than the market" (*Risk and Blame: Essays in Cultural Theory* [London: Routledge, 1992], 162); in doing so, Mauss countered the tradition within English Utilitarianism that saw competitive individualism as the primary engine of social interaction (74).

91. "Coolidge Projects Inland Waterways for Flood," *New York Times*, 4 October 1927, *ProQuest Historical Newspapers*.

Chapter 3

1. Barry, *Rising Tide*, 284.

2. Modris Ecksteins, *Rites of Spring: The Great War and the Birth of the Modern Age* (Boston: Houghton Mifflin, 1989), 242–52. To the French, he was "*homme de reve, homme oiseau*, a modern Icarus who, unlike his mythical forebear, had dispelled tragedy" (244); public receptions of Lindbergh across Europe were "frenzied and carnivalesque" (246). While Lindbergh's person charmed the tradition-loving side of European society, his successful feat assured that, to enthusiasts of the modern, "man and machine had become one in this act of daring" (251).

3. Robert D. Heinl, "Air Hero's Arrival in New York Told Vividly over Radio," *Washington Post*, 14 June 1927, 4; the article described his appearance in both Washington, D.C., and New York City.

4. "Flood and Flight as News," *New York Times*, 29 May 1927, n.p., *ProQuest Historical Newspapers*.

5. Editorial, *The Nation* 124.3232 (15 June 1927): 655. As Cleveland Chase put it in the *New York Times*: "The Mississippi flood, still at the height of its devastating course, was pushed off the front pages by Lindbergh's flight." "Fighting the 'Father of Waters,'" 27 November 1927, BR9, *ProQuest Historical Newspapers*.

6. L. C. Speers, "Louisiana Parishes Rotting in the Flood," *New York Times*, 11 July 1927, *ProQuest Historical Newspapers*.

7. Dickson, "Flood Changes Region into Valley of Sorrow."

8. Ibid.

9. Nixon, *Slow Violence*, 2.

10. "Flood and Flight as News," n.p.

11. Taylor, untitled ms., 7.

12. Beck, *Risk Society*, 47. Beck explains: "While class societies are capable of being organized as nation states, risk societies bring about 'communities of danger' that ultimately can only be comprised in the United Nations." In the 1927, these "communities of danger" were not supranational.

13. Douglas, *Risk and Blame*, 8. Douglas is doubtful, though, whether blaming is an ideal or necessary social behavior. She wonders if a better model is that of a "no-fault culture," for members of such a culture "irrigate their social system with a lavish flow of gifts." "As between justice and mercy," she concludes, "it seems that laying blame accurately is much less important for maintaining public safety than the generous treatment of the victim" (17). Gifts, as I have just argued, do not simply and healthily "irrigate a system" in a neutral, restorative manner. As Mauss argued, gift-giving is a form of social contest; the gift-giver always hopes to take something back. Giving can be just as much about "building community consensus" as can blaming. And the act of giving can obscure the giver's initiating role in the recipient's condition of distress. Gifts, as theorists after Mauss have pointed out, can be a form of poison. See Gloria Goodwin Raheja, *The Poison in the Gift: Ritual, Prestation, and the Dominant Caste in a North Indian Village* (Chicago: University of Chicago Press, 1988); and Lewis Hyde, *The Gift: Imagination and the Erotic Life of Property* (New York: Vintage, 1983).

14. Rogers, "I don't butt in . . . ," *Will Rogers' Weekly Articles*, ed. James M. Smallwood (Stillwater: Oklahoma State University Press, 1980), 43.

15. Marcel Mauss had written that "charity wounds him who receives, and our whole moral effort is directed toward suppressing the unconscious harmful patronage of the rich almoner" (*The Gift*, 63).

16. Editorial, *Commercial Appeal*, 17 April 1927, n.p.

17. "The Burden of Floods: Who Should Bear It?" *Commercial Appeal*, 24 April 1927, n.p.

18. "Stand Together, Pull Together and Victory Is Certain," *Commercial Appeal*, 22 May 1927, n.p.

19. "Herbert Hoover Asks More Aid for Victims," *Commercial Appeal*, 29 May 1927, 1.

20. "Levee Construction Is for the Government; Not for Individuals," *Commercial Appeal*, 14 June 1927.

21. "A National Obligation," *Atlanta Constitution*, 15 May 1927, C2-c2, *ProQuest Historical Newspapers*.

22. "Chain the Mississippi!" *Atlanta Constitution*, 19 June 1927, C2-c2, *ProQuest Historical Newspapers*.

23. M. Ashby Jones, D.D., "Text and Pretext: The Mississippi River—A Dare," *Atlanta Constitution*, 15 May 1927, C2, *ProQuest Historical Newspapers*.

24. Dickson, "America, Its Dander Up, Vows Revenge on River," 3.

25. Hodding Carter, *Lower Mississippi* (New York: Rinehart, 1942), 263, 280–81.
26. Lincoln to J. C. Conklin, August 1863, qtd. in James M. McPherson, *Battle Cry of Freedom: The Civil War Era* (New York: Oxford University Press, 1988), 638.
27. Simpich, "The Great Mississippi Flood of 1927," 257.
28. Maria Mattingly Maloney, "Orphans of the Mississippi," *New York Herald Tribune*, 29 May 1927.
29. Murphy, "Overflow Notes," 224–25, 230.
30. "Wasted Irony," *Wall Street Journal*, 7 June 1927, n.p., *ProQuest Historical Newspapers*. *Barron's* editorial reprinted here. *Barron's* further suggested that the southerners showed a regrettable "obliviousness" to the humor in such a piece of "satire"; moreover, "intensely sensitive people have seldom any sense of humor, and some of our methods of education leave a tendency to hysteria in the attitude towards life which is no asset to us when we come to deal with large national problems."
31. "The Lesson of the Mississippi Flood," *Chicago Daily Tribune*, 18 April 1927, 10.
32. Walter Parker, "Curbing the Mississippi," *The Nation* 124.3227 (11 May 1927): 521.
33. Ibid., 522.
34. Simpich, "The Great Mississippi Flood of 1927," 285.
35. "The Mississippi," *Manchester Guardian*, 14 May 1927, 15.
36. Jess Dorman, "The Mississippi," *Los Angeles Times*, 16 May 1927, A4.
37. Saxon, *Father Mississippi*, 408, 399.
38. "Trees Would Save Millions from an Erosion by Floods," *Washington Post*, 11 December 1927, *ProQuest Historical Newspapers*.
39. "Voice of the People from the Flood" (op-ed page), *Chicago Daily Tribune*, 30 April 1927, *ProQuest Historical Newspapers*. An editorial a year later cast Chicago's solidarity with the Lower Valley in a more suspicious light: "Is Flood Control Jeopardized by Scandal?" *Chicago Daily Tribune*, 19 April 1928, *ProQuest Historical Newspapers* detailed how upper midwestern timber interests stood to benefit by the federal government buying land in upper tributaries to establish flood-controlling reservoirs.
40. See H. L. Mencken, *A Religious Orgy in Tennessee: A Reporter's Account of the Scopes Monkey Trial* (Brooklyn: Melville House, 2010).
41. Flood sermon by Reverend Ben Cox of the Central Baptist Church in Memphis, quoted in Daniel, *Deep'n as It Come*, 115–16.
42. "When Enmity Is Forgotten," *Commercial Appeal*, 19 April 1927, n.p.
43. Nelson, qtd. in *Afro-American*, 28 April 1928, n.p., *ProQuest Historical Newspapers*.
44. "Reserved for Whites," *Chicago Defender*, 4 June 1927, 1-A2, *ProQuest Historical Newspapers*.
45. "Withstanding the Flood," 20.
46. Here is what Michael Warner calls, in "Publics and Counterpublics," *Public Culture* 14.1 (2002): 66, a "cross-citational field" of journalism, a phrase that indicates how modern publics operate in a self-consciously complex and comparative arena. As "discourse . . . move[s] in different directions" across this field, its movement allows various publics to "develop reflexivity," to become differentiated as a "we." It allows readers to feel as if they "[participate] in the circulation of judgments" rather than languish as "a passive theatrical audience" (67).

47. White, "The Negro and the Flood," 688–89, reprinted in the *Chicago Defender*, 2 July 1927, A1.
48. Barry, *Rising Tide*, 322.
49. Apparently other preachers read the flood as a godsend: Louis Lautier reported that "Bishop Robert E Jones, of Methodist Episcopal Church addressed the National Negro Business League, declaring that the flood 'was a God send in emancipating Negroes in southern states along the river.'" "Bishop Jones Tells Business League Flood a Godsend," *Afro-American*, 20 August 1927, *ProQuest Historical Newspapers*.
50. William Pickens, "Gasoline, Thrown on Husband, Ignited," *New York Amsterdam News*, 4 May 1927, 1, *ProQuest Historical Newspapers*.
51. Williams Pickens, "God and the Preachers," *New York Amsterdam News*, 18 May 1927, *ProQuest Historical Newspapers*.
52. Two weeks after Pickens's article, another journalist in the same paper persisted in reading the flood providentially: "His hand wrought the havoc of this flood to avenge the crimes committed against these poor, ignorant farm hands by money-mad plantation owners." The author hoped, somewhat inconsistently, that the flood would help black and white to "come one bit nearer a real brotherhood, a real understanding of each other," "Where Tragedy and Comedy Walk Hand in Hand." *New York Amsterdam News*, 1 June 1927, 14, *ProQuest Historical Newspapers*.
53. Ida B. Wells, "Brand Ministers in Flood Area as Betrayers," *Chicago Defender*, 16 July 1927, 1, *ProQuest Historical Newspapers*.
54. Ida B. Wells, "Flood Refugees Are Held as Slaves in Mississippi Camp," *Chicago Defender*, 30 July 1927, 1-A11, *ProQuest Historical Newspapers*.
55. Wells, "Brand Ministers," 1, 4.
56. Wells, "Flood Refugees," 1-A11.
57. Ibid.
58. Douglas, *Risk and Blame*, 17.
59. See Patricia A. Schechter, *Ida B. Wells-Barnett and American Reform, 1880–1930* (Chapel Hill: University of North Carolina Press, 2001) on Wells-Barnett's full career as a crusader, especially her navigation of and resistance to gendered expectations for female reformers.
60. William Pickens, "The South's Fairness," *New York Amsterdam News*, 22 June 1927, 22, *ProQuest Historical Newspapers*.
61. J. Winston Harrington, "Work or Go Hungry Edict Perils Race," *Chicago Defender*, 11 June 1927, 1-1, *ProQuest Historical Newspapers*.
62. George S. Schuyler remembered of *The Crisis*, in the fortieth anniversary issue of the magazine (March 1951): "Then came *The Crisis*, like a clear, strong breeze cutting through the miasma of Negrophobism. Here for the first time with brilliance, militancy, facts, photographs and persuasiveness, a well-edited magazine challenged the whole concept of white supremacy then nationally accepted. . . . It is no exaggeration to say that the early *Crisis* created an intellectual revolution in the most out-of-way places. . . . It became the bible of the militant Negro of the day and 'must' reading for the growing number of his white champions." www.thecrisismagazine.com/history2.html.
63. We know that she was a white female based on recorded correspondence between

Claude Barnett and Robert Moton, quoted in Barry, *Rising Tide*, 389. All my attempts to figure out this woman's identity have proved futile; possibilities include Mary White Ovington, Lillian Wald, and Florence Kelley, all white women in activist social work connected with the NAACP.

64. Du Bois, "Peonage," *The Crisis* 34 (November 1927): 311.
65. W.E.B. Du Bois, "Flood," *The Crisis* 34 (July 1927): 108.
66. W.E.B. Du Bois, "Peonage," 311.
67. W.E.B. Du Bois, "Red Cross Slavery," *The Crisis* 34 (June 1927): 130. Du Bois quoted and italicized sections of the Jackson, MS *Daily News*, 30 April 1927.
68. "The Flood, the Red Cross and the National Guard," *The Crisis*, March 1928, 101.
69. "The Flood, the Red Cross and the National Guard," *The Crisis*, 28 January 1928, 7.
70. Ibid., 6.
71. H. L. Mencken, "The Mississippi Flood," *Evening Sun*, 23 May 1927, n.p.
72. Natalie J. Ring has recently argued that a northern conception of the South as a "problem" needing northern solution continued to exist even in those decades around the end of the nineteenth century when the "romance of reunion" narrative was thriving; she argues that "demarcating the region as a backward space reinforced the hegemony of the nation-state and created a sense of urgency surrounding sectional reunion" (*Problem South*, 3). This attitude toward the South was tied in with Progressive and imperial narratives of reform; many aspects of the management of the "southern problem" were either colonialist or "perceived to be colonial" (10).
73. Kellogg, "Behind the Levees," 279.
74. Arthur Kellogg, "Up from the Bottomlands," *Survey Graphic* 58.5 (July 1927): 360, 365, 366.
75. Craig Dale, "Human Wreckage Is Flood Problem," *Chicago Daily News*, 19 August 1927, "DR-224/72 Mississippi River Valley Flood 3/30/27 Newspapers, Clippings, Etc.," Central File, 1917–1934, box 742, Collection ANRC—130/77/17/01, NARA. All Dale articles are from this file.
76. Craig Dale, "Moral Shaken by Flood Havoc," *Chicago Daily News*, 19 August 1927.
77. Craig Dale, "Four Horsemen Ride Flood Area," *Chicago Daily News*, 17 August 1927, 1.
78. Dale, "Human Wreckage Is Flood Problem."
79. Craig Dale, "Flood Cruel to Negroes in South," *Chicago Daily News*, 22 August 1927.
80. Craig Dale, "Disease Spreads in Flood's Wake," *Chicago Daily News*, 23 August 1927.
81. See Jay Watson, *Reading for the Body: The Recalcitrant Materiality of Southern Fiction, 1893–1985* (Athens: University of Georgia Press, 2012) on how "images of diseased or lethargic southern bodies . . . circulated in national publications" at the turn of the twentieth century; these "haunt[ed] the nation and its progressivist social and political discourses" (16). See also Todd L. Savitt and James Harvey Young, eds., *Disease and Distinctiveness in the American South* (Knoxville: University of Tennessee Press, 1988); within this collection, James O. Breeden writes that "the high incidence of disease [pellagra, hookworm, yellow fever, and malaria] and its effects retarded social and economic development and contributed to the national

image of southern backwardness," problems largely controlled by World War II, through a combination of extraregional funding and intraregional campaigns and structures (in "Disease as a Factor in Southern Distinctiveness," 8, 14–15). Dale's articles hit a major nerve, in part because of real health problems but also because they failed to acknowledge extensive efforts within the South to combat disease.

82. See Hoover and Maj. Genl. Edgar Jadwin, "Mississippi Flood Control," joint statement delivered at Memphis, Tennessee, 30 April 1927, typescript in Hoover Papers.

83. "Red Cross Worker Ordered Fired," *Afro-American*, 24 December 1927, 1, *ProQuest Historical Newspapers*.

84. "Propaganda," *Afro-American*, 21 January 1928, 6, *ProQuest Historical Newspapers*.

85. See separate coverage of Rogers's congressional appearance in "Will Rogers Urges Federal Flood Aid before Committee," *Washington Post*, 13 January 1928, *ProQuest Historical Newspapers*. Rogers had testified: "It seems to me that the Nation should pay for all of it. We should not try to keep them half drowned."

86. "Propaganda."

Chapter 4

1. Chris Albertson, *Bessie* (New Haven: Yale University Press, 2003 [1972]), 102. Maud Smith affirms that this was the address where Smith wrote "Back Water Blues"; because Smith and Jack Gee had bought a house in Philadelphia in 1926, and had bought housing for relatives on Kater Street, my assumption is that the Christian Street house was hers, rather than Clarence and Maud's. See Carman Moore, *Somebody's Angel Child: The Story of Bessie Smith* (New York: Thomas Crowell, 1969), largely based on interviews with Smith's husband, Jack Gee, in the 1960s (84, 86).

2. The full advertisement on the car's side read "Jack Gee Presents Bessie Smith—The Empress of the Blues." Moore, *Somebody's Angel Child*, 80.

3. Albertson, *Bessie*, 41, 43, 45; this information is for the 1925 tour.

4. Ibid., 62–65. Smith sold over four million records from 1924 to 1929; see Michelle R. Scott, *Blue Empress in Black Chattanooga: Bessie Smith and the Emerging Urban South* (Urbana: University of Illinois Press, 2008), 2. Albertson argues that it was "only in the South that Bessie had a substantial following of whites" (*Bessie*, 45; see also 64), but the nationwide magazine *Music Trades* announced on 16 February 1924 in "Dealers Expect Big Sale of Blues Records by Bessie Smith" that "her records enjoy a considerable demand among white people . . . especially noted among professional white entertainers" (qtd. in Albertson, *Bessie*, 64).

5. The *Pittsburgh Courier* covered a whites-only performance of hers at Club 81 on 13 February 1924 at which the whites "filled the house" (qtd. in Albertson, *Bessie*, 65–66).

6. Smith was one of the great "popular" as opposed to "folk" or "country" blues singers. David Evans distinguishes the modes this way: "The folk blues aesthetic emphasized truth in the lyrics, and musical and structural freedom within the context of the traditional and familiar, while the aesthetics of the [popular or urban] blues songwriters emphasized storytelling, lyrical originality, and novelty within fixed musical structures" (*Big Road Blues: Tradition and Creativity in the Folk Blues*

[Berkeley: University of California Press, 1982], 61). In terms of narrative continuity, country blues singers tended to move more freely across topics, stanza by stanza, adding and swerving improvisationally, whereas the popular blues that from its start was a recorded, and often orchestral, form tended to need more coherence and deliberate musical composition. Once the country blues started being recorded in sheet music form (1912) and through the phonograph (1926), and once the popular or urban blues was disseminated to rural places via tent shows, radio, phonograph, and sheet music, there was much cross-pollination between the two (59, 70). Of Smith's particular mixture, Hayden Carruth writes that she "took the country blues, in the purity of its lamentation and bitterness, and transformed it into an urban art, retaining the power of its origins within its newly sophisticated meanings" and sense of "irony"; her particular forte, in his mind, was how she could "propel syntax against meter." *Sitting In: Selected Writings on Jazz, Blues, and Related Topics* (Iowa City: University of Iowa Press, 1993), 148, 151.

7. David Evans, "'Back-Water Blues': The Story behind the Song," *Popular Music* 26.1 (2006): 99. See also Richard M. Mizelle Jr.'s treatment of "Back-Water Blues" and Smith's other flood song, "Homeless Blues," in *Backwater Blues: The Mississippi Flood of 1927 in the African American Imagination* (Minneapolis: University of Minnesota Press, 2014), 29–31, 49–50. Mizelle sees in these songs and a number of other flood blues a valuable archive of African American flood experience.
8. Abbé Niles asserted in 1926 that blues had, by that point, "penetrated the national consciousness" and become an "integral part of our music." "The Story of the Blues," in *Blues: An Anthology*, ed. W. C. Handy (Mineola, NY: Dover, 2012 [1926]), 20.
9. Albertson, *Bessie*, 146. A scanning of Cincinnati papers from early January through 6 February 1927 found no advertisements of Smith's *Harlem Frolics* performing in that city.
10. Ibid.
11. Evans, "Back-Water Blues," 110–13. Evans effectively disproves the information that Jack Gee passed on to Carman Moore, namely that Smith wrote the song while the company headed north from Alabama to Chattanooga in late December; see Moore, *Somebody's Angel Child*, 87.
12. Scott, *Blue Empress in Black Chattanooga*, 57.
13. There was also, on 26 and 27 December, a current flood taking place in Chattanooga where Chattanooga Creek joined with the Tennessee River, displacing two thousand families and inundating industrial plants in the lowlands where Smith grew up; see Evans, "Back-Water Blues," 108.
14. Barry, *Rising Tide*, 181.
15. Ibid., 176–82.
16. Albertson, *Bessie*, 146.
17. *Pittsburgh Courier*, 21 May 1927, *ProQuest Historical Newspapers*.
18. "Among the Theatres 'Preaching Records' Vie with Blues as Best Sellers Mississippi Flood Increases Calls for 'Muddy Waters' and 'Back Water' Blues," *Afro-American*, 18 June 1927, *ProQuest Historical Newspapers*. According to David Evans, Smith recorded "Muddy Water," a Tin Pan Alley song written by white composers, on 2 March, and it was released on 20 April; her rendition of this saccharine song "leaves

the listener feeling uneasy about the song's cheerful portrait of the Old South" ("Back-Water Blues," 100). Albertson avers that Smith sings "the most banal lyrics with conviction" (*Bessie*, 150).

19. Evans, "Back-Water Blues," 99.
20. Albertson, *Bessie*, 155, 157.
21. See Daphne Duval Harrison, *Black Pearls: Blues Queens of the 1920s* (New Brunswick, NJ: Rutgers University Press, 1988) on the popularity of phonographs among southern blacks in the 1920s (57); overall national record sales were at 104 million in 1927, a figure that declined precipitously with the arrival of nationwide radio (and the Depression) to 6 million in 1932 (61).
22. Moore describes Smith being struck by "the great magic of recordings as a means of reaching into the nation" (*Somebody's Angel Child*, 73).
23. Albertson, *Bessie*, 42.
24. Gunther Schuller, *Early Jazz: Its Roots and Musical Development* (New York: Oxford University Press, 1968), 239, 228–29.
25. While the country blues is marked by a tradition of narrative "incoherence," in which singers intentionally and creatively add and shift themes, the classic blues tended to shape songs into a single story. See Evans, *Big Road Blues*, 52.
26. Albertson, *Bessie*, 42.
27. Schuller, *Early Jazz*, 228, 238.
28. Van Vechten, *Jazz Record* (1947), qtd. in Albertson, *Bessie*, 172.
29. Ibid.. This memory came from April 1928 when Smith appeared at the 55th Street apartment of Van Vechten and his wife during the run of her "Musical Comedy Triumph" at the Lafayette called *Mississippi Days* (169); the niece's quote is on 175.
30. Barker quoted in Albertson, *Bessie*, 155.
31. Ralph Ellison, "The Blues," *New York Review of Books*, 6 February 1964, n.p., http://www.nybooks.com/articles/archives/1964/feb/06/the-blues/?pagination=false.
32. Carman Moore suggests that, as a child, Smith sang in a choir that made a trip to Memphis (*Somebody's Angel Child*, 21).
33. Scott, *Blues Empress*, 66, 91–96, 114. Moore writes that Smith "was raised to adulthood in back of theaters, in tents, and on the streets—a strange, new breed of outdoor girl" (*Somebody's Angel Child*, 40).
34. "James P. Johnson Dies, But Leaves Large Legacy," *Downbeat*, 1 April 1956.
35. Nick Morrison, "Stride Piano: Bottom-End Jazz," NPR.org, 12 April 2010.
36. "James P. Johnson Dies, But Leaves Large Legacy."
37. Albertson, *Bessie*, 147.
38. William T. Dargan, *Lining Out the Word: Dr. Watts Hymn Singing in the Music of Black Americans* (Berkeley: University of California Press, 2006), 214–17.
39. Steven J. Morrison, in "Downhome Tragedy: The Blues and the Mississippi Flood of 1927," *Southern Folklore* 51 (1994): 265–84, argues that what became typical of the flood blues was an alteration between a third-person chronicle of events and a first-person experiential account (268). As the first blues recorder of the 1927 super-flood, Smith no doubt had influence on this structure.
40. Robert Frost plays with the conversation between his being consumed by his own "inner" weather and a tree's concern with "outer weather" in "A Tree at My Window," *West-Running Brook* (New York: Henry Holt, 1928), 25.

41. Smith's shifting from third to first person confirms James H. Cone's observation that the blues is a form simultaneously empirical and lyrical and that when it invokes the absurd, it is a "factual" more than philosophical "absurdity." *The Spirituals and the Blues: An Interpretation* (New York: Seabury Press, 1972), 119, quotes on 112.

42. Adam Gussow, *Seems Like Murder Here: Southern Violence and the Blues Tradition* (Chicago: University of Chicago Press, 2002), 27.

43. See ibid., chap. 1, for a discussion of how lynching violence made its way into blues lyrics and shaped the blues tradition.

44. Carman Moore says of Smith's moan: "As she sang, certain words just disappeared into pure humming sound. . . . she became at such times a singer no more, but a burnishing saxophone or a trombone of the gods" (*Somebody's Angel Child*, 46).

45. Hazel V. Carby argues in "It Jus Be's Dat Way Sometime: The Sexual Politics of Women's Blues," in *The Jazz Cadence of American Culture*, ed. Robert G. O'Meally (New York: Columbia University Press, 1998) that female blues singers could articulate "the possibilities of movement" (476); they were "organic intellectuals," who "not only were . . . a part of the community that was the subject of their song but . . . also a product of the rural-to-urban movement" (476). "Back Water Blues" then represents a paradox in that it showcases a cosmopolitan, mobile celebrity singing about the sadness of having to move, of having nowhere to move, and thus of being unable to move any more.

46. Morrison argues in "Downhome Tragedy" that "Back Water Blues" tells of an "exhausted submission" to "the forces of nature" (273) and the fate of becoming a "person without a place" (275). He also singles out Smith and Charlie Patton (who wrote and recorded "High Water Everywhere" parts I and II in 1929) for the "intimacy and immediacy" of their experience-based songs as opposed to the spate of more generic renditions by singers removed from the flood itself (279). I agree that Smith depicts an "exhausted submission" but also describes the paradox of knowing more and having less—of acquiring knowledge and losing the foundation of self.

47. Niles, "The Story of the Blues," 17.

48. Cone, *The Spirituals and the Blues*, 110.

49. Ralph Waldo Emerson, "Nature," in *Ralph Waldo Emerson: Selected Essays, Lectures and Poems* (New York: Random House, 2006), 18–19.

50. For a contrasting argument about Romanticism, see W. Jackson Bate, *Romantic Ecology: Wordsworth and the Environmental Tradition* (London: Routledge, 2013 [1991]), where he identifies the "Romantic ideology" as not exclusively about transcendence but also dedicated to "a theory of ecosystems and unalienated labor" (10). Karl Kroeber argues likewise in *Ecological Literary Criticism: Romantic Imagining and the Biology of Mind* (New York: Columbia University Press, 1994) that Romantic poets were not "seekers after an unattainable transcendence" but rather "forerunners of a new biological, materialistic understanding of humanity's place in the natural cosmos" (2). See also James C. McKusick, *Green Writing: Romanticism and Ecology* (New York: Palgrave Macmillan, 2010 [2000]); and Onno Oerlemans, *Romanticism and the Materiality of Nature* (Toronto: University of Toronto Press, 2002).

51. Unlike Smith's contemporaries such as Sterling Brown, Langston Hughes, and Zora Neale Hurston, who had access to and explored the Western literary canon, there is no indication that Smith's ancient sources stretched beyond the Old and New Testaments. It was more that a similar predicament—in terms of land use and economic stratification, and the perennial vulnerability of the small farmer to dispossession by a large or more powerful landholder—characterized both her and Virgil's writing context. They both, moreover, emerged out of similar traditions of folk singing, often competitively, about love, hardship, and land loss. Though the georgic genre might seem to foreground farm labor more than pastoral and thus be a more fitting tradition, the classical pastoral, before the tradition was watered down in the early modern period, bespoke the particular relation to land loss that seems especially relevant here. After all, Smith is not singing about rural labor exactly; she's singing about displacement.

52. Raymond Williams, *The Country and the City* (New York: Oxford University Press, 1975), 15, 16.

53. *Virgil's Eclogues*, trans. Len Krisak, intro. Gregson Davis (Philadelphia: University of Pennsylvania Press, 2010), ix, vii.

54. Ibid., xiii.

55. Williams, *The Country and the City*, 18.

56. Though Smith works in the more urban or popular vein of the blues, there was much influence back and forth in these years between urban and country blues. Her southern upbringing, her potential derivation of this song from a vernacular Nashville tune, and the root of all blues singing in spiritual verse connects "Back Water Blues" with folk forms. Smith, and other Vaudeville singers, did sing and record these saccharine Dixie tunes—take her cover of "Muddy Water (a Mississippi Moan)," for instance—but I would argue that such a recording was more a response to the popular market than expressive of Smith's artistic and social vision.

57. Ralph Ellison, "Richard Wright's Blues," *Antioch Review* 5.2 (Summer 1945), reprinted in 50.1/2 (Winter/Spring 1992): 62.

58. Ralph Ellison, "The Blues," *New York Review of Books*, review of LeRoi Jones, *Blues People* (6 February 1964): n.p. Ellison is discussing the blues in the context of a more general African American influence on mainstream U.S. culture through "song and dance."

59. Angela Y. Davis, *Blues Legacies and Black Feminism* (New York: Vintage, 1998), 101.

60. Harrison, *Black Pearls*, 4.

61. Albertson, *Bessie*, 157, 156.

62. Ibid., 158–59.

63. The following truncated list of flood recordings is taken from David Evans's exhaustive and authoritative survey of the more than two dozen 1927 flood songs, "High Water Everywhere: Blues and Gospel Commentary on the 1927 Mississippi River Flood," *Nobody Knows Where the Blues Come From* (Jackson: University Press of Mississippi, 2006), 15, 17–18, 22–23, 9–39, which includes the lyrics of the songs mentioned in this paragraph.

64. Ibid., 40–42.

Chapter 5

1. *Billboard*, 7 May 1927, 5, *ProQuest Historical Newspapers*.
2. *Billboard*, 21 May, 1927, 66, *ProQuest Historical Newspapers*.
3. *Billboard*, 4 June 1927, 68, *ProQuest Historical Newspapers*. See *Billboard*, 2 October 1920, 3, for their help wanted advertisement, *ProQuest Historical Newspapers*.
4. Reprinted in *Billboard*, 21 May 1927, 38, from the *Winona (MS) Times* editorial. Notice exists, too, of Hughie Fitz the acrobatical clown who was down in the flood area "doing his bit for the entertainment of the refugees." *Billboard*, 4 June 1927, 9, *ProQuest Historical Newspapers*.
5. Martinelli to Charles H. Douglass, an African American theater owner, Macon, Georgia. On Charles H. Douglass and his Douglass Theater, see Jason L. Ellerbee, "African American Theaters in Georgia: Preserving an Entertainment Legacy" (Master's thesis in Historic Preservation, University of Georgia, 2004), 40–53, http://getd.galib.uga.edu/public/ellerbee_jason_l_200408_mhp/ellerbee_jason_l_200408_mhp.pdf and www.douglasstheatre.org.
6. "Tickets for Flood Benefit Friday Get Big Response," *Atlanta Constitution*, 4 May 1927, 16–16, *ProQuest Historical Newspapers*.
7. Burt A. Folkart, "Mary Foy; One of Last 3 in Zany Family," obituary, 17 December 1987, http://articles.latimes.com/1987-12-17/news/mn-29386_1_vaudeville.
8. E. F. Albee, *Vaudeville News and New York Star*, 25 February 1928, qtd. in Anthony Slide, "Eddie Foy," *The Encyclopedia of Vaudeville* (Westport, CT: Greenwood Press, 1994), 188. Albee added that "probably he was the favorite of more entire American families than any other stage artist."
9. Frank Cullen, with Florence Hackman and Donald McNeilly, *Vaudeville Old & New: An Encyclopedia of Variety Performers in America*, vol. 1 (New York: Routledge, 2007), 409–10.
10. The Foy Family, "Chips of the Old Block," Vitaphone film short 2580 (1928), http://www.youtube.com/watch?v=qZmGzNAmicw.
11. Charles Foy, qtd. in "Tickets for Flood Benefit Friday Get Big Response," 16.
12. Recall the advertisement for the Charles T. Buell & Company carnival kit of enlarged flood photographs I mentioned at the start of chapter 2; through a "viewing box," a carnival attendee in Minnesota or Maine could transport herself to the "marvelous attraction"—the self-made circus—down south. "Advertisement," *Billboard*, 28 May 1927, 100.
13. Richard Schechner, *Environmental Theater: An Expanded New Edition* (New York: Applause, 1994 [1973]), xxviii, 17.
14. Ibid., xx, xi.
15. Dickie and Foot, introduction to *Disastro*, 11–12.
16. The reporter continued: "What is the greatest news story of all time?" The reporter wondered rhetorically, "ADAM eating the apple? The landing of the ark on Ararat?"
17. *Oxford English Dictionary*, 2nd ed..
18. In *Slow Violence*, Nixon addresses the eco-catastrophic at a still slower scale, when degradation is not necessarily marked by spectacular events.
19. This is how Joseph Wood Krutch characterized Vaudeville in "Contemporaneity," *The Nation* 124.3215 (16 February 1927): 194.

20. Cullen, Hackman, and McNeilly, *Vaudeville Old & New*, xi.
21. Krutch, *The Nation* 122 (13 January 1926): 41.
22. Cullen, Hackman, and McNeilly, *Vaudeville Old & New*, xv.
23. Robert W. Snyder, *Voice of the City: Vaudeville and Popular Culture in New York* (New York: Oxford University Press, 1989), 66–67.
24. As Snyder points out, critics of the Keith-Albee near monopoly on big Vaudeville "likened it to an octopus, with a Times Square booking office brain and theatre circuit tentacles" (*Voice of the City*, 83).
25. See Snyder, *Voice of the City*, xv, 43–44; and Cullen, Hackman, and McNeilly, *Vaudeville Old & New*, xxii. Strausbaugh, in *Black Like You*, argues that "the vaudeville stage presented images of an integrated America that were a theatrical fantasy, a lie. But maybe it also was presenting an ideal, an image of possibility, of the future" (134).
26. Douglas Gilbert, *American Vaudeville: Its Life and Times* (New York: Dover, 1968 [1940]), 206.
27. Snyder, *Voice of the City*, xvi, xv, 161.
28. Gilbert, *American Vaudeville*, 61, 70, 72.
29. Ibid., 251, 385.
30. Ibid., 393.
31. Lippmann, *American Inquisitors*, 5, 4.
32. Snyder, *Voice of the City*, xv.
33. Pantti and Wahl-Jorgensen, "Not an Act of God," 118.
34. Performance and theater studies scholars have offered robust counterclaims to traditional public sphere theory about the possibilities—and in particular the knowledge-making or consciousness-changing possibilities—of the stage. These scholars point out how cultures that prize the lettered archive and are attached to "the real" misjudged the way knowledge is communicated and in particular have underestimated how it might be communicated through performance. See Diana Taylor, *The Archive and the Repertoire: Performing Cultural Memory in the Americas* (Durham: Duke University Press, 2003), 28. She argues that "part of what performance and performance studies allows us to *do*, then, is take seriously the repertoire of embodied practices as an important system of knowing and transmitting knowledge" (26) and asserts that knowing occurs not through disembodied reasoning and the exact transmission of print but rather through embodied "scenarios" being passed along and played with (28–33). Peggy Phelan, in *Unmarked: The Politics of Performance* (New York: Routledge, 1993), points out that the media and publics always exist in reciprocal relations, that the media does not simply impose its version of truth on the public but takes up mass behaviors in a "dialogic . . . manner" (21). She discusses how "the visible real is employed as a truth-effect for the establishment of [various] discursive and representational notions of the real" (3)—visibility can thus become a social and epistemological "trap" (6); performance can, however, sidestep these traps by engaging with the "phantasmatic" (4). Deception and revelation are not antithetical terms in the theater; instead, memory and experience can emerge in flexible reenactment, angled at but not copied from that real. Moreover, as David Krasner suggests in *Resistance, Parody, and Double Consciousness in African American Theatre, 1895–1910* (New York: St. Martin's Press, 1997), audience members are not passive receptacles of staged displays;

rather, they can be "coproducers in the performance as active creators of meaning" (134).

35. The Cameraman, "Colorful News 'Movies,'" *New York Amsterdam News*, 22 June 1927, 22, *ProQuest Historical Newspapers*.

36. Walter Benjamin, "The Author as Producer," in *Understanding Brecht*, trans. Anna Bostock (New York: Verso, 1998 [1966]), 101.

37. Benjamin, along with underscoring this potential in something funny to ignite ideas, defends what he calls "reception in a state of distraction" ("The Work of Art in the Age of Mechanical Reproduction," 240). In an era of mass entertainment, "art" is just as likely to be experienced by people "noticing [an] object in incidental fashion" as it is through their being absorbed into a work through "concentration" (240). Instead of this binary distraction/concentration brought on by low or high art consumption, I would suggest that Vaudeville comedy occurs through attraction as it makes audience members pay communal attention to a riff or joke.

38. L. C. Speers, "The Red Cross Takes up a Titanic Task," *New York Times*, 8 May 1927, *ProQuest Historical Newspapers*.

39. "Bostonians Stage Show to Aid Flood Refugees," *Chicago Defender*, 28 May 1927, *ProQuest Historical Newspapers*. News clipping in "Boston—National Theatre (II)" folder at Houghton Library Theatre Collection, Harvard University.

40. "In Vaudeville," *New York Times*, 12 June 1927, xi, *ProQuest Historical Newspapers*. For a description of the interborough Vaudeville network ca. 1915, see Snyder, *Voice of the City*, 82–83.

41. "Flood Fund Here Passes a Million," *New York Times*, 4 May 1927, *ProQuest Historical Newspapers*.

42. Dickson, "Negroes Real Heroes of Mississippi's Rampage," 3.

43. Al Jolson, famous for singing in blackface even before the release of *The Jazz Singer* in the fall of 1927, did a radio benefit broadcast from Chicago in late April. "WRC Relief Program for Victims of Flood," *Washington Post*, 30 April 1927, 7.

44. *Los Angeles Daily Times*, 7 May 1927, 8, *ProQuest Historical Newspapers*.

45. John Strausbaugh argues that "as a general rule, it seems that minstrels' presentations were one part 'authentic' to three parts comic caricature and sentimental fantasy" but then qualifies this generalization as he points out the complex circulations of minstrel culture from rural black "folk" culture to popular white minstrelsy only to be reappropriated by black performers (*Black Like You*, 72).

46. As David Evans has noted when analyzing the spate of river songs produced around and just after the 1927 flood that fail to mention the disaster: "It was as if American popular culture could not focus on the tragedy and pain of this massive current event and had to fall back on nostalgia and stereotypes" ("High Water Everywhere," 14); the same could be said of the more escapist blackface acts staged during the benefits.

47. Snyder, *Voice of the City*, 257.

48. Chappy Gardner, "Along the Rialto: Lafayette Charity," *Pittsburgh Courier*, 21 May 1927, *ProQuest Historical Newspapers*.

49. The Lafayette was, from 1915, co-leased and co-managed by the black drama critic Lester A. Walton until, in 1919, it came under, in Walton's words, "colored management and control." Mary Francesca Thompson, "The Lafayette Players: 1915–1932"

(PhD diss., University of Michigan, 1972), 163–64, 128–29, *ProQuest Dissertations and Theses.*

50. The Lafayette Players included Charles Gilpin and Clarence Muse; they staged *Salomé, Jekyll and Hyde, Othello,* and a part-operatic version of *Faust.* The touring stock company showed African Americans doing canonical theater to audiences of both races around the country (Thompson, "The Lafayette Players," 50, 150, 54, 102, 139, 187, 197). See Krasner, *Beautiful Pageant,* on New York black audiences' participation in this rhetoric of skin tones (266).

51. "Flood Benefit Here on May 10: Lafayette Theatre Presenting One of the Greatest Shows Ever Presented in Harlem," *New York Amsterdam News,* 4 May 1927, ProQuest Historical Newspapers. Four days later, the *Chicago Defender* attested that the benefit had been specifically for "the race victims" of the flood. Nardy, "Stage Stuff," *Chicago Defender,* 14 May 1927, *ProQuest Historical Newspapers.*

52. See Krasner, *Beautiful Pageant,* on the Lafayette's campaign to "reach the better class of colored people" (213).

53. Nardy, "Stage Stuff"; Gardner, "Along the Rialto." Krasner argues that such celebrities were "admired somewhat like conquering heroes" (*Beautiful Pageant,* 267).

54. Flournoy Miller, "London and Darkeydom," Flournoy E. Miller Papers, box 1, folder 2, manuscript drafts, p. 3, Schomburg Library, New York Public Library. He continued: "We changed our act but theatre managers would not stand for us to change the Boxing."

55. See entry for Miller and Lyles in Anthony Slide, *The Encyclopedia of Vaudeville* (Westport, CT: Greenwood Press, 1994), 345–46. Mel Watkins writes that *Shuffle Along* "usher[ed] in a new era of successful black musicals on Broadway." *On the Real Side: Laughing, Lying and Signifying—the Underground Tradition of African-American Humor That Transformed American Culture, from Slavery to Richard Pryor* (New York: Simon and Schuster, 1994), 162. Langston Hughes wrote that *Shuffle Along* "gave just the proper push—a pre-Charleston kick—to that Negro vogue of the '20s, that spread of books, African sculpture, music and dancing" (qtd. in Brown, *Babylon Girls,* 197). See also Krasner, *Beautiful Pageant,* chap. 11 (239–88) on the musical, which he calls "the most popular musical of the Harlem Renaissance" (239).

56. In 1929, the pair appeared in *Great Day,* the Broadway musical inspired by the 1927 flood, about a young white engineer who holds back the river from his sweetheart's plantation; with lyrics by William Rose and Edward Eliscu, and with black bandleader Lois Deppe leading fifty members of the Fisk Jubilee Singers, it was staged at the Colonial Theatre beginning on 16 September. *Gotham Life* (27 October 1929, n.p.) reported that Miller and Lyles, "whose popularity is almost legendary, did their stuff, and how." Given that this plotting once more situated black performers as either a spiritual-choral or comedic interlude to the main white, romantic action, Miller and Lyles seemed to have had less opportunity to craft a genially subversive show in this case. Listen to the lyrics to the title song "Great Day" to get a quick bead on its orientation.

57. Flournoy E. Miller, "My Fifty Years in Show Business," ms., Flournoy E. Miller Papers, 2, 3, 1.

58. Kip Lornell writes that Richards and Pringle's "arguably included the most talented

performers on the minstrel circuit" in the 1890s. Editorial headnote for Lynn Abbott and Doug Seroff, "Richards and Pringle's Original Georgia Minstrels and Billy Kersands, 1889–1895," in *From Jubilee to Hip Hop: Readings in African-American Music*, ed. Lornell (Upper Saddle River, NJ: Prentice Hall, 2010), 6.

59. *Indianapolis Freeman* correspondent quoted in Abbott and Seroff, "Richards and Pringle's," 6.

60. Ibid., 7.

61. When Richards and Pringle's played New Orleans in 1887, they played to a majority white audience, but in Memphis in 1896 the ratio was 4,000 blacks to 1,000 whites; it is difficult to say then what the racial ratio was in the New Madrid theater, but it was very likely a racially mixed audience. See Abbott and Seroff, "Richards and Pringle's," 6.

62. Miller, "My Fifty Years in Show Business," 2, 3.

63. Jessie Fauset, "The Gift of Laughter," in *The New Negro*, ed. Gates and Jarrett, 517, 518.

64. Of this general trend in black Vaudeville, Mel Watkins writes, "The performers who initially broke the color line [in the North] were forced to reflect the old stereotypes if they wanted work. Yet, as 'crossover' entertainers, their ascent was crucial to the evolution of black comedy and entertainment" (*On the Real Side*, 155). See also Daphne A. Brooks, *Bodies in Dissent: Spectacular Performances of Race and Freedom, 1850–1910* (Durham: Duke University Press, 2006) on how both minstrelsy and "coon" songs functioned as "a gateway to new professional ventures" for black performers (213).

65. "Miller and Lyles Hope for Theatre Devoted to Negro," *Pittsburgh Courier*, 22 May 1926, 10, *ProQuest Historical Newspapers*. Miller and Lyles also wrote and staged a serious play, *The Flat Below*, in May 1922 at the Lafayette; Krasner, *Beautiful Pageant*, 267.

66. As such, here is a different model of minstrel-busting black theater than that outlined by Brooks in *Bodies in Dissent* for the generation before Miller and Lyles, one based, as she puts it, on "[invoking] an aesthetics of fantasy as a counterhegemonic response to the concept of an essential territory" of blackness (268) and on performing a kind of "Brechtian drag" (254) that forecloses on a "desired 'black' etiological core" (250). Miller and Lyles seem to believe in a "core" of both identity and art, and in the necessary fusion of the two. For an analysis of the complex and fraught conditions of performance for African Americans during slavery, and in particular, ways that the pleasures of enslaved people were used to give the lie to the fundamental pains of bondage, see Saidiya V. Hartman, *Scenes of Subjection: Terror, Slavery, and Self-Making in Nineteenth-Century America* (Oxford: Oxford University Press, 1997). On black discursive modernism defined by a tension between "mastery of [minstrel] form and the deformation of mastery," and the role of Harlem therein, see Houston A. Baker Jr., *Modernism and the Harlem Renaissance* (Chicago: University of Chicago Press, 1987), 99.

67. "Miller and Lyles Hope for Theatre Devoted to Negro," 10.

68. The original act that they first performed at Fisk University to raise money for a science building was a "boxing dance." "Miller and Lyles Partners since College Days at Fisk," *Afro-American*, 30 July 1927, 8, *ProQuest Historical Newspapers*.

69. "Miller and Lyles Hope for Theatre Devoted to Negro," 10.

70. Music historian Joel Rudinow, in *Soul Music: Tracking the Spiritual Roots of Pop from Plato to Motown* (Ann Arbor: University of Michigan Press, 2010), explains syncopation as a "'displacement' of accent from presumed normal expectations," an "upsetting [of] rhythmic expectations" (121).

71. The pair was also known for a routine they called "Indefinite Talk," in which each interrupted the other before crucial information was given in a sentence but somehow knew what the content was, a kind of magically understood gapped communication; they also did what they called "mutilatin' the language" ("I's regusted"). Watkins judged that the pair "exacted more influence on the transition of black American stage humor than any other performers in the early twentieth century" (*On the Real Side*, 173).

72. For example, Steve, when asking "Didn't your boss raise you?" continues to move the conversation in its expected direction, from "salaries" to "wages" to "raise[s]," establishing a back-and-forth rhythm. But Sam, in his response, explodes—my pun intended—the existing signification of the word "raise" *and* the plot expectations about normal working conditions—in effect, the temporal and semiotic rhythm of the scene—introducing a fantastically violent element into the everyday.

73. This is not to ignore how Darwinian theory was also co-opted to naturalize imperial and racist hierarchies of worth.

74. Miller and Lyles as "A Pair of Black Aces," "Evolution," recorded Perfect Records, 12602, 18 October 1927. For their discography, see http://www.honkingduck.com/discography/discog_artist.php?like=MILLER%20%26%20LYLES.

75. Percy Hammond, "The Colored Folks in Another Child-like Imitation of Dull, White Extravaganza," *New York Herald Tribune*, 13 July 1927, n.p.

76. Alison Smith, review of *Rang Tang*, "The Stage," *The World*, 13 July 1927, n.p.

77. Ibid.

78. Miller and Lyles, "The Lost Aviators," Banner Records, 2173 (31 October 1927). A typescript of a slightly longer and more formally worded version of this scene, called "Non-Stop Flight," is in the Flournoy E. Miller Papers.

79. George Schuyler, "Blessed Are the Sons of Ham," *The Nation* 124.3220 (23 March 1927).

80. The Cameraman, "Colorful News 'Movies,'" *New York Amsterdam News*, 6 July 1927, 20, *ProQuest Historical Newspapers*.

81. Brooks, *Bodies in Dissent*, 5.

82. Schuyler, "Blessed Are the Sons of Ham."

83. Gilroy, *Black Atlantic*, 55.

84. Zora Neale Hurston, *Their Eyes Were Watching God* (New York: Perennial, 1990 [1937]), 51. For an analysis of Sam and Lige's conversation as predictive of the flood that overtakes Janie and Tea Cake at the end of the novel, see my essay, "Zora Neale Hurston and the Environmental Ethic of Risk," in *American Studies, Ecocriticism, and Citizenship: Thinking and Acting in the Local and Global Commons*, ed. Joni Adamson and Kimberly Ruffin (New York: Routledge, 2013).

85. Indeed, the Majority Leader of the Senate, Joe Robinson, announced Rogers's death in 1935 on the Senate floor attesting that Rogers was "probably the most widely

known private citizen and certainly the best beloved." Qtd. in Ben Yagoda, *Will Rogers: A Biography* (New York: Knopf, 1993), xi.

86. Peter C. Collins, "Will Rogers: Symbolic Man, Journalist, and Film Image," *Journal of Popular Culture* 9.4 (Spring 1976): 851.

87. Daniel Heath Justice, *Our Fire Survives the Storm: A Cherokee Literary History* (Minneapolis: University of Minnesota Press, 2006), 132.

88. "Simple Life and Kindly Manner Marked Life of Will Rogers," Fred Stone Scrapbook No. 25, p. 43, quoted in Collins, "Will Rogers," 858.

89. The New Orleans benefit on 1 June 1927 raised $48,000; see photo in *The Papers of Will Rogers: From the Broadway Stage to the National Stage (September 1915–July 1928*, ed. Steven K. Gragert and M. Jane Johansson (Norman: University of Oklahoma Press, 1996), 4:497. See *Will Rogers' Daily Telegrams*, ed. James M. Smallwood, Steven K. Gragert, assistant editor (Stillwater: Oklahoma State University Press, 1978), 1:92–95 and *Weekly Articles: Coolidge Years, 1927–1929* (Stillwater: Oklahoma State University Press, 1981), 3:40, 42. In later years, Rogers would go on more "tours of mercy" for other environmental disasters, prompting one to comment on Rogers's "Christ-like spirit of giving" (qtd. in Collins, "Will Rogers," 857).

90. Telegram from B. Patton Harrison to Will Rogers, 1 June 1927; see also telegram from John Barton Payne to Rogers, 1 June 1927 (Payne was the chairman of the American National Red Cross), both in *The Papers of Will Rogers*, 4:497, 498.

91. "Two Benefits Yield $20,000 Flood Fund," *New York Times*, 2 May 1927, *ProQuest Historical Newspapers*.

92. Yagoda, *Will Rogers*, 9, 13.

93. See ibid., 281, on a particularly vehement anti-Jacksonian speech made by Rogers.

94. Will Rogers, quoted in Justice, *Our Fire Survives the Storm*, 119.

95. Michael Rogin describes minstrelsy as "a white form of appropriative access to imagined black experience, with varying mixtures of fantasy and authenticity, mockery and envy, ecstasy and contempt." "Nowhere Left to Stand: The Burnt Cork Roots of Popular Culture," *Cineaste* 26.2 (2001).

96. Rogers thought *Birth of a Nation* was the "best old Picture there is" (Yagoda, *Will Rogers*, 231).

97. *The Will Rogers Scrapbook*, ed. Bryan B. Sterling (New York: Grosset and Dunlap, 1976), 59, 56.

98. On the experience of Africans and African Americans in Indian Territory, see Tiya Miles and Sharon Holland, introduction to *Crossing Waters, Crossing Worlds: The African Diaspora in Indian Country* (Durham: Duke University Press, 2006), 8–9; they describe how Indian Territory existed in the minds of black migrants as an idealized "haven" (8) at the turn of the century until these migrants encountered segregationist policies upon their arrival.

99. Rogers, Good Gulf Show radio broadcast, 14 April 1935, in Steven K. Gragert, ed., *Radio Broadcasts of Will Rogers* (Stillwater: Oklahoma State University Press, 1983), 121.

100. Will Rogers, "Will Rogers Urges Beating Up Owner of One-Crop Farm," *Washington Post*, 14 February 1927, 4, *ProQuest Historical Newspapers*.

101. Rogers, *Radio Broadcasts of Will Rogers*, 119.

102. Will Rogers, *Weekly Articles of Will Rogers: Roosevelt Years, 1933–1935*, ed. James

M. Smallwood and Steven K. Gragert (Stillwater: Oklahoma State University Press, 1981), 126.

103. Yagoda, *Will Rogers*, 221.

104. Barry, *Rising Tide*, 275, 109.

105. Rogers, "I Don't Butt in in Family Rows!" (no. 236), *Will Rogers' Weekly Articles*, vol. 3, ed. James M. Smallwood and Steven K. Gragert (Stillwater: Oklahoma State University Press, 1981), 42.

106. Will Rogers, "Dimes for Flood Victims," *Washington Post*, May 8, 1927, 8.

107. Will Rogers, "Will Rogers Wants Gray Trial Writers to Urge Flood Aid," *Washington Post*, 29 April 1927, 5, *ProQuest Historical Newspapers*.

108. Will Rogers, "Congress and the Mississippi," *Washington Post*, 15 May 1927, SM8, *ProQuest Historical Newspapers*.

109. Will Rogers, "Will Rogers Couples Cameras and Murderers," *New York Times*, 31 December 1927, 19, *ProQuest Historical Newspapers*.

110. Harry Carr, "The Lancer," *Los Angeles Times*, 31 May 1927, *ProQuest Historical Newspapers*.

111. Will Rogers, "Let's Give a Dime to the Flood Victims," *Weekly Articles*, 3:27.

112. John Crawford, "Will Rogers Knows More than He Pretends," 14 December 1924, BR2, *ProQuest Historical Newspapers*.

113. Will Rogers, "Congress Will Make River Behave," *Weekly Articles*, 3:28.

114. Rogers, "I Don't Butt in in Family Rows!" *Weekly Articles*, 3:43; see Justice, *Our Fire Survives the Storm*, on Rogers's critique of U.S. imperialism in Puerto Rico, Hawaii, Cuba, and the Philippines "which mirrored and perfected the brutal erasure of Indian sovereignty in the former Indian territory" (124).

115. Justice, *Our Fire Survives the Storm*, 124.

116. See Yagoda, *Will Rogers*, 232–33, for a description of the interview, which took place as part of Rogers's only semi-ironic diplomatic tour. Rogers reported that Mussolini "laughed and put his hands on both my shoulders and said in English, 'You can tell 'em Mussolini, R-e-g-u-l-a-r G-u-y. . . . Mussolini no Napoleon, want fight, always look mad; Mussolini, laugh, gay, like good time same as everybody else, maybe more so'—and he winked." I suspect that Rogers is actually "puncturing" Mussolini's own PR self-stylization as "of the people" more than purveying it here.

117. Collins argues that this was a signature Rogers rhetorical strategy ("Will Rogers," 863).

118. "Propaganda."

119. Walter Benjamin, "Prescriptions for Comedy Writers," *Radio Benjamin*, ed. Lecia Rosenthal, trans. Jonathan Lutes with Lisa Harries Schumann and Diana K. Reese (London: Verso, 2014), 360, 366.

Modernism within a Second Nature

1. Cleveland B. Chase, "Fighting the 'Father of Waters,'" *New York Times*, 27 November 1927, BR9, *ProQuest Historical Newspapers*.

2. James W. Thomas, *Lyle Saxon: A Critical Biography* (Birmingham, AL: Summa, 1991), 89–97, Saxon qtd. on 90. Saxon's manuscript journal from these weeks per-

forming flood rescue is housed at the Tulane University Library: Saxon, "Correspondence 1927 Jan–June," 4-1-44, Saxon Collection.

3. Saxon, *Father Mississippi*, 301, 304, 311, 310, 302, 313.

4. Ibid., 408, 307; Saxon qtd. in Thomas, *Lyle Saxon*, 97.

5. Saxon, *Father Mississippi*, 279.

6. On entanglements of "folk" celebration with movements as diverse as fascist nationalism, southern agrarianism, and Booker T. Washington's racial uplift program, as well as Zora Neale Hurston's alternate understanding of folk culture as migratory and evolving, see my "Zora Neale Hurston and the Environmental Ethic of Risk," 22.

7. Sterling A. Brown, "Ma Rainey," in *Folk-Say: A Regional Miscellany*, ed. Benjamin A. Botkin (Norman: University of Oklahoma Press, 1930), 278. Houston A. Baker Jr., in *Modernism and the Harlem Renaissance*, positions Sterling Brown's poem "Ma Rainey" as representing the arrival of the "indisputably modern moment in Afro-American discourse" (92); in particular, "it was the blending . . . of class and mass—*poetic* mastery discovered as a function of deformative *folk* sound—[which] constitutes the essence of black discursive modernism" (93). Jayna Brown takes exception to Brown's contrasting the "authentic" black folk suffering in the flood as against northern, light-skinned cabaret dancers, "situating them as willful and uncaring urban courtiers against their poor rural brethren" (*Babylon Girls*, 236).

8. Sterling A. Brown, "The Blues as Folk Poetry," in *Folk-Say* (1930), 339, 324, 329, 330, 331. Given my book's contention that "the earth" in the rural South is modern and artefactual, a "second nature," separations of earth-bound folk from earth-separated moderns become more difficult.

9. Mary Austin, "American Folk," in *Folk-Say* (1930), 287, 289, 288.

10. J. Frank Dobie, "Provincialism," *Folk-Say* (1930), 321.

11. Sterling A. Brown, "Children of the Mississippi," *Southern Road* (New York: Harcourt, Brace, 1932), 67–69.

12. In another flood poem, "Foreclosure," it is the animated and personified river who is the "treacherous" protagonist: though he had "built up [banks] for his children," "in his dotage / Whimsical and drunkenly turbulent, [he] / Cuts away the banks, steals away the loam" (*Southern Road*, 73).

13. Ruth Bass, "Ole Miss," in *Folk-Say: A Regional Miscellany*, ed. Benjamin A. Botkin (Norman: University of Oklahoma Press, 1931), 48, 50, 49, 55, 68, 56.

14. Walter Benjamin, "The Mississippi Flood of 1927" ["Die Mississippi-Überschwemmung 1927"], in *Radio Benjamin*, ed. Lecia Rosenthal, trans. Jonathan Lutes with Lisa Harries Schumann and Diana K. Reese (London: Verso, 2014), 260.

15. Walter Benjamin, "Reflections on Radio" (1930-31), in *Radio Benjamin*, 454; Benjamin elaborates: "Never has there been a genuine cultural institution that was not legitimized by the expertise it inculcated in the audience through its forms and technologies" (453).

16. Walter Benjamin, "Theses on the Philosophy of History," in *Illuminations*, ed. Hannah Arendt , trans. Harry Zohn (New York: Schocken, 1968), 257–58, 259, 261, 263.

17. Benjamin, "The Mississippi Flood of 1927," 265.

18. Esther Leslie, interview on "The Benjamin Broadcasts," *Archive on 4*, 24 May, 2014, http://www.bbc.co.uk/radio/player/b044b3lj.
19. Ibid., 260, 261, 262.
20. Ibid., 260.
21. Quoted in Barry, *Rising Tide*, 275; "dictators" were appointed in all the worst-hit states to run individual flood relief commissions.
22. See Barry, *Rising Tide*, for an in-depth account of the situation around the dynamiting (231–58).
23. Benjamin, "The Mississippi Flood of 1927," 265.
24. Walter Benjamin, "The Railway Disaster at the Firth of Tay," in *Radio Benjamin*, 260, 252.
25. Robin Walz, *Modernism* (Harlow, UK: Pearson Education, 2008), 16–17; Rita Barnard, "Modern American Fiction," in *Cambridge Companion to American Modernism*, ed. Walter B. Kalaidjian (New York: Cambridge University Press, 2005), 40. On modernization and embodiment, see Tim Armstrong, *Modernism, Technology, and the Body* (New York: Cambridge University Press, 1998), who discusses the contradictory sense of both bodily extension and bodily fragmentation or decomposition, especially 96–101. See Watson, *Reading for the Body*, for a summary of recent scholarship on modernism viewed as "the expressive response to a new sensorium created by the mechanical modes of information storage and transmission" (90); Watson places Hurston within this phenomenon of modernist writing (87–134).
26. Pericles Lewis, *The Cambridge Introduction to Modernism* (New York: Cambridge University Press, 2007), 11–17, quote on 11.
27. Although, of course, the eighteenth century expressed its own skepticism about the viability of reason and of political structures dependent upon human reason; the gothic genre on both sides of the Atlantic exemplified such alarmed uncertainty.
28. Michael H. Levenson, *A Genealogy of Modernism: A Study of English Literary Doctrine, 1908-1922* (New York: Cambridge University Press, 1984), 2.
29. See Eric Auerbach's classic description of literary modernism as typified by Virginia Woolf in "The Brown Stocking" chapter of *Mimesis: The Representation of Reality in Western Literature* (Princeton: Princeton University Press, 2013), 525–53.
30. Levenson, *Genealogy*, 10.
31. Anne Raine, "Ecocriticism and Modernism," *Oxford Handbooks Online* (March 2014).
32. Raine observes that "engaging with modernism has not been a first priority for eco-criticism" ("Ecocriticism and Modernism," 2). She cites Carol Cantrell's work ("The Flesh of the World: Virginia Woolf's *Between the Acts*," in *The Green Studies Reader: From Romanticism to Ecocriticism*, ed. Lawrence Coupe [London: Routledge, 2000]), Douglas Mao, *Solid Objects: Modernism and the Test of Production* (Princeton: Princeton University Press, 1998), and a few other brief treatments of individual writers as "just beginning to work out what an ecocritical or planetary account of modernism might look like" (2). See also John Parham, ed., *The Environmental Tradition in English Literature* (London: Ashgate, 2002), with chapters on Woolf, D. H. Lawrence, and Ted Hughes. As I'll discuss, Faulkner has received eco-critical attention, but the focus tends to be on his work after the mid-1930s.

The field has had a strong connection to Romanticism and Transcendentalism since the 1990s; see Bate, *Romantic Ecology* and Lawrence Buell, *The Environmental Imagination: Thoreau, Nature Writing, and the Formation of American Culture* (Cambridge, MA: Harvard University Press, 1995). In recent years, the field has embraced the early modern period, Victorian writers, and contemporary transnational literature and culture, often in connection with the Environmental Justice movement. For the American early modern milieu, see, for example, an early work of feminist ecocriticism, Annette Kolodny, *The Lay of the Land: Metaphor as Experience and History in American Life and Letters* (Chapel Hill: University of North Carolina Press, 1975), and Timothy Sweet, *American Georgics: Economy and Environment in American Literature, 1580–1864* (Philadelphia: University of Pennsylvania Press, 2002); Gabriel Egan, *Green Shakespeare: From Ecopolitics to Ecocriticism* (New York: Routledge, 2006); Robert N. Watson, *Back to Nature: The Green and the Real in the Late Renaissance* (Philadelphia: University of Pennsylvania Press, 2011); Simon C. Estok, *Ecocriticism and Shakespeare: Reading Ecophobia* (New York: Palgrave Macmillan, 2011); *Ecocritical Shakespeare*, ed. Lynne Bruckner and Daniel Brayton (London: Ashgate, 2011); Ken Hiltner, *What Else Is Pastoral? Renaissance Literature and the Environment* (Ithaca, NY: Cornell University Press, 2011); Daniel Brayton, *Shakespeare's Ocean: An Ecocritical Exploration* (Charlottesville: University of Virginia Press, 2012); and John Parham, *Green Man Hopkins: Poetry and the Victorian Ecological Imagination* (Amsterdam: Editions Rodopi, 2010). And, finally, for studies that take a largely contemporary and transnational approach, see Ursula Heise, *Sense of Place and Sense of Planet: The Environmental Imagination of the Global* (New York: Oxford University Press, 2008); Nixon, *Slow Violence*; and Adamson and Ruffin, *American Studies, Ecocriticism, and Citizenship*.

33. Lawrence Buell's attention, in *Writing for an Endangered World: Literature, Culture, and Environment in the U.S. and Beyond* (Cambridge, MA: Harvard University Press, 2001), to modernist authors (including both Wright and Faulkner), the modernizing South, urban environmental experience, breaking down the dichotomy of rural/urban, and generally situating Anglophone modernism as a response to "first nature becoming reproduced by second nature" (245) is an important exception to the above characterization; all of these features, along with his chapter titled "Watershed Aesthetics" (243–65), have provided an important impetus for this book.

Chapter 6

1. See Persky, *The Burden of Dependency* on the longstanding southern perception of existing as a colonial economy vis-à-vis an external, capitalized power; on Faulkner's contemporaries—as varied ideologically as Donald Davidson, W. J. Cash, and Rupert Vance—taking this view, see 123, 128, 144. Pascale Casanova attests that Faulkner has "offered the novelists of the poorest countries the possibility of giving acceptable literary form to the most repugnant realities," acting as a "formidable force for accelerating literary time" (*The World Republic of Letters*, trans. M. B. DeBevoise [Cambridge, MA: Harvard University Press, 2004], 337). Though

Casanova does not mention Faulkner's connection of the rural tropics and semi-tropics with environmental degradation and disaster, this seems to me one of the ways in which Faulkner may continue to be a "force" for writers and readers in the Global South.

2. For recent work on the importance not only of a symbolic or mythic "Nature" but of southern environmental history in Faulkner's work, see Donald M. Kartiganer and Ann J. Abadie, eds., *Faulkner and the Natural World: Faulkner and Yoknapatawpha, 1996* (Jackson: University Press of Mississippi, 1999); Lawrence Buell's contribution, "Faulkner and the Claims of the Natural World," in particular, attends to "environmental actuality" (4); Joseph R. Urgo and Ann J. Abadie, *Faulkner and the Ecology of the South: Faulkner and Yoknapatawpha, 2003* (Jackson: University Press of Mississippi, 2005); Bart H. Welling, "A Meeting with Old Ben: Seeing and Writing Nature in Faulkner's *Go Down, Moses,*" *Mississippi Quarterly* 55.4 (2002): 461–96; and Matthew Wynn Sivils, "Faulkner's Ecological Disturbances," *Mississippi Quarterly* 59.3/4 (Summer 2006): 489–502. Critics have assumed that Faulkner does not begin representing, and thinking through, the Flood of 1927 until he wrote *If I Forget Thee, Jerusalem* in the late 1930s. Robert Jackson, in "The Southern Disaster Complex," *Mississippi Quarterly* 63.3/4 (Summer 2010), argues that Faulkner engages in a broader southern disaster rhetoric but that, in his tendency to use classical allusion, renders those disasters elemental and blameless. I would argue, to the contrary, that Faulkner does represent the environmental and historical underpinnings of disaster but uses classical tragedy to claim for southern history an epic—and sometimes mock-epic—gravitas.

3. See Lucinda Hardwick MacKethan, *The Dream of Arcady: Place and Time in Southern Literature* (Baton Rouge: Louisiana State University Press, 1980) on the persistence of a pastoral mode throughout Faulkner's career (153–80).

4. *Flags in the Dust*, the now reconstituted longer novel out of which *Sartoris* (1929) was drawn, was begun in 1926 and finished in September 1927 (see Joseph Blotner, *Faulkner: A Biography* [New York: Random House, 1974], 1:531–57); in it he is certainly considering how fast cars, airplanes, and modern war clattered up against small-town Mississippi, but I do not detect flood musings in it. I suspect that the book already had its own concerns established by the spring of 1927 and that it took Faulkner a bit of time to begin his imaginative processing of the flood.

5. Faulkner told Harrison Smith in February 1934 that the theme he would explore in *Absalom, Absalom!* involved how "a man . . . outraged the land, and the land then turned and destroyed the man's family." Qtd. in Charles Aiken, *William Faulkner and the Southern Landscape* (Athens: University of Georgia Press, 2009), 151.

6. In 2001, Lawrence Buell positioned Faulkner's fiction as a response to the modernization of his region, especially to the "ruthless exploitation of rurality by industry and agribusiness" (*Writing for an Endangered World*, 171). Buell assumed that Faulkner misinterpreted the 1927 flood as a natural occurrence and writes, "Had Faulkner realized that the flood was exacerbated by unwise manipulations of the river [and] . . . by a long succession of engineering feats," then "Old Man" might have been the eco-critique that *Go Down, Moses* was of the timber industry, and Faulkner might have "developed a coherent environmental ethic" (176). As chapter 3 demonstrated, the diagnosis of the flood as anthropogenic was all over the south-

ern, and national, public sphere in 1927; recovering Faulkner's early awareness of the catastrophic consequences of poor watershed management allows us to extend our understanding of him as a career-long environmental writer and to recover what was indeed a "coherent" if evolving "environmental ethic."

7. See Blotner's extensive discussion of the importance of A. E. Housman's poetry for Faulkner's youthful poetry (*Faulkner*, 1:183–87); he remarks how "Faulkner's lyrics . . . so often sound[ed] the elegiac note with the pastoral" (187). The material is slightly different in Blotner's two-volume and his condensed, one-volume, biography of Faulkner; I have thus consulted and will cite both editions.

8. Ibid., 1:82.

9. A fellow University of Mississippi student, Louis Cochran, remembering how other students estimated Faulkner, commented that some "thought him queer" (qtd. in Joseph Blotner, *Faulkner: A Biography* [one-volume edition] [New York: Random House, 1984], 80).

10. William Faulkner, *The Wild Palms* [*If I Forget Thee, Jerusalem*] (New York: Vintage, 1995 [1939]), 20.

11. William Faulkner, "Mississippi," *Holiday* (April 1954): 45, reprinted in *William Faulkner: Critical Collection*, ed. Leland H. Cox (Detroit: Gale, 1982), 33–60.

12. To Philip Weinstein's point in "'Make It New': Faulkner and Modernism," in *A Companion to William Faulkner* ed. Richard C. Moreland (Malden, MA: Blackwell, 2007), that Faulkner's "gifts" as a modernist pointed him not to contemporaneous external events but "inward" (353), I would say that he *did* focus on major events of his time but represented them by delineating how they reached that inward—perceptual, phenomenological, psychological—place.

13. William Faulkner, *The Sound and the Fury* (New York: Vintage, 1990 [1929]), 3.

14. For an overview of this scholarship, see the chapter titled "Psychological Criticism" in *A Companion to Faulkner Studies*, ed. Charles A. Peek and Robert W. Hamblin, which traces psychoanalytic readings of *The Sound and the Fury* back to 1957. See also *Faulkner and Psychology: Faulkner and Yoknapatawpha, 1991*, ed. Donald M. Kartiganer and Ann J. Abadie (Jackson: University Press of Mississippi, 1994), especially the two essays on *The Sound and the Fury*. The locus classicus of this approach is John T. Irwin, *Doubling and Incest/Repetition and Revenge: A Speculative Reading of Faulkner* (Baltimore: Johns Hopkins University Press, 1975); see, for a recent claim to Freud's ongoing relevance to Faulkner Studies, Michael Zeitlin, "Returning to Freud and *The Sound and the Fury*," *Faulkner Journal* 13.1/2 (Fall 1997): 57–77.

15. The one essay to address ecology in *The Sound and the Fury* reads "ecology" as the "venue" in which "dysfunctional family relationship[s]" find "expression"; in other words, nonhuman nature is primarily a figural site rather than a constitutive domain. Eric Gary Anderson, "Environed Blood: Ecology and Violence in *The Sound and the Fury* and *Sanctuary*," in *Faulkner and the Ecology of the South*, ed. Urgo and Abadie, 35, 38.

16. Faulkner to Morton Goldman (18 February 1935), in *Selected Letters of William Faulkner*, ed. Joseph Blotner (New York: Random House, 1977), 89.

17. William Faulkner, *As I Lay Dying* (New York: Vintage, 1990 [1930]), 45; this is Dr. Peabody's diagnosis.

18. Hortense Spillers, in "Topographical Topics: Faulknerian Space," *Mississippi Quarterly* 57 (2004): 535–68, shows how pervasively Faulkner spatializes history, and historicizes space; in particular, she writes that the risk-saturated "poetics" of the Mississippi "might be described as a topographical obsession" (549) for Faulkner and that no matter which river Faulkner wrote about, he was always thinking about the Mississippi (554).
19. Sivils points out that environmental experience, for Faulkner, was always connected to "race, poverty, class, and other social factors" and touches upon Faulkner's notation of land use in *Sound and the Fury*. "Faulkner's Ecological Disturbances," 489, 492.
20. In saying this, I mean to augment rather than dismiss appraisals—like the one Weinstein offers in "'Make It New': Faulkner and Modernism" (344–45)—of Faulkner's handling of the Freudian world he encountered.
21. Faulkner finished this sentence by saying: "but I have never read him. Neither did Shakespeare. I doubt if Melville did either, and I am sure Moby Dick didn't." In that final phrase, he suggests that fundamental truths, unlike human systems of organization of that truth that invariably fail to capture it (like psychoanalysis), are invested in nature ("The Art of Fiction XII: William Faulkner," *Paris Review* [Spring 1956], in *William Faulkner: Critical Collection*, 20).
22. This conversation between inner and outer weather, between a man tossed by storms within and a tree by winds without, comes from Robert Frost, "The Tree at My Window," *West-Running Brook* (New York: Holt, 1928), 25.
23. Sigmund Freud, "The 'Uncanny,'" in *The Standard Edition of the Complete Psychological Works of Sigmund Freud, Volume XVII (1917–1919): An Infantile Neurosis and Other Works*, trans. J. Strachey (London: Hogarth Press, 1955), 248, 221, 225, Psychoanalytic Electronic Publishing April 2011.
24. Ibid., 221–22.
25. Ibid., 222–23.
26. *Oxford Eagle*, 26 May 1927, 1.
27. Blotner, *Faulkner*, 1:288, 323.
28. See William Alexander Percy's largely self-exculpatory account of his, and by proxy his father's, policies of concentration camp management in *Lanterns on the Levee: Recollections of a Planter's Son* (Baton Rouge: Louisiana State University Press, 1973 [1941]), 242–69. It appears that Percy allowed his own intentions—to evacuate black sharecroppers—to be countermanded by his father LeRoy Percy's decision to keep his laborers in Greenville so that they would not relocate; though the childhood chapters of his memoir show Will Percy capable of depicting African American characters with admiration and sympathy, he fails to portray any black character as a fully realized adult, even, or especially, his African American driver and lover, Ford (on Percy's homosexuality, see Barry, *Rising Tide*, 420–21). Because his account of the flood is marked by this strong defensiveness and paternalism, it is a less interesting text than Lyle Saxon's account, so I have not given it treatment in this book; moreover, the Percy family dominates Barry's narrative in *Rising Tide*. Faulkner's close friend Ben Wasson, whom he visited often in the early 1920s in Greenville and who perhaps communicated to Faulkner about the explosiveness of the local situation in a way that white southern presses would not have, was living

in Greenwich Village and working in the publishing industry while Faulkner was revising *Sound and the Fury*; see Blotner, *Faulkner*, 1:366, 582–83.

29. Blotner, *Faulkner*, 1:394, 524, 555, 583.

30. Saxon, *Father Mississippi*, 290.

31. Lyle Saxon, *New York Herald Tribune*, Book Section, 13 October 1929. On the Saxon connection, see Blotner, *Faulkner*, 1:583, 587, 592, 632.

32. On how contemporaneous southerners viewed "the role of the southern compradores in furthering northern business interests," see Persky, *Burden of Dependency*, 113.

33. Spillers, in "Topographical Topics: Faulknerian Space," points out that, for Quentin, "the river is back there waiting. . . . way back for Quentin to a piece of psychic life that has gotten away from him" (548).

34. Stephen H. Kellert, in *In the Wake of Chaos: Unpredictable Order in Dynamical Systems* (Chicago: University of Chicago Press, 1993), is here describing Lev Landau's 1944 work on turbulence (9).

35. Qtd. in Blotner, *Faulkner*, 1:371.

36. See my *American Curiosity: Cultures of Natural History in the Colonial British Atlantic World* (Chapel Hill: University of North Carolina Press, 2006), chaps. 5 and 6.

37. Freud, "The 'Uncanny,'" 239.

38. "The Basement Blues," in *Blues: An Anthology*, ed. W. C. Handy (New York: Boni, 1926), rev. ed. Jerry Silverman (New York: Macmillan, 1972), 154–57. On Faulkner the teenager listening to Handy at dances, see Blotner, *Faulkner*, 1:155.

39. Faulkner, introduction to *The Sound and the Fury* (1946), reprinted in *William Faulkner: Essays, Speeches and Public Letters*, ed. James B. Meriwether (New York: Modern Library, 2004), 299.

40. Donna Haraway might call the epistemology Caddy learns from Frony and other black members of the household "*situated knowledge*," a phrase she devised in "Situated Knowledges: The Science Question in Feminism and the Privilege of Partial Perspective," *Feminist Studies* 14.3 (Autumn 1988): 581. Haraway distinguishes this "feminist critical empiricism" from "the god trick of seeing everything from nowhere" (582) that modern optical technologies render into everyday practice; situated knowledges, to the contrary, resist our "tempting myths" that this vision is "a route to disembodiment" and "transcendence" (582).

41. See Charles A. Peek's excellent essay "'That Evening Sun(g)': Blues Inscribing Black Spaces in White Stories," *Southern Quarterly* 42.3 (Spring 2004): 130–50. For the chronology of Faulkner's composition of Nancy's story, see Blotner, *Faulkner*, 1:565–566. Curiously, H. L. Mencken was its first editor and publisher, convincing Faulkner to change Jesus' name lest it offend readers.

42. Her position suggests another blues song, Handy and Dave Elman's "Make Me One Pallet on Your Floor" (1923).

43. William Faulkner, "Pantaloon in Black," *Go Down, Moses* (New York: Vintage, 1990), 142.

44. "Build Up the Levees," *Commercial Appeal*, 17 April 1927, n.p.

45. Saikku, *This Delta, This Land*, 86.

46. Associating a knoll and a graveyard brings to mind the Indian burial mounds that kept people safe in the 1927 flood.

47. One could argue that Louis Hatcher typifies the kind of "Watershed Aesthetics" and epistemology that Lawrence Buell ends his *Writing for an Endangered World* by advocating: "Thinking 'watershed' . . . challenges parochialism not only of jurisdictional borders of whatever sort but also of 'natural' borders that fail to take larger interdependencies into account, interdependencies that finally reach out to include the whole planet" (264). Quentin remembers Hatcher's insight while he himself is making a series of mental connections: between the Charles River watershed and that of the Mississippi; Boston's Atlantic port and the Gulf South's; the country and the city; and the ethnic strife of Boston with the racial strife of Mississippi. All of this mental work of avowing interdependency on Quentin's part suggests that he is attempting, with Hatcher's guidance, to herald a spiritually attuned watershed cosmology and ethic but does not see himself as personally eligible to enter its promised land.

48. William Faulkner, "That Evening Sun," in *Selected Short Stories of William Faulkner* (New York: Modern Library, 1993), 96.

49. Jason also registers the connection between his family's physical and his region's environmental disempowerment when he links Benjy's castration with deforestation and the larger timber industry: "I could hear the Great American Gelding snoring away like a planing mill" (263).

50. Ralph Ellison, "The Blues," *New York Review of Books*, 6 February 1964.

51. I am using the phrase "environmental unconscious" in a more direct nod to Freud—arguing that the flood constitutes the repressed content of *The Sound and the Fury*—than does Lawrence Buell in *Writing for an Endangered World*; Buell coins the phrase to indicate both human blockages and breakthroughs concerning perception and articulation about environments (22).

52. Faulkner was clearly interested in how people are affected by their environments, and his literary project has some overlap with the work of the contributors to *Folk-Say* I mentioned earlier. I would argue, though, that Faulkner would not have imagined that an environment produces one kind of "folk" but that environmental history prods humans in myriad and unpredictable ways.

53. See, for example, John Limon, "Addie in No Man's Land," in *Faulkner and War: Faulkner and Yoknapatawpha*, ed. Noel Polk and Ann J. Abadie (Oxford: University Press of Mississippi, 2001); and Ted Atkinson, *Faulkner and the Great Depression: Aesthetics, Ideology, and Cultural Politics* (Athens: University of Georgia Press, 2006). Atkinson writes that "*As I Lay Dying* reads as arguably the first quintessential Depression novel" (194).

54. Dewey, *The Public and Its Problems*, 131.

55. Limon, "Addie in No Man's Land," 39, 45. Cheryl Lester understands the novel to be an allegory of the "collective upheaval of traditional rural life" ("As They Lay Dying: Rural Depopulation and Social Dislocation as a Structure of Feeling," *Faulkner Journal* 21.1/2 [Fall 2005/Spring 2006]: 28). Susan Willis likewise argues that "the family's migration is a geographic metaphor describing [the] demographic change" of agriculturalism to urbanism ("Learning from the Banana," *American Quarterly* 39.4 [Winter 1987]: 587). By contrast, John T. Matthews argues that the Bundrens' rural mode was not removed from modernity but rather had "already been *constituted* by the dialectical history of capitalist agriculture, commodified economic and

social relations, and the homogenization of mass culture in the nineteenth-century South" ("*As I Lay Dying* in the Machine Age," *boundary* 2 19.1 [1992]: 74); and Jolene Hubbs argues that the novel is not so much about migration toward modernity/urbanization but about the ways in which modernity impinges on the rural world ("William Faulkner's Rural Modernism," *Mississippi Quarterly* 61.3 [2008]: 461–75). Agreeing with Matthews and Hubbs, I read the river scenes not as a symbolic crossing into modernity but rather as a key symptom of modernity's decades-long presence in the rural world.

56. The title of *As I Lay Dying*, in its quotation of Agamemnon's speech to Odysseus in Book XI of the *Odyssey*, does, however, add a layer of classical epic to the modern southern political milieu.

57. Blotner, *Faulkner*, 144.

58. See Albert D. Kirwan, *Revolt of the Rednecks: Mississippi Politics, 1876–1925* (New York: Harper, 1951), 103–21, quote on 118. And see Matthews, "*As I Lay Dying* in the Machine Age" (82), for mention of Governors Whitfield and Vardaman.

59. James C. Cobb, *The Most Southern Place on Earth: The Mississippi Delta and the Roots of Regional Identity* (Oxford: Oxford University Press, 1992), 146–47.

60. Kirwan, *Revolt*, 144, 164–77.

61. Ibid., 146. "The White Chief" wore his hair long and flowing like men of an earlier generation and appeared at rallies in an eight-wheeled lumber cart pulled by white oxen, where his supporters wore red ties. All were theatrically embracing the epithets "cattle" and "rednecks" that had been angrily given to them by LeRoy Percy. See Blotner, *Faulkner*, 129–32, 144.

62. Whitfield's victory was attributed to the influence of the new female vote (Kirwan, *Revolt*, 303–5). That Whitfield is a man of the cloth, given to oratorical fervor and a kind of passionate consummation with his congregation in open-air meetings, also suggests Faulkner's sly nod to the South's strong conversion to Methodism in the 1740s under the spell of the famous eighteenth-century itinerant Methodist minister George Whitefield (pronounced Whitfield).

63. Wilbur J. Cash, "The Mind of the South," *American Mercury* 18.70 (October 1929): 192, 189, 186, 187, 188.

64. See, for example, Willis, "Learning from the Banana," who sees Addie as representing "the unmediated connection with organic process," something Faulkner treats in a "disparaging mode" (588); Mary Jane Dickerson argues in "Some Sources of Faulkner's Myth in *As I Lay Dying*," *Mississippi Quarterly* (Summer 1966): 132–42 that specifically, in Addie and Dewey Dell, we see the Demeter-Persephone relationship (134) or really an inverted version of that myth, since both want to abjure their fertility.

65. I would argue that she is not then "a maternal Eve at one with the immemorial earth" (even if ironized) as Andre Bleikasten argues in *Faulkner's "As I Lay Dying,"* trans. Roger Little (Bloomington: Indiana University Press, 1973), 76, 77 but an index of the vulnerability and quasi-absurdity of cotton monoculture. As Candace Waid puts it in *The Signifying Eye: Seeing Faulkner's Art* (Athens: University of Georgia Press, 2013), "Like the cotton, Dewey Dell is harvested: reaped at the end of the row" (92); moreover, Dewey Dell "embodies the wages of materialism" as set against Addie's matriarchal power (86).

66. Watson G. Branch, "Darl Bundren's 'Cubistic' Vision," in *William Faulkner's "As I Lay Dying": A Critical Casebook*, ed. Dianne L. Cox (New York: Garland, 1985), 119.

67. Armstrong writes that because of technologies like the telephone, men "live in wider distances, and think in larger figures" (*Modernism, Technology, and the Body*, 83); he calls this process within modernity, and modernist culture, a "mechano-morphism" of the body (84). World War I, moreover, is linked to both a "man-machine fantasy" of powerful extension and bodily disintegration (95).

68. William Faulkner to Mrs. M. C. Faulkner, 18 August 1925 and 22 September 1925, *Selected Letters of William Faulkner*, ed. Blotner, 13, 24. See also Homer Pettey, "Perception and the Destruction of Being in *As I Lay Dying*," *Faulkner Journal* 19.1 (2003): 27–46, who elaborates that Faulkner learned from Cezanne that art, more than representing the world, needed to materialize perception (27–28) and from the Futurists that art could mix memory and sight (28n1).

69. Quoted in Richard Cork, *Vorticism and Abstract Art in the First Machine Age: Volume One, Origins and Development* (London: Gordon Fraser, 1976), 283.

70. See Leah Dickerman, introduction to *Dada: Zurich, Berlin, Hanover, Cologne, New York, Paris* (Washington, DC: National Gallery of Art/DAP, 2005), 7, 9.

71. See Brigid Doherty, "See: 'We Are All Neurasthenics'! or, the Trauma of Dada Montage," *Critical Inquiry* 24.1 (Autumn 1997), esp. 111–12.

72. Tristan Tzara, "Dada Manifesto," in *Dada Painters and Poets: An Anthology*, ed. Robert Motherwell (Boston: G. K. Hall, 1981 [1951]), 78.

73. Tristan Tzara, "An Introduction to Dada," in *Dada Painters and Poets*, ed. Motherwell, 403.

74. Dickerman, introduction to *Dada*, 7.

75. Richard Huelsenbeck, quoting his own German Dadaist manifesto in "En Avant Dada: A History of Dadaism" (1920), in *Dada Painters and Poets*, ed. Motherwell, 24.

76. *Faulkner in the University*, ed. Frederick L. Gwynn and Joseph L. Blotner (Charlottesville: University Press of Virginia, 1959), 87.

77. Or, "It wont balance" (96).

78. William Faulkner, *Absalom, Absalom!* (New York: Vintage, 1990), 142.

79. Cash sent a letter to Odum in 1929 laying out his ideas for the book-length *Mind of the South*; see Fred C. Hobson, *Tell About the South: The Southern Rage to Explain* (Baton Rouge: Louisiana State University Press, 1983), 245. On Odum, see also George Tindall, "The Significance of Howard W. Odum," *Journal of Southern History* 24 (August 1958): 285–307; and Morton Sosna, *In Search of the Silent South* (New York: Columbia University Press, 1977), 42–59.

80. Daniel Joseph Singal, *The War Within: From Victorian to Modernist Thought in the South, 1919–1945* (Chapel Hill: University of North Carolina Press, 1982), 116, 131. Odum also termed his method "descriptive studies" or "regional portraiture" (131). Odum became increasingly interested, in the 1930s, in thinking about how the southern region could be reintegrated into the United States, restoring in the process a sense of national balance; see his magnum opus, *Southern Regions of the United States* (Chapel Hill: University of North Carolina Press, 1936).

81. This phrase belongs to a 1925 article in *Social Forces* that Odum edited, by a Kentucky-born sociologist named Luther Lee Bernard, called "The Concept of

Progress: III. The Scientific Phase" (37). See Hobson, *Tell About the South*, on how the southern sociologist seemed to "abhor the concrete, the organic, and the religious" and favored "the abstract, the theoretical, and the scientific"; he tells how Nashville Agrarian Donald Davidson feared that the "southern sociologist of the 1920s and 1930s would transform the entire South into a gigantic laboratory for social experimentation" (181).

82. Singal, *The War Within*, 133. Singal argues that it was "this grounding in organicism that helped guide Odum to portraiture" (133).

83. As regards William Faulkner's awareness of the new southern self-criticism, it seems quite likely, as someone who through New York and New Orleans literary circles must have become aware of Mencken's *American Mercury* and as someone who had his ear to the ground about the place of the South in the national imagination, that he would have known Cash's 1929 "The Mind of the South." In terms of the new sociology dedicated to quantification and equilibrium, I think it likely that Faulkner would have, as he traveled in cosmopolitan intellectual circles in the 1920s, been apprised of this pervasive language and mentality of social analysis. That Odum was positively cited by Cash and that Odum's apparently heretical *Journal of Social Forces* was all over the southern papers in 1925 suggests that Faulkner would have known who the University of North Carolina sociologist was and even been exposed to excerpts from the journal.

84. In the figure of Cash, there is probably too a satire of the physical sciences, especially engineering, whose tools were revealed to be, at their worst, dangerous and, at their best, ineffectual in the 1927 flood.

85. Aiken, *William Faulkner and the Southern Landscape*, 145, 147; quote is from Eugene W. Hilgard, 1860.

86. Cora corroborates this impression as she sees Addie's body as "wasted," making "no more of a hump" under the quilt "than a rail would"; this overindustrialized iron rail body fittingly has eyes like "sockets of iron" (8).

87. Jethro Tull was a well-known early eighteenth-century English innovator of the "New Husbandry" of mechanized farming, an implement designer, and writer of the treatise *The horse-Hoeing husbandry*, in which he says such practical things as "fine Language will not fill a Farmer's Barn" (Jethro Tull, *The horse-Hoeing husbandry: or, an essay on the principles of tillage and vegetation. Wherein is shewn a method of introducing a sort of vineyard-culture into the corn-fields* [Dublin: Rhames, 1733], iv). See Ernest Clarke, "Tull, Jethro (bap. 1674, d. 1741)," rev. G. E. Mingay, *Oxford Dictionary of National Biography* (New York: Oxford University Press, 2004).

88. Bleikasten, in *Faulkner's "As I Lay Dying*," appreciates the "liquid catastrophe" (112) at the novel's center, as well as the interpenetration of characters and environment, but interprets the water more symbolically and existentially than as a symptom of history (111–12).

89. Faulkner, "Mississippi," 45.

90. Christopher T. White, in "The Modern Magnetic Animal: *As I Lay Dying* and the Uncanny Zoology of Modernism," *Journal of Modern Literature* 31.3 (Spring 2008): 81–101, argues that animals in the novel "expose the limitations of *logos*" and the traditional philosophical privileging of "the (human) subject" (82); they "[haunt]

the text" (84). Certainly the animated, or animal, force that seems here to dispatch a part-goat emissary to foil the humans' plot seems to exemplify the "limitations" of human communication, epistemology, and sociality. Darl's attention to the language of this animal (its "clucks" and "murmurs" [141]) and his wanting to dissolve into its force pegs him as "insane" within human law.

91. Reck, "Utter Desolation Rules Flood Stricken Region"; Brickell, "Again the Old Dragon Mississippi Fumes."

92. When Jewel's body is joined to his horse, their combined form undergoes a dynamic apotheosis. Moreover, a martial quality attaches to Jewel as he is described as having a "wooden" face staring out of "the visor of a helmet" (94).

93. See Blotner, *Faulkner*, 550; Faulkner said this in response to a query from the *Chicago Daily Tribune* in the summer of 1927.

94. See chapter 72, titled "The Monkey-Rope," in Herman Melville, *Moby Dick, or, The Whale* (1851).

95. Faulkner produces an inversion of the *Moby Dick* epilogue in which the "coffin lifebuoy" rockets out of the vortex to save Ishmael, as if it was sent by his bosom friend Queequeg so that Vitalism, mystic indecipherability, and amity might not die. In other words, Melville's novel ends on a profoundly Romantic gesture of vestigial Vitalism.

96. Armstid explains that Cash repeatedly asks for his tools; the family "shoved them under the side of the bed, where he could reach his hand and touch them" (186).

97. Cash's revelation about the social construction of mental normativity is reminiscent of Quentin's insights on the topic of race after he meets Deacon and Mr. Compson's on the topic of virginity.

98. Dale, "Human Wreckage Is Flood Problem."

99. At the novel's end, when Peabody suggests that the family behead their father at the nearest sawmill, he voices the rage against Anse nobody from within the family will. I suspect he produces in the children an ambivalent sense of vindication and shame not unlike liberal southerners might have felt when reading one of Mencken's barbed assaults on southern yokeldom.

100. See 209, 213, and 224 for a record of Jewel's nonwhite skin.

101. Erin E. Edwards, in "Extremities of the Body: The Anoptic Corporeality of *As I Lay Dying*," *Modern Fiction Studies* 55.4 (Winter 2009): 739–64, argues that there is "a blind, often grotesque familiarity with an ambient corporeality" (743), a familiarity that produces "epistemological aporia" (743); she also points out that "the natural world and one's sense of place are already Other, already an opaquely monitoring force that awakens self-reflection" (754). I very much agree with this reading but would argue that this isn't a kind of ahistorical corporeality at work but Faulkner's representation of the disturbed corporeality of a modernized nature.

102. Interestingly, Calvin Bedient describes "Darl's mind" as "flowing everywhere like the flood waters of the river—but flowing because unformed, because it has no home in itself, no principle of containment" ("Pride and Nakedness: *As I Lay Dying*," in *William Faulkner Critical Collection*, 209). For Bedient, the river is a metaphor for epistemology; I would argue, by contrast, that, along with the war, it is the river's derangement by modernization that leaves his mind without a "home."

103. Cathy Caruth explains that "since the traumatic event is not experienced as it oc-

curs, it is fully evident only in connection with another place, and in another time" (Caruth, ed., *Trauma: Explorations in Memory* [Baltimore: Johns Hopkins University Press, 1995], 8).

104. Dickson, "Flood Changes Region into Valley of Sorrow," 1.

105. Williams, *Americans and Their Forests*, 252.

106. Atkinson situates Darl's revolt against property in the context of rural unrest begun in the 1920s (*Faulkner and the Great Depression*, 186).

107. Hoover speaks of property redistribution in his interview with Alexander, "Herbert Hoover Wins Hearts of Folks."

108. See Louis D. Rubin, ed., *I'll Take My Stand: The South and the Agrarian Tradition by Twelve Southerners* (New York: Harper and Brothers, 1930).

109. Tzara, "Dada Manifesto," 78; Hugo Ball, "Dada Fragments" (1916–17), reprinted in *Dada Painters and Poets*, ed. Motherwell, 51.

110. In 1906, John Philip Sousa bewailed "The Menace of Mechanical Music" represented by the gramophone because it would be a poor "substitute for human skill, intelligence, and soul" and injure "artistic manifestation." *Appleton's Magazine* 8.3 (September 1906): 278, quoted in Sebastian D. G. Knowles, "Death by Gramophone," *Journal of Modern Literature* 27.1 (2003): 2.

111. Lester argues in "As They Lay Dying" that the family's journey has shown how the forces of modernity "simultaneously solicit and reject them as middle class subjects, while neutralizing . . . the counter-hegemonic or alternative pressure they might otherwise exert as working-class subjects" (31).

112. A term coined by the short story writer O. Henry in *Cabbages and Kings* (New York: Doubleday, 1904), his fictional study of Honduras, its mixture of oligarchical rule and laborers' poverty, and its reliance on one export cultivar.

113. See Hosam Aboul-Ela, *Other South: Faulkner, Coloniality, and the Mariategui Tradition* (Pittsburgh: University of Pittsburgh Press, 2007) for more elaboration on how postbellum white southerners saw themselves as part of the United States' imperial periphery; Ring, in *Problem South*, explains that within the push to develop tropical medicine for a new American empire, the U.S. South also came to be treated as a "tropical Other, as a diseased and degenerate space" (84), afflicted with a "tropical pathology" (85). See also her fourth chapter, "The Poor White Problem as the 'New Race Question'" (135–74), for help in analyzing the Bundrens' blackening skin; and Antonio Gramsci, "Some Aspects of the Southern Question," *Selections from Political Writings, 1921–1926* (London: Electric Book Company, 1978).

114. Cash, "The Mind of the South," 192.

115. This appraisal comes from the protagonist of Faulkner's "Delta Autumn," in *Go Down, Moses* (New York: Vintage, 1990 [1942]), 347.

116. I am making a slightly different point here than does Matthews in "*As I Lay Dying* in the Machine Age," when he argues that Faulkner "needed to exorcise the strictly aestheticist impulse of his modernism" and forge instead a mode that was "critical, self-reflective" (91). I agree with Matthews that Faulkner achieved a "critical" relation to life in this novel, but I would say that—through his avant-garde artist character—he draws for himself a kind of limit-case of activist art.

117. Faulkner's Civil War and Reconstruction-era novel, *The Unvanquished*, was also published during this interval, in 1938.

118. William Faulkner, *Light in August* (New York: Vintage, 1990), 6, 5. See Lawrence Buell's treatment of the environmental aspects of the novel in *Writing for an Endangered World*, 172–74.

119. William Faulkner, *Absalom, Absalom!* (New York: Vintage, 1972), 9.

120. Barbara Foley explains that proletarian or social realist literature and art achieved cultural prominence even if it never reached the mass audience it sought. *Radical Representations: Politics and Form in U.S. Proletarian Fiction, 1929–1941* (Durham: Duke University Press, 1993), 107.

121. See Atkinson's *Faulkner and The Great Depression* for a book-length treatment of Faulkner's 1930s fiction, especially Faulkner's response to fascism and agricultural issues. On how Faulkner's reputation after World War II was built on his being positioned by critics like Malcolm Cowley as writing literature affirmative of the nation and universal in its aesthetic achievement—as opposed to historically embedded or radical—see Lawrence Schwartz, *Creating Faulkner's Reputation: The Politics of Modern Literary Criticism* (Knoxville: University of Tennessee Press, 1988).

122. "Wild Palms" was not exactly a new story; as Joseph Blotner explains, Faulkner had written a short story along the lines of the beginning chapter of *Wild Palms* at some point before September. On 15 September, Faulkner started to write it again, apparently imagining it this time as the beginning of a longer work. *Faulkner*, 2:385; on the details of his New York City trip, see 386–89.

123. See Carla Kaplan, *Zora Neale Hurston: A Life in Letters* (New York: Knopf, 2007), 404–7.

124. Richard Wright, "Between Laughter and Tears," *New Masses*, 5 October 1937, 25.

125. Lucy Tompkins, "In the Florida Glades," *New York Times Book Review*, 26 September 1937, 29 excerpted in Adele S. Newson, *Zora Neale Hurston: A Reference Guide* (Boston: G. K. Hall, 1987), 11. Perhaps, too, Hurston's use of the flood to translate her heroine's problematic and violent lover into the sweet projection of her heroine's wishes suggested the cathartic potential of water for heartbreak; Hurston, too, started her flood novel as a means to get over a failed romance, in her words, to "embalm all the tenderness of my passion" for a 1931 liaison. Kaplan, *Zora Neale Hurston*, 183.

126. William Faulkner to Richard Wright, n.d., Richard Wright Papers, Series II, Correspondence, Personal Correspondence, JWJ MSS 3, box 97, folder 1328, Beinecke Library, Yale University.

127. For a comprehensive history, see David Welky, *The Thousand-Year Flood: The Ohio-Mississippi Disaster of 1937* (Chicago: University of Chicago Press, 2011).

128. Emil Ludwig, *The Nile: The Life-Story of a River*, trans. Mary H. Lindsay (New York: Viking, 1937), vii, x.

129. Lorentz, "Prologue," in *The River* (Farm Security Administration, 1937).

130. William Faulkner, interview with Joan Williams, qtd. in Thomas L. McHaney, *William Faulkner's "The Wild Palms": A Study* (Jackson: University Press of Mississippi, 1975), 24.

131. See McHaney, *William Faulkner's "The Wild Palms,"* 22, 24; and Blotner, *Faulkner*, 2:389, 406, 408.

132. McHaney, *William Faulkner's "The Wild Palms,"* 13, 34, 51, 54, 56, 64–65, 85–86.

McHaney draws, too, on an article by Cleanth Brooks, "The Tradition of Romantic Love and *The Wild Palms*," *Mississippi Quarterly* 25.3 (Summer 1972): 265–87.

133. McHaney, *William Faulkner's "The Wild Palms*," 87.

134. Editors demanded that Faulkner change his title to *The Wild Palms*, fearing that the other title would, according to Blotner, "hurt the book's sales by arousing Anti-Semitic feeling" (*Faulkner*, 2:399). It would be fascinating and important to pursue—though it is beyond the purview of this chapter—whether or how Faulkner was thinking about the Jewish diaspora as he contemplated the general modern condition of environmental alienation.

135. Cynthia Dobbs puts it well when she says that in his 1939 novel, "Faulkner makes external, physical, and literal a sense of disorientation that in his earlier novels he renders in primarily intrapsychic and social terms"; "Faulkner makes central a figure from natural history—the Mississippi Flood of 1927—to expand this sense of radical disorientation to include the very landscape on which his characters attempt to ground themselves" ("Flooded: The Excesses of Geography, Gender, and Capitalism in Faulkner's *If I Forget Thee, Jerusalem*," *American Literature* 73.4 [December 2001]: 817–18). I would argue that Faulkner had been using the flood as early as 1928 to indicate "radical disorientation" but makes the eco-historical cause of that disorientation newly explicit here; Dobbs argues that Faulkner dwells on the flood and the river's "radical fluidity" (811) to query the logics of gender and capitalism.

136. I am making a different point than that of Cecelia Tichi, who argues that when Faulkner addresses ecological concerns, he turns to "social realism" ("'Old Man': Shackles, Chains, and Water Water Everywhere," in *Faulkner and the Ecology of the South*, ed. Urgo and Abadie, 3). I would agree with Atkinson's characterization of Faulkner's 1930s writing on agrarian issues, namely that he produced an "ambivalent agrarianism in the context of competing ideological positions" coming out of both the right and left in response to the land crises of the 1930s (*Faulkner and the Great Depression*, 175).

137. James T. Farrell, *A Note on Literary Criticism* (New York: Vanguard, 1936), 87.

138. Louis Adamic, "What the Proletariat Reads," *Saturday Review of Literature* 11 (1 December 1934); Alan Colmer, "Portrait of the Artist as a Proletarian," *Saturday Review of Literature* 16 (31 July 1937): 14; V. F. Calverton, "Proletarianitis," *Saturday Review of Literature* 15 (9 January 1937): 16, all quoted in Foley, *Radical Representations*, 102–3.

139. As Donald H. Grubbs explains, the uproar over prison farms in the South and the fact that these often unfairly jailed convicts' work was thus extracted as slave labor made national news and reached President Roosevelt's desk in 1936; a federal grand jury indicted an Arkansas deputy sheriff "for aiding and abetting in holding in slavery," an indictment that elated "liberals across the nation" (*Cry from the Cotton*, 116–17, quote on 117). That Faulkner shows how prison laborers had been put in perilous danger working the 1927 flood must have struck a key with the late 1930s national indignation about unjust prison farm labor.

140. Sivils argues that the flood in "Old Man" shows Faulkner's "understanding of disturbances—including floods—as socially linked ecological catastrophes originating from environmental abuse" ("Faulkner's Ecological Disturbances," 498). I agree

but would point out that the link Faulkner forges in this chapter between industrialization and flooding is fairly lost in later chapters as he imagines the river resuming its customary feistiness against humanity's easily overwhelmed modern mechanisms.

141. Dickson, "Negroes Real Heroes of Mississippi's Rampage," 3.

142. Ted Atkinson discusses how, in *As I Lay Dying*, the nonfamilial narration "both cues and sanctions laughter" at the family's expense; in "Old Man," the third-person narrator assumes that role (*Faulkner and the Great Depression*, 182).

143. I agree with the point of Ramon Saldivar and Sylvan Goldberg that this "vision of human agency subordinated to the will of a natural world older and more powerful than humans is curiously at odds with the environmental history that lies behind the flood." "The Faulknerian Anthropocene: Scales of Time and History in *The Wild Palms* and *Go Down, Moses*," in *The New Cambridge Companion to William Faulkner*, ed. John T. Matthews (Cambridge: Cambridge University Press, 2015), 198.

144. And when the pair is in the remote woods of Wisconsin or the mountains of Utah, they subsist strictly on canned food and are not tutored in wilderness skills by their environment's challenges; rather, they aestheticize the scenery. Part of northern Wisconsin is in the Mississippi's watershed, but my guess, given the rest of their itinerary, is that Charlotte and Harry are residing beyond its bounds.

145. Mary Austin, "American Folk," *Folk-Say* (1930), 287.

146. McHaney argues that "Old Man" is a kind of "modern fertility rite as set against the aborticidal tragedy of Harry and Charlotte." *William Faulkner's "The Wild Palms*," 112.

147. Quoted in Blotner, *Faulkner*, 2:399.

148. There is certainly a similarity between this wilderness idyll and that "androcentric wilderness narrative" that runs throughout the American canon, including in Faulkner's "The Bear" (see Buell, *The Environmental Imagination*, 35); the tall convict's fear of his pregnant passenger's body and his later misogynistic statement would support such a reading. But the fact that, as the narrator says, he and the woman "had jointly suffered all the crises emotional social economic and even moral" (213) and that her nursing body and her wit are now peacefully a part of his days and the "rich oblivious darkness" (220) lead me to see this as a kind of atavistic familial or social idyll where production and reproduction and nature are all mutually intact.

Chapter 7

1. See Barry, *Rising Tide*, 314–17.

2. He tells of this episode in *Black Boy: A Record of Childhood and Youth* [American Hunger] (New York: Harper, 2005 [1945]) and called it his "terror upon the river" (51–53, quote on 53).

3. On his reading of Communist print culture, see *Black Boy*, 316–20. He felt that this literature "oversimplified the experience of those whom they sought to lead. In their effort to recruit masses, they had missed the meaning of the lives of the masses, had conceived of people in too abstract a manner. I would make voyages,

discoveries, explorations with words and try to put some of that meaning back" (320).

4. Karl Marx, *Economic and Philosophical Manuscripts of 1844*, ed. Dirk J. Struik, trans. Martin Milligan (New York: International Press, 1964), 106.

5. Henri Lefebvre, *The Production of Space*, trans. Donald Nicholson-Smith (Malden, MA: Blackwell, 1991), 345.

6. Trigant Burrow, *The Social Basis of Consciousness: A Study in Organic Psychology Based upon a Synthetic and Societal Concept of the Neuroses* (New York: Harcourt, 1927), 119, 249.

7. Carla Cappetti, for example, figures the relation between the Chicago School and Wright as one of "intellectual grafting" and specifies that "Environment" in *Black Boy* and *American Hunger* "becomes an all inclusive term" against which the individual "must strive for self-realization" ("Sociology of an Existence: Wright and the Chicago School," in *Richard Wright: Critical Perspectives Past and Present*, ed. Henry Louis Gates Jr. and K. A. Appiah [New York: Amistad Press, 1993], 255, 258). For a fuller treatment of Wright's "sociological imagination," see Cappetti, *Writing Chicago: Modernism, Ethnography, and the Novel* (New York: Columbia University Press, 1993).

8. In 1987, the Reverend Benjamin Chavis, executive director of the United Church of Christ Commission for Racial Justice, originated the term "environmental racism" in a report linking the siting of hazardous waste facilities close to communities of color; in 1991, delegates at the First National People of Color Environmental Leadership Summit in Washington, DC, devised a seventeen-point "Principles of Environmental Justice" statement. See Giovanna Di Chiro, "Nature as Community: The Convergence of Environment and Social Justice," in *Uncommon Ground: Rethinking the Human Place in Nature*, ed. William Cronon (New York: Norton, 1996), 304. As Adams, Evans, and Stein put it in their introduction to *The Environmental Justice Reader: Politics, Poetics, & Pedagogy*, ed. Joni Adamson, Mei Mei Evans, and Rachel Stein (Tucson: University of Arizona Press, 2002), "Environmental justice movements call attention to the ways disparate distribution of wealth and power often leads to correlative social upheaval and the unequal distribution of environmental degradation and/or toxicity" (5). For the intersection of racial and economic inequity and environmental justice issues in the South, see any number of studies by Robert Bullard; in *The Wrong Complexion for Protection: How the Government Response to Disaster Endangers African American Communities* (New York: New York University Press, 2012), Bullard and Beverly Wright call the government response to the 1927 flood a "classic case of environmental injustice" (56).

9. Wright, "Between Laughter and Tears," quoted in *Zora Neale Hurston: Critical Perspectives Past and Present*, ed. Henry Louis Gates Jr. and K. A. Appiah (New York: Amistad, 1993), 18.

10. Zora Neale Hurston, in her review of *Uncle Tom's Children*, *Saturday Review of Literature* (2 April 1938), reprinted in *Richard Wright: Critical Perspectives Past and Present*, calls out Wright for his preoccupation with "spectacular" violence, noting that it is also "the favorite Negro theme" (3).

11. See, for example, Charles J. Rolo, "This, Too, Is America," in *Richard Wright's "Black Boy" (American Hunger)*, ed. William L. Andrews and Douglas Taylor (New York:

Oxford University Press, 2003), 27. The quotes are from *Black Boy* by Richard Wright.

12. William Howard, in "Richard Wright's Flood Stories and the Great Mississippi River Flood of 1927: Social and Historical Backgrounds," *Southern Literary Journal* 16.2 (Spring 1984): 44–62, was the first and only scholar really to contextualize Wright's flood stories; Howard asserted that "the flurry of journalistic activity attending the flood of 1927 exposed him to alternative points of view (like those of Mencken) that must have spurred his imagination as much as the flood itself" (44). An important beginning, this article only set out to establish the connection between Wright and the flood, not to perform close readings of Wright's work in the light of such a connection. Richard M. Mizelle Jr., *Backwater Blues: The Mississippi Flood of 1927 in the African American Imagination* (Minneapolis: University of Minnesota Press, 2014), and especially its chapter on Wright, "Burning Waters Rise: Richard Wright's *Blues Voice* and the Double Environmental Burden of Race," marks a recent contribution along these lines. Mizelle argues that Wright's flood stories "constitute the first published creative intellectual engagement with the historical experiences of African Americans during the 1927 flood, rooted in the sociology of black newspapers and his own intense familiarity with race and racism" (70). As I've been arguing, the creative outpouring of black expression during and after the flood is more extensive than Mizelle allows; I do agree that Wright's and other black-authored texts "dispel the historical myth of black environmental illiteracy" (72).

13. H. L. Mencken, "The Mississippi Flood," *Evening Sun*, 23 May 1927, n.p.

14. "Another Mencken Absurdity," *Commercial Appeal*, 28 May 1927, n.p.

15. Wright described arriving "early at work" on 28 May 1927, going into "the bank lobby where the Negro porter was mopping," picking up the *Commercial Appeal*, and beginning "my free reading of the press" (*Black Boy*, 244).

16. Wright tells of a carpenter in the neighborhood who made him look carefully at a racist cartoon in a newspaper Wright was selling (*Black Boy*, 129).

17. "Stand Together, Pull Together and Victory Is Certain," *Commercial Appeal*, 22 May 1927, n.p.

18. "The Burden of Floods: Who Should Bear It?"

19. Queen and Mann, *Social Pathology*, 435–36.

20. Though Dickson's series was not syndicated in the *Commercial Appeal*, it was printed in many major papers (in Atlanta, New York, Chicago, and Los Angeles) that circulated in Memphis. I cannot prove from external evidence that Wright read Dickson's stories, but internal evidence strongly suggests it, as I will soon show.

21. Harris Dickson, "One Tiny Tragedy Tells Horrors of Flood Area," *Los Angeles Times*, 7 June 1927, 4.

22. See Wright, *Black Boy*, 165–68. Wright's first appearance in print, at fifteen, had been with a local black paper, the Jackson *Southern Register*, and he had received encouragement from its editor, Malcolm Rodgers.

23. When Wright worked for the *Southern Register*, he would ask Rodgers to read the black papers and magazines arriving from around the nation, including the *Chicago Defender*, the *Pittsburgh Courier*, and the *Baltimore Afro-American*, as well as

The Crisis and *Opportunity*; see Margaret Walker, *Richard Wright Daemonic Genius: A Portrait of the Man, A Critical Look at His Work* (New York: Warner, 1988), 28. All these papers and magazines reported on the flood: see the editorial "Withstanding the Flood," 20; Jesse O. Thomas, "In the Path of the Flood," *Opportunity* 5 (August 1927): 236–37; William N. Jones, "Death Stalks in Mississippi Flood Path," *Afro-American*, 30 April 1927, n.p.; and White, "The Negro and the Flood," 688–89.

24. Harrington, "Use Troops in Flood Area to Imprison Farm Hands," 1–1.

25. Wells, "Flood Refugees Are Held as Slaves in Mississippi Camp," 1-A11.

26. Wright typed his address on the typescript draft of "Down by the Riverside," drafts, typescript, corrected/1936 n.d., in the Richard Wright Papers, Series I, Writings, Books, *Uncle Tom's Children*, Beinecke Rare Book and Manuscript Library, Yale University Library, New Haven.

27. Tuskegee Institute, Department of Records and Research, *Negro Year Book: An Annual Encyclopedia of the Negro, 1921–22*, ed. Monroe N. Work (Tuskegee, AL: Negro Year Book Company, 1922), 426. Wright knew Barnett well enough to suggest him as a referee for his Guggenheim application in 1938 and shared drafts of his flood stories with Associated Negro Press reporter Frank Marshall Davis (Hazel Rowley, *Richard Wright: The Life and Times* [New York: Holt, 2001], 157, 116).

28. For an alternate account of Wright's spatial imagination, see Thadious Davis, *Southscapes*; Davis describes how Wright becomes an author through the cultural space of the Federal Writers' Project (135–37) but also through a "spatial and psychological distancing from the putative ecosystem in both his own family and his environment" (157). I will soon contend that Wright, in *Black Boy*, establishes that his foundational emotional and creative lexicon comes from early experiences of rural southern nature, a lexicon that even outlasts Jim Crow spatialization protocols.

29. Along with Cappetti, *Writing Chicago*, see Michael Fabre, *The Unfinished Quest of Richard Wright*, trans. Isabel Barzun, 2nd ed. (Urbana: University of Illinois Press, 1993), 232, 571n38; Rowley, *Richard Wright*, 81–82.

30. Richard Wright, introduction to St. Clair Drake and Horace R. Cayton, *Black Metropolis: A Study of Negro Life in a Northern City* (New York: Harcourt, 1945), xvii.

31. Ibid., xviii. Wright also mentioned the influence of Robert Redfield's *Tepoztlan: A Mexican Village* (Chicago: University of Chicago Press, 1930), in which Redfield did take physical geography seriously but still sought to render his data into a study of "the general type of change whereby primitive man becomes civilized man, the rustic becomes the urbanite" (14).

32. See Rowley, *Richard Wright*, 81–82.

33. My ensuing argument differs from Lawrence Buell's point about Wright's indebtedness to Chicago Sociology as a way to transfer that field's empirical bona fides to *Native Son* (*Writing for an Endangered World*, 142).

34. Horace Cayton, "Reflections on Richard Wright: A Symposium on an Exiled Native Son," quoted in Rowley, *Richard Wright*, 81. For an institutional history, see Martin Bulmer, *The Chicago School of Sociology: Institutionalization, Diversity, and the Rise of Sociological Research* (Chicago: University of Chicago Press, 1984).

35. Qtd. in Bulmer, *Chicago School*, 76.

36. Bulmer, *Chicago School*, 37.
37. Robert Park, Ernest Burgess, and Roderick McKenzie, *The City* (Chicago: University of Chicago Press, 1967), 64, 56. This model of social organization-disorganization-reorganization comes from a Chicago sociologist who preceded them, W. I. Thomas, and sought to explain how the rules that previously distinguished and controlled a group might be loosened and then re-formed; see Bulmer, *Chicago School*, 31, 61.
38. Chapter 3 in Park, Burgess, and McKenzie, *The City*, is titled "The Ecological Approach to the Study of the Human Community"; for the use of the "climax stage" concept, see 77.
39. On Clements, see Worster, "The Ecology of Order and Chaos," 3, 4. On the narrative, and Darwinian, underpinnings of the Clements-Gleason debate, see Debra Journet, "Ecological Theories as Cultural Narratives: F. E. Clements's and H. A. Gleason's 'Stories' of Community Succession," *Written Communication* 8.4 (October 1991), 446–72.
40. Robert Park and Ernest Burgess, *Introduction to the Science of Sociology* (Chicago: University of Chicago Press, 1921), 44, 162. Herbert Spencer, who wrote in the mid-nineteenth century across the fields of biology, philosophy, sociology, and psychology, engaged selectively with both Lamarck and Darwin to propose that, at all scales of life, organisms were evolving toward greater differentiation and complexity, all the while producing an ever more concordant network. Spencer wrote that "universally a patient self-rectification" (469) was occurring. As changes internal to organisms and in the outer environment act reciprocally upon each other, they would eventually achieve an end state of "harmony" (469) and "equilibrium" (476). "A Theory of Population, Deduced from the General Law of Animal Fertility," *Westminster Review* 57.112, n.s., 1 (January and April 1852), www.victorian-web.org; on Spencer's theories of "progression towards perfection," see Mark Francis, *Herbert Spencer and the Invention of Modern Life* (Durham, UK: Acumen, 2007), 196.
41. Lowell Juilliard Carr noted that in the United States, "where nature is supposed to be most completely subdued, there were 938 disasters in the forty-eight years from 1881 to 1928" ("Disaster and the Sequence-Pattern Concept of Social Change," 209); after these, he asserted, came an "eventually renewed equilibrium" (207).
42. Prince, *Catastrophe and Social Change*, 139; Queen and Mann, *Social Pathology*, 435–36, 437.
43. Wright, *Writers Club Bulletin*, Columbia University, 1 (1938): 15, qtd. in Fabre, *The Unfinished Quest of Richard Wright*, 21.
44. Burrow, *The Social Basis of Consciousness*, 11, 59, 87, 118, 249, 34, 115, 127, 128, 132, 249.
45. "Ethics" had been published in *American Stuff*, an anthology of the Federal Writers' Project. See Richard Yarborough, introduction to *Uncle Tom's Children* (New York: Perennial, 1993), xviii–xix. Wright had been reading these stories in draft form to fellow writers, radicals, and intellectuals at the (mostly white) John Reed Club and the (black) South Side Writers' Group (Rowley, *Richard Wright*, 89, 116–17). Wright remembered that at the John Reed Club, fellow writers would "tear [his stories] to bits, analyze each line, each paragraph ruthlessly, without fear or favor,"

a process that produced in him "a sense of objectivity about his work" (qtd. on 89). He also read drafts of these stories to Joyce Gourfain and Arna Bontemps (93, 111).

46. On "Ethics" as a text that gives the subsequent volume of fiction the status of a sociological study, see Watson, *Reading for the Body*, 161; and Robert Bone, "Richard Wright and the Chicago Renaissance," *Callaloo* 9.3 (Summer 1986): 457. Watson is especially interested in how "Ethics" establishes a "pedagogy of [bodily] pain" (161, 163).

47. Richard Wright, "The Ethics of Living Jim Crow," *Uncle Tom's Children* (New York: Harper Perennial, 1991), 7.

48. Yarborough, introduction to ibid., x.

49. Richard Wright, "How 'Bigger' Was Born," *Native Son* (New York: Harper Perennial, 1993), 531.

50. Yarborough, introduction, xxiii.

51. Watson argues: "As the green of the southern pastoral here revealingly merges with the green of American wealth, Wright stresses that the material sources of white authority ultimately lie ... in an object-rich world and the exemption from embodiment it promises" (*Reading for the Body*, 167).

52. McKenzie, "The Ecological Approach," in *The City*, 64–65.

53. Park, "The Mind of the Hobo: Reflections upon the Relation between Mentality and Locomotion," in *The City*, 159.

54. Marx wrote: "The object which labor produces—labor's product—confronts it as *something alien*, as a *power independent* of the producer. The product of labor is labor which has been embodied in an object, which has become material: it is the *objectification* of labor" (*Economic and Philosophical Manuscripts of 1844*, 108).

55. Marx, *Economic and Philosophical Manuscripts of 1844*, 109, 112, 114. Scholars have shown that Marx was not only concerned with temporal paradigms but engaged with issues of both space and nature. See, for example, David Harvey, *Spaces of Capital: Towards a Critical Geography* (London: Routledge, 2001), especially industrial capitalism's built environments (247–48) and Marx's argument that imperialism could not offer a "spatial fix" to capitalism's social dilemmas (299–300); and Paul Burkett, *Marx and Nature: A Red and Green Perspective* (New York: St. Martin's Press, 1999), especially Marx's consideration of the instability of nature (114) and its despoliation by industrial capitalism (107–43).

56. Marx, *Economic and Philosophical Manuscripts of 1844*, 113.

57. I would disagree, then, with Davis's assertion in *Southscapes* that after the first scene in *Black Boy* (of house burning), Wright remains "inviolately unassimilated to his surroundings" (155).

58. Lefebvre, *The Production of Space*, 19. Joshua Scott Stone, in his dissertation, "American Ethni/Cities: Critical Geography, Subject Formation, and the Urban Representations of Abraham Cahan, Richard Wright, and James Baldwin" (Paper 501, *Open Access Dissertations*, 2010), makes a similar argument, namely that Wright differed from the Chicago School's spatial theorization and anticipated Lefebvre (112, 136, 138); Stone describes Wright's "critical urbanism" and argues that Wright was attending to the northern racialization of space that was especially ineradicable because unacknowledged behind a claim of "spatial neutrality" (116).

59. Lefebvre, *The Production of Space*, 90, 345, 11, 166, 32, 376, 93.

60. On the southern practices of spatial signage, see Elizabeth Abel, *Signs of the Times: The Visual Politics of Jim Crow* (Berkeley: University of California Press, 2010).

61. In his reading of "Down by the Riverside," Abdul R. JanMohamed reads Mann's running toward the river as "a belated and positive, if paradoxical, appropriation of his own death as a way of undermining the master's use of the threat of death as a mode of coercion" (*The Death-Bound-Subject: Richard Wright's Archaeology of Death* [Durham: Duke University Press, 2005], 56). More generally, JanMohamed sees Mann's character, and his "pressured situation," as designed by Wright to allow him "to explore the subjectivating effects of social death" under Jim Crow (52) and reads the flood as an allegory for the "general condition of the world" (53); in other words, the flood, representing imminent peril, materializes the threat of death perpetually hanging over black males in a racist South. I am arguing, by contrast, that Wright is signifying upon the mediation of the specific historical flood of 1927 and is critiquing not only national forms of Jim Crow racism but also Mann's abandoning his memory, his suspicion, and his world-making imaginative faculties. It is both a systemic and a character critique.

62. The Cameraman, "Grotesque Journalism," *New York Amsterdam News*, 22 June 1927, 22.

63. John Dewey, *Experience and Nature* (Chicago: Open Court, 1925), 41; Henry Gleason, "The Individualistic Concept of the Plant Association," *Bulletin of the Torrey Botanical Club* 53.1 (January 1926): 16; Frank Knight, *Risk, Uncertainty and Profit* (Boston: Houghton Mifflin, 1921), 201–2.

64. Will Irwin opined that this "long siege by the Mississippi" had been brought on by a "coincidence of the weather" that produced in the tributaries "a sinister rhythm" ("Can We Tame the Mississippi?" 406).

65. I would slightly amend Watson's point that in *Uncle Tom's Children*, we see the violent "intrusion of whiteness onto the scene of black making" (*Reading for the Body*, 168) and that it is Heartfield who alone "precipitat[es] the fall" of Mann's epic power (181); in the case of Mann, that "intrusion" onto Mann's scene of forensic/artistic world-making is preceded by his own submission of these powers to existing, mediated symbolism.

66. Mann may also have in mind the Christian spiritual that he and his kin had sung before embarking on their river crossing that proclaimed that "*Down by the riverside / Ah ain gonna study war no mo*" (73). In this song, the riverside is a place to commune with the Prince of Peace.

67. "Withstanding the Flood," n.p.

68. Ralph Ellison, "Richard Wright's Blues," *Antioch Review* 50.1/2, 50th anniversary issue (Winter–Spring 1992 [1945]): 61–74, quote on 62.

69. One of the kinds of changes Wright made as he was revising this novella was to designate and continually draw attention to the color scheme of the story. Heartfield's boat, green in the typescript, becomes "white"; Mrs. Heartfield gains the designation "white" (17); the "flare," first described as "roving," becomes "yellow" (18) (typescript [original], 70); the "hills" become "Green slopes" (54); the "young soldiers" are given the designation "white" (22); see also 24, 25, 29, 30, 56 for more additions of "white." All of these hues (white, yellow, red, and green), functioning cooperatively, amount to more than just a general environmental assault but con-

spire to create a specifically visual formula of domination, in which the racial category "white" commandeers the chromal spectrum. Mann's thoughts of murdering the Heartfield mother and children appears as an absorption of whiteness into black: "He wished that their white bodies were at the bottom of the black waters"; "he wanted to leave them here for the black waters to swallow" (print version, 108, 110). But it is "the rushing black water" that "tilt[s]" the house and hurls him into "black space" (111), and effectively intervenes in his murderous plans. It is blackness that swallows *him* into its higher ethics, that returns him to his better angels.

70. Maurice O. Wallace has argued that *Native Son* is Wright's meditation on "the picture-taking racial gaze that fixes . . . black male subjects within a rigid and limited grid of representational possibilities" and of "the primacy of the picture over the person in the white mind" (*Constructing the Black Masculine: Identity and Ideality in African-American Men's Literature and Culture, 1775–1995* [Durham: Duke University Press, 2002], 135). By contrast, Sara Blair makes the argument that in *Native Son*, Wright not only makes a "critique of racism as a visual operation" but also "mark[s] his investment in Bigger *as* a sometime contestant—however fatally ill-matched—on the visual field" (*Harlem Crossroads: Black Writers and the Photograph in the Twentieth Century* [Princeton: Princeton University Press, 2007], 63). In "Down by the Riverside," Wright is already thinking about how a visual regime of racial codification and visual technologies that produce racial "truth" doom his black protagonist. I would also concur with Blair, for Mann, like Bigger, is imagined as a "contestant" in the visual field and is indeed its temporary winner.

71. Richard Wright, *Twelve Million Black Voices: A Folk History of the Negro in the United States of America* (London: Lindsay Drummond, 1947).

72. Andres Mario Zervigón, *John Heartfield and the Agitated Image: Photography, Persuasion, and the Rise of Avant-Garde Photomontage* (Chicago: University of Chicago Press, 2012), 239. Zervigón argues that in the 1930s, "Heartfield's photomontage was becoming *the* form of an emerging, radical-left proletarian art" (239). Zervigón summarizes: his images "taught audiences how to adopt radical eyes whose piercing vision could perceive a social reality that Weimar's surface culture generally occluded" (232).

73. The copy read: "We know only one race, we recognize only one enemy—the exploiting class." *A-I-Z* 10.26 (4 July 1931): 517.

74. Douglas Kahn, *John Heartfield: Art and Mass Media* (New York: Tanam, 1985), 71.

75. Zervigón, *John Heartfield*, 139. He borrows the phrase "nervous breakdown" from Chicago *Daily News* reporter Ben Hecht, who visited Berlin in 1919 and met Heartfield (139).

76. Kahn, *John Heartfield*, 2; Devin Fore, *Realism after Modernism: The Rehumanization of Art and Literature* (Cambridge, MA: MIT Press, 2012), 266. Fore points out that Heartfield used visual and verbal "elements that were not just public, but avowedly and militantly clichéd" (304); the same should be said of Wright as he signified upon popular flood media.

77. This image appeared in *A-I-Z* 11.29 (17 July 1932): 675.

78. In the first typescript, the line reads: "a glare of light played over the water and found him" (21).

79. Burrow, *The Social Basis of Consciousness*, 128.

80. Ibid., 249.

81. Frederick Douglass, *Narrative of the Life of Frederick Douglass, an American Slave* (New York: Dover, 1995 [1845]), 38.

82. On Wright's engagement with leftist journalism beginning in 1933, see Rowley, *Richard Wright*, 74–79.

83. I borrow the phrase from John Michael Vlach's study, *Back of the Big House: The Architecture of Plantation Slavery* (Chapel Hill: University of North Carolina Press, 1993).

84. W.E.B. Du Bois, *The Souls of Black Folk* (Rockville, MD: Manor, 2008), 19.

85. Marx, *Economic and Philosophical Manuscripts of 1844*, 114.

86. Eliot Kleinberg, *Black Cloud: The Great Hurricane of 1928* (New York: Carroll & Graf, 2003), xiv. Roughly 2,400 people died that night, about one-third of the local population, making it the second deadliest hurricane in U.S. history. Yet it is deceptive to think about the *hurricane* killing such a mass of people; it was merely the instigating event. Only eleven died in the hurricane damage at Palm Beach, for example. The vast majority were victims of the storm-surge flooding of Okeechobee some forty miles inland. More than three-quarters of the dead there were African American and Afro-Caribbean.

87. As Hurston's narrator puts it, using free indirect discourse, in *Their Eyes Were Watching God* (New York: Perennial, 1990): "The folks let the people do the thinking. If the castles thought themselves secure, the cabins needn't worry. . . . The bossman might have the thing stopped before morning anyway" (158). See also my "Zora Neale Hurston and the Environmental Ethic of Risk," 21–36.

88. Wright, "Between Laughter and Tears." Alain Locke, dean of the Harlem Renaissance, concurred in an *Opportunity* review from 1 June 1938 that "her gift for poetic phrase, for rare dialect, and folk humor keep her flashing on the surface of her community and her characters from diving down either to the inner psychology of characterization or to sharp analysis of the social background." *Zora Neale Hurston*, ed. Gates and Appiah, 18.

89. In one of the earlier scenes of the novel, characters are debating the possible existence of a "great big ole scoundrel beast" who, as one speaker claims, "eats up all de folks outa de house and den eat de house." His interlocutor is skeptical: "'taint no sich a varmint nowhere dat kin eat no house!" He sure does exist, the first man, Sam Watson, claims: "Dey caught him over dere in Egypt. Seem lak he used tuh hang around dere and eat up dem Pharaohs' tombstones." Sam, who has been arguing for the overarching power of nature throughout the debate, concludes by saying, "Nature is high in uh varmint lakdat" (66). What Sam is describing here is the power of water operating in a floodplain. He points to the Nile's cyclical inundation of its banks and, without knowing it, presages Lake Okeechobee's own flooding. The narrator will take up this figure again to describe the power of the water in the lake to exceed humanly engineered constraints: the storm "woke up old Okechobee [sic] and the monster began to roll in his bed" (158).

90. Hurston, *Saturday Review of Literature*, 2 April 1938, in *Richard Wright: Critical Perspectives*, 3.

Conclusion

1. See Charles C. Eldredge, *John Steuart Curry's Hoover and the Flood: Painting Modern History* (Chapel Hill: University of North Carolina Press in association with the Morris Museum of Art, 2007), for an extensive treatment of this reproduced painting, including its position within early twentieth-century flood imagery, within the European and American traditions of history painting, and within the political milieu of 1940; quote on 8. I would like to thank Chuck Grench for letting me know of Eldredge's book.

2. Eldredge, *Hoover and the Flood*, 11, 72–73.

3. Henry R. Luce, "The American Century," *Life* 17 (February 1941), reprinted in *Diplomatic History* 23.2 (Spring 1999): 165, 171.

4. The AP photographer James N. Keen took the picture; for a reproduction, see Eldredge, *Hoover and the Flood*, 41. Eldredge formally analyzes the image on 7–8.

5. Luce, "The American Century," 166.

6. See Jennifer Rae Greeson's analysis of this process during the nineteenth century in *Our South: Geographic Fantasy and the Rise of National Literature* (Cambridge, MA: Harvard University Press, 2010).

7. The secondary literature on empire and environment is most extensive for European empires and especially the former British Empire and includes coverage of how environmental despoliation was closely associated with awareness of environmental vulnerability and the field of ecology. See Grove, *Green Imperialism*; Alfred W. Crosby, *Ecological Imperialism: The Biological Expansion of Europe, 900–1900* (Cambridge: Cambridge University Press, 2004 [1986]); and William Beinart and Lotte Hughes, *Environment and Empire* (Oxford: Oxford University Press, 2007). For scholarship on U.S. environmental imperialism, see Joni Adamson, *American Indian Literature, Environmental Justice, and Ecocriticism: The Middle Place* (Tucson: University of Arizona Press, 2001); and Elizabeth DeLoughrey and George B. Handley, eds., *Postcolonial Ecologies: Literatures of the Environment* (New York: Oxford University Press, 2011), especially on U.S. tourism and "militourism" in the Caribbean and the Pacific Islands. Though U.S. attitudes and habits certainly derive from and are continuous with modernizing imperial Europe, one can trace an American pattern of environmental prodigality beyond its national borders in, for a few examples, the exportation of the plantation system beyond the U.S. South as U.S. fruit corporations transformed Central American countries into "Banana Republics"; the exportation of extractive practices in the harvesting of rubber in Amazonia during the 1940s or minerals needed in consumer technology in Africa today; U.S. nuclear testing and nuclear aggression in Asia and its aftermath; the 1984 Bhopal Disaster in India inside an American majority-owned Union Carbide pesticide plant; Chief Economist of the World Bank Lawrence Summers's advocating a plan to dump wealthy nations' toxins in Africa (see Nixon, *Slow Violence*, 18–19); and, finally, Americans' disproportionate consumption of energy and thus emission of climate-changing carbons.

8. The critique of bungled federal engineering we saw in 1927 returned as residents in New Orleans came to call the 2005 disaster the "federal flood"; see John Swenson,

New Atlantis: Musicians Battle for the Survival of New Orleans (New York: Oxford University Press, 2011), 267n1.

9. Klein, in *Shock Doctrine*, describes how "it is in these malleable moments, when we are psychologically unmoored and physically uprooted" by catastrophe, that a "disaster capitalism" brings about "orchestrated raids on the public sphere" (21). Making the maintenance of the Mississippi levee system federal and *public*, though, in the late 1920s did not necessarily help laborers in the Delta.

10. Barry, in *Rising Tide*, explains how Delta planters and politicians, in order to get the federal government to agree to shoulder all the costs of the levee system, agreed to desist in calling for a special session of Congress to meet to appropriate rehabilitation funds; because of this deal, Hoover could say to a New Orleans Rotary Club: "We rescued Main Street with Main Street. . . . It is upon such independence and self-government that is based the greatness of the United States" (qtd. on 375). The national press, before this deal was struck, was critical of Congress; Barry calls this a "watershed, when the nation first demanded that the federal government assume a new kind of responsibility for its citizens" (374).

11. Lars Clausen, "Social Differentiation and the Long-Term Origin of Disasters," *Natural Hazards* 6 (1992): 182.

12. This characterization belongs to theater critic Hilton Als in "The Shadow Act: Kara Walker's Vision," *New Yorker*, 8 October 2007.

13. Natasha Trethewey, *Beyond Katrina: A Meditation on the Mississippi Gulf Coast* (Athens: University of Georgia Press, 2010).

14. See, for example, Jed Horne, *Breach of Faith: Hurricane Katrina and the Near Death of a Great American City* (New York: Random House, 2006), which won the Pulitzer Prize; Douglas Brinkley, *The Great Deluge* (New York: William Morrow, 2006); Michael Eric Dyson, *Come Hell or High Water: Hurricane Katrina and the Color of Disaster* (New York: Basic Civitas, 2007); and Ivor van Heerden with Mike Bryan, *The Storm: What Went Wrong and Why during Hurricane Katrina: The Inside Story from One Louisiana Scientist* (New York: Viking, 2006).

15. On the ways in which the New Orleans levee disaster should provoke policy, historiography, and intellectual thinking that move beyond the limiting analytical category of the nation-state, see Wai-Chee Dimock, "World History According to Katrina," in *States of Emergency: The Object of American Studies*, ed. Russ Castronovo and Susan Kay Gillman (Chapel Hill: University of North Carolina Press, 2009), 143–60.

16. Dewey, *The Public and Its Problems*, 131.

17. Ibid., 183–84; Dewey, *Experience and Nature*, 41.

18. Dewey, *Experience and Nature*, 70. See Hugh P. McDonald, *John Dewey and Environmental Philosophy* (Albany: SUNY Press, 2004) for a discussion of Dewey's environmental thinking and ethics. McDonald summarizes: since, for Dewey, the Cartesian "metaphysics of the subject is the source of the devaluation of the environment, and the subject is treated as a detached substance," Dewey's "critique of substance, subject, and interaction provides a pragmatic alternative in which the 'subject' is entirely superceded"; what becomes paramount then are the transactions between organisms and environments (155).

19. Environmental historian Donald Worster has discussed the challenges of environmentalist messaging in a cosmos ecologists have since the 1970s defined not as stable but as inherently dynamic, even chaotic ("The Ecology of Order and Chaos," 1–18).

20. See Heise, *Sense of Place and Sense of Planet* for an argument on why cultivating citizens' local environmental belonging cannot alone enable us to grapple with today's environmental issues; she calls for an attitude of "eco-cosmopolitanism."

21. James Weldon Johnson, *God's Trombones: Seven Negro Sermons in Verse* (New York: Viking, 1927), 1.

22. See Jeannine DeLombard, "Aaron Douglas," *American National Biography Online*, www.anb.org.

23. Johnson, *God's Trombones*, 34, 35.

24. Pickens, "God and the Preachers."

25. "Gasoline, Thrown on Husband, Ignited," 1.

26. George Best, *A True Discourse of the Late Voyages of Discoverie . . . of Martin Frobisher . . .* (London, 1578), 30–32.

PERMISSIONS
ACKNOWLEDGMENTS

Grateful acknowledgment is made for permission to reprint the following previously published material. The author has made every effort to trace and acknowledge copyright holders, but if any have been overlooked inadvertently we would be grateful for notification of any corrections to be incorporated in future printings or editions of this book.

Portions of Chapter 6 were originally published in a slightly revised form in "Faulkner and the Outer Weather of 1927," *American Literary History* 24.1 (Spring 2012): 34–58, reprinted with permission of Oxford University Press and "*As I Lay Dying* and the Modern Aesthetics of Ecological Crisis," in *The New Cambridge Companion to William Faulkner*, ed. John T. Matthews (Cambridge: Cambridge University Press, 2015), 74–91 © Cambridge University Press 2015, reprinted with permission.

Excerpts are included from *Black Boy* by Richard Wright. Copyright © 1937, 1942, 1944, 1945 by Richard Wright, renewed © 1973 by Ellen Wright. Reprinted by permission of HarperCollins Publishers and Jonathan Cape of The Random House Group Ltd.

Excerpts are included from *Uncle Tom's Children* by Richard Wright. Copyright © 1936, 1937, 1938 by Richard Wright. Copyright © renewed 1964, 1965, 1966 by Ellen Wright. Reprinted by permission of HarperCollins Publishers and Jonathan Cape of The Random House Group Ltd.

"Backwater Blues" by Bessie Smith Copyright ©1927 (renewed), 1974 Frank Music Corp. All rights reserved. Reprinted by permission of Hal Leonard Corporation.

Excerpts from *As I Lay Dying* by William Faulkner, copyright © 1930 and renewed 1958 by William Faulkner. Used by permission of Random House, an imprint and division of Penguin Random House LLC. Used in the eBook by permission from W.W. Norton & Company, Inc. All rights reserved.

Excerpts from *The Sound and the Fury* by William Faulkner, copyright © 1929 and renewed 1957 by William Faulkner. Used by permission of Random House, an imprint and division of Penguin Random House LLC. Used in the eBook by permission from W.W. Norton & Company, Inc. All rights reserved.

Excerpts from *The Wild Palms* by William Faulkner, copyright © 1939 and renewed 1967 by Mrs. William Faulkner and Mrs. Paul D. Summers. Used by permission of Random House, an imprint and division of Penguin Random House LLC. Used in the eBook by permission from W.W. Norton & Company, Inc. All rights reserved.

Excerpts from Flournoy E. Miller, "My Fifty Years in Show Business," undated manuscript, by permission of the New York Public Library and Ms. Fredi Gordon.

INDEX

Aboul-Ela, Hosam, *Other South,* 354n113
Addie (Faulkner character), 205, 213, 217, 218, 219, 222–23, 226, 350nn64–65, 352n86
African American medical workers, 118
African American physicians, 116
African Americans, 30, 70, 114; in Alley, 85–86; and Anderson, 203; and body, 8–9, 17, 41, 110; civic organizations of, 31; and Colored Advisory Commission, 42; and Curry, 278, 279; and Dale, 122; and Dickson, 86–88, 262; direction of rescue by, 46, 118, 279, 288; education of, 69, 83; and farming, 14, 29, 42, 121–22, 123; and Faulkner, 194, 202–3, 205, 207, 208, 210, 212, 224, 237, 241, 282; and Harris, 237; and Hoover, 82, 83, 114, 279, 312n93; and Hurston, 231, 275; and invention of race, 8–9; and Johnson, 134; and Kellogg, 121–22; and knowledge, 202, 203–5; labor of, 8, 14, 29–34, 35, 41–42, 44, 45, 46, 47, 111, 112, 113, 115, 116, 123, 279; media representations of, 32, 82–89, 94, 121–22, 154, 155, 156–57, 237, 247, 310n57; merchant class of, 29; migration by, 7, 32, 33, 34, 132, 143; and political rights, 30, 31, 111, 116, 308n40, 309n49; poor, 29, 110, 113; professional class of, 29; and property, 83; retrogression of, 7, 31, 34; and risk, 17, 34, 123, 168, 301n40; and Rogers, 170–71, 174, 175, 176, 177; and Saxon, 181–82; shootings of, 115, 118; and Sinclair, 266; and Bessie Smith, 125, 131, 132, 134, 142, 143, 144; as social service workers, 43; and Taylor, 2; and unfulfilled promises of Civil War, 56; and vaudeville, 156–69; and R. Wright, 244, 245, 247, 250, 251, 254, 255, 256, 259–60, 261, 263, 265, 268, 270, 271, 274. *See also* blackness; black press; Jim Crow; lynching; race; racial violence; racism; Red Cross Camps; slavery
African Americans nurses, 43
African American social workers, 82
African American sociologists, 252
African American women, 45, 47
African colonization societies, 32
Agamben, Giorgio, 8, 9
Agamemnon, 90–91
agrarianism, 227
Agrarians, 236, 241
agriculture, 110; and Anthropocene, 5; and Faulkner, 192, 213, 218–19, 220, 221; industrial, 27, 48, 226; and Kellogg, 121–22; and monoculture, 7, 11, 24, 27, 48, 110, 173, 213, 221, 273, 307n30; in post-flood regions, 48; post-Reconstruction, 20–31; and prairie, 27; and Rogers, 173; and R. Wright, 273. *See also* farmers
Agriculture Department, 121
Aiken, Charles S., 219
Alabama, 131, 266
Alario, Margarita, "The Paradoxes of Modernity," 299n26
Albee, E. F., 153